Yamaha FZS1000 Fazer
Service and Repair Manual

by Matthew Coombs

(4287 - 264)

Models covered

FZS1000 Fazer. 998cc. 2001 to 2005
FZS1000S Fazer. 998cc. 2003 to 2005

© Haynes Publishing 2006

ABCDE
FGHIJ
KLMNO
PQR

A book in the **Haynes Service and Repair Manual Series**

All rights reserved. No part of this book may be reproduced or transmitted in any form or by any means, electronic or mechanical, including photocopying, recording or by any information storage or retrieval system, without permission in writing from the copyright holder.

ISBN 978 1 78521 284 0

British Library Cataloguing in Publication Data
A catalogue record for this book is available from the British Library

Library of Congress Control Number 2005930654

Printed in the USA

Haynes Publishing
Sparkford, Yeovil, Somerset BA22 7JJ, England

Haynes North America, Inc
861 Lawrence Drive, Newbury Park, California 91320, USA

Haynes Publishing Nordiska AB
Box 1504, 751 45 UPPSALA, Sweden

Contents

LIVING WITH YOUR YAMAHA FAZER

Introduction

Yamaha – musical instruments to Motorcycles	Page	0•4
Acknowledgements	Page	0•8
About this manual	Page	0•8
Identification numbers	Page	0•9
Buying spare parts	Page	0•9
Model development	Page	0•10
Bike spec	Page	0•10
Safety first!	Page	0•12

Daily (pre-ride) checks

Engine oil level	Page	0•13
Brake fluid level	Page	0•14
Coolant level	Page	0•15
Tyres	Page	0•16
Suspension, steering and final drive	Page	0•16
Legal and safety	Page	0•16

MAINTENANCE

Routine maintenance and servicing

Specifications	Page	1•2
Recommended lubricants and fluids	Page	1•2
Component locations	Page	1•3
Maintenance schedule	Page	1•4
Maintenance procedures	Page	1•6

Contents

REPAIRS AND OVERHAUL

Engine, transmission and associated systems

Engine, clutch and transmission	Page	2•1
Cooling system	Page	3•1
Fuel and exhaust systems	Page	4•1
Ignition system	Page	5•1

Chassis components

Frame, suspension and final drive	Page	6•1
Brakes, wheels and tyres	Page	7•1
Frame and bodywork	Page	8•1

Electrical system — Page 9•1

Wiring diagrams — Page 9•23

REFERENCE

Tools and Workshop Tips	Page	REF•2
Security	Page	REF•20
Lubricants and fluids	Page	REF•23
Conversion Factors	Page	REF•26
MOT test checks	Page	REF•27
Storage	Page	REF•32
Fault finding	Page	REF•35
Fault finding equipment	Page	REF•44
Technical terms explained	Page	REF•48

Index — Page REF•52

Yamaha
Musical instruments to motorcycles

**The FS1E -
first bike of many sixteen year olds in the UK**

The Yamaha Motor Company

The Yamaha name can be traced back to 1889, when Torakusu Yamaha founded the Yamaha Organ Manufacturing Company. Such was the success of the company, that in 1897 it became Nippon Gakki Limited and manufactured a wide range of reed organs and pianos.

During World War II, Nippon Gakki's manufacturing base was utilised by the Japanese authorities to produce propellers and fuel tanks for their aviation industry. The end of the war brought about a huge public demand for low cost transport and many firms decided to utilise their obsolete aircraft tooling for the production of motorcycles. Nippon Gakki's first motorcycle went on sale in February 1955 and was named the 125 YA-1 Red Dragonfly. This machine was a copy of the German DKW RT125 motorcycle, featuring a single cylinder two-stroke engine with a four-speed gearbox. Due to the outstanding success of this model the motorcycle operation was separated from Nippon Gakki in July 1955 and the Yamaha Motor Company was formed.

The YA-1 also received acclaim by winning two of Japan's biggest road races, the Mount Fuji Climbing race and the Asama Volcano race. The high level of public demand for the YA-1 led to the development of a whole series of two-stroke singles and twins.

Having made a large impact on their home market, Yamahas were exported to the USA in 1958 and to the UK in 1962. In the UK the signing of an Anglo-Japanese trade agreement during 1962 enabled the sale of Japanese lightweight motorcycles and scooters in Britain. At that time, competition between the many motorcycle producers in Japan had reduced numbers significantly and by the end of the sixties, only the big-four which are familiar with today remained.

Yamaha Europe was founded in 1968 and based in Holland. Although originally set up to market marine products, the Dutch base is now the official European Headquarters and distribution centre. Yamaha motorcycles are built at factories in Holland, Denmark, Norway, Italy, France, Spain and Portugal. Yamahas are imported into the UK by Yamaha Motor UK Ltd, formerly Mitsui Machinery Sales (UK) Ltd. Mitsui and Co. were originally a trading house, handling the shipping, distribution and marketing of Japanese products into western countries. Ultimately Mitsui Machinery Sales was formed to handle Yamaha motorcycles and outboard motors.

Based on the technology derived from its motorcycle operation, Yamaha have produced many other products, such as automobile and lightweight aircraft engines, marine engines and boats, generators, pumps, ATVs, snowmobiles, golf cars, industrial robots, lawnmowers, swimming pools and archery equipment.

Two-strokes first

Part of Yamaha's success was a whole string of innovations in the two-stroke world. Autolube engine lubrication, torque induction, multi-ported engines, reed valves and power valves kept their two-strokes at the forefront of technology. Many advances were achieved with the use of racing as a development laboratory. They went to the USA in the late 1950s with an air-cooled 250cc twin but didn't hit the GPs until the early 1960s when Fumio Ito scored a hat-trick of sixth places in the Isle of Man TT, the Dutch TT and the Belgian GP. This experiment gave rise to the idea of the over-the-counter racer, an idea that became reality in the TD1, the first in an unmatched series of two-stroke racers that were the standard issue for privateers at national and international level for years and helped Yamaha develop their road engines. While privateers raced the twins, Yamaha built the outrageously complicated vee-four 250 for Phil Read and followed it with a vee-four 125 that Bill Ivy lapped the Isle of Man on at over 100mph! When the FIM regulations were changed to limit the smaller GP classes to two cylinders, these exotic bikes died but set the scene for an unparalleled dynasty of mass-produced racers based on the same technology as the road bikes.

In the 1960s and 70s the two-stroke engined YAS3 125, YDS1 to YDS7 250 and YR5 350 formed the core of Yamaha's range. By the mid-70s they had been superseded by the RD (Race-Developed) 125, 250, and 350 range of two-stroke twins, featuring improved 7-port engines with reed valve induction. Braking was improved by the use of an hydraulic brake on the front wheel of DX models, instead of the drum arrangement used previously, and cast alloy wheels were available as an option on later RD models. The RD350 was replaced by the RD400 in 1976.

Running parallel with the RD twins was a range of single-cylinder two-strokes. Used in a variety of chassis types, the engine was used in the popular 50 cc FS1-E moped, the V50 to 90 step-thrus, RS100 and 125, YB100 and the DT trail range.

The TD racers got water-cooling in 1973 to become the TZs, the most successful and numerous over-the-counter racers ever built. That same year, Jarno Saarinen became the first rider to win a 500cc GP on a four-cylinder two-stroke on the new in-line four which was effectively a pair of TZs side-by-side. TZs won everywhere – including the Daytona 200 and 500 races when overbored to 351cc. A 700cc TZ also appeared, one year later taken out to 750cc. Steve Baker won the first Formula 750 world title – one of the precursors of Superbike – on one in 1977. The following year Kenny Roberts won Yamaha's first world 500 title and would be succeeded by Wayne Rainey and Eddie Lawson before Mick Doohan and the NSR500 took over.

The air-cooled single and twin cylinder RD road bikes were eventually replaced by the LC series in 1980, featuring liquid-cooled engines, radical new styling, spiral pattern cast wheels and cantilever rear suspension (Yamaha's Monoshock). Of all the LC models, the RD350LC, or RD350R as it was later known, has made the most impact in the market. Later models had YPVS (Yamaha Power Valve System) engines, another first for Yamaha – this was essentially a valve located in the exhaust ports which was electronically operated to alter port timing to achieve maximum power output. The RD500LC was the largest two-stroke made by Yamaha and differed from the other LCs by the use of its vee-four cylinder engine.

With the exception of the RD350R, now manufactured in Brazil, the LC range has been discontinued. Two-stroke engined models have given way to environmental pressure, and thus with a few exceptions, such as the TZR125 and TZR250, are used only in scooters and small capacity bikes.

The distinctive paintwork and trim of the RD models

Introduction

The Four-strokes

Yamaha concentrated solely on two-stroke models until 1970 when the XS1 was produced, their first four-stroke motorcycle. It was perhaps Yamaha's success with two-strokes that postponed an earlier move into the four-stroke motorcycle market, although their work with Toyota during the 1960s had given them a sound base in four-stroke technology.

The XS1 had a 650 cc twin-cylinder SOHC engine and was later to become known as the XS650, appearing also in the popular SE custom form. Yamaha introduced a three cylinder 750 cc engine in 1976, fitted in a sport-tourer frame and called the XS750, TX750 in the USA. The XS750 established itself well in the sport tourer class and remained in production with very few changes until uprated to 850 cc in 1980.

Other four-strokes followed in 1976, with the introduction of the XS250/360/400 series twins. The XS range was strengthened in 1978 by the four-cylinder XS1100.

The 1980s saw a new family of four-strokes, the XJ550, 650, 750 and 900 Fours. Improvements over the XS range amounted to a slimmer DOHC engine unit due to the relocation of the alternator behind the cylinders, electronic ignition and uprated braking and suspension systems. Models were available mainly in standard trim, although custom-styled Maxims were produced especially for the US market. The XJ650T was the first model from Yamaha to have a turbo-charged engine. Although these early XJ models have now been discontinued, their roots live on in the XJ600S and XJ900S Diversion (Seca II) models.

The XS650 led the way for Yamaha's four-stroke range

The FZR prefix encompasses the pure sports Yamaha models. With the exception of the 16-valve FZR400 and FZR600 models, the FZ/FZR750 and FZR1000 used 20-valve engines, two exhaust valves and three inlet

Yamaha's XS750 was produced from 1976 to 1982 and then uprated to 850 cc

valves per cylinder. This concept was called Genesis and gave improved gas flow to the combustion chambers. Other features of the new engine were the use of down-draught carburetors and the engine's inclined angle in the frame, plus the change to liquid-cooling. Lightweight Deltabox design aluminium frames and uprated suspension improved the bikes's handling. The Genesis engine lives on in the YZF750 and 1000 models.

The Genesis concept was the basis of Yamaha's foray into four-stroke racing, first with a bike known simply as 'The Genesis', an FZ750 motor in a TT Formula 1 bike with which the factory attempted to steal the Honda RVF750's thunder at important events like the Suzuka 8 Hours and the Bol d'Or although they never fielded it for a whole World Championship season. That had to wait for the advent of the World Superbike Championship, although there was no full works team until 1995, instead it was left to individual importers to support teams. It was the Australian Dealer Team Yamaha which scored the factory's first World Superbike win in the series debut year of 1988. The rider? Mick Doohan. Slightly, embarrassingly, it was the steel framed FZ750 rather than the FZR homologation special that won races. The OW01 was a race winner, mainly in the hands of Fabrizio Pirovano, the factory's most successful Superbike racer with ten victories, but national success in the UK, Japan, and in the Daytona 200 has not been translated into World Championships for any of Yamaha's 750s.

The vee-twin engine has been the mainstay of the XV Virago range. Since 1981 XVs have been produced in 535, 700, 750, 920, 1000 and 1100 engine sizes, all using the same basic air-cooled sohc vee-twin engine. Other uses of vee engines have been in the XZ550 of the early 1980s, the XVZ12 Venture and the mighty VMX-12 V-Max.

A new family of four-strokes was released in 1980 with the introduction of the XJ range

Yamaha has always been a sporting-orientated company whose motto could be 'Racing Improves the Breed', so it's no surprise that the latest generation of lightweight sportsters are at the cutting edge of performance on and off the track. The R6 won more races than any other machine in the inaugural year of the World Supersports Championship, the R7 won a race in its debut year in World Superbike in the hands of the mercurial Noriyuki Haga, and the mighty 1000cc R1 ended Honda's domination of the Isle of Man F1 TT when David Jefferies won three races in a week in 1999.

In Grand Prix racing, the factory took several years to get over the shock of Wayne Rainey's crippling accident. and first 500cc win since the American's enforced retirement didn't come until 1998 when Simon Crafar won at Donington Park. For 1999, Yamaha refocussed their ambitions and signed Italian superstar Max Biaggi plus Spanish trier Carlos Checa for the works team, while dashing young Frenchman Regis Laconi and tough little Aussie Gary McCoy rode for the WCM satellite team. Both teams got a win in the '99 season and with a new TZ250 being developed for 2000 it looks as if Yamaha's spirit of competition will go on unabated into the new Millenium.

One litre Fazer

Let's face it, cutting edge sport bikes are extreme. Extreme not only in performance but also in what they do well. If you want to go very fast all the time or your riding is confined to the expert group at trackdays then the latest full-on sports bike is probably just what you want. However, if you occasionally want to ride in town, in traffic, with a pillion, then it's a different story.

The manufacturers have been trying to accomplish this trick for a long time. Even as far back as the early 1980s, the Yamaha stable contained their new-fangled FZR water-cooled models and the FJ range of air-cooled models, but they had very little in common. Suzuki should probably be credited with getting the concept right first with their Bandit range. However, the Bandits used old-generation oil/air-cooled motors first seen in early GSX-Rs wrapped in a steel tube chassis to produce useable performance at an affordable price.

That's the route Yamaha took for the first Fazer, the FZS600, but they went one step further with the big Fazer. Like the Bandits, and Honda's Hornets, Yamaha took a step

The XV535 Virago vee-twin

Introduction

back in time with the cycle parts: steel tube chassis, conventional front forks, big comfortable seat, and even – gasp – a centrestand. However, they had a new idea about the power plant: they took the motor out of their top of the range superbike and, with minimal modifications, put it in the big new Fazer. The Fazer got the original carburetted class-leading YZF-R1 motor with minimal modifications. Carb size came down from 40 to 37mm thus endowing the motor with more midrange and torque, and a ten-percent heavier crankshaft damped down the donor R1's rev-happy tendencies. By comparison, the Fazer was a substantial 33 kg heavier than the R1 and the wheelbase a couple of inches longer which makes the handling less nervous and matches the bike's dynamics to its engine characteristics. Don't get the idea that the Fazer was a cheap job, though. You can probably spot a few bits sourced from the parts bins of previous models, but the brakes and wheels are straight off the R1.

Everyone knows what an R1 is and what it's meant for, but what about the Fazer? Any thoughts that it was a streetfighter in the mould of the Triumph Speed Triple didn't survive the first press roadtests, and despite the tubular steel chassis there isn't much retro about the Fazer as there is with big twin-shock air-cooled bikes like Yamaha's XJR1300. If you were in any doubt, the price tag told you it wasn't a budget bike built down to a price. One American magazine came up with the perfect description: 'Super Standard', which sums it up nicely. A British magazine went so far as to wonder if it was 'the perfect road bike'.

The Fazer will traverse any given stretch of road this side of a race track as fast as anything on two wheels while carrying one or two people in comfort, and riders with long limbs or creaky joints won't need to visit their osteopaths after a day in the saddle. To say it has a large fuel tank and a centrestand makes it sound like a tourer but it isn't. It gets lumped into the Standard or Streetbike category in those end-of-year awards page fillers, although it is also often road tested alongside sports tourers like the VFR Honda. Pigeonholing the Fazer is difficult if not impossible. The one thing everyone agrees on is that it's a very competent motorcycle.

Yamaha appear to have got it right first time because changes to the first generation Fazer have been few, apart from the addition of the S model with its black engine and black swingarm. The reason that a lot of Fazers look different is the range of official Yamaha accessories: higher screens, crash protection mushrooms and a very trick looking carbon-fibre front mudguard are popular with owners.

Although not covered in this manual, a fuel-injected Fazer 1000 replaced the first generation model in 2006. Once again this model has inherited its power plant from the YZF-R1, thus the concept stays the same, but the realisation of it moves on.

Acknowledgements

Our thanks are due to Taylors Motorcycles of Crewkerne who supplied the machine featured in the illustrations throughout this manual. We would also like to thank NGK Spark Plugs (UK) Ltd for supplying the colour spark plug condition photographs and the Avon Rubber Company for supplying information on tyre fitting and Draper Tools Ltd for some of the workshop tools shown.

The 2001 FZS1000

The 2005 FZS1000S

About this manual

The aim of this manual is to help you get the best value from your motorcycle. It can do so in several ways. It can help you decide what work must be done, even if you choose to have it done by a dealer; it provides information and procedures for routine maintenance and servicing; and it offers diagnostic and repair procedures to follow when trouble occurs.

We hope you use the manual to tackle the work yourself. For many simpler jobs, doing it yourself may be quicker than arranging an appointment to get the motorcycle into a dealer and making the trips to leave it and pick it up. More importantly, a lot of money can be saved by avoiding the expense the shop must pass on to you to cover its labour and overhead costs. An added benefit is the sense of satisfaction and accomplishment that you feel after doing the job yourself.

References to the left or right side of the motorcycle assume you are sitting on the seat, facing forward.

We take great pride in the accuracy of information given in this manual, but motorcycle manufacturers make alterations and design changes during the production run of a particular motorcycle of which they do not inform us. No liability can be accepted by the authors or publishers for loss, damage or injury caused by any errors in, or omissions from, the information given.

Illegal Copying

It is the policy of Haynes Publishing to actively protect its Copyrights and Trade Marks. Legal action will be taken against anyone who unlawfully copies the cover or contents of this Manual. This includes all forms of unauthorised copying including digital, mechanical, and electronic in any form. Authorisation from Haynes Publishing will only be provided expressly and in writing. Illegal copying will also be reported to the appropriate statutory authorities.

Identification numbers 0•9

Frame and engine numbers

The frame serial number is stamped into the right-hand side of the steering head. The engine number is stamped into the crankcase on the right-hand side of the engine. The model code label is on the top of the frame cross-piece under the seat. These numbers should be recorded and kept in a safe place so they can be furnished to law enforcement officials in the event of a theft. There is also a carburettor identification number on the intake side of each carburettor body.

The frame serial number, engine serial number, carburettor identification number and model code should be recorded and kept in a handy place (such as with your driver's licence) so that they are always available when purchasing or ordering parts for your machine.

The procedures in this manual identify the bikes by year. The model codes (Europe) or suffix letters (US) for all years are tabled below.

Buying spare parts

Once you have found all the identification numbers, record them for reference when buying parts. Since the manufacturers change specifications, parts and vendors (companies that manufacture various components on the machine), providing the ID numbers is the only way to be reasonably sure that you are buying the correct parts.

Whenever possible, take the worn part to the dealer so direct comparison with the new component can be made. Along the trail from the manufacturer to the parts shelf, there are numerous places that the part can end up with the wrong number or be listed incorrectly.

The two places to purchase new parts for your motorcycle – the accessory store and the franchised dealer – differ in the type of parts they carry. While dealers can obtain virtually every part for your motorcycle, the accessory dealer is usually limited to normal high wear items such as shock absorbers, tune-up parts, various engine gaskets, cables, chains, brake parts, etc. Rarely will an accessory outlet have major suspension components, cylinders, transmission gears, or cases.

Used parts can be obtained for roughly half the price of new ones, but you can't always be sure of what you're getting. Once again, take your worn part to the breaker for direct comparison.

Whether buying new, used or rebuilt parts, the best course is to deal directly with someone who specialises in parts for your particular make.

Europe models	Year	Model code
FZS1000 Fazer	2001	5LV1
FZS1000 Fazer	2002	5LV8
FZS1000 Fazer	2003	5LVF
FZS1000S Fazer	2003	5LVN
FZS1000 Fazer	2004	1C21
FZS1000S Fazer	2004	1C25
FZS1000 Fazer	2005	1C28
FZS1000S Fazer	2005	1C2A

US 49-state models	Year	US California models	Year
FZS1000 N	2001	FZS1000 NC	2001
FZS1000 P	2002	FZS1000 PC	2002
FZS1000 R	2003	FZS1000 RC	2003
FZS1000 SP R	2003	FZS1000 SP RC	2003
FZS1000 S	2004	FZS1000 SC	2004
FZS1000 T	2005	FZS1000 TC	2005

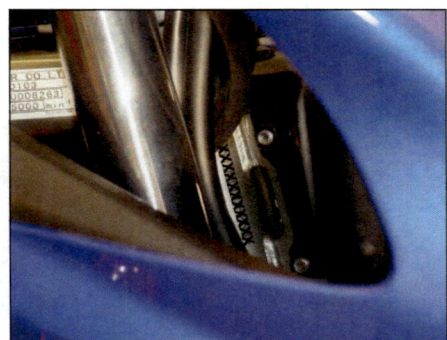

The frame number is stamped into the right-hand side of the steering head

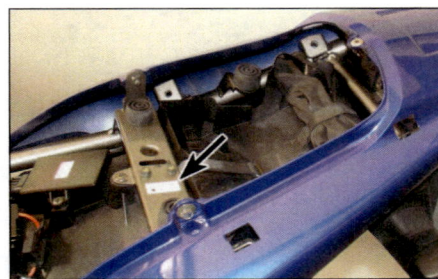

The model code or suffix label (arrowed) is stuck to the frame

The engine number is stamped into the crankcase on the right-hand side of the engine

Model development

The Fazer 1000 was launched in 2001. It uses a de-tuned version of the 2001 R1 engine, providing more torque and mid-range power, and sits in a tubular steel frame instead of the alloy beam frame of its sportier donor. The only difference to the engine internals is that the clutch uses conventional coil springs as opposed to the diaphragm spring used on the R1. Externally the engine covers have been changed to improve the looks now that the engine is fully exposed.

The Fazer has remained essentially unchanged over its production life, with the only significant development being the use of floating discs on the front brake system from 2003. Also in 2003 the S version was launched, giving the option of having a black engine and swingarm.

Bike Spec

Dimensions and weights

Overall length	2125 mm
Overall width	765 mm
Overall height	1190 mm
Wheelbase	1450 mm
Seat height	820 mm
Ground clearance	140 mm
Weight (wet)	
California models	232 kg
All other models	231 kg
Weight (dry)	
California models	209 kg
All other models	208 kg
Maximum load (total of rider, passenger, luggage and accessories)	
California models	188 kg
All other models	189 kg

Bike spec

Engine
Type	Four-stroke in-line four cylinder
Capacity	998cc
Bore	74 mm
Stroke	58 mm
Compression ratio	11.4 to 1
Cooling system	Liquid cooled
Clutch	Wet multi-plate with cable release
Transmission	Six-speed constant mesh
Final drive	Chain and sprockets
Camshafts	DOHC, chain driven
Fuel system	4 x Mikuni BSR37 carburettors, regular unleaded fuel
Exhaust system	Four-into-one with EXUP valve
Ignition system	Digital transistorised electronic

Chassis
Frame type	Tubular steel cradle
Rake and Trail	26°, 104 mm
Fuel tank capacity	
Total (inc. reserve)	21 litres
Reserve	4 litres
Front suspension	
Type	Oil-damped, coil sprung telescopic forks
Travel	140 mm
Adjustment	Spring pre-load, rebound and compression damping
Rear suspension	
Type	Single coil sprung and oil/gas damped shock absorber with rising rate linkage, aluminium swingarm
Travel (at wheel axle)	135 mm
Adjustment	Spring pre-load, rebound damping and compression damping
Wheels	Cast alloy, front 3.5 x 17 inch, rear 5.5 x 17 inch
Tyres (standard – refer to owners handbook or Yamaha dealer for other fittings)	
Front	120/70-ZR17 (58W) tubeless
Rear	180/55-ZR17 (73W) tubeless
Front brake	Twin 298 mm discs with twin opposed-piston calipers
Rear brake	Single 267 mm disc with single opposed-piston caliper

Safety first!

Professional mechanics are trained in safe working procedures. However enthusiastic you may be about getting on with the job at hand, take the time to ensure that your safety is not put at risk. A moment's lack of attention can result in an accident, as can failure to observe simple precautions.

There will always be new ways of having accidents, and the following is not a comprehensive list of all dangers; it is intended rather to make you aware of the risks and to encourage a safe approach to all work you carry out on your bike.

Asbestos

● Certain friction, insulating, sealing and other products - such as brake pads, clutch linings, gaskets, etc. - contain asbestos. Extreme care must be taken to avoid inhalation of dust from such products since it is hazardous to health. If in doubt, assume that they do contain asbestos.

Fire

● Remember at all times that petrol is highly flammable. Never smoke or have any kind of naked flame around, when working on the vehicle. But the risk does not end there - a spark caused by an electrical short-circuit, by two metal surfaces contacting each other, by careless use of tools, or even by static electricity built up in your body under certain conditions, can ignite petrol vapour, which in a confined space is highly explosive. Never use petrol as a cleaning solvent. Use an approved safety solvent.

● Always disconnect the battery earth terminal before working on any part of the fuel or electrical system, and never risk spilling fuel on to a hot engine or exhaust.

● It is recommended that a fire extinguisher of a type suitable for fuel and electrical fires is kept handy in the garage or workplace at all times. Never try to extinguish a fuel or electrical fire with water.

Fumes

● Certain fumes are highly toxic and can quickly cause unconsciousness and even death if inhaled to any extent. Petrol vapour comes into this category, as do the vapours from certain solvents such as trichloro-ethylene. Any draining or pouring of such volatile fluids should be done in a well ventilated area.

● When using cleaning fluids and solvents, read the instructions carefully. Never use materials from unmarked containers - they may give off poisonous vapours.

● Never run the engine of a motor vehicle in an enclosed space such as a garage. Exhaust fumes contain carbon monoxide which is extremely poisonous; if you need to run the engine, always do so in the open air or at least have the rear of the vehicle outside the workplace.

The battery

● Never cause a spark, or allow a naked light near the vehicle's battery. It will normally be giving off a certain amount of hydrogen gas, which is highly explosive.

● Always disconnect the battery ground (earth) terminal before working on the fuel or electrical systems (except where noted).

● If possible, loosen the filler plugs or cover when charging the battery from an external source. Do not charge at an excessive rate or the battery may burst.

● Take care when topping up, cleaning or carrying the battery. The acid electrolyte, evenwhen diluted, is very corrosive and should not be allowed to contact the eyes or skin. Always wear rubber gloves and goggles or a face shield. If you ever need to prepare electrolyte yourself, always add the acid slowly to the water; never add the water to the acid.

Electricity

● When using an electric power tool, inspection light etc., always ensure that the appliance is correctly connected to its plug and that, where necessary, it is properly grounded (earthed). Do not use such appliances in damp conditions and, again, beware of creating a spark or applying excessive heat in the vicinity of fuel or fuel vapour. Also ensure that the appliances meet national safety standards.

● A severe electric shock can result from touching certain parts of the electrical system, such as the spark plug wires (HT leads), when the engine is running or being cranked, particularly if components are damp or the insulation is defective. Where an electronic ignition system is used, the secondary (HT) voltage is much higher and could prove fatal.

Remember...

✗ **Don't** start the engine without first ascertaining that the transmission is in neutral.

✗ **Don't** suddenly remove the pressure cap from a hot cooling system - cover it with a cloth and release the pressure gradually first, or you may be scalded by escaping coolant.

✗ **Don't** attempt to drain oil until you are sure it has cooled sufficiently to avoid scalding you.

✗ **Don't** grasp any part of the engine or exhaust system without first ascertaining that it is cool enough not to burn you.

✗ **Don't** allow brake fluid or antifreeze to contact the machine's paintwork or plastic components.

✗ **Don't** siphon toxic liquids such as fuel, hydraulic fluid or antifreeze by mouth, or allow them to remain on your skin.

✗ **Don't** inhale dust - it may be injurious to health (see Asbestos heading).

✗ **Don't** allow any spilled oil or grease to remain on the floor - wipe it up right away, before someone slips on it.

✗ **Don't** use ill-fitting spanners or other tools which may slip and cause injury.

✗ **Don't** lift a heavy component which may be beyond your capability - get assistance.

✗ **Don't** rush to finish a job or take unverified short cuts.

✗ **Don't** allow children or animals in or around an unattended vehicle.

✗ **Don't** inflate a tyre above the recommended pressure. Apart from overstressing the carcass, in extreme cases the tyre may blow off forcibly.

✔ **Do** ensure that the machine is supported securely at all times. This is especially important when the machine is blocked up to aid wheel or fork removal.

✔ **Do** take care when attempting to loosen a stubborn nut or bolt. It is generally better to pull on a spanner, rather than push, so that if you slip, you fall away from the machine rather than onto it.

✔ **Do** wear eye protection when using power tools such as drill, sander, bench grinder etc.

✔ **Do** use a barrier cream on your hands prior to undertaking dirty jobs - it will protect your skin from infection as well as making the dirt easier to remove afterwards; but make sure your hands aren't left slippery. Note that long-term contact with used engine oil can be a health hazard.

✔ **Do** keep loose clothing (cuffs, ties etc. and long hair) well out of the way of moving mechanical parts.

✔ **Do** remove rings, wristwatch etc., before working on the vehicle - especially the electrical system.

✔ **Do** keep your work area tidy - it is only too easy to fall over articles left lying around.

✔ **Do** exercise caution when compressing springs for removal or installation. Ensure that the tension is applied and released in a controlled manner, using suitable tools which preclude the possibility of the spring escaping violently.

✔ **Do** ensure that any lifting tackle used has a safe working load rating adequate for the job.

✔ **Do** get someone to check periodically that all is well, when working alone on the vehicle.

✔ **Do** carry out work in a logical sequence and check that everything is correctly assembled and tightened afterwards.

✔ **Do** remember that your vehicle's safety affects that of yourself and others. If in doubt on any point, get professional advice.

● If in spite of following these precautions, you are unfortunate enough to injure yourself, seek medical attention as soon as possible.

Daily (pre-ride) checks 0•13

Note: *The daily (pre-ride) checks outlined in the owner's manual covers those items which should be inspected on a daily basis.*

Engine oil level

Before you start:
✔ Support the motorcycle on its centrestand. Make sure it is on level ground.
✔ Start the engine and let it idle for several minutes to allow it to reach normal operating temperature.
Caution: Do not run the engine in an enclosed space such as a garage or workshop.
✔ Leave the motorcycle undisturbed for a few minutes to allow the oil level to stabilise.

Bike care:
● If you have to add oil frequently, you should check whether you have any oil leaks. If there is no sign of oil leakage from the joints and gaskets the engine could be burning oil (see *Fault Finding*).

The correct oil
● Modern, high-revving engines place great demands on their oil. It is very important that you always top up with a good quality oil of the specified type and viscosity, and do not overfill the engine.
Caution: Do not use chemical additives or oils with a grade of CD or higher, or use oils labelled "ENERGY CONSERVING II". Such additives or oils could cause clutch slip.

Oil type	API grade SE, SF or SG
Oil viscosity UK models US models	 SAE 10W30 or 20W40* SAE 20W40*
*Refer to the viscosity table to select the oil best suited to your conditions.	

Oil viscosity table; select the oil best suited to the conditions

1 Wipe the oil level inspection window, located on the right-hand side of the engine, so that it is clean.

2 With the motorcycle level and vertical, the oil should lie between the maximum and minimum marks on the window (arrowed).

3 If the oil level is near, on or below the minimum line, remove the filler cap from the top of the clutch cover.

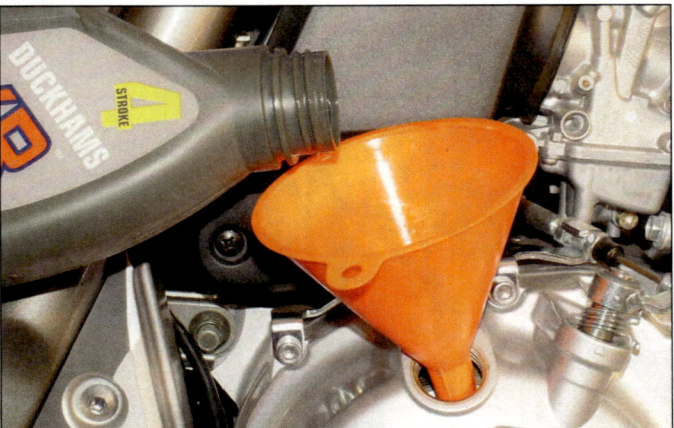

4 Top the engine up with the recommended grade and type of oil, so that it is almost up to the maximum level on the window. Install the filler cap.

0•14 Daily (pre-ride) checks

Brake fluid levels

⚠️ **Warning: Brake hydraulic fluid can harm your eyes and damage painted surfaces, so use extreme caution when handling and pouring it and cover surrounding surfaces with rag. Do not use fluid that has been standing open for some time, as it absorbs moisture from the air which can cause a dangerous loss of braking effectiveness.**

Before you start:
✔ When checking the front brake fluid level support the motorcycle in on its centrestand. Turn the handlebars to the right until the top of the front master cylinder, which is on the right handlebar, is as level as possible.
✔ When checking the rear brake fluid level support the motorcycle in on its centrestand on level ground. The rear master cylinder reservoir is located behind the right-hand side panel – the level line is are visible with the panel in place.
✔ Make sure you have the correct hydraulic fluid. DOT 4 is recommended.
✔ If topping up is necessary, wrap a rag around the reservoir being worked on to ensure that any spillage does not come into contact with painted surfaces.

Bike care:
● The fluid in the front and rear brake master cylinder reservoirs will drop slightly as the brake pads wear down.
● If any fluid reservoir requires repeated topping-up this is an indication of an hydraulic leak somewhere in the system, which should be investigated immediately.
● Check for signs of fluid leakage from the hydraulic hoses and brake system components – if found, rectify immediately (see Chapter 7).
● Check the operation of both brakes before taking the machine on the road; if there is evidence of air in the system (spongy feel to lever or pedal), it must be bled as described in Chapter 7.

FRONT BRAKE

1 The front brake fluid level is visible in the inspection window in the reservoir body – it must be above the LOWER level line (arrowed).

2 If the level is on or below the LOWER level line, undo the reservoir cover screws then remove the cover, the diaphragm plate and the diaphragm.

3 Top up with new clean DOT 4 hydraulic fluid, until the level is above the LOWER level line on the window, but not above the level line (arrowed) on the inside of the reservoir wall. Take care to avoid spills (see **Warning** above).

4 Wipe any traces of moisture out of the diaphragm using a clean absorbent and lint-free cloth.

5 Ensure that the diaphragm is correctly seated before installing the plate and cover. Secure the cover with its screws.

Daily (pre-ride) checks 0•15

REAR BRAKE

6 The rear brake fluid level is visible through the reservoir body – it must be above the LOWER level line (arrowed).

7 If the level is on or below the LOWER level line, remove the reservoir mounting screw and displace the reservoir to provide clearance.

8 Support the reservoir upright, then unscrew the cap and remove the diaphragm plate and the diaphragm.

9 Top up with new clean DOT 4 hydraulic fluid, until the level is above the lower level line. Take care to avoid spills (see **Warning** on page 0•14). Do not overfill.

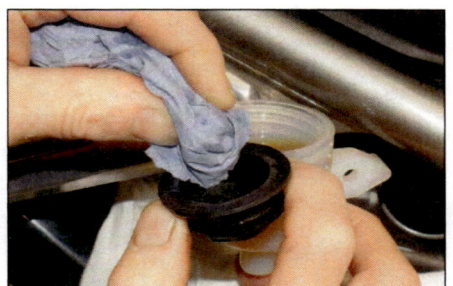

10 Wipe any traces of moisture out of the diaphragm using a clean absorbent and lint-free cloth.

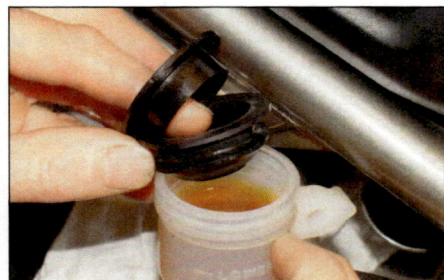

11 Ensure that the diaphragm is correctly seated before installing the plate and cap. Tighten the cap securely. Install the reservoir and tighten the mounting screw.

Coolant level

 Warning: DO NOT remove the cooling system pressure cap to add coolant. Topping up is done via the coolant reservoir tank filler. DO NOT leave open containers of coolant about, as it is poisonous.

Before you start:
✔ Make sure you have a supply of coolant available – a mixture of 50% distilled water and 50% corrosion inhibited ethylene glycol anti-freeze is needed. **Note:** *Yamaha specify that soft tap water can be used, but NOT hard water. If in doubt, boil the water first or use only distilled water.*
✔ Always check the coolant level when the engine is cold. If the engine has been running allow it cool down fully.
✔ Support the motorcycle on its centrestand. Make sure it is on level ground.

Bike care:
● Use only the specified coolant mixture. It is important that anti-freeze is used in the system all year round, and not just in the winter. Do not top the system up using only water, as the system will become too diluted.
● Do not overfill the reservoir. If the coolant is significantly above the FULL level line at any time, the surplus should be siphoned or drained off to prevent the possibility of it being expelled out of the overflow hose.
● If the coolant level falls steadily, check the system for leaks (see Chapter 1). If no leaks are found and the level continues to fall, it is recommended that the machine be taken to a Yamaha dealer for a pressure test.

1 The reservoir is mounted behind the engine on the right-hand side. With the motorcycle level and vertical the coolant should lie between the FULL and LOW level lines (arrowed) on the reservoir.

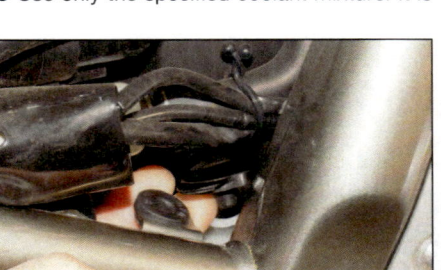

2 If the coolant level is near, on or below the LOW level line, remove the right-hand side panel (see Chapter 8), then remove the reservoir filler cap.

3 Top the coolant up with the recommended coolant mixture so that it is almost up to the FULL level line. Fit the cap securely, then install the side panel (see Chapter 8).

Daily (pre-ride) checks

Tyres

The correct pressures:
- Tyre pressures change with temperature and atmospheric pressure, therefore any change in the weather will affect the pressure of the tyre.
- The tyres must be checked when **cold**, not immediately after riding. Note that incorrect tyre pressures will cause abnormal tread wear and unsafe handling. Extremely low tyre pressures may cause the tyre to slip on the rim or come off.
- Use an accurate pressure gauge. Many garage forecourt gauges are wildly inaccurate. If you buy your own, spend as much as you can justify on a quality gauge.
- Correct air pressure will increase tyre life and provide maximum stability, handling capability and ride comfort.

Tyre care:
- Check the tyres carefully for cuts, tears, embedded nails or other sharp objects and excessive wear. Operation of the motorcycle with excessively worn tyres is extremely hazardous, as traction and handling are directly affected.
- Check the condition of the tyre valve and ensure the dust cap is in place.
- Pick out any stones or nails which may have become embedded in the tyre tread. If left, they will eventually penetrate through the casing and cause a puncture.
- If tyre damage is apparent, or unexplained loss of pressure is experienced, seek the advice of a tyre fitting specialist without delay.

Loading*/speed	Front	Rear
Up to 90 kg (198 lb) load	36 psi (2.5 Bar)	39 psi (2.7 Bar)
90 kg (198 lb) up to max. load of 196 kg (432 lb)	36 psi (2.5 Bar)	42 psi (2.9 Bar)
High speed riding	36 psi (2.5 Bar)	42 psi (2.9 Bar)

Load is the total weight of the rider, passenger, luggage and any accessories – see Bike spec

Tyre tread depth:
- At the time of writing UK law requires that tread depth must be at least 1 mm over the entire tread breadth all the way around the tyre, with no bald patches. Many riders, however, consider 2 mm tread depth minimum to be a safer limit. Yamaha recommend a minimum of 1.6 mm.
- Many tyres now incorporate wear indicators in the tread. Identify the triangular pointer or TWI mark on the tyre sidewall to locate the indicator bar and renew the tyre if the tread has worn down to the bar.

1 Check the tyre pressures when the tyres are **cold** and keep them properly inflated.

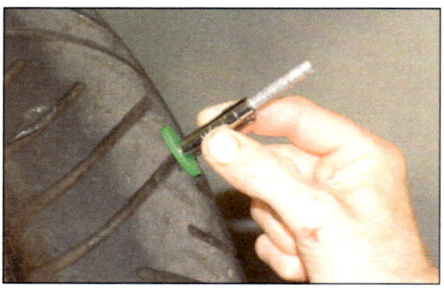

2 Measure tread depth at the centre of the tyre using a tread depth gauge.

3 Tyre tread wear indicator bar (arrowed) and its location marking (usually either an arrow, a triangle or the letters TWI as shown) on the sidewall.

Suspension, steering and final drive checks

Suspension and Steering:
- Check that the front and rear suspension operates smoothly without binding (see Chapter 1).
- Check that the suspension is adjusted as required (see Chapter 6).
- Check that the steering moves smoothly from lock-to-lock (see Chapter 1).

Final drive:
- Check that the drive chain slack isn't excessive, and adjust it if necessary (see Chapter 1).
- If the chain looks dry, lubricate it (see Chapter 1).

Legal and safety checks

Lighting and signalling:
- Take a minute to check that the headlight, tail light, brake light, instrument lights and turn signals all work correctly.
- Check that the horn sounds when the switch is operated.
- A working speedometer graduated in mph is a statutory requirement in the UK.

Safety:
- Check that the throttle grip rotates smoothly and snaps shut when released, in all steering positions. Also check for the correct amount of freeplay (see Chapter 1).
- Check that the brake lever and pedal, clutch lever and gearchange lever operate smoothly. Lubricate them at the specified intervals or when necessary (see Chapter 1).
- Check that the engine shuts off when the kill switch is operated. Check the starter interlock circuit (see Chapter 1).
- Check that the stand return springs hold the stands securely up when retracted.

Fuel:
- This may seem obvious, but check that you have enough fuel to complete your journey. If you notice signs of fuel leakage – rectify the cause immediately.
- Ensure you use the correct grade fuel – see Chapter 4 Specifications.

Chapter 1
Routine maintenance and Servicing

Contents

Air filter cleaning and renewal 5	Fuel filter renewal 24
Battery check 11	Fuel hose renewal 33
Battery charging, removal and installation .... see Chapter 9	Fuel system, EXUP system and air induction system (AIS) check .. 6
Brake fluid level check .... see *Daily (pre-ride) checks*	Headlight beam adjustment 29
Brake hose renewal 28	Idle speed check and adjustment 3
Brake seal renewal and fluid change 27	Nut and bolt check 15
Brake pad wear check 8	Sidestand and centrestand check 14
Brake system check 9	Spark plug check and adjustment 2
Carburettor synchronisation 4	Stand, lever pivot and cable lubrication 18
Clutch check and adjustment 10	Starter interlock circuit check 14
Coolant level check .... see *Daily (pre-ride) checks*	Steering head bearing check and adjustment 20
Cooling system check 16	Steering head bearing lubrication 23
Coolant change 26	Suspension check 19
Drive chain and sprocket check, adjustment and lubrication 1	Swingarm and suspension linkage bearing lubrication 22
Engine compression check 30	Throttle and choke cable check 17
Engine oil pressure check 31	Tyre pressure and tread depth .... see *Daily (pre-ride) checks*
Engine oil and filter change 21	Valve clearance check and adjustment 25
Engine oil change 7	Wheel bearing check 13
Engine oil level check .... see *Daily (pre-ride) checks*	Wheel and tyre check 12
Front fork oil change 33	

Degrees of difficulty

Easy, suitable for novice with little experience	**Fairly easy,** suitable for beginner with some experience	**Fairly difficult,** suitable for competent DIY mechanic	**Difficult,** suitable for experienced DIY mechanic	**Very difficult,** suitable for expert DIY or professional 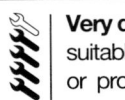

Specifications

Engine
Spark plugs
    Type .... NGK CR9E or Nippondenso U27ESR-N
    Electrode gap .... 0.7 to 0.8 mm
Engine idle speed .... 1050 to 1150 rpm
Cylinder identification .... numbered 1 to 4 from left to right
Carburettor synchronisation – intake vacuum at idle .... 225 mmHg
Carburettor synchronisation – max. difference between carburettors .. 10 mmHg
Valve clearances (COLD engine)
    Intake valves .... 0.11 to 0.20 mm
    Exhaust valves .... 0.21 to 0.25 mm
Cylinder compression
    Standard .... 206 psi (14.5 Bar)
    Maximum .... 230 psi (16.2 Bar)
    Minimum .... 179 psi (12.6 Bar)
    Max. difference between cylinders .... 14.5 psi (1.0 Bar)

Cycle parts
Drive chain slack .... 40 to 45 mm
Drive chain stretch limit.... .... 150.1 mm
Rear brake pedal height .... 35 to 40 mm
Throttle cable freeplay at twistgrip flange .... 3 to 5 mm
EXUP cable freeplay .... 1.5 mm
Clutch cable freeplay .... 10 to 15 mm
Tyre pressures (cold) .... see *Daily (pre-ride) checks*

Recommended lubricants and fluids
Engine oil type .... see *Daily (pre-ride) checks*
Engine oil capacity
    Oil change .... 2.8 litres
    Oil and filter change .... 3.0 litres
    Following engine overhaul – dry engine, new filter .... 3.7 litres
Coolant type .... 50% distilled water, 50% corrosion inhibited ethylene glycol anti-freeze. **Note:** *Yamaha specify that soft tap water can be used, but NOT hard water. If in doubt, boil the water first or use only distilled water.*
Coolant capacity .... 2.4 litres
Brake/clutch fluid .... DOT 4
Fork oil type .... Yamaha suspension oil '01' or 5W fork oil
Drive chain .... Engine oil or chain lubricant suitable for O-ring chains
Steering head bearings .... Lithium-based multi-purpose grease
Swingarm pivot and bearings .... Lithium-based multi-purpose grease
Suspension linkage bearings .... Lithium-based multi-purpose grease
Bearing seal lips .... Lithium-based multi-purpose grease
Gearchange lever, clutch lever, front brake lever,
    rear brake pedal, sidestand pivots .... Lithium-based multi-purpose grease
Cables .... Aerosol cable lubricant
Throttle grip .... Multi-purpose grease or dry film lubricant

Torque wrench settings
Brake torque arm nuts .... 23 Nm
Cooling system drain bolt .... 7 Nm
EXUP pulley cover bolts .... 10 Nm
Fork clamp bolts (top yoke) .... 30 Nm
Handlebar clamp bolts .... 23 Nm
Oil drain bolt .... 43 Nm
Oil filter .... 17 Nm
Oil gallery bolt .... 10 Nm
Rear axle nut .... 150 Nm
Spark plugs .... 13 Nm
Steering head bearing adjuster nut using service tool
    Initial setting .... 52 Nm
    Final setting .... 18 Nm
Steering stem nut .... 110 Nm
Timing rotor/pick-up coil cover bolts .... 12 Nm

Component locations 1•3

Component locations on the right hand side

1 Rear brake fluid reservoir
2 Fuel filter
3 Coolant reservoir
4 Air filter
5 Pressure cap
6 Front brake fluid reservoir
7 Throttle cable adjuster
8 Oil filler cap
9 Oil level inspection window
10 Rear brake light switch
11 Rear brake pedal adjuster

Components locations on the left hand side

1 Clutch cable adjuster
2 Steering head bearing adjuster
3 Air induction system valve
4 Idle speed adjuster
5 Fuel tap strainer
6 Battery
7 Drive chain adjuster
8 EXUP valve
9 Oil drain plug
10 Coolant drain plug
11 Oil filter
12 Front fork seals

Maintenance schedule – Europe models

Note: *The daily (pre-ride) checks outlined in the owner's handbook cover those items which should be inspected on a daily basis. Always also perform the pre-ride inspection at every maintenance interval (in addition to the procedures listed). The intervals listed below are the intervals recommended by the manufacturer for each particular operation during the model years covered in this manual. Your owner's handbook may have different intervals for your model.*

Daily (pre-ride)
☐ See *Daily (pre-ride) checks* at the beginning of this manual.

After the initial 1000 km (600 m)
Note: *This check is usually performed by a Yamaha dealer after the first 600 miles (1000 km) from new. Thereafter, maintenance is carried out according to the following intervals of the schedule.*

Every 1000 km (600 m)
☐ Check, adjust, clean and lubricate the drive chain (Section 1)

Every 10,000 km (6000 m)
☐ Check the spark plug gaps (Section 2)
☐ Check and adjust the idle speed (Section 3)
☐ Check/adjust the carburettor synchronisation (Section 4)
☐ Clean and check the air filter element (Section 5)
☐ Check the fuel system and EXUP system (Section 6)
☐ Check the air induction system (AIS) (Section 6)
☐ Change the engine oil (Section 7)
☐ Check the brake pads (Section 8)
☐ Check the brake system and brake light switch operation (Section 9)
☐ Check the clutch (Section 10)
☐ Check the battery (Section 11)
☐ Check the condition of the wheels and tyres (Section 12)
☐ Check the wheel bearings (Section 13)
☐ Check the sidestand, centrestand and interlock circuit operation (Section 14)
☐ Check the tightness of all nuts, bolts and fasteners (Section 15)
☐ Check the cooling system (Section 16)
☐ Check and adjust the throttle and choke cables (Section 17)

Every 10,000 km (6000 m) (continued)
☐ Lubricate the clutch/gearchange/brake lever/brake pedal/sidestand pivots and the throttle/choke cables (Section 18)
☐ Check the suspension (Section 19)
☐ Check and adjust the steering head bearings (Section 20)

Every 20,000 km (12,400 m)
Carry out all the items under the 10,000 km (6000 m) check, plus the following
☐ Fit new spark plugs (Section 2)
☐ Fit a new air filter (Section 5)
☐ Change the engine oil and filter (Section 21)
☐ Re-grease the swingarm and suspension linkage bearings (Section 22).
☐ Re-grease the steering head bearings (Section 23).
☐ Check the in-line fuel filter (Section 24)

Every 40,000 km (25,000 m)
☐ Check and adjust the valve clearances (Section 25)

Every two years
☐ Renew the brake seals and change the fluid (Section 27)

Every three years
☐ Change the coolant (Section 26)

Every four years
☐ Fit new brake hoses (Section 28)

Non-scheduled maintenance
☐ Check and adjust the headlight beam (Section 29)
☐ Check engine compression (Section 30)
☐ Check engine oil pressure (Section 31)
☐ Fit new fuel hoses (Section 32)
☐ Change the front fork oil (Section 33)

Maintenance schedule – US models

Note: *The daily (pre-ride) checks outlined in the owner's handbook cover those items which should be inspected on a daily basis. Always also perform the pre-ride inspection at every maintenance interval (in addition to the procedures listed). The intervals listed below are the intervals recommended by the manufacturer for each particular operation during the model years covered in this manual. Your owner's handbook may have different intervals for your model.*

Daily (pre-ride)
- [ ] See *Daily (pre-ride) checks* at the beginning of this manual.

After the initial 600 miles (1000 km)
Note: *This check is usually performed by a Yamaha dealer after the first 600 miles (1000 km) from new. Thereafter, maintenance is carried out according to the following intervals of the schedule.*

Every 600 m (1000 km)
- [ ] Check, adjust, clean and lubricate the drive chain (Section 1)

Every 4000 m (6400 km) or 6 months
- [ ] Check the spark plug gaps (Section 2)
- [ ] Check and adjust the idle speed (Section 3)
- [ ] Check/adjust the carburettor synchronisation (Section 4)
- [ ] Clean and check the air filter element (Section 5)
- [ ] Check the fuel system and EXUP system (Section 6)
- [ ] Check the air induction system (AIS) (Section 6)
- [ ] Change the engine oil (Section 7)
- [ ] Check the brake pads (Section 8)
- [ ] Check the brake system and brake light switch operation (Section 9)
- [ ] Check the clutch (Section 10)
- [ ] Check the battery (Section 11)
- [ ] Check the condition of the wheels and tyres (Section 12)
- [ ] Check the wheel bearings (Section 13)
- [ ] Check the sidestand, centrestand and interlock circuit operation (Section 14)
- [ ] Check the tightness of all nuts, bolts and fasteners (Section 15)
- [ ] Check the cooling system (Section 16)
- [ ] Check and adjust the throttle and choke cables (Section 17)
- [ ] Lubricate the clutch/gearchange/brake lever/brake pedal/sidestand pivots and the throttle/choke cables (Section 18)
- [ ] Check the suspension (Section 19)
- [ ] Check and adjust the steering head bearings (Section 20)

Every 8000 m (12,800 km) or 12 months
Carry out all the items under the 4000 m (6400 km) check, plus the following
- [ ] Fit new spark plugs (Section 2)
- [ ] Fit a new air filter (Section 5)
- [ ] Change the engine oil and filter (Section 21)

Every 12,000 m (20,000 km) or 18 months
- [ ] Check the EVAP system (Section 6)

Every 16,000 m (25,600 km) or two years
- [ ] Change the coolant (Section 26)
- [ ] Re-grease the swingarm and suspension linkage bearings (Section 22).
- [ ] Re-grease the steering head bearings (Section 23).

Every 20,000 miles (32,000 km)
- [ ] Fit a new in-line fuel filter (Section 24)

Every 26,000 miles (42,000 km)
- [ ] Check and adjust the valve clearances (Section 25)

Every two years
- [ ] Renew the brake seals and change the fluid (Section 27)

Every four years
- [ ] Fit new brake hoses (Section 28)

Non-scheduled maintenance
- [ ] Check and adjust the headlight beam (Section 29)
- [ ] Check engine compression (Section 30)
- [ ] Check engine oil pressure (Section 31)
- [ ] Fit new fuel hoses (Section 32)
- [ ] Change the front fork oil (Section 33)

1•6 Introduction

1 This Chapter is designed to help the home mechanic maintain his/her motorcycle for safety, economy, long life and peak performance.

2 Deciding where to start or plug into the routine maintenance schedule depends on several factors. If the warranty period on your motorcycle has just expired, and if it has been maintained according to the warranty standards, you may want to pick up routine maintenance as it coincides with the next mileage or calendar interval. If you have owned the machine for some time but have never performed any maintenance on it, then you may want to start at the beginning and include all frequent procedures to ensure that nothing important is overlooked. If you have just had a major engine overhaul, then you should start the engine maintenance routines from the beginning. If you have a used machine and have no knowledge of its history or maintenance record, you should combine all the checks into one large initial service and then settle into the maintenance schedule prescribed.

3 Before beginning any maintenance or repair, clean the machine thoroughly, especially around the oil filter, spark plugs, valve cover, side panels, carburettors, etc. Cleaning will help ensure that dirt does not contaminate the engine and will allow you to detect wear and damage that could otherwise easily go unnoticed.

4 Certain maintenance information is sometimes printed on decals attached to the motorcycle. If any information on the decals differs from that included here, use the information on the decal.

1 Drive chain and sprocket check, adjustment and lubrication

Check

1 The drive chain stretches with use. A neglected drive chain won't last long and can quickly damage the sprockets. Routine chain adjustment and lubrication isn't difficult and will ensure maximum chain and sprocket life.

2 To check the chain, support the bike on its centrestand, and shift the transmission into neutral. Make sure the ignition switch is OFF.

3 Push up on the bottom run of the chain and measure the slack midway between the two sprockets **(see illustration)**, then compare your measurement to that listed in this Chapter's Specifications. Since the chain will rarely wear evenly, resulting in a tight spot, rotate the rear wheel so that another section of chain can be checked; do this several times to check the entire length of chain. Any adjustment should be based upon the measurement taken at the tightest point.

4 The above chain slack check will suffice for regular maintenance, but every now and then it is important to check the chain for wear. Check the amount of chain wear (stretch) by measuring a ten-link section with it held taut, and comparing the measurement to the limit in the Specifications. Ideally this should be done with the chain removed, although it is possible to take the measurement on the bike if the chainguard is removed; the measurement is taken on the chain's top run, midway between the sprockets. Take three measurements in different places on the chain, noting that the measurement should be taken between the rollers of the 1st and 11th roller surfaces **(see illustration)**. If the chain has stretched beyond the limit specified, replace it with a new one (see Chapter 6).

5 In some cases where lubrication has been neglected, corrosion and galling may cause the links to bind and kink, which effectively shortens the chain's length and makes it tight. Thoroughly clean and work free any such links, then highlight them with a marker pen or paint. After the bike has been ridden repeat the measurement for slack in the highlighted area. If the chain has kinked again and is still tight, replace it with a new one. A rusty, kinked or worn chain will damage the sprockets and can damage transmission bearings. If in any doubt as to the condition of a chain, it is far better to install a new one than risk damage to other components and possibly yourself.

6 Check the entire length of the chain for damaged rollers, loose links and pins, and missing O-rings and replace with a new one if necessary. **Note:** *Never install a new chain on old sprockets, and never use the old chain if you install new sprockets – replace the chain and sprockets as a set.*

7 Remove the front sprocket cover (see Chapter 6). Check the teeth on the engine sprocket and the rear wheel sprocket for wear **(see illustration)**. If the sprocket teeth are worn excessively, or you are fitting a new chain, renew the chain and sprockets as a set.

8 Inspect the drive chain slider on the swingarm for excessive wear and replace it with a new one if necessary (see Chapter 6, Section 14).

Adjustment

9 Support the bike on its centrestand. Rotate the rear wheel until the chain is positioned with the tightest point at the centre of its bottom.

10 Slacken the nuts on the brake torque arm bolts **(see illustration)**. Slacken the axle nut **(see illustration)**.

11 Slacken the adjuster locknut on each side of the swingarm, then turn the adjuster bolts evenly as required until the amount of freeplay

1.3 Push up on the chain and measure the slack

1.4 Check the amount of stretch by measuring a 10-link section as shown

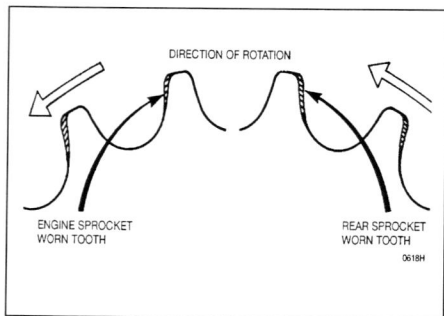

1.7 Check the sprockets in the areas indicated to see if they are worn excessively

1.10a Slacken the nuts on the torque arm bolts (arrowed) . . .

1.10b . . . then slacken the rear axle nut (arrowed)

Routine Maintenance and Servicing

1.11a Slacken the locknut (A) and turn the adjuster (B) as required

1.11b Check the relative position of the back edge of the adjustment marker with the marks on the swingarm

1.13 Tighten the axle nut to the specified torque

specified at the beginning of the Chapter is obtained at the centre of the bottom run of the chain **(see illustration)**. If the bolts are turned in because the chain is too tight push or kick the wheel forwards to take up the clearance and create the slack. Following chain adjustment, check that the back edge of each chain adjustment marker is in the same position in relation to the marks on the swingarm **(see illustration)**. It is important that each adjuster aligns with the same mark; if not, the rear wheel will be out of alignment with the front. Mae sure that there is no clearance between the adjuster bolt head and the front of the adjustment marker – push or kick the wheel forwards to eliminate any freeplay.

 HAYNES HiNT *Refer to Chapter 7 for information on checking wheel alignment.*

12 If there is a difference in the chain adjuster positions, adjust one of them so that its position is exactly the same as the other, then check the chain freeplay as described above and readjust if necessary.

13 Tighten the axle nut to the torque setting specified at the beginning of the Chapter, then tighten the adjuster bolt locknuts **(see illustration)**. Recheck the adjustment. Now tighten the brake torque arm bolt nuts to the specified torque.

Lubrication

14 If required, wash the chain in paraffin (kerosene), then wipe it off and allow it to dry, using compressed air if available.

Caution: *Don't use petrol (gasoline), solvent or other cleaning fluids which might damage the internal sealing properties of the chain's O-rings. Don't use high-pressure water or cleaning brushes. The entire process shouldn't take longer than ten minutes – if it does, the O-rings in the chain rollers could be damaged.*

15 The best time to lubricate the chain is after the motorcycle has been ridden. When the chain is warm, the lubricant will penetrate the joints between the side plates better than when cold. **Note:** *Yamaha specifies engine oil or chain lube that is specifically for O-ring chains; do not use chain lube that is not specifically for O-ring chains, as it may contain solvents that could damage the O-rings.* Apply the lubricant to the area where the side plates overlap – not the middle of the rollers **(see illustration)**.

 HAYNES HiNT *Apply the lubricant to the top of the lower chain run, so centrifugal force will work it into the chain when the bike is moving. After applying the lubricant, let it soak in a few minutes before wiping off any excess.*

⚠ **Warning:** *Take care not to get any lubricant on the tyres or brake system components. If any of the lubricant inadvertently contacts them, clean it off thoroughly using a suitable solvent or dedicated brake cleaner before riding the machine.*

2 Spark plug check and adjustment

Every 6000 miles (10,000 km) – Europe models

Every 4000 miles (6400 km) – US models

1 Make sure your spark plug socket is the correct size before attempting to remove the plugs – a suitable one is supplied in the motorcycle's tool kit which is stored under the seat.

2 Work on one plug at a time. Clean any debris off the plug cap seal. Pull the cap off the spark plug **(see illustration)**. Using compressed air if available, clean the area around the base of the spark plugs to prevent any dirt falling into the engine when the plugs are removed.

3 Using either the plug removing tool supplied in the bike's toolkit or a deep socket or commercial plug wrench of your own, unscrew the plug from the cylinder head **(see illustration)**.

4 Inspect the electrodes for wear. Both the centre and side electrodes should have square edges and the side electrodes should be of uniform thickness. Look for excessive deposits and evidence of a cracked or chipped insulator around the centre electrode. Compare your spark plugs to the colour spark plug reading chart at the end of this manual. Check the threads, the washer and the

1.15 Apply the lubricant to the overlap between the sideplates

2.2 Pull the cap up off the spark plug

2.3 Unscrewing the spark plug using the Yamaha tool

1•8 Routine Maintenance and Servicing

2.7a Using a wire type gauge to measure the spark plug electrode gap

2.7b Using a feeler gauge to measure the spark plug electrode gap

2.7c Adjust the electrode gap by bending the side electrode only

ceramic insulator body for cracks and other damage.

5 If the electrodes are not excessively worn, and if the deposits can be easily removed with a wire brush, and there are no cracks or chips visible in the insulator, the plugs can be re-used. If in doubt concerning the condition of the plugs, replace them with new ones, as the expense is minimal. Note that the spark plugs should be replaced with new ones at every second service interval, i.e. every 12,400 miles (20,000 km) on Europe models and every 8000 miles on US models.

6 Cleaning spark plugs by sandblasting is permitted, provided you clean the plugs with a high flash-point solvent afterwards.

7 Before installing the plug, make sure it is the correct type and heat range and check the gap between the electrodes **(see illustrations)**. Compare the gap to that specified and adjust as necessary. If the gap must be adjusted, bend the side electrode only and be very careful not to chip or crack the insulator nose **(see illustration)**. Make sure the sealing washer is in place on the plug before installing it.

8 Fit the plug into the end of the tool, then use the tool to insert the plug **(see illustration)**. Since the cylinder head is made of aluminium, which is a soft metal and easily damaged, thread the plug as far as possible into the head turning the tool by hand. Once the plug is finger-tight, the job can be finished with a spanner on the tool supplied or a socket drive **(see illustration 2.3)**. If a torque wrench can be applied, tighten the spark plug to the torque setting specified at the beginning of the Chapter. Otherwise, tighten them according the instructions on the box – generally if new plugs are being used, tighten them by 1/2 a turn after the washer has seated, and if the old plugs are being reused, tighten them by 1/8 to 1/4 turn after they have seated. Do not over-tighten them.

> **HAYNES HiNT** *As the plugs are quite recessed, you can slip a short length of hose over the end of the plug to use as a tool to thread it into place. The hose will grip the plug well enough to turn it, but will start to slip if the plug begins to cross-thread in the hole – this will prevent damaged threads.*

9 Fit the spark plug cap, making sure it locates correctly **(see illustration 2.2)**.

> **HAYNES HiNT** *Stripped plug threads in the cylinder head can be repaired with a thread insert – see Section 2 of 'Tools and Workshop Tips' in the Reference section.*

3 Idle speed check and adjustment

Every 6000 miles (10,000 km) – Europe models

Every 4000 miles (6400 km) – US models

1 The idle speed should be checked and adjusted before and after the carburettors are synchronised (balanced), after checking the valve clearances, and when it is obviously too high or too low. Before adjusting the idle speed, make sure the spark plugs are clean and their gaps are correct, and that the air filter is clean. If a valve clearance check is part of the service you are performing, do that first (see Section 25). Also, turn the handlebars from side-to-side and check the idle speed does not change as you do. If it does, the throttle cables may not be adjusted or routed correctly, or may be worn out. This is a dangerous condition that can cause loss of control of the bike. Be sure to correct this problem before proceeding.

2 The engine should be at normal operating temperature, which is usually reached after 10 to 15 minutes of stop-and-go riding. Make sure the transmission is in neutral, and place the motorcycle on its centrestand. Check the idle speed reading on the tachometer with that specified at the beginning of this Chapter.

3 The idle speed adjuster is located on the left-hand side of the motorcycle between the carburettor and the air filter housing **(see illustration)**. If adjustment is required, turn the adjuster until the speed listed in this Chapter's Specifications is obtained. Turn the knob clockwise to increase idle speed, and anti-clockwise to decrease it.

4 Snap the throttle open and shut a few times, then recheck the idle speed. If necessary, repeat the adjustment procedure.

5 If a smooth, steady idle cannot be achieved, the fuel/air mixture may be incorrect (check the pilot screw settings – see Chapter 4 Specifications) or the carburettors may need synchronising (see Section 4), or

2.8 Thread the plug as far as possible turning the tool by hand

3.3 Idle speed adjuster knob (arrowed)

Routine Maintenance and Servicing

4.4a Detach the AIS system hose (arrowed) from the union on the No. 4 duct . . .

4.4b . . . and the blanking caps (arrowed) from the rest . . .

4.4c . . . and attach the gauge hoses in their place

the AIS system may be faulty. Also check the intake manifold rubbers for cracks which will cause an air leak, resulting in a weak mixture.

4 Carburettor synchronisation

Every 6000 miles (10,000 km) – Europe models

Every 4000 miles (6400 km) – US models

⚠ **Warning:** *Petrol (gasoline) is extremely flammable, so take extra precautions when you work on any part of the fuel system. Don't smoke or allow open flames or bare light bulbs near the work area, and don't work in a garage where a natural gas-type appliance is present. If you spill any fuel on your skin, rinse it off immediately with soap and water. When you perform any kind of work on the fuel system, wear safety glasses and have a fire extinguisher suitable for a Class B type fire (flammable liquids) on hand.*

⚠ **Warning:** *Take great care not to burn your hand on the hot engine unit when accessing the gauge take-off points at the intake manifolds. Do not allow exhaust gases to build up in the work area; either perform the check outside or use an exhaust gas extraction system.*

1 Carburettor synchronisation (or balancing as it is often termed) is simply the process of adjusting the carburettors so that they pass the same amount of fuel/air mixture to each cylinder. This is done by measuring the vacuum produced in each cylinder. Carburettors that are out of synchronisation will result in increased fuel consumption, increased engine temperature, erratic idling, less than ideal throttle response and higher vibration levels. If a valve clearance check is part of the service you are performing, do that first (see Section 25).

2 To properly synchronise the carburettors you will need a set of vacuum gauges or a manometer. These instruments measure engine vacuum, and can be obtained from motorcycle dealers or mail order parts suppliers. The equipment used should be suitable for a four cylinder engine and come complete with the necessary adapters and hoses to fit the take-off points. **Note:** *Because of the nature of the synchronisation procedure and the need for special instruments, most owners leave the task to a Yamaha dealer.*

3 Start the engine and let it run until it reaches normal operating temperature, then check that the idle speed is correctly set, and adjust it if necessary (see Section 3). Raise the fuel tank (see Chapter 4).

4 Release the clamp securing the AIS system hose to the take-off union on the intake duct for cylinder No. 4 (right-hand cylinder) and attach the No. 4 gauge or manometer hose in its place **(see illustration)**. Remove the blanking caps from the take-off points on the intake ducts for cylinders Nos. 1, 2, and 3 and attach the other gauge or manometer hoses **(see illustrations)**. Make sure the No. 1 gauge is attached to the hose from the No. 1 (left-hand) intake duct, and so on.

5 Visually identify the three synchronisation screws which are situated in between the carburettors and are accessed from the top **(see illustration)**. The two outer ones are visible from behind the large bore vent hoses and are accessed with the screwdriver at a slight backward angle. The centre one is more easily visible and is accessed with the screwdriver to the right of the cable bracket and at a slight forwards angle.

6 Start the engine and let it idle. If the gauges are fitted with damping adjustment, set this so that the needle flutter is just eliminated but so that they can still respond to small changes in pressure.

7 The vacuum readings for all cylinders should be the same **(see illustration)**. If the vacuum readings differ, proceed as follows.

8 Synchronise the carburettors by turning the screws situated in between each carburettor, in the throttle linkage **(see illustration 4.5)**. **Note:** *Do not press on the screws whilst adjusting them, otherwise a false reading will be obtained.* First synchronise No. 1 carburettor to No. 2 using the left-hand synchronising screw until the readings are the same. Then synchronise No. 3 carburettor to No. 4 using the right-hand screw. Finally synchronise Nos. 1 and 2 carburettors to Nos. 3 and 4 using the centre screw. When all the carburettors are synchronised, open and close the throttle quickly to settle the linkage, and recheck the gauge readings, readjusting if necessary.

9 When the adjustment is complete, adjust the idle speed (see Section 3), and check the throttle cable freeplay (see Section 17). Remove the gauges and refit the blanking caps and AIS hose, making sure they are fully pushed onto their unions and secured by their clamps **(see illustrations 4.4c, b and a)**. Lower the fuel tank (see Chapter 4).

4.5 Left-hand screw (A) for synchronising carburettor 1 to 2, and centre screw (B) for synchronising pairs 1 and 2 to 3 and 4

4.7 Carburettor synchronisation set-up

1•10 Routine Maintenance and Servicing

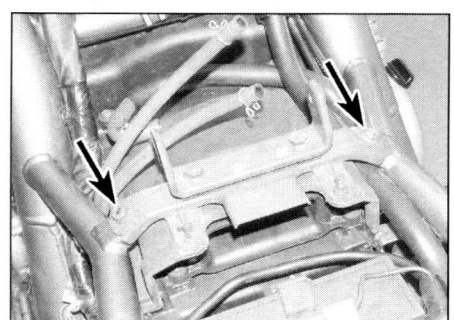

5.2a Unscrew the bolts (arrowed) . . .

5.2b . . . then free the grommets and remove the bracket and rubber cover

5.3a Undo the screws (arrowed) . . .

5 Air filter cleaning and renewal

Every 6000 miles (10,000 km) – Europe models

Every 4000 miles (6400 km) – US models

1 Remove the fuel tank (see Chapter 4). Remove the side panels (see Chapter 8).
2 Unscrew the tank bracket mounting bolts **(see illustration)**. Free the side panel mounting grommets from their pegs on the frame and remove the bracket along with the rubber cover, noting how they fit **(see illustration)**.

3 Undo the screws securing the air filter cover, then remove the cover and withdraw the filter from the housing **(see illustrations)**.
4 Tap the filter on a hard surface to dislodge any large particles of dirt. If compressed air is available, use it to clean the element, directing the air in the opposite direction of normal airflow (i.e. from the outside to the inside) **(see illustration)**.

 HAYNES HiNT *If using compressed air to clean the element, place either your hand, a rag, or a piece of card on the inside of the element to prevent any dust and debris being blown from one side of the element into the other.*

Caution: If the machine is continually ridden in dusty conditions, the filter should be cleaned more frequently.
5 Check the element for signs of damage. If it is torn or cannot be cleaned, or is obviously beyond further use, replace it with a new one. If the machine is used in excessively wet or dusty conditions the filter should be serviced more frequently.
6 Install the filter element, making sure it is properly seated **(see illustration 5.3)**. Fit the air filter cover, making sure the rubber seal is in place in the rim **(see illustrations 5.3 and a)**.
7 Install the tank bracket with the rubber cover and fit the grommets back onto their pegs, using a smear of oil to help them into place if necessary – make sure the shorter bolt is installed on the right-hand side (if the longer bolt is fitted there its end will press on the fuel supply hose) **(see illustrations 5.2b and a)**. Install the side panels (see Chapter 8), then the fuel tank (see Chapter 4).
8 Check that the filter in the air filter housing drain hose has not become blocked, and clean it if necessary **(see illustration)** – the hose comes out of the left-hand side of the housing.
9 Check the crankcase breather hose between the engine and the front of the air filter housing for loose connections, cracks and deterioration, and replace it with a new one if necessary **(see illustration)**.

5.3b . . . then lift off the cover . . .

5.3c . . . and withdraw the element

5.4 Direct the air in the opposite direction to normal airflow

5.8 Check the drain hose filter . . .

5.9 . . . and the crankcase breather hose (arrowed)

Routine Maintenance and Servicing

6 Fuel system, EXUP system and air induction system (AIS) check

Every 6000 miles (10,000 km) – Europe models

Every 4000 miles (6400 km) – US models

 Warning: *Petrol (gasoline) is extremely flammable, so take extra precautions when you work on any part of the fuel system. Don't smoke or allow open flames or bare light bulbs near the work area, and don't work in a garage where a natural gas-type appliance is present. If you spill any fuel on your skin, rinse it off immediately with soap and water. When you perform any kind of work on the fuel system, wear safety glasses and have a fire extinguisher suitable for a Class B type fire (flammable liquids) on hand.*

Fuel system check

1 Raise the fuel tank (see Chapter 4). Remove the right-hand side panel (see Chapter 8). Check the tank, fuel tap and fuel hoses, and the in-line filter and fuel pump, for signs of leakage, deterioration or damage **(see illustrations)**; in particular check that there is no leakage from the fuel hoses. Replace any hoses which are cracked or have deteriorated with new ones (see Section 33).

2 If the tap has been leaking from the face, tightening the assembly screws on the face may help. Slacken the screws a little first, then tighten them evenly and a little at a time to ensure the cover seats properly on the tap body. If leakage persists, remove the tap (see Chapter 4), then undo the screws on the face of the tap and disassemble it, noting how the components fit. Inspect all components for wear or damage, and replace the seal with a new one. None of the other components are available individually, so if they are damaged fit a new tap. If the tap has been leaking from the base, tightening the mounting screws may help. Otherwise, remove the tap and fit a new O-ring (see Chapter 4). Remove any corrosion or paint bubbles before installing the tap.

3 If there is evidence of fuel leakage from any of the carburettors, first locate the source – if it is from the bottom, tighten the float chamber drain screw. Otherwise refer to Chapter 4).

4 On California models, check the EVAP system hoses and canister for loose connections, cracks and deterioration and replace them with new ones if necessary.

Fuel filter cleaning and renewal

5 An in-line fuel filter is fitted in the hose from the fuel tap to the fuel pump **(see illustration)**. Remove the right-hand side panel (see Chapter 8). If the filter is dirty or clogged,

6.1a Check the tap and hoses ...

replace it with a new one – this type of filter cannot be cleaned. Displace the fuel pump from its mount. Have a rag handy to soak up any residual fuel, then release the clamps and disconnect the hoses from the filter, noting which fits where. Release the filter from its holder and discard it. Install the new filter so that its arrow points in the direction of fuel flow (i.e. towards the pump). Fit the hoses onto the unions on the filter and secure them with the clamps. Start the engine and check that there are no leaks.

6 A fuel strainer is mounted in the tank and is integral with the fuel tap. Cleaning of the strainer is not part of the maintenance schedule, but is advised after a high mileage has been covered or if fuel starvation problems are suspected. Remove the fuel tank and the fuel tap (see Chapter 4). Clean the gauze strainer to remove all traces of dirt and fuel sediment. Check the gauze for holes. If any are found, a new tap should be fitted – the strainer is not available separately. If the strainer is dirty, check the condition of the inside of your tank – if there is evidence of rust, drain and clean the tank (see Chapter 4).

EXUP system check

7 When the ignition is first switched ON, the EXUP system performs its own self-diagnosis. If a fault occurs, the tachometer will be seen to display zero rpm for 3 seconds, then 7000 rpm for 2.5 seconds, then the actual engine speed for 3 seconds, whereupon it will repeat the cycle until the engine is switched off. Note that the motorcycle can be ridden even though a fault has been diagnosed,

6.1b ... and the pump and filter (arrowed) as described

though a difference in performance will be noticed.

8 Raise the fuel tank (see Chapter 4).

9 Unscrew the bolts securing the EXUP pulley cover on the exhaust and remove the cover **(see illustration)**.

10 Start the engine and increase the revs. The servo, located under the front of the fuel tank on the left-hand side, should start to turn and continue as the revs rise, and be fully turned at around 5000 rpm. As it turns, simultaneously check that the pulley on the exhaust is turning the valve. If the servo turns but the pulley does not, remove the cables and check, lubricate or replace them, as necessary (see Chapter 4). If the pulley operates, but the movement of the valve is sticky or not complete, first check the cables, and if they are good, disassemble the valve for cleaning and inspection (see Chapter 4). If the servo does not operate, refer to Chapter 4 for further tests.

11 The EXUP pulley and valve are prone to corrosion, due to their exposed location. The pulley cover and valve cover bolts can seize, the cable ends can seize in their sockets in the pulley, and the valve shaft can seize in its bushes. Keep the area well lubricated with WD40 or a suitable equivalent. It is highly advisable to disassemble the system from time to time (according to the conditions you ride in) and lubricate the shaft, bushes, cable ends and bolts with copper-based grease (see Chapter 4).

12 Measure the amount of freeplay in each EXUP cable as shown and check that it is as specified at the beginning of the Chapter **(see**

6.6 In-line fuel filter (arrowed)

6.9 Unscrew the bolts (arrowed) and remove the cover

1•12 Routine Maintenance and Servicing

illustration). If not, slacken the lockring on the adjuster in each cable and turn the adjusters in to create freeplay in the cable (see illustration). Now turn the cable pulley on the valve until the notch in the pulley aligns with the hole in the housing, then insert a 4 mm pin into the hole (see illustration). Turn each cable adjuster out until there is no cable freeplay, then turn each in by 1/2 turn, then tighten the lockrings. Remove the pin from the hole and check that the freeplay is as specified and equal for each cable. Readjust as required if necessary.

13 Apply some copper grease to the cover bolt threads. Install the cover and tighten the bolts to the torque setting specified at the beginning of the Chapter (see illustration 6.9). Lower the fuel tank (see Chapter 4).

Air induction system (AIS) check)

14 If the valves clearances are all correct and the carburettors have been synchronised, and have no other faults, yet the idle speed cannot be set properly, it is possible that the AIS is faulty. Further information on the function of the system is in Chapter 4.

15 Raise the fuel tank (see Chapter 4). Check the air cut-off valve and reed valve unit on the top of the engine for signs of physical damage (see illustration) and replace it with a new one if necessary (see Chapter 4).

16 Check the AIS hoses and pipes for signs of deterioration or damage, and check that they are all securely connected with the hoses clamped at each end. Replace any hoses which are cracked or deteriorated with new ones (see Chapter 4).

17 Remove the valve unit and disassemble it (see Chapter 4). Check the reeds for cracks, warpage and any other damage or deterioration. Also check the contact areas between the reeds and the reed holders, and the holders themselves, for any signs of damage or deterioration. Any carbon deposits or other foreign particles can be cleaned off using a high flash-point solvent.

18 Any further testing of the air induction system requires the use of exhaust gas analysers and temperature sensors. If the system is thought to be faulty, take the bike to a Yamaha dealer for assessment. Make sure that the idle speed, valve clearances and carburettor synchronisation have all been checked before assuming that the AIS is faulty.

6.12a Check the freeplay in the cables

6.12c Insert the pin into the hole so it locks the pulley

6.12b EXUP cable freeplay adjuster lockrings (A) and adjusters (B)

6.15 The valve unit (arrowed) is below the frame tube

7 Engine oil change

Every 6000 miles (10,000 km) – Europe models

Every 4000 miles (6400 km) – US models

⚠ Warning: Be careful when draining the oil, as the exhaust pipes, the engine, and the oil itself can cause severe burns.

1 Consistent routine oil and filter changes are the single most important maintenance procedure you can perform on a motorcycle. The oil not only lubricates the internal parts of the engine, transmission and clutch, but it also acts as a coolant, a cleaner, a sealant, and as corrosion protection. Because of these demands, the oil takes a terrific amount of abuse and should be changed often with new oil of the recommended grade and type. Saving a little money on the difference in cost between a good oil and a cheap oil won't pay off if the engine is damaged. The oil filter should be changed with every second oil change.

2 Before changing the oil, warm up the engine so the oil will drain easily.

3 Position a clean drain tray below the engine. Unscrew the oil filler cap from the clutch cover to vent it and to act as a reminder that there is no oil in the engine (see illustration).

4 Unscrew the oil drain bolt from the underside of the engine and allow the oil to flow into the drain tray (see illustrations).

7.3 Remove the oil filler cap from the clutch cover

7.4a Unscrew the crankcase oil drain plug . . .

7.4b . . . and allow the oil to drain

Routine Maintenance and Servicing

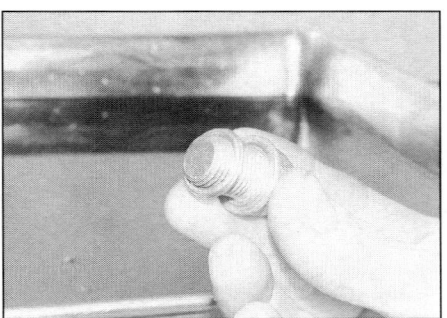

7.4c Replace the sealing washer with a new one

7.5 Install the drain plug and tighten it to the specified torque

Check the condition of the sealing washer on the bolt and discard it if it is damaged or worn – it will probably be necessary to cut the old one off using pliers **(see illustration)**. It is always advisable to use a new one even if the old one looks all right.

5 When the oil has completely drained, fit the bolt into the crankcase, preferably using a new sealing washer, and tighten it to the torque setting specified at the beginning of the Chapter **(see illustration)**. Avoid overtightening, as you will damage the sump.

6 Refill the engine to the proper level using the recommended type and amount of oil (see *Daily (pre-ride) checks*). With the motorcycle level and vertical, the oil level should lie between the maximum and minimum level lines on the inspection window (see *Daily (pre-ride) checks*). Install the filler cap **(see illustration 7.3)**. Start the engine and let it run for two or three minutes. Stop the engine, wait a few minutes, then check the oil level. If necessary, add more oil to bring the level up to the maximum level line on the window. Check that there are no leaks around the drain plug. If there are, and you didn't use a new sealing washer, drain the oil again and replace the washer with a new one.

7 Every so often, and especially as Yamaha do not fit an oil pressure switch and warning light (the system fitted uses an oil level sensor), it is advisable to perform an oil pressure check (see Section 31).

8 The old oil drained from the engine cannot be re-used and should be disposed of properly. Check with your local refuse disposal company, disposal facility or environmental agency to see whether they will accept the used oil for recycling. Don't pour used oil into drains or onto the ground.

HAYNES HiNT *Check the old oil carefully – if it is very metallic coloured, then the engine is experiencing wear from break-in (new engine) or from insufficient lubrication. If there are flakes or chips of metal in the oil, then something is drastically wrong internally and the engine will have to be disassembled for inspection and repair. If there are pieces of fibre-like material in the oil, the clutch is experiencing excessive wear and should be checked.*

Note: It is antisocial and illegal to dump oil down the drain. To find the location of your local oil recycling bank in the UK, call this number free. In the USA, note that any oil supplier must accept used oil for recycling.

8 Brake pad wear check

Every 6000 miles (10,000 km) – Europe models

Every 4000 miles (6400 km) – US models

1 Each brake pad has wear indicators that can be viewed without removing the pads from the caliper.
2 On original equipment brake pads the turned-in corners of the pad backing material form the wear indicators – when they are almost contacting the disc itself the pads must be replaced with new ones **(see illustration)**. The indicators are visible by looking at the relevant corner of the pads **(see illustration)**. The groove cut into the friction material can also be used as a wear indicator – the pad is worn when the groove is no longer visible **(see illustration)**. *Note: Some after-market pads may not have the turned-in corners, in which case use the groove as the wear indicator.*
Caution: Do not allow the pads to wear to the extent that the indicators contact the disc itself, as the disc will be damaged.
3 If the pads are worn to the indicators, new ones must be installed. If the pads are dirty or if you are in doubt as to the amount of friction material remaining, remove them for inspection (see Chapter 7). If required, measure the amount of friction material remaining – the absolute minimum is 0.5 mm.
4 Refer to Chapter 7 for details of pad renewal.

9 Brake system check

Every 6000 miles (10,000 km) – Europe models

Every 4000 miles (6400 km) – US models

1 A routine general check of the brake system will ensure that any problems are discovered

8.2a Brake pad wear indicators and minimum thickness groove

8.2b Brake pad wear indicator (arrowed) – rear brake shown

8.2c Friction material groove (A) and turned in corner (B) – front pad

1•14 Routine Maintenance and Servicing

9.3 Check the brake hose for cracks, bulges and leaking fluid

9.5 Hold the brake light switch (A) and turn the adjuster nut (B)

9.6 Adjusting the front brake lever span

and remedied before the rider's safety is jeopardised.

2 Check the brake lever and pedal for loose mountings, improper or rough action, excessive play, bends, and other damage. Lubricate the lever and pedal at the specified interval or as required (see Section 18). Replace any damaged parts with new ones (see Chapter 7).

3 Make sure all brake component fasteners are tight. Check the brake pads for wear (see Section 8) and make sure the fluid level in the reservoirs is correct (see *Daily (pre-ride) checks*). Look for leaks at the hose connections and check for cracks in the hoses themselves **(see illustration)**. If the lever or pedal is spongy, bleed the brakes (see Chapter 7). Change the brake fluid every two years (see Section 27) and replace the hoses with new ones if they deteriorate, or every four years irrespective of their condition (see Section 28). Replace the master cylinder and caliper seals with new ones every two years, or if leakage from them is evident (see Section 27).

4 Make sure the brake light operates when the front brake lever is pulled in. The front brake light switch, mounted on the underside of the master cylinder, is not adjustable; if it fails to operate properly, check it (see Chapter 9).

5 Make sure the brake light is activated just before the rear brake takes effect. If adjustment is necessary, hold the switch and turn the adjuster nut on the switch body until the brake light is activated when required **(see illustration)**. If the brake light comes on too late, turn the nut clockwise. If the brake light comes on too soon or is permanently on, turn the nut anti-clockwise. If the switch doesn't operate the brake light, check it (see Chapter 9).

6 The front brake lever has a span adjuster which alters the distance of the lever from the handlebar. Each setting is identified by a number on the adjuster which aligns with the arrow on the lever bracket. Pull the lever away from the handlebar and turn the adjuster ring until the setting which best suits the rider is obtained **(see illustration)**. There are four settings – setting 1 gives the largest span, and setting 4 the smallest. When making adjustment ensure that the pin set in the lever bracket is engaged in its detent in the adjuster.

7 Check the position of the brake pedal (brake pedal height). Yamaha recommend the distance between the tip of the brake pedal and the top of the rider's footrest should be as specified at the beginning of the Chapter **(see illustration)**. If the pedal height is incorrect, or if the rider's preference is different, slacken the clevis locknut on the master cylinder pushrod, then turn the pushrod using a spanner on the hex at the top of the rod until the pedal is at the correct or desired height **(see illustration)**. After adjustment check that the pushrod end is still visible in the hole in the clevis. On completion tighten the locknut. Adjust the rear brake light switch after adjusting the pedal height (see Step 5).

10 Clutch check and adjustment

Every 6000 miles (10,000 km) – Europe models

Every 4000 miles (6400 km) – US models

1 Check that the clutch lever operates smoothly and easily.

2 If the lever action is heavy or stiff, remove the cable (see Chapter 2) and lubricate it (see Section 18). If the inner cable still does not run smoothly in the outer cable, replace it with a new one. Install the lubricated or new cable (see Chapter 2). If the action is still stiff, remove the lever and check for damage or distortion, or any other cause, and remedy as necessary. Clean and lubricate the pivot and contact areas (see Section 18). If the lever is good, refer to Chapter 2 and check the release mechanism in the cover and the clutch itself.

3 With the cable operating smoothly, check that the clutch lever is correctly adjusted. Periodic adjustment is necessary to compensate for wear in the clutch plates and stretch of the cable. Check that the amount of freeplay at the clutch lever end is within the specifications listed at the beginning of the Chapter **(see illustration)**.

4 If adjustment is required, on 2001 and 2002 models first slacken the adjuster lockring. On

9.7a Measure the distance between the top of the footpeg and the top of the brake pedal as shown

9.7b Slacken the locknut (A) and turn the pushrod using the hex (B) making sure the rod end is still visible in the hole (C)

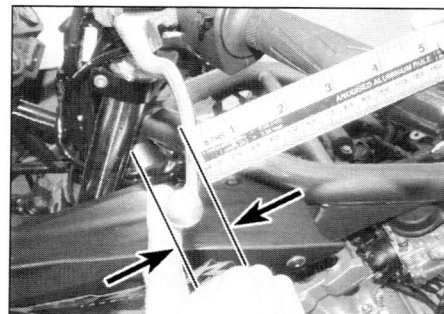

10.3 Check the amount of freeplay in the cable as shown

Routine Maintenance and Servicing

all models turn the adjuster in or out until the required amount of freeplay is obtained **(see illustration)**. To increase freeplay, turn the adjuster clockwise (into the lever bracket). To reduce freeplay, turn the adjuster anti-clockwise (out of the lever bracket). On 2001 and 2002 models tighten the locking ring securely.

5 If all the adjustment has been taken up at the lever, reset the adjuster to give the maximum amount of freeplay, then set the correct amount of freeplay by repositioning the threaded section of in the cable bracket on the right-hand side of the engine. Slacken the nuts securing the cable in its bracket and adjust them as required until the cable is positioned to give the correct freeplay **(see illustration)**. To increase freeplay, thread the nuts up the cable (towards the handlebar end). To reduce freeplay, thread them down the cable. Tighten the nuts against the bracket. Subsequent adjustments can now be made using the lever adjuster only.

11 Battery check

Every 6000 miles (10,000 km) – Europe models

Every 4000 miles (6400 km) – US models

1 All models are fitted with a sealed (maintenance-free) battery. **Note:** *Do not attempt to remove the battery caps to check the electrolyte level or battery specific gravity. Removal will damage the caps, resulting in electrolyte leakage and battery damage.*

2 All that should be done is to check that the terminals are clean and tight and that the casing is not damaged or leaking. See Chapter 9 for further details.

3 If the machine is not in regular use, disconnect the battery and give it a refresher charge every month to six weeks (see Chapter 9).

12 Wheel and tyre check

Every 6000 miles (10,000 km) – Europe models

Every 4000 miles (6400 km) – US models

Wheels

1 Cast wheels are virtually maintenance free, but they should be kept clean and checked periodically for cracks and other damage. Also check the wheel runout and alignment (see Chapter 7). Never attempt to repair

10.4 Turn the adjuster as described to set the correct freeplay

damaged cast wheels; they must be replaced with new ones. Check the valve rubber for signs of damage or deterioration and have it replaced with a new one if necessary. Also, make sure the valve cap is in place and tight.

Tyres

2 Check the tyre condition and tread depth thoroughly – see *Daily (pre-ride) checks*.

13 Wheel bearing check

Every 6000 miles (10,000 km) – Europe models

Every 4000 miles (6400 km) – US models

1 Wheel bearings will wear over a period of time and result in handling problems.

2 Support the motorcycle on its centrestand. To check the front wheel place a jack under the engine, with a piece of wood between the jack head and the sump to cushion and spread the load, and raise the front wheel off the ground. Check for any play in the bearings by pushing and pulling the wheel against the hub **(see illustration)**. Also spin the wheel and check that it rotates smoothly.

3 If any play is detected in the front wheel hub, or if the wheel does not rotate smoothly and freely (and this is not due to brake or transmission drag), the wheel bearings must be removed and inspected for wear or damage (see Chapter 7).

13.2 Checking for play in the wheel bearings

10.5 Slacken and adjust the nuts (arrowed) as described

4 On the rear wheel there should be a small amount of freeplay because it is fitted with a needle roller bearing in one side, which by nature exhibits more freeplay than conventional caged ball bearings. However, if the freeplay is excessive, or if the wheel does not rotate smoothly (and this is not due to brake or transmission drag), inspect the bearings for wear and damage and replace them with new ones if necessary (see Chapter 7). Note that once a needle bearing has been removed, it cannot be reused.

14 Sidestand, centrestand and starter interlock circuit check

Every 6000 miles (10,000 km) – Europe models

Every 4000 miles (6400 km) – US models

Sidestand and centrestand

1 The stand return springs must be capable of retracting the stands fully and holding them retracted when the motorcycle is in use. If a spring is sagged or broken it must be replaced with a new one.

2 Lubricate the stand pivot regularly (see Section 18).

Starter interlock circuit

3 The sidestand switch prevents the motorcycle being started if it is in gear and the stand is down, and cuts the engine if the stand is put down while it is running and in gear. Check its operation by shifting the transmission into neutral, retracting the stand and starting the engine. Pull in the clutch lever and select a gear. Extend the sidestand. The engine should stop as the sidestand is extended. If the sidestand switch does not operate as described, check its circuit (see Chapter 9). The clutch switch is also part of the same circuit – to check it, retract the sidestand, then select a gear. With the clutch lever pulled in, start the engine – if the engine starts, the switch is good. Otherwise, check the circuit (see Chapter 9).

1•16 Routine Maintenance and Servicing

15 Nut and bolt check

Every 6000 miles (10,000 km) – Europe models

Every 4000 miles (6400 km) – US models

1 Since vibration of the machine tends to loosen fasteners, all nuts, bolts, screws, etc. should be periodically checked for proper tightness. Also check the exhaust system ports and joints for signs of gas leakage, and if tightening the fasteners does not cure the problem remove the exhaust system and replace all gaskets and seals with new ones (see Chapter 4).

2 Pay particular attention to the following:
 Spark plugs
 Engine oil and coolant drain bolts
 Gearchange lever, brake and clutch lever, and brake pedal bolts
 Footrest and stand bolts
 Engine mounting bolts
 Shock absorber and suspension linkage bolts and swingarm pivot bolt nut
 Handlebar clamp bolts
 Front axle bolt and axle clamp bolts
 Front fork clamp bolts (top and bottom yoke)
 Steering stem nut
 Rear axle nut
 Front sprocket nut and rear sprocket nuts and studs
 Brake caliper mounting bolts
 Brake hose banjo bolts and caliper bleed valves
 Brake disc bolts
 Exhaust system bolts/nuts

3 If a torque wrench is available, use it along with the torque specifications at the beginning of this and other Chapters.

16 Cooling system check

Every 6000 miles (10,000 km) – Europe models

Every 4000 miles (6400 km) – US models

Warning: The engine must be cool before beginning this procedure.

1 Check the coolant level (see *Daily (pre-ride) checks*).

2 Check the cooling system for evidence of leakage. Examine each rubber coolant hose along its entire length **(see illustration)**. Look for cracks, abrasions and other damage. Squeeze each hose at various points. They should feel firm, yet pliable, and return to their original shape when released. If they are dried out or hard, replace them with new ones.

16.2a Check all the hoses and joints as described

Models equipped with a carburettor warmer circuit have a small-bore delivery hose from the thermostat housing to the right-hand side of the carburettor assembly and a return hose from the other side of the carburettors to the thermostat housing. Raise the fuel tank (see Chapter 4) for full access to the hoses and check the hose condition; note that the delivery hose contains an in-line check valve **(see illustration)**.

3 Check for evidence of leaks at each cooling system joint. If necessary, tighten the hose clips carefully to prevent future leaks.

4 To prevent leakage of water from the cooling system to the lubrication system and vice versa, two seals are fitted on the pump shaft. On the bottom of the sump there is a drain hole fed by a pipe coming from the pump **(see illustration)**. If either seal fails, the drain allows the coolant or oil to escape and prevents them mixing. The seal on the water pump side is of the mechanical type which bears on the rear face of the impeller. The second seal, which is mounted behind the mechanical seal, is of the normal feathered lip type. If on inspection the drain hole shows signs of coolant leakage, remove the pump and replace the mechanical seal with a new one. If it is oil that is leaking, or if the leakage is white and with the texture of emulsion, replace both seals with new ones (the mechanical seal has to be removed in order to remove the oil seal, and it cannot be reused). Refer to Chapter 3 for seal renewal.

5 Check the radiator for leaks and other damage. Leaks in the radiator leave tell-tale scale deposits or coolant stains on the

16.4 The drain hole (arrowed) is on the bottom of the sump

16.2b Check valve (arrowed) in carburettor warmer circuit hose

outside of the core below the leak. If leaks are noted, remove the radiator (see Chapter 3) and have it repaired by a professional.

Caution: Do not use a liquid leak stopping compound to try to repair leaks.

6 Check the radiator fins for mud, dirt and insects, which may impede the flow of air through the radiator. If the fins are dirty, remove the radiator (see Chapter 3) and clean it, using water or low pressure compressed air directed through the fins from the rear side. If the fins are bent or distorted, straighten them carefully with a screwdriver. If the air flow is restricted by bent or damaged fins over more than 30% of the radiator's surface area, install a new radiator.

7 Remove the right-hand cockpit trim panel (see Chapter 8). Remove the pressure cap from the radiator filler neck by turning it anti-clockwise until it reaches a stop **(see illustration)**. If you hear a hissing sound (indicating that there is still pressure in the system), wait until it stops. Now press down on the cap and continue turning the cap until it can be removed. Check the condition of the coolant in the system. If it is rust-coloured or if accumulations of scale are visible, drain, flush and refill the system with new coolant (See Section 26). Check the cap seal for cracks and other damage. If in doubt about the pressure cap's condition, have it tested by a Yamaha dealer or replace it with a new one. Install the cap by turning it clockwise until it reaches the first stop, then push down on the cap and continue turning until it can turn no further.

8 Check the antifreeze content of the coolant

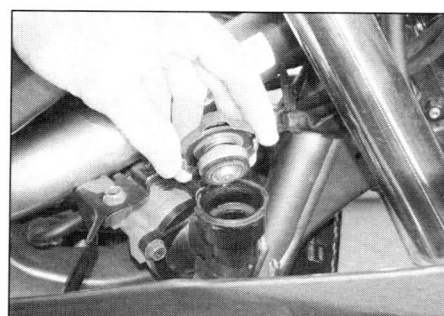

16.7 Remove the pressure cap as described

Routine Maintenance and Servicing

17.3 Measure the amount of freeplay in the throttle as shown

17.4 Slacken the lockring (arrowed) and turn the adjuster as required

17.6 Slacken the top nut (A) and slide the cable in the bracket until the bottom nut (B) is clear of the lug, then thread it up or down as required

with an antifreeze hydrometer. Sometimes coolant looks like it is in good condition, but it might be too weak to offer adequate protection. If the hydrometer indicates a weak mixture, drain, flush and refill the system (see Section 26).

9 Start the engine and let it reach normal operating temperature, then check for leaks again. As the coolant temperature increases beyond normal, the fan should come on automatically and the temperature should begin to drop. If it does not drop, refer to Chapter 3 and check the thermo switch, fan motor and fan circuit.

10 If the coolant level is consistently low, and no evidence of leaks can be found, have the entire system pressure-checked by a Yamaha dealer.

17 Throttle and choke cable check

Every 6000 miles (10,000 km) – Europe models

Every 4000 miles (6400 km) – US models

Throttle cables

1 Make sure the throttle twistgrip rotates easily from fully closed to fully open and returns automatically from fully open to fully closed when released. Do this with the front wheel turned at various angles to make sure the cables aren't binding at any point.

2 If the throttle sticks, this is probably due to a cable fault. Remove the cables (see Chapter 4) and lubricate them (see Section 18). If the inner cables still do not run smoothly in the outer cables, replace them with new ones. With the cables removed, check that the twistgrip runs smoothly and freely around the handlebar – dirt and debris combined with a lack of lubrication can cause the action to be stiff. Install the lubricated or new cables, making sure they are correctly routed (see Chapter 4). If this fails to improve the operation of the throttle, the fault could lie in the carburettors. Remove them and check

the action of the throttle linkage and butterflies (see Chapter 4).

3 With the throttle operating smoothly, check for a small amount of freeplay in the cables, measured in terms of the amount of twistgrip rotation before the throttle opens, and compare the amount to that listed in this Chapter's Specifications **(see illustration)**. If it is incorrect, adjust the cables to correct it as follows.

4 Loosen the adjuster lockring **(see illustration)**. Turn the adjuster until the specified amount of freeplay is obtained (see this Chapter's Specifications), then retighten the lockring. Turn the adjuster in to increase freeplay and out to reduce it. Refit the rubber boot on completion.

5 If the adjuster has reached its limit of adjustment, reset it so that the freeplay is at a maximum, then adjust the cable at the carburettor end as follows. Raise the fuel tank (see Chapter 4).

6 Slacken the accelerator (opening) cable top nut and slide the cable down in the bracket until the bottom nut is clear of the lug, then thread the bottom nut up or down as required – thread it down to reduce freeplay, and thread it up to increase it **(see illustration)**. Draw the cable up into the bracket so the bottom nut becomes captive against the lug, then tighten the top nut down onto the bracket. Further adjustments can now be made at the throttle end. If the cable cannot be adjusted as specified, replace the cable with a new one (see Chapter 4).

> ⚠ **Warning: Turn the handlebars all the way through their travel with the engine idling. Idle speed should not change. If it does, the cable may be routed incorrectly. Correct this condition before riding the bike.**

7 Check that the throttle twistgrip operates smoothly and snaps shut quickly when released. Install the fuel tank (see Chapter 4).

Choke cable

8 If the choke does not operate smoothly this is probably due to a cable fault. Remove the cable (see Chapter 4) and lubricate it (see Section 18). If the inner cable still does not run smoothly in the outer cable, replace it with a new one. Install the cable, routing it so it takes the smoothest route possible.

9 If this fails to improve the operation of the choke, check that the lever is not binding in the switch housing. If the lever action is good, the fault could lie in the carburettors rather than the cable, necessitating their removal and inspection of the choke plungers (see Chapter 4).

10 Make sure there is a small amount of freeplay in the cable before the plungers move. If there isn't, check that the cable is seating correctly at the carburettor end – raise the fuel tank (see Chapter 4) for access. You can create some freeplay in the cable by slackening the outer cable clamp screw on the carburettor and sliding the cable further into the clamp. Otherwise, replace the cable with a new one.

18 Stand, lever pivot and cable lubrication

Every 6000 miles (10,000 km) – Europe models

Every 4000 miles (6400 km) – US models

1 Since the controls, cables and various other components of a motorcycle are exposed to the elements, they should be lubricated periodically to ensure safe and trouble-free operation.

2 The footrests, clutch and brake levers, brake pedal, gearchange lever linkage and stand pivots should be lubricated frequently. In order that the lubricant is applied where it will do the most good, the component should be disassembled. The lubricant recommended by Yamaha for each application is listed at the beginning of the Chapter. If chain or cable lubricant is being used, it can be applied to the pivot joint gaps and will usually work its way into the areas where friction occurs, so less disassembly of the component is needed (however it is always better to do so and clean off all corrosion, dirt and old lubricant first). If motor oil or light grease is being used, apply it sparingly as it may attract dirt (which could

1•18 Routine Maintenance and Servicing

18.3 Lubricating a cable with a pressure lubricator. Make sure the tool seals around the inner cable

19.7 Checking for play in the swingarm bearings

19.8 Checking for play in the suspension linkage bearings

cause the controls to bind or wear at an accelerated rate). **Note:** *One of the best lubricants for the control lever pivots is a dry-film lubricant (available from many sources by different names).*

3 To lubricate the throttle, choke and clutch cables, disconnect the relevant cable at its upper end, then lubricate the cable with a pressure adapter and aerosol lubricant **(see illustration)**. See Chapter 4 for the throttle and choke cable removal procedures, and Chapter 2 for the clutch cable.

19 Suspension check

Every 6000 miles (10,000 km) – Europe models

Every 4000 miles (6400 km) – US models

1 The suspension components must be maintained in top operating condition to ensure rider safety. Loose, worn or damaged suspension parts decrease the motorcycle's stability and control.

Front suspension

2 While standing alongside the motorcycle, apply the front brake and push on the handlebars to compress the forks several times. See if they move up and down smoothly without binding. If binding is felt, the forks should be disassembled and inspected (see Chapter 6).

3 Inspect the area above and around each dust seal for signs of scratches, corrosion and pitting, and oil leakage, then carefully lever up the dust seal using a flat-bladed screwdriver and inspect the area around the fork seal. If leakage is evident, the seals in each fork must be replaced with new ones (see Chapter 6). If there is pitting in the chrome tubes within the extent of fork travel, you should consider replacing them with new ones as it will eventually cause the seals to fail. If there is evidence of corrosion between the seal retaining ring and its groove spray the area with a penetrative lubricant, otherwise the ring will be difficult to remove if needed. Press the dust seal back into place on completion..

4 Check the tightness of all suspension nuts and bolts to be sure none have worked loose, applying the torque settings at the beginning of Chapter 6 if you have a torque wrench.

Rear suspension

5 Inspect the rear shock absorber for damage and fluid leakage and tightness of its mountings. If leakage is found, the shock must be replaced with a new one (see Chapter 6).

6 With the aid of an assistant to support the bike, compress the rear suspension several times. It should move up and down freely without binding. If any binding is felt, the worn or faulty component must be identified and checked (see Chapter 6). The problem could be due to either the shock absorber, the suspension linkage components or the swingarm components.

7 Support the motorcycle on its centrestand. Grab the swingarm and rock it from side to side – there should be no discernible movement at the rear **(see illustration)**. If there's a little movement or a slight clicking can be heard, inspect the tightness of all the swingarm and rear suspension mounting bolts and nuts, referring to the procedures and torque settings specified at the beginning of Chapter 6, and re-check for movement.

8 Next, grasp the top of the rear wheel and pull it upwards – there should be no discernible freeplay before the shock absorber begins to compress **(see illustration)**. Any freeplay felt in either check indicates worn bearings in the suspension linkage or swingarm, or worn suspension mountings. The worn components must be identified and replaced with new ones (see Chapter 6).

9 To make an accurate assessment of the swingarm bearings, remove the rear wheel (see Chapter 7) and the nut and bolt securing the suspension linkage rods to the swingarm (see Chapter 6). Grasp the rear of the swingarm with one hand and place your other hand at the junction of the swingarm and frame. Try to move the rear of the swingarm from side to side. Any wear (play) in the bearings should be felt as movement between the swingarm and the frame at the front. If there is any play, the swingarm will be felt to move forward and backward at the front (not from side-to-side). Alternatively, measure the amount of freeplay at the swingarm end – Yamaha specify a maximum of 1 mm. Next, move the swingarm up and down through its full travel. It should move freely, without any binding or rough spots. If any play in the swingarm is noted or if the swingarm does not move freely, the bearings must be removed for inspection or renewal (see Chapter 6).

20 Steering head bearing check and adjustment

Every 6000 miles (10,000 km) – Europe models

Every 4000 miles (6400 km) – US models

1 Steering head bearings can become dented, rough or loose during normal use of the machine. In extreme cases, worn or loose steering head bearings can cause steering wobble – a condition that is potentially dangerous.

Check

2 Support the motorcycle on its centrestand on level ground. Place a jack under the engine, with a piece of wood between the jack head and the sump to cushion and spread the load, and raise the front wheel off the ground. Alternatively have an assistant push down on the rear of the bike.

3 Point the front wheel straight-ahead and move the handlebars slowly from side-to-side. Any dents or roughness in the bearing races will be felt and the bars will not move smoothly and freely. Again point the wheel straight-ahead, and tap the front of the wheel to one side. The wheel should 'fall' under its own weight to the limit of its lock, indicating that the bearings are not too tight. Check for similar movement to the other side. If the steering doesn't perform as described, and

Routine Maintenance and Servicing 1•19

20.4 Checking for play in the steering head bearings

20.6 Unscrew the bolt (arrowed) and displace the guide

20.8a Slacken the fork clamp bolt (arrowed) on each side . . .

it's not due to the resistance of cables or hoses, then the bearings should be adjusted as described below.

4 Next, grasp the bottom of the forks and gently pull and push them forward and backward **(see illustration)**. Any looseness or freeplay in the steering head bearings will be felt as front-to-rear movement of the forks. If play is felt, adjust the bearings as described below.

> **HAYNES HiNT** *Make sure you are not mistaking any movement between the bike and stand or jack, or between the stand or jack and the ground, for freeplay in the bearings. Do not pull and push the forks too hard – a gentle movement is all that is needed. Freeplay in the forks themselves due to worn bushes can also be misinterpreted as steering head bearing play – do not confuse the two.*

Adjustment

5 Support the motorcycle on its centrestand on level ground. Remove the fuel tank (see Chapter 4) and the fairing (see Chapter 8). **Note:** *Although it is not strictly necessary to remove the fuel tank and fairing, doing so will prevent the possibility of damage, should a tool slip.*
6 Unscrew the bolt securing the front brake hose guide to the top yoke and displace it **(see illustration)**.

20.8b . . . then unscrew the steering stem nut and remove the washer

7 Displace the handlebars (see Chapter 6).
8 Slacken fork clamp bolts in the top yoke **(see illustration)**. Unscrew the steering stem nut and remove it along with its washer **(see illustration)**.
9 Gently ease the top yoke upwards off the fork tubes and position it clear, using a rag to protect the tank or other components **(see illustration)**.
10 Remove the tabbed lock washer, noting how it fits, then unscrew and remove the locknut, using either a C-spanner, a peg spanner or a drift located in one of the notches if required – though it should only be finger-tight, and remove the rubber washer **(see illustrations)**.
11 To adjust the bearings as specified by Yamaha, a special service tool (Pt. No. 90890-01403 for Europe models, or YU-33975 for US

20.9 Ease the top yoke up off the steering stem and forks

models) and a torque wrench are required. If the tool is available, first slacken the adjuster nut, then tighten it to the initial torque setting specified at the beginning of the Chapter with the torque wrench positioned at 90° to the tool's centreline as shown **(see illustration)**. Now slacken the nut so that it is loose, then tighten it to the final torque setting specified. Check that the steering is still able to move freely from side to side, but that all freeplay is eliminated.
12 If the Yamaha tool is not available, using either a C-spanner, a peg spanner or a drift located in one of the notches, slacken the

20.10a Remove the tabbed lockwasher

20.10b The locknut should only be finger-tight but use a C-spanner if required

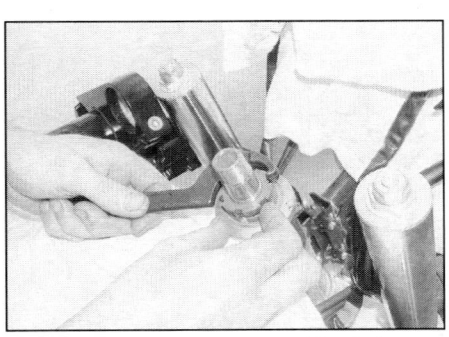

20.11 Set the torque wrench at right-angles (90°) to the service tool

Routine Maintenance and Servicing

20.12 If the tool is not available, adjust the bearings as described

20.13 Fit the locknut and tighten it as described

21.2a Using a filter wrench . . .

adjuster nut slightly until pressure is just released, then tighten it until all freeplay is removed, then tighten it a little more **(see illustration)**. This pre-loads the bearings. Now slacken the nut, then tighten it again, setting it so that all freeplay is just removed, yet the steering is able to move freely from side to side. To do this tighten the nut only a little at a time, and after each tightening repeat the checks outlined above (Steps 2 to 4) until the bearings are correctly set. The object is to set the adjuster nut so that the bearings are under a very light loading, just enough to remove any freeplay.

Caution: Take great care not to apply excessive pressure because this will cause premature failure of the bearings.

13 With the bearings correctly adjusted install the rubber washer and the locknut **(see illustration)**. Tighten the locknut finger-tight, then tighten it further until its notches align with those in the adjuster nut, but make sure it is not so tight that the rubber washer starts to be squeezed out the side. Install the tabbed lock washer so that the tabs fit into the notches in both the locknut and adjuster nut **(see illustration 20.10a)**.

14 Fit the top yoke onto the steering stem **(see illustration 20.9)**, then install the washer and steering stem nut and tighten it to the torque setting specified at the beginning of Chapter **(see illustration 20.8b)**. Now tighten both the fork clamp bolts to the specified torque setting **(see illustration 20.8a)**.

15 Install the handlebars (see Chapter 6).

16 Mount the front brake hose guide on the top yoke and tighten the bolt **(see illustration 20.6)**.

17 Re-check the bearing adjustment as described above and re-adjust if necessary.

18 Install the fuel tank if removed (see Chapter 4), and the fairing if removed (see Chapter 8).

21 Engine oil and filter change

Every 12,400 miles (20,000 km) – Europe models

Every 8000 miles (12,800 km) – US models

 Warning: Be careful when draining the oil, as the exhaust pipes, the engine, and the oil itself can cause severe burns.

1 Drain the engine oil as described in Section 7, Steps 2 to 5.

2 Now place the drain tray below the oil filter, which is at the front of the engine. Unscrew the oil filter using a commercially available filter removing wrench and socket extension and tip any residual oil into the drain tray **(see illustrations)**. If one is not available and you use a strap or chain-type removing tool be very careful not to touch the exhaust if it is still hot or warm – it is best to let it cool down first. Wipe any oil off the exhaust pipes to prevent too much smoke when you start the engine.

3 Smear clean engine oil onto the rubber seal on the new filter, then manoeuvre it into position and screw it onto the engine until the seal just seats **(see illustration)**. If the filter wrench is being used, tighten the filter to the torque setting specified at the beginning of the Chapter **(see illustration 21.2b)**. Otherwise, tighten the filter as tight as possible by hand, or by the number of turns specified on the filter or its packaging. **Note:** *Do not use a strap or chain tool to tighten the filter as you will damage it.*

4 Refill the engine to the proper level as described in Section 7, Steps 6 and 7.

5 Note the advice in Section 7 for disposing of used oil. Remember to drain all the old oil from the filter (you can punch a hole in the filter to ensure it drains fully) into the drain pan. Note that the old filter should be taken to the oil disposal facility rather than disposed of with the household rubbish.

22 Swingarm and suspension linkage bearing lubrication

Every 12,400 miles (20,000 km) – Europe models

Every 16,000 miles (25,600 km) – US models

1 Over a period of time the grease will harden and dirt will penetrate the bearings.

2 The rear suspension components are not equipped with grease nipples. Remove the

21.2b . . . and extension bar, unscrew the filter . . .

21.2c . . . and drain it into the tray

21.3 Smear some clean oil onto the seal then thread the filter onto the engine

Routine Maintenance and Servicing

swingarm and the suspension linkage as described in Chapter 6 for greasing of the bearings.

23 Steering head bearing lubrication

Every 12,400 miles (20,000 km) – Europe models

Every 16,000 miles (25,600 km) – US models

1 Over a period of time the grease will harden or may be washed out of the bearings by incorrect use of jet washes.
2 Disassemble the steering head for re-greasing of the bearings. Refer to Chapter 6 for details.

24 Fuel filter renewal

Every 12,400 miles (20,000 km) – Europe models

Every 20,000 miles (32,000 km) – US models

1 Refer to Section 6 and replace the in-line fuel filter with a new one.

25 Valve clearance check and adjustment

Every 25,000 miles (40,000 km) – Europe models

Every 26,000 miles (42,000 km) – US models

1 The engine must be completely cool for this maintenance procedure, so let the machine sit overnight before beginning.
2 Remove the valve cover (see Chapter 2).

25.4 Unscrew the bolts (arrowed) and remove the cover, noting the wiring clamp (A)

Each cylinder is referred to by a number. They are numbered 1 to 4 from left to right, viewed as normally seated on the bike.
3 Make a chart or sketch of all valve positions so that a note of each clearance can be made against the relevant valve.
4 Unscrew the bolts securing the timing rotor/pick-up coil cover on the right-hand side of the engine and remove the cover, noting the wiring clamp **(see illustration)**. Discard the gasket, as a new one must be used. Remove the dowels from either the crankcase or the cover if they are loose.
5 Turn the engine using a spanner or socket on the timing rotor bolt, turning it in a clockwise direction only, until the 'T' mark faces back and aligns with the crankcase mating surfaces **(see illustration)**, and the camshaft lobes for the No. 1 (left-hand) cylinder face away from each other – in this position the No. 1 cylinder is at TDC (Top Dead Centre) on the compression stroke **(see illustration)**. If the cam lobes are facing towards each other, rotate the engine clockwise 360° (one full turn) so that the 'T' mark again aligns with the crankcase mating surfaces. The camshaft lobes will now be facing away from each other.
6 With No. 1 cylinder at TDC on the compression stroke, check the clearances on the No. 1 cylinder intake and exhaust valves. Insert a feeler gauge of the same thickness as the correct valve clearance (see

Specifications) between the camshaft lobe and follower of each valve and check that it is a firm sliding fit – you should feel a slight drag when the you pull the gauge out **(see illustration)**. If not, use the feeler gauges to obtain the exact clearance. Record the measured clearance on the chart.
7 Now turn the engine clockwise 180° (half a turn) so that the 'T' mark faces forward and aligns with the crankcase mating surfaces and the camshaft lobes for the No. 2 cylinder are facing away from each other. The No. 2 cylinder is now at TDC on the compression stroke. Measure the clearances of the No. 2 cylinder valves using the method described in Step 6.
8 Now turn the engine clockwise 180° (half a turn) so that the 'T' mark faces back and aligns with the crankcase mating surfaces and the camshaft lobes for the No. 4 cylinder are facing away from each other. The No. 4 cylinder is now at TDC on the compression stroke. Measure the clearances of the No. 4 cylinder valves using the method described in Step 6.
9 Now turn the engine clockwise 180° (half a turn) so that the 'T' mark faces forward and aligns with the crankcase mating surfaces and the camshaft lobes for the No. 3 cylinder are facing away from each other. The No. 3 cylinder is now at TDC on the compression stroke. Measure the clearances of the No. 3 cylinder valves using the method described in Step 6.
10 When all clearances have been measured and charted, identify whether the clearance on any valve falls outside that specified. If it does, the shim between the cam follower and the valve must be replaced with one of a thickness which will restore the correct clearance.
11 Shim replacement requires removal of the camshafts (see Chapter 2). There is no need to remove both camshafts if shims from only one side of the engine need replacing. Place rags over the spark plug holes and the cam chain tunnel to prevent a shim from dropping into the engine on removal.
12 With the camshaft removed, lift out the cam follower of the valve in question, then retrieve the shim from inside the follower **(see**

25.5a Turn the engine until the 'T' mark aligns with the crankcase mating surfaces . . .

25.5b . . . and the camshaft lobes for No. 1 cylinder face away from each other as shown

25.6 Measuring the clearance using a feeler gauge

Routine Maintenance and Servicing

25.12a Lift out the follower . . .

25.12b . . . and remove the shim from inside the follower

25.13 Measure the shim using a micrometer

MEASURED VALVE CLEARANCE	\multicolumn{25}{c}{PRESENT SHIM SIZE}
	120	125	130	135	140	145	150	155	160	165	170	175	180	185	190	195	200	205	210	215	220	225	230	235	240
0.00 – 0.02 mm									120	125	130	135	140	145	150	155	160	165	170	175	180	185	190	195	200	205	210	215	220	225
0.03 – 0.07 mm							120	125	130	135	140	145	150	155	160	165	170	175	180	185	190	195	200	205	210	215	220	225	230
0.08 – 0.10 mm		120	125	130	135	140	145	150	155	160	165	170	175	180	185	190	195	200	205	210	215	220	225	230	235
0.11 – 0.20 mm	\multicolumn{25}{c}{SPECIFIED CLEARANCE/NO ADJUSTMENT REQUIRED}
0.21 – 0.22 mm	125	130	135	140	145	150	155	160	165	170	175	180	185	190	195	200	205	210	215	220	225	230	235	240
0.23 – 0.27 mm	130	135	140	145	150	155	160	165	170	175	180	185	190	195	200	205	210	215	220	225	230	235	240
0.28 – 0.32 mm	135	140	145	150	155	160	165	170	175	180	185	190	195	200	205	210	215	220	225	230	235	240
0.33 – 0.37 mm	140	145	150	155	160	165	170	175	180	185	190	195	200	205	210	215	220	225	230	235	240
0.38 – 0.42 mm	145	150	155	160	165	170	175	180	185	190	195	200	205	210	215	220	225	230	235	240
0.43 – 0.47 mm	150	155	160	165	170	175	180	185	190	195	200	205	210	215	220	225	230	235	240
0.48 – 0.52 mm	155	160	165	170	175	180	185	190	195	200	205	210	215	220	225	230	235	240
0.53 – 0.57 mm	160	165	170	175	180	185	190	195	200	205	210	215	220	225	230	235	240
0.58 – 0.62 mm	165	170	175	180	185	190	195	200	205	210	215	220	225	230	235	240
0.63 – 0.67 mm	170	175	180	185	190	195	200	205	210	215	220	225	230	235	240
0.68 – 0.72 mm	175	180	185	190	195	200	205	210	215	220	225	230	235	240
0.73 – 0.77 mm	180	185	190	195	200	205	210	215	220	225	230	235	240
0.78 – 0.82 mm	185	190	195	200	205	210	215	220	225	230	235	240
0.83 – 0.87 mm	190	195	200	205	210	215	220	225	230	235	240
0.88 – 0.92 mm	195	200	205	210	215	220	225	230	235	240
0.93 – 0.97 mm	200	205	210	215	220	225	230	235	240
0.98 – 1.02 mm	205	210	215	220	225	230	235	240
1.03 – 1.07 mm	210	215	220	225	230	235	240
1.08 – 1.12 mm	215	220	225	230	235	240
1.13 – 1.17 mm	220	225	230	235	240
1.18 – 1.22 mm	225	230	235	240
1.23 – 1.27 mm	230	235	240
1.28 – 1.32 mm	235	240
1.33 – 1.37 mm	240

25.14a Shim selection chart – intake camshaft

MEASURED VALVE CLEARANCE	\multicolumn{25}{c}{PRESENT SHIM NUMBER}
	120	125	130	135	140	145	150	155	160	165	170	175	180	185	190	195	200	205	210	215	220	225	230	235	240
0.00 – 0.02 mm											120	125	130	135	140	145	150	155	160	165	170	175	180	185	190	195	200	205	210	215
0.03 – 0.07 mm									120	125	130	135	140	145	150	155	160	165	170	175	180	185	190	195	200	205	210	215	220
0.08 – 0.12 mm							120	125	130	135	140	145	150	155	160	165	170	175	180	185	190	195	200	205	210	215	220	225
0.13 – 0.17 mm			120	125	130	135	140	145	150	155	160	165	170	175	180	185	190	195	200	205	210	215	220	225	230
0.18 – 0.20 mm		120	125	130	135	140	145	150	155	160	165	170	175	180	185	190	195	200	205	210	215	220	225	230	235
0.21 – 0.30 mm	\multicolumn{25}{c}{SPECIFIED CLEARANCE/NO ADJUSTMENT REQUIRED}
0.31 – 0.32 mm	125	130	135	140	145	150	155	160	165	170	175	180	185	190	195	200	205	210	215	220	225	230	235	240
0.33 – 0.37 mm	130	135	140	145	150	155	160	165	170	175	180	185	190	195	200	205	210	215	220	225	230	235	240
0.38 – 0.42 mm	135	140	145	150	155	160	165	170	175	180	185	190	195	200	205	210	215	220	225	230	235	240
0.43 – 0.47 mm	140	145	150	155	160	165	170	175	180	185	190	195	200	205	210	215	220	225	230	235	240
0.48 – 0.52 mm	145	150	155	160	165	170	175	180	185	190	195	200	205	210	215	220	225	230	235	240
0.53 – 0.57 mm	150	155	160	165	170	175	180	185	190	195	200	205	210	215	220	225	230	235	240
0.58 – 0.62 mm	155	160	165	170	175	180	185	190	195	200	205	210	215	220	225	230	235	240
0.63 – 0.67 mm	160	165	170	175	180	185	190	195	200	205	210	215	220	225	230	235	240
0.68 – 0.72 mm	165	170	175	180	185	190	195	200	205	210	215	220	225	230	235	240
0.73 – 0.77 mm	170	175	180	185	190	195	200	205	210	215	220	225	230	235	240
0.78 – 0.82 mm	175	180	185	190	195	200	205	210	215	220	225	230	235	240
0.83 – 0.87 mm	180	185	190	195	200	205	210	215	220	225	230	235	240
0.88 – 0.92 mm	185	190	195	200	205	210	215	220	225	230	235	240
0.93 – 0.97 mm	190	195	200	205	210	215	220	225	230	235	240
0.98 – 1.02 mm	195	200	205	210	215	220	225	230	235	240
1.03 – 1.07 mm	200	205	210	215	220	225	230	235	240
1.08 – 1.12 mm	205	210	215	220	225	230	235	240
1.13 – 1.17 mm	210	215	220	225	230	235	240
1.18 – 1.22 mm	215	220	225	230	235	240
1.23 – 1.27 mm	220	225	230	235	240
1.28 – 1.32 mm	225	230	235	240
1.33 – 1.37 mm	230	235	240
1.38 – 1.42 mm	235	240
1.43 – 1.47 mm	240

25.14b Shim selection chart – exhaust camshaft

Routine Maintenance and Servicing

25.15a Fit the shim into the recess in the top of the valve . . .

25.15b . . . then install the follower

25.17a Locate the new gasket onto the dowels (arrowed)

25.17b Locate the pivot pin (A) in the hole (B)

illustrations). The follower is best removed with a magnet or using the suction created by a valve lapping tool, but fingers may suffice, and long nosed pliers can be used with care – do not grip the follower tightly as you could score it. If the shim is not in the follower, pick it out of the top of the valve using either a magnet, a small screwdriver with a dab of grease on it (the shim will stick to the grease), or a screwdriver and a pair of pliers **(see illustration 25.15a)**. Do not allow the shim to fall into the engine.

13 A size mark should be stamped on the upper face of the shim – a shim marked 175 is 1.75 mm thick. If the mark is not visible, the shim thickness will have to be measured. It is recommended that the shim is measured, anyway, to check that it has not worn **(see illustration)**.

14 Using the appropriate shim selection chart, find where the measured valve clearance and existing shim thickness values intersect and read off the shim size required **(see illustrations)**. **Note:** *If the existing shim is marked with a number not ending in 0 or 5, round it up or down as appropriate to the nearest number ending in 0 or 5, so that the chart can be used.* Shims are available in 0.05 mm increments from 1.20 mm to 2.40 mm. **Note:** *If the required replacement shim is greater than 2.40 mm (the largest available), the valve is probably not seating correctly due to a build-up of carbon deposits and should be checked and cleaned or resurfaced as required (see Chapter 2).*

15 Obtain the replacement shim, then lubricate it with molybdenum disulphide grease and fit it into its recess in the top of the valve, with the size mark facing up **(see illustration)**. Check that the shim is correctly seated, then lubricate the follower with molybdenum disulphide oil (a 50/50 mixture of molybdenum disulphide grease and engine oil) and fit it onto the valve, checking that it fits easily and can be turned freely **(see illustration)**. Repeat the process for any other valves until the clearances are correct, then install the camshafts (see Chapter 2).

16 Rotate the crankshaft several turns to seat the new shim(s), then check the clearances again.

17 Install all disturbed components in a reverse of the removal sequence. Install the timing rotor/pick-up coil cover using a new gasket, and do not forget the dowels if removed **(see illustration)**. Locate the cam chain tensioner blade pivot pin in the hole in the cover **(see illustration)**. Tighten the cover bolts to the torque setting specified at the beginning of the Chapter, not forgetting the wiring clamp **(see illustration 25.4)**.

26 Coolant change

Every three years – Europe models

Every 16,000 miles (25,600 km) – US models

⚠️ **Warning:** *Allow the engine to cool completely before performing this maintenance operation. Also, don't allow antifreeze to come into contact with your skin or the painted surfaces of the motorcycle. Rinse off spills immediately with plenty of water. Antifreeze is highly toxic if ingested. Never leave antifreeze lying around in an open container or in puddles on the floor; children and pets are attracted by its sweet smell and may drink it. Check with local authorities (councils) about disposing of antifreeze. Many communities have collection centres where antifreeze can be disposed of safely. Antifreeze is also combustible, so don't store it near open flames.*

26.2a Unscrew the drain plug . . .

26.2b . . . and allow the coolant to drain

Draining

1 Support the motorcycle on its centrestand on level ground. Remove the right-hand cockpit trim panel (see Chapter 8). Remove the pressure cap from the radiator filler neck by turning it anti-clockwise until it reaches a stop **(see illustration 16.7)**. If you hear a hissing sound (indicating there is still pressure in the system), wait until it stops. Now press down on the cap and continue turning the cap until it can be removed. Also remove the filler cap from the coolant reservoir.

2 Position a suitable container beneath the drain plug on the coolant pipe coming out of the front of the engine. Remove the drain plug and allow the coolant to completely drain from the system **(see illustrations)**. Retain the old sealing washer for use during flushing.

3 Access to the reservoir itself for draining purposes is difficult. One way is to detach the

Routine Maintenance and Servicing

26.3 Detach the overflow hose from the filler neck

26.12 Fill the system using the correct mixture as described

overflow hose from the radiator filler neck, then draw it out from the bike, noting its routing, and place it at a lower level than the bottom of the reservoir – raise the fuel tank (see Chapter 4) to see the hose, and remove the right-hand side panel (see Chapter 8) so you can remove the reservoir cap **(see illustration)**. Reconnect the hose to the filler neck on completion. Alternatives are to remove the reservoir (see Chapter 3) or to draw the contents out via the filler neck using a syringe.

Flushing

4 Flush the system with clean tap water by inserting a garden hose in the radiator filler neck. Allow the water to run through the system until it is clear and flows cleanly out of the drain hole. If the radiator is extremely corroded, remove it (see Chapter 3) and have it cleaned professionally. Also flush the reservoir if drained.
5 Clean the drain hole, then install the drain plug using the old sealing washer. Fit the hose and cap onto the reservoir.
6 Fill the cooling system with clean water mixed with a flushing compound. Make sure the flushing compound is compatible with aluminium components, and follow the manufacturer's instructions carefully. Install the pressure cap.
7 Start the engine and allow it to reach normal operating temperature. Let it run for about ten minutes.
8 Stop the engine. Let it cool for a while, then cover the pressure cap with a heavy rag and turn it anti-clockwise to the first stop, releasing any pressure that may be present in the system. Once the hissing stops, push down on the cap and remove it completely.

9 Drain the system once again.
10 Fill the system with clean water and repeat the procedure in Steps 7 to 9.

Refilling

11 Fit a new sealing washer onto the drain plug and tighten it to the torque setting specified at the beginning of the Chapter (the old washer can be reused if it is not damaged or deformed, though it is always better to use a new one) **(see illustration 26.2a)**.
12 Fill the system via the radiator filler neck with the proper coolant mixture (see this Chapter's Specifications) **(see illustration)**. **Note:** *Pour the coolant in slowly to minimise the amount of air entering the system.* When the system appears full, move the bike off its stand and shake it slightly to dissipate the coolant, then place the bike back on the auxiliary stand and top the system up.
13 When the system is full (all the way up to the top of the radiator filler neck), install the pressure cap **(see illustration 16.7)**. Now fill the coolant reservoir to the FULL level line (see *Daily (pre-ride) checks*).
14 Start the engine and allow it to idle for 2 to 3 minutes. Flick the throttle twistgrip part open 3 or 4 times, so that the engine speed rises to approximately 4000 – 5000 rpm, then stop the engine.
15 Let the engine cool, then remove the pressure cap as described in Step 1. Check that the coolant level is still up to the top of the radiator or filler neck. If it is low, add the specified mixture until it reaches the top. Refit the pressure cap.
16 Check the coolant level in the reservoir and top up if necessary.
17 Check the system for leaks.
18 Do not dispose of the old coolant by

pouring it down the drain. Instead pour it into a heavy plastic container, cap it tightly and take it into an authorised disposal site or service station – see **Warning** at the beginning of this Section.
19 Install the cockpit trim and side panels (see Chapter 8).

27 Brake seal renewal and fluid change

Every two years

1 The seals will deteriorate over a period of time and lose their effectiveness, leading to sticky operation or fluid loss, or the ingress of air and dirt. Refer to Chapter 7 and disassemble the front and rear brake master cylinders and calipers for seal renewal.
2 Each brake system should be filled with fresh brake fluid and bled of air as described in Chapter 7.

28 Brake hose renewal

Every four years

1 The flexible hoses will deteriorate with age and should be replaced with new ones every four years regardless of their apparent condition.
2 Refer to Chapter 7 and disconnect the hoses from the master cylinders and calipers. Always replace the banjo union sealing washers with new ones.

Routine Maintenance and Servicing

Non-scheduled maintenance

29 Headlight beam adjustment

Note: *An improperly adjusted headlight may cause problems for oncoming traffic or provide poor, unsafe illumination of the road ahead. Before adjusting the headlight aim, be sure to consult with local traffic laws and regulations – for UK models refer to MOT Test Checks in the Reference section.*

1 The headlight beam can be adjusted both horizontally and vertically. Before making any adjustment, check that the tyre pressures are correct and the suspension is adjusted as required. Make any adjustments to the headlight aim with the machine on level ground, with the fuel tank half full and with an assistant sitting on the seat. If the bike is usually ridden with a passenger on the back, have a second assistant to do this. Remove the cockpit trim panels (see Chapter 8).
2 Vertical adjustment is made by turning the adjuster screw on the bottom outer corner of each headlight unit **(see illustration)**. Turn it anti-clockwise to raise the beam, and clockwise to lower it.
3 Horizontal adjustment is made by turning the adjuster knob on the top inner corner of each headlight unit **(see illustration 29.2)**. For the left-hand beam, turn it anti-clockwise to move the beam to the right, and clockwise to move it to the left. For the right-hand beam, turn it clockwise to move the beam to the right, and anti-clockwise to move it to the left.

30 Engine compression check

1 Among other things, poor engine performance may be caused by leaking valves, incorrect valve clearances, a leaking head gasket, or worn pistons, rings and/or cylinder walls. A cylinder compression check will help pinpoint these conditions and can also indicate the presence of excessive carbon deposits in the cylinder head.
2 The only tools required are a compression gauge and a spark plug wrench. A compression gauge with a threaded end for the spark plug hole is preferable to the type which requires hand pressure to maintain a tight seal. Depending on the outcome of the initial test, a squirt-type oil can may also be needed.
3 Make sure the valve clearances are correctly set (see Section 25) and that the cylinder head nuts are tightened to the correct torque setting (see Chapter 2).
4 Refer to *Fault Finding Equipment* in the *Reference* section for details of the compression test. Refer to the specifications at the beginning of this Chapter for compression figures.

29.2 Vertical adjuster (A), horizontal adjuster (B)

31 Engine oil pressure check

1 None of the models covered in this manual are fitted with an oil pressure switch and warning light, only an oil level sensor and light (see Chapter 9 for further information). If a lubrication problem is suspected, first check the oil level (see *Daily (pre-ride) checks*).
2 If the oil level is correct, an oil pressure check must be carried out next. The check provides useful information about the condition of the engine's lubrication system.
3 To check the oil pressure, slacken the oil gallery bolt in the front of the cylinder head on the right-hand end – there is no need to remove it. Start the engine and allow it to idle.
4 After a short while oil should begin to seep out from the oil gallery plug. If no oil has appeared after one minute, stop the engine immediately. If the oil does not appear after one minute, either the pressure regulator is stuck open, the oil pump is faulty, the oil strainer or filter is blocked, or there is other engine damage.
5 Begin diagnosis by checking the oil filter, strainer and regulator, then the oil pump (see Chapter 2). If no problems are found with those items, it may well be that the bearing oil clearances are excessive and the engine needs to be overhauled.
6 If the oil appears very quickly and spurts out, the pressure may be too high, meaning either an oil passage is clogged, the regulator is stuck closed or the wrong grade of oil is being used.
7 Tighten the oil gallery bolt to the torque setting specified at the beginning of the Chapter.
8 Refer to Chapter 2 and rectify any problems before running the engine again.
9 If the oil pressure and oil level are both good, then the oil level sensor or its warning light may be faulty. Check them and the circuit and replace with a new one if necessary (see Chapter 9).

32 Fuel hose renewal

Warning: *Petrol (gasoline) is extremely flammable, so take extra precautions when you work on any part of the fuel system. Don't smoke or allow open flames or bare light bulbs near the work area, and don't work in a garage where a natural gas-type appliance is present. If you spill any fuel on your skin, rinse it off immediately with soap and water. When you perform any kind of work on the fuel system, wear safety glasses and have a fire extinguisher suitable for a Class B type fire (flammable liquids) on hand.*

1 The fuel delivery hoses should be replaced with new ones after a few years, regardless of their condition. it is also advisable to replace all other fuel system hoses (breather, drain and vacuum hoses) at the same time.
2 Remove the fuel tank (see Chapter 4). Disconnect the fuel hoses from the fuel tap, filter, fuel pump and from the carburettors, noting the routing of each hose and where it connects (see Chapter 4 if required). It is advisable to make a sketch of the various hoses before removing them, to ensure they are correctly installed.
3 Secure each new hose to its unions using new clamps. Run the engine and check that there are no leaks before taking the machine out on the road.

33 Front fork oil change

1 Fork oil degrades over a period of time and loses its damping qualities. Refer to the fork oil change procedure in Chapter 6. The forks do not need to be completely disassembled.

Notes

Chapter 2
Engine, clutch and transmission

Contents

Alternator ..... see Chapter 9	Major engine repair – general note 3
Cam chain, tensioner, tensioner blade and guide blade 8	Neutral switch ..... see Chapter 9
Camshafts and followers 9	Oil and filter change ..... see Chapter 1
Clutch 12	Oil cooler 6
Clutch maintenance ..... see Chapter 1	Oil level check ..... see Daily (pre-ride) checks
Clutch cable 13	Oil pressure check ..... see Chapter 1
Component access 2	Oil pump 17
Connecting rods 22	Oil sump, oil strainer and pressure relief valve 16
Crankcase separation and reassembly 18	Pick-up coil assembly ..... see Chapter 5
Crankcase and cylinder bore inspection and servicing 19	Pistons 23
Crankshaft and main bearings 21	Piston rings 24
Cylinder head removal and installation 10	Running-in procedure 28
Cylinder head and valve overhaul 11	Selector drum and forks 27
Cylinder compression check ..... see Chapter 1 and Reference	Spark plugs ..... see Chapter 1
Engine removal and installation 4	Starter clutch and idle/reduction gear 14
Engine disassembly and reassembly general information 5	Starter motor ..... see Chapter 9
Gearchange mechanism 15	Transmission shaft disassembly, inspection and reassembly 26
General information 1	Transmission shaft removal and installation 25
Idle speed check and adjustment ..... see Chapter 1	Valve clearance check ..... see Chapter 1
Main and connecting rod bearing information 20	Valve cover 7

Degrees of difficulty

Easy, suitable for novice with little experience	Fairly easy, suitable for beginner with some experience	Fairly difficult, suitable for competent DIY mechanic	Difficult, suitable for experienced DIY mechanic	Very difficult, suitable for expert DIY or professional

Specifications

General
Type	Four-stroke in-line four
Capacity	998 cc
Bore	74 mm
Stroke	58 mm
Compression ratio	11.4 to 1
Cylinder numbering	1 to 4 from left to right
Cooling system	Liquid cooled
Clutch	Wet multi-plate
Transmission	Six-speed constant mesh
Final drive	Chain

Camshafts
Intake lobe height	
Standard	32.50 to 32.60 mm
Service limit (min)	32.40 mm
Exhaust lobe height	
Standard	32.95 to 33.05 mm
Service limit (min)	32.85 mm
Journal diameter	24.459 to 24.472 mm
Holder diameter	24.500 to 24.521 mm
Journal oil clearance	0.028 to 0.062 mm
Runout (max)	0.03 mm

Engine, clutch and transmission

Cylinder head
Warpage (max) .... 0.10 mm

Valves, guides and springs
Valve clearances .... see Chapter 1
Intake valve
  Stem diameter
    Standard .... 3.975 to 3.900 mm
    Service limit (min) .... 3.945 mm
  Guide bore diameter
    Standard .... 4.000 to 4.012 mm
    Service limit (max) .... 4.050 mm
  Stem-to-guide clearance
    Standard .... 0.010 to 0.037 mm
    Service limit (max) .... 0.08 mm
  Head diameter .... 22.9 to 23.1 mm
  Face width .... 1.76 to 2.90 mm
  Seat width .... 0.9 to 1.1 mm
  Margin thickness .... 0.5 to 0.9 mm
  Valve lift .... 7.45 to 7.65 mm
Exhaust valve
  Stem diameter
    Standard .... 4.465 to 4.480 mm
    Service limit (min) .... 4.430 mm
  Guide bore diameter
    Standard .... 4.500 to 4.512 mm
    Service limit (max) .... 4.550 mm
  Stem-to-guide clearance
    Standard .... 0.020 to 0.047 mm
    Service limit (max) .... 0.10 mm
  Head diameter .... 24.4 to 24.6 mm
  Face width .... 1.76 to 2.90 mm
  Seat width .... 0.9 to 1.1 mm
  Margin thickness .... 0.5 to 0.9 mm
  Valve lift .... 7.75 to 7.95 mm
Valve stem runout (max) .... 0.01 mm
Valve springs free length
  Intake .... 38.90 mm
  Exhaust .... 40.67 mm
Valve spring bend (max)
  Intake .... 1.7 mm
  Exhaust .... 1.8 mm

Clutch
Clutch plate assembly thickness .... 43.1 to 43.9 mm
Friction plates
  Type A
    Quantity 8
    Thickness
      Standard .... 2.92 to 3.08 mm
      Service limit (min) .... 2.8 mm
  Type B
    Quantity 1
    Thickness
      Standard .... 3.42 to 3.58 mm
      Service limit (min) .... 3.32 mm
Plain plates (standard thickness – see Section 12)
  Quantity 8
  Thickness .... 1.9 to 2.1 mm
  Warpage (max) .... 0.1 mm
Clutch spring free length .... 50 mm

Cylinder bores
Bore .... 74.000 to 74.010 mm
Ovality (out-of-round) (max) .... 0.05 mm
Taper (max) .... 0.05 mm
Cylinder compression .... see Chapter 1

Engine, clutch and transmission 2•3

Lubrication system
Engine oil pressure	6.4 psi (0.45 Bar) @ 1100 rpm
Relief valve opening pressure	69.7 to 81.1 psi (4.8 to 5.6 Bar)
Filter bypass valve opening pressure	25.6 to 31.3 psi (1.8 to 2.2 Bar)

Oil pump
  Inner rotor tip-to-outer rotor clearance
    Standard .... 0.09 to 0.15 mm
    Service limit .... 0.23 mm
  Outer rotor-to-housing clearance
    Standard .... 0.03 to 0.08 mm
    Service limit .... 0.15 mm
  Rotor end-float
    Standard .... 0.06 to 0.11 mm
    Service limit .... 0.18 mm

Crankshaft and bearings
Main bearing oil clearance .... 0.029 to 0.053 mm
Runout (max) .... 0.03 mm

Connecting rods
Big-end side clearance .... 0.160 to 0.262 mm
Big-end oil clearance .... 0.031 to 0.055 mm

Pistons
Piston diameter (measured 5 mm up from skirt, at 90° to piston
  pin axis) .... 73.955 to 73.970 mm
Piston-to-bore clearance
  Standard
    2001 and 2002 models .... 0.030 to 0.055 mm
    2003-on models .... 0.010 to 0.035 mm
  Service limit (max) .... 0.12 mm
Piston pin diameter .... 16.991 to 17.000 mm
Piston pin bore diameter in piston .... 17.002 to 17.013 mm
Piston pin-to-piston pin bore clearance
  Standard .... 0.002 to 0.022 mm
  Service limit .... 0.072 mm

Piston rings
Top ring
  Type .... Barrel
  Ring width .... 2.75 mm
  Ring thickness .... 0.9 mm
  Ring end gap (installed) .... 0.32 to 0.44 mm
  Piston ring-to-groove clearance .... 0.030 to 0.065 mm
2nd ring
  Type .... Taper
  Ring width .... 2.8 mm
  Ring thickness .... 0.8 mm
  Ring end gap (installed) .... 0.43 to 0.58 mm
  Piston ring-to-groove clearance .... 0.020 to 0.055 mm
Oil ring
  Ring width .... 2.6 mm
  Ring thickness .... 1.5 mm
  Side-rail end gap (installed) .... 0.10 to 0.35 mm

Transmission
Gear ratios (no. of teeth)
  Primary reduction .... 1.581 to 1 (68/43T)
  Final reduction .... 2.750 to 1 (44/16T)
  1st gear .... 2.500 to 1 (35/14T)
  2nd gear .... 1.842 to 1 (35/19T)
  3rd gear .... 1.500 to 1 (30/20T)
  4th gear .... 1.333 to 1 (28/21T)
  5th gear .... 1.200 to 1 (30/25T)
  6th gear .... 1.115 to 1 (29/26T)
Shaft runout (max) .... 0.08 mm

Selector drum and forks
Selector fork shaft runout (max) .... 0.1 mm

Torque wrench settings

Cam chain tensioner cap bolt	10 Nm
Cam chain tensioner mounting bolts	10 Nm
Camshaft holder bolts	10 Nm
Camshaft sprocket bolts	24 Nm
Clutch cover bolts	12 Nm
Clutch nut	70 Nm
Clutch spring bolts	8 Nm
Connecting rod cap nuts (see Section 22)	
Initial setting	20 Nm
Final setting	36 Nm
Coolant outlet pipe bolt	10 Nm
Coolant pipe bolts	10 Nm
Crankcase 9 mm bolts (Nos. 1 to 10)	
First stage	15 Nm
Second stage	+ 45 to 50°
Crankcase 8 mm bolts (Nos. 21 and 22)	24 Nm
Crankcase 6 mm bolts (Nos. 16 and 24)	14 Nm
Crankcase 6 mm bolts (all other bolts)	12 Nm
Cylinder head nuts	
First stage	20 Nm
Second stage	50 Nm
Cylinder head bolts	12 Nm
Engine mounting bolts	
Lower rear mounting bolt nut	55 Nm
Upper rear mounting bolt nut	55 Nm
Frame cross-piece-to-cradle bolts	33 Nm
Frame cross-piece-to-engine bolts	55 Nm
Frame cradle-to main frame bolts	24 Nm
Front sprocket cover support plate bolts	10 Nm
Gearchange shaft centralising spring locating pin	22 Nm
Oil baffle plate bolts	10 Nm
Oil cooler bolt	35 Nm
Oil pipe bolts	10 Nm
Oil pump drive chainguard	10 Nm
Oil strainer bolts	10 Nm
Oil sump bolts	10 Nm
Oil pump housing bolts	10 Nm
Oil/water pump assembly driven sprocket bolt	15 Nm
Oil/water pump assembly mounting bolts and sprocket cover bolts	10 Nm
Selector drum retaining plate bolts	10 Nm
Starter clutch bolts	12 Nm
Timing rotor bolt	60 Nm
Timing rotor/pick-up coil cover bolts	12 Nm
Transmission input shaft bearing housing Torx screws	12 Nm
Valve cover bolts	12 Nm

1 General information

The engine/transmission unit is a liquid-cooled in-line four, with five valves per cylinder. The valves are operated by double overhead camshafts which are chain driven off the right-hand end of the crankshaft. The engine/transmission assembly is constructed from aluminium alloy. The crankcase is divided horizontally.

The crankcase incorporates a wet sump, pressure-fed lubrication system which uses a chain-driven oil pump, an oil filter, a relief valve and an oil level sensor. The pump is driven by a chain and sprockets, with the drive sprocket locating into the starter driven sprocket on the back of the clutch housing. The oil is cooled by a cooler which is fed off the engine's water cooling system.

The alternator is on the left-hand end of the crankshaft, and the starter clutch is on the back of the clutch housing.

Power from the crankshaft is routed to the transmission via the clutch. The clutch is of the wet, multi-plate type and is gear-driven off the crankshaft. The transmission is a six-speed constant-mesh unit. Final drive to the rear wheel is by chain and sprockets.

2 Component access

Operations possible with the engine in the frame

The components and assemblies listed below can be removed without having to remove the engine from the frame. If however,

a number of areas require attention at the same time, removal of the engine is recommended.
  Valve cover
  Camshafts
  Cam chain
  Clutch and starter clutch
  Gearchange mechanism
  Alternator
  Starter motor
  Pick-up coil assembly
  Oil filter and cooler
  Oil sump, oil strainer and oil pressure relief valve
  Oil pump and water pump

Operations requiring engine removal

It is necessary to remove the engine from the frame to gain access to the following components.
  Cylinder head
  Crankshaft and bearings
  Connecting rods and bearings
  Cylinder bores, pistons and piston rings
  Transmission shafts
  Selector drum and forks

3 Major engine repair general note

1 It is not always easy to determine when, or if, an engine should be completely overhauled, as a number of factors must be considered.
2 High mileage is not necessarily an indication that an overhaul is needed, while low mileage, on the other hand, does not preclude the need for an overhaul. Frequency of servicing is probably the single most important consideration. An engine that has regular and frequent oil and filter changes, as well as other required maintenance, will most likely give many miles of reliable service. Conversely, a neglected engine, or one which has not been run-in properly, may require an overhaul very early in its life.
3 Exhaust smoke and excessive oil consumption are both indications that piston rings and/or valve guides are in need of attention, although make sure that the fault is not due to oil leakage.
4 If the engine is making obvious knocking or rumbling noises, the connecting rods and/or main bearings are probably at fault.
5 Loss of power, rough running, excessive valve train noise and high fuel consumption rates may also point to the need for an overhaul, especially if they are all present at the same time. If a complete tune-up does not remedy the situation, major mechanical work is the only solution.
6 An engine overhaul generally involves restoring the internal parts to the specifications of a new engine. During a major overhaul, the piston rings and main and connecting rod bearings are usually replaced with new ones. Generally, the valve seats are re-ground, since they are usually in less than perfect condition at this point. The end result should be a like new engine that will give as many trouble-free miles as the original.
7 Before beginning the engine overhaul, read through the related procedures to familiarise yourself with the scope and requirements of the job. Overhauling an engine is not all that difficult, but it is time-consuming. Plan on the motorcycle being tied up for a minimum of two weeks. Check on the availability of parts and make sure that any necessary special tools, equipment and supplies are obtained in advance.
8 Most work can be done with typical workshop hand tools, although a number of precision measuring tools are required for inspecting parts to determine if they must be renewed. Often a dealer will handle the inspection of parts and offer advice concerning reconditioning and replacement. As a general rule, time is the primary cost of an overhaul so it does not pay to install worn or substandard parts.
9 As a final note, to ensure maximum life and minimum trouble from a rebuilt engine, everything must be assembled with care in a spotlessly clean environment.

4 Engine removal and installation

Caution: *The engine is very heavy. Engine removal and installation should be carried out with the aid of at least one assistant. Personal injury or damage could occur if the engine falls or is dropped. An hydraulic or mechanical floor jack should be used to support and lower or raise the engine, if possible.*

Removal

1 Support the motorcycle on its centrestand on level ground. It is advisable to apply the front brake by tying the lever back to the handlebar – this will prevent the bike toppling off the stand if it is jolted while removing the engine. Work can be made easier by raising the machine to a suitable working height on an hydraulic ramp or a suitable platform. Make sure the motorcycle is secure and will not topple over (see Section 1 of *Tools and Workshop Tips* in the *Reference* section). When disconnecting any wiring, cables and hoses mark or tag them as a reminder to where they connect.
2 If the engine is dirty, particularly around its mountings, wash it thoroughly before starting any major dismantling work. This will make work much easier and rule out the possibility of caked-on lumps of dirt falling into some vital component.
3 Remove the seat, side panels and fairing (see Chapter 8).
4 Remove the fuel tank (see Chapter 4).
5 Drain the engine oil and the coolant (see Chapter 1).
6 Remove the carburettors (see Chapter 4). Plug the intake manifolds with clean rag. Remove the AIS system valve unit along with its hoses (see Chapter 4).
7 Disconnect the negative (–) lead from the battery, then disconnect the positive (+) lead (see Chapter 9). If required, remove the starter motor (see Chapter 9). If the starter motor is left in place, unscrew the rear mounting bolt and detach the earth lead, then lift the rubber terminal cover, unscrew terminal the nut and detach the power lead **(see illustrations)**. Secure the leads clear of the engine.
8 Remove the ignition HT coils and leads (see Chapter 5).
9 Make a note or sketch of all the cooling system hoses between the radiator and the engine. Remove the radiator (see Chapter 3), but detach the hoses from their unions on the engine components rather than from the radiator itself, then remove the radiator along with the hoses, noting their routing, and releasing them from any clips or ties. Also remove the thermostat housing along with the outlet pipe hose from the valve cover (see Chapter 3).
10 Remove the exhaust system (see Chapter 4).
11 Slacken the gearchange lever linkage rod locknuts, then unscrew the rod and separate it from the lever and the arm (the rod is reverse-threaded on one end, so will unscrew from both lever and arm simultaneously when turned in

4.7a Unscrew the bolt and detach the earth lead . . .

4.7b . . . then unscrew the nut and detach the power lead

2•6 Engine, clutch and transmission

4.11a Slacken the locknuts, then thread the rod off the lever and arm . . .

4.11b . . . and withdraw it from the frame

4.11c Note the alignment of the punch mark with the slit, then unscrew the bolt and slide the arm off the shaft

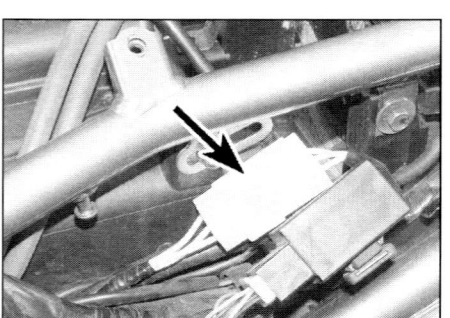

4.13 Disconnect the alternator wiring connector (arrowed) . . .

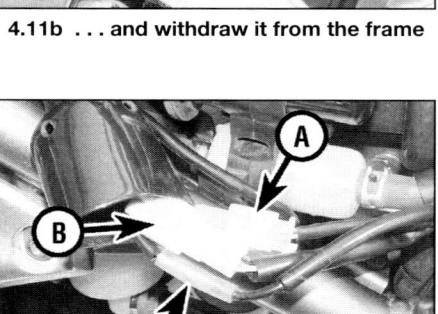

4.15 . . . the pick-up coil wiring connector (A), the neutral switch wiring connector (B), and the and the speed sensor wiring connector (C)

the one direction) **(see illustration)**. Note how far the rod is threaded into the lever and arm, as this determines the height of the lever relative to the footrest. Withdraw the rod from the frame **(see illustration)**. If required, unscrew the linkage arm pinch bolt and slide the arm off the shaft, noting how the punch mark on the shaft aligns with the slit in the arm **(see illustration)**. If no mark is visible, make your own before removing the arm, so that it can be correctly aligned with the shaft on installation.

12 Remove the front sprocket (see Chapter 6).

13 Trace the alternator wiring from the alternator on the left-hand side of the engine and disconnect it at the connector **(see illustration)**. Release the wiring from any clips or ties, noting its routing, and coil it so that it does not impede engine removal.

14 Trace the oil level sensor wiring from the bottom of the engine and disconnect it at the connector. Release the wiring from any clips or ties, noting its routing, and coil it so that it does not impede engine removal.

15 Trace the ignition pick-up coil wiring from the coil on the right-hand side of the engine and disconnect it at the connector **(see illustration)**. Release the wiring from any clips or ties, noting its routing, and coil it so that it does not impede engine removal.

16 Trace the neutral switch wiring from the back of the engine and disconnect it at the connector **(see illustration 4.15)**. Release the wiring from any clips or ties, noting its routing, and coil it so that it does not impede engine removal.

17 Trace the speed sensor wiring from the back of the engine and disconnect it at the connector **(see illustration 4.15)**. Release the wiring from any clips or ties, noting its routing, and feed it down to the switch.

18 Detach the clutch cable from the release mechanism arm (see Section 15).

19 Detach the crankcase breather hose from the crankcase and air filter housing and remove it **(see illustration)**.

20 At this point, position an hydraulic or mechanical jack under the engine with a block of wood between the jack head and crankcase. Make sure the jack is centrally positioned so the engine will not topple in any direction when the last mounting bolt is removed. Take the weight of the engine on the jack. It is also advisable to place a block of wood between the rear wheel and the ground, or under the swingarm, in case the bike tilts back onto the rear wheel when the engine is removed.

21 Unscrew the nuts and withdraw the bolts securing the front cross-piece to the right-hand frame cradle – on all the cross-piece mounts note which bolts fit where and which have washers **(see illustration)**. Unscrew the

4.19 Remove the crankcase breather hose (arrowed)

4.21a Unscrew the nuts and withdraw the bolts securing the cross-piece to the frame cradles . . .

Engine, clutch and transmission 2•7

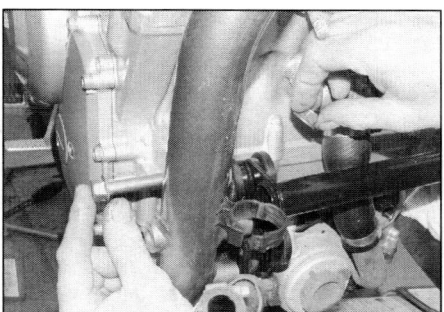
4.21b ... and to the engine ...

4.21c ... and remove the cross-piece

4.22 Remove the right-hand cradle section of the frame

4.23a Unscrew the bolt and remove the bracket

4.23b Unscrew the bolt (arrowed) ...

4.23c ... and draw the pipe out of the engine

nuts and withdraw the bolts securing the front cross-piece to the left-hand frame cradle. Unscrew the nuts and withdraw the bolts securing the cross-piece to the engine and remove the cross-piece **(see illustrations)**. Note the arrangement of the bushes and seals.

22 Unscrew the bolts securing the right-hand cradle to the main frame and remove the cradle **(see illustration)**.

23 To prevent the possibility of damaging the front mudguard when removing the engine, unscrew the bolt securing the radiator mounting bracket to the front of the engine and remove it, noting how it fits **(see illustration)**. If required, remove the oil cooler (see Section 7). If required, unscrew the bolt securing the water pump inlet pipe to the left-hand side of the engine and pull it out **(see illustrations)**. Also if required, slacken the clamps securing the coolant hoses to the inlet union and the oil cooler (if not removed) on the front of the engine and detach the hoses, then unscrew the bolt securing the coolant pipe to the engine and pull it out **(see illustrations)**. Discard the pipe O-rings, as new ones must be used.

24 Check around the engine and frame to make sure that all wiring, cables and hoses that need to be disconnected have been disconnected, and that any that remain connected to the engine are not retained by any clips, guides or brackets connected to the frame. Check that any protruding mounting brackets will not get in the way, and remove them if necessary. Cover the left-hand frame

4.23d Slacken the clamp screws (A) and detach the hoses, then unscrew the bolt (B) ...

cradle in some rag to prevent the possibility of chipping it when manoeuvring the engine out **(see illustration)**.

4.23e ... and draw the pipe out of the engine

25 Make sure the engine is supported by the jack, and have an assistant hold it **(see illustration)**. Unscrew the nut on the upper

4.24 Protect the frame by wrapping some rag around it

4.25a Make sure the jack is supporting the engine

2•8 Engine, clutch and transmission

4.25b Unscrew the nut . . .

4.25c . . . then withdraw the bolt

rear mounting bolt then withdraw the bolt **(see illustrations)**. Unscrew the nut on the lower rear mounting bolt then withdraw the bolt. Carefully manoeuvre the engine out of the right-hand side of the frame, taking care not to damage the left-hand cradle section.

Installation

26 Before installing the engine, remove the seals from each end of the metal buses in the front cross-piece, then withdraw the bushes – if they have become corroded they may need to be drifted out **(see illustrations)**. Clean any corrosion of the bushes and their bores and smear them and the seals with grease before refitting them. Check the condition of the met-elastic buses – if they are deformed or deteriorated a new cross-piece will have to be fitted as they bushes are not listed as being available separately.

27 Installation is the reverse of removal, noting the following points:
- Make sure no wires, cables or hoses become trapped between the engine and the frame when installing the engine.
- Many of the engine mounting bolts are of different size and length. Make sure the correct bolt is installed in its correct location. On the front cross-piece the M8 bolts fit through the met-elastic bushes in the bottom frame mount, the longer M10 bolts fit through the top frame mount and have washers **(see illustration 4.21a)**, and the shorter M10 bolts fit through the engine mount **(see illustration 4.21b)**. Install all of the bolts and nuts finger-tight only until they are all located, then tighten them in the order below to their torque settings specified at the beginning of the Chapter.

4.26a Remove the seals . . .

- First tighten the lower and upper rear mounting bolt nuts to the torque setting specified at the beginning of the Chapter. Now tighten the frame cross-piece-to-cradle bolt nuts to the specified torque, followed by the cross-piece-to-engine bolt nuts. Finally tighten the right-hand frame cradle-to-main frame bolts to the specified torque.
- Use new gaskets on the exhaust pipe connections, and new O-rings smeared with grease on the coolant pipes. Tighten the pipe bolts to the specified torque setting.
- Make sure all wires, cables and hoses are correctly routed and connected, and secured by any clips or ties.
- Refill the engine with oil and coolant to the correct levels (see Chapter 1 and Daily checks).
- Adjust the throttle and clutch cable freeplay and engine idle speed (see Chapter 1).
- Adjust the drive chain slack (see Chapter 1).
- Start the engine and check for any oil or coolant leaks before installing the body panels.

5 Engine disassembly and reassembly general information

Disassembly

1 Before disassembling the engine, thoroughly clean and degrease its external surfaces. This will prevent contamination of the engine internals, and will also make working a lot easier and cleaner. A high flashpoint solvent, such as paraffin (kerosene) can be used, or better still, a proprietary engine

4.26b . . . and withdraw the bushes

degreaser such as Gunk. Use old paintbrushes and toothbrushes to work the solvent into the various recesses of the casings. Take care to exclude solvent or water from the electrical components and intake and exhaust ports.

 Warning: The use of petrol (gasoline) as a cleaning agent should be avoided because of the risk of fire.

2 When clean and dry, position the engine on the workbench, leaving suitable clear area for working. Make sure the engine is stable – some strategically placed blocks of wood under the crankcase or engine covers will help support it and keep it stable while you work. Gather a selection of small containers, plastic bags and some labels so that parts can be grouped together in an easily identifiable manner. Also get some paper and a pen so that notes can be taken. You will also need a supply of clean rag, which should be as absorbent as possible.

3 Before commencing work, read through the appropriate section so that some idea of the necessary procedure can be gained. When removing components note that great force is seldom required, unless specified (checking the specified torque setting of the particular bolt being removed will indicate how tight it is, and therefore how much force should be needed). In many cases, a component's reluctance to be removed is indicative of an incorrect approach or removal method – if in any doubt, re-check with the text.

4 When disassembling the engine, keep 'mated' parts together (including gears, pistons, connecting rods, valves, etc. that have been in contact with each other during engine operation). These 'mated' parts must be reused or replaced as an assembly. It is worth obtaining a large sheet of card and marking it according to the layout of the engine so that parts can be placed on it and stored in relation to their position in the engine as they are removed.

5 A complete engine / transmission disassembly should be done in the following general order with reference to the appropriate Sections (or Chapters, where indicated).

Remove the valve cover
Remove the camshafts
Remove the cylinder head
Remove the clutch and starter clutch
Remove the pick-up coil assembly (see Chapter 5)
Remove the alternator (see Chapter 9)
Remove the starter motor (see Chapter 9)
Remove the gearchange mechanism
Remove the oil sump
Remove the oil pump/water pump
Separate the crankcase halves
Remove the crankshaft
Remove the connecting rods and pistons
Remove the transmission output shaft
Remove the selector drum and forks
Remove the transmission input shaft

Reassembly

6 Reassembly is accomplished by reversing the general disassembly sequence.

Engine, clutch and transmission 2•9

6.3 Slacken the clamp screws (arrowed) and detach the hoses

6.4a Bend down the lockwasher tab(s) ...

6.4b ... then unscrew the bolt and remove the washer, noting the O-ring (arrowed) on the bolt

6 Oil cooler

Note: *The oil cooler can be removed with the engine in the frame. If the engine has been removed, ignore the steps which do not apply.*

Removal

1 The cooler is located on the front of the engine. Drain the engine oil and the cooling system (see Chapter 1).
2 For best access remove the exhaust system (see Chapter 4).
3 Slacken the clamp securing each hose to the cooler and detach the hoses **(see illustration)**.
4 Bend down the tabs on the cooler bolt lockwasher **(see illustration)**. Unscrew the bolt using a socket and remove the lockwasher **(see illustration)**. Remove the cooler, noting how the tab locates between the lugs on the crankcase. Discard the cooler and bolt O-rings, as new ones must be used.
5 Check the cooler body for cracks and dents and any evidence of coolant leakage and replace it with a new one, if necessary. Also check the hoses for splits, cracks, hardening and deterioration and fit new ones, if required.

6.6a Fit a new O-ring into the groove in the cooler

Installation

6 Installation is the reverse of removal, noting the following:
● Clean the mating surfaces of the crankcase and the cooler with a rag and some thinners.
● Use a new O-ring on the cooler body and smear it with clean engine oil. Make sure it seats in its groove **(see illustration)**.
● Locate the tab on the cooler between the lugs on the crankcase **(see illustration)**.
● Use a new lockwasher if the tabs on it are weakened or deformed – Yamaha

6.6b Locate the tab (A) between the lugs (B)

recommend using a new one regardless. Use a new O-ring on the cooler bolt **(see illustration 6.4b)**. Tighten the bolt to the torque setting specified at the beginning of the Chapter **(see illustration)**.
● Bend up the lockwasher tabs to secure the bolt **(see illustration)**.
● Make sure the coolant hoses are pressed fully onto their unions and are secured by the clamps **(see illustration 6.3)**.
● Fill the engine with the correct quantity of oil (see Chapter 1).
● Refill the cooling system (see Chapter 1).

6.6c Tighten the bolt to the specified torque

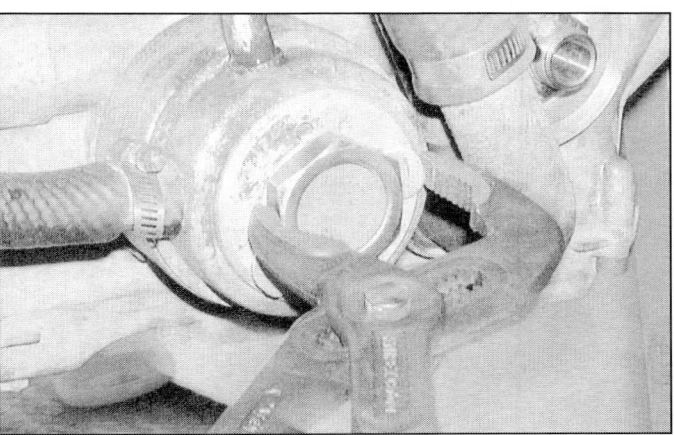

6.6d Bend up the tabs to secure the bolt

2•10 Engine, clutch and transmission

7.2a Unscrew the cover bolts (arrowed) . . .

7.2b . . . and lift the cover off the engine

7.3 Check the grommets on the bolts for cracks and deterioration

7.5 Make sure the gasket locates correctly in the cover

7.6 Apply the sealant to the cut-outs in the head

7 Valve cover

Note: *The valve cover can be removed with the engine in the frame. If the engine has been removed, ignore the steps which do not apply.*

Removal

1 Remove the carburettors (see Chapter 4), and the radiator, the thermostat housing and the outlet pipes from the valve cover (see Chapter 3).
2 Unscrew the bolts securing the valve cover and remove it **(see illustrations)**. If the cover is stuck, do not try to lever it off with a screwdriver. Tap it gently around the sides with a rubber hammer or block of wood to dislodge it.

Installation

3 Examine the valve cover gasket for signs of damage or deterioration and fit a new one, if necessary. Similarly check the rubber grommets on the cover bolts for cracks, hardening and deterioration **(see illustration)**.
4 Clean the mating surfaces of the cylinder head and the valve cover with lacquer thinner, acetone or brake system cleaner.
5 Fit the gasket into the valve cover, making sure it locates correctly into the groove **(see illustration)**. Use a few dabs of grease to keep it in place while the cover is fitted.
6 Apply a suitable sealant to the cut-outs in the cylinder head where the gasket half-circles fit **(see illustration)**. Position the valve cover on the cylinder head, making sure the gasket stays in place **(see illustration 7.2b)**. Install the cover bolts and tighten them to the torque setting specified at the beginning of the Chapter.
7 Install the remaining components in the reverse order of removal.

8 Cam chain, tensioner, tensioner blade and guide blade

Note: *The cam chain, tensioner and guides can be removed with the engine in the frame.*

Cam chain

Removal

1 Remove the camshafts (see Section 9).
2 Unscrew the bolt securing the timing rotor and remove the rotor, noting how it fits **(see illustrations)**. To prevent the crankshaft

8.2a Unscrew the bolt and remove the washer . . .

8.2b . . . then draw the rotor off the shaft

8.2c Counter-holding the crankshaft using a strap on the alternator rotor

Engine, clutch and transmission 2•11

8.3a Draw the chain off the sprocket and out of the engine

8.3b Draw the sprocket off the shaft . . .

8.3c . . . and remove the locating pin

turning, either select a gear and apply the rear brake (if the engine is in the frame), or remove the alternator cover (see Chapter 9) and use a rotor holding strap **(see illustration)**.

3 Draw the cam chain off its sprocket and out of the engine **(see illustration)**. If required, draw the sprocket off the crankshaft, noting which way round it fits, and remove the timing rotor/sprocket locating pin **(see illustrations)**.

Inspection

4 Check the chain for binding, kinks and any obvious damage and replace it with a new one, if necessary. Check the camshaft and crankshaft sprocket teeth for wear and renew the cam chain, camshaft sprockets and crankshaft sprocket as a set, if necessary.

Installation

5 Installation of the chain is the reverse of removal. Make sure the marked side of the timing rotor faces out. Tighten the rotor bolt to the torque setting specified at the beginning of the Chapter, counter-holding the crankshaft as on removal **(see illustration)**.

Cam chain tensioner

Removal

6 Unscrew the tensioner cap bolt and remove the sealing washer **(see illustration)**.

7 Slacken the tensioner mounting bolts slightly **(see illustration)**. Insert a small flat-bladed screwdriver in the end of the tensioner

8.5 Tighten the rotor bolt to the specified torque

so that it engages the slotted plunger **(see illustration)**. Turn the screwdriver clockwise until the plunger is fully retracted and hold it in this position while unscrewing the tensioner mounting bolts. Withdraw the tensioner from the engine, then release the screwdriver – the plunger will spring back out once the screwdriver is removed, but can be easily reset on installation.

8 Discard the gasket, as a new one must be used on installation. Do not dismantle the tensioner.

Inspection

9 Check that the plunger moves smoothly when drawn into the tensioner (by turning the screwdriver) and springs back out freely when the screwdriver is released **(see illustration)**.

10 If the tensioner or any of its components

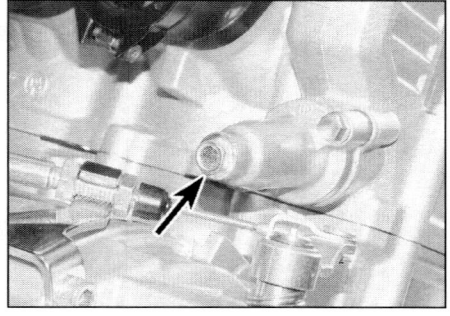

8.6 Unscrew the bolt (arrowed) and remove the washer

are worn or damaged, or if the plunger does not run smoothly and freely or is seized in the body, the tensioner must be replaced with a new one – internal components are not available.

Installation

11 Ensure the tensioner and cylinder block surfaces are clean and dry. Fit a new gasket onto the tensioner.

12 Insert a small flat-bladed screwdriver in the end of the tensioner so that it engages the slotted plunger, then turn it clockwise until the plunger is fully retracted **(see illustration 8.9)**. Hold the screwdriver so the plunger remains retracted while the tensioner and its bolts are installed and while the bolts are tightened to the torque setting specified at the beginning of the Chapter – make sure the tensioner is

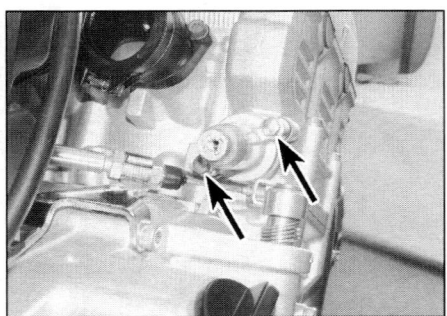

8.7a Slacken the bolts (arrowed) . . .

8.7b . . . then insert the screwdriver, retract the plunger and remove the tensioner as described

8.9 Check the operation of the tensioner as described

2•12 Engine, clutch and transmission

8.12a Install the tensioner with the UP mark at the top

8.12b Install the cap bolt using a new washer

8.14 Lift the front guide out of the engine using pliers

8.15a Withdraw the pivot pin . . .

8.15b . . . and lift the blade out of the top of the engine

installed with the 'UP' mark facing up, **(see illustration)**. Relax your grip on the screwdriver and check that it turns as the tensioner extends to take up chain slack, then remove the screwdriver. Install the tensioner cap bolt with a new sealing washer and tighten it to the specified torque **(see illustration)**.

Tensioner blade and guide blade

Removal

13 Remove the valve cover (see Section 7).
14 To remove the cam chain front guide, lift it out of the front of the cam chain tunnel, noting which way round it fits and how it locates **(see illustration)**.
15 To remove the cam chain tensioner blade, first remove the cam chain tensioner (see above) and the intake camshaft (see Section 9). Withdraw the tensioner blade pivot pin, then draw the blade out of the top of the engine, noting which way round it fits **(see illustrations)**.

Inspection

16 Check the sliding surfaces of the blades for excessive wear, deep grooves, cracking and other obvious damage, and renew them if necessary.

Installation

17 Slide the front guide blade into the front of the cam chain tunnel **(see illustration 8.14)**, making sure it locates correctly onto its seat and its lugs locate in their cut-outs **(see illustration)**.
18 Apply some clean engine oil to the tensioner blade pivot pin, then install the blade and insert the pin **(see illustrations 8.15b and a)**. Install the intake camshaft (see Section 9) and the tensioner (see above).
19 Install the valve cover (see Section 7).

9 Camshafts and followers

Note: *The camshafts can be removed with the engine in the frame. Place rags over the spark plug holes and the cam chain tunnel to prevent components from dropping into the engine on removal.*

Removal

1 Remove the valve cover (see Section 7).
2 Unscrew the bolts securing the timing rotor/pick-up coil cover on the right-hand side of the engine and remove the cover, noting the wiring clamp **(see illustration)**. Discard

8.17 Make sure the guide blade locates correctly

9.2 Unscrew the bolts (arrowed) and remove the cover, noting the wiring clamp (A)

Engine, clutch and transmission 2•13

9.3a Turn the engine until the 'T' mark aligns with the crankcase mating surfaces...

9.3b ... and the camshaft lobes for No. 1 cylinder face away from each other as shown

9.3c Intake camshaft alignment marks

the gasket, as a new one must be used. Remove the dowels from either the crankcase or the cover, if they are loose.

3 Turn the engine using a spanner or socket on the timing rotor bolt, turning it in a clockwise direction only, until the 'T' mark faces back and aligns with the crankcase mating surfaces **(see illustration)**, and the camshaft lobes for the No. 1 (left-hand) cylinder face away from each other, and the dot on each camshaft faces up and aligns with the arrow on the camshaft holder **(see illustrations)**. If the cam lobes are facing towards each other and the dots are facing down, rotate the engine clockwise 360° (one full turn) so that the 'T' mark again aligns with the crankcase mating surfaces. The camshaft lobes will now be facing away from each other and the dots will be facing up and aligned with the arrows, meaning the No. 1 cylinder is at TDC (Top Dead Centre) on the compression stroke.

4 Before disturbing the camshafts, make a note of the timing markings described above and how they align. If you are in any doubt as to the alignment of the markings, or if they are not visible, make your own alignment marks between all components, and also between a tooth on each sprocket (including the crankshaft sprocket) and its corresponding link on the chain, before disturbing them. These markings ensure that the valve timing can be correctly set up on assembly without difficulty. As it is easy to be a tooth out on installation, marking between a tooth on each sprocket and its link in the chain is especially useful.

5 Remove the cam chain tensioner (see Section 8).

6 Remove the cam chain guide blade (see Section 8).

7 Before removing the camshaft holders, make a note of which fits where, as they must be installed in the same place. The large holders for each camshaft are marked 'L' and 'R' (for Left and Right), and the intake ones have eight bolts each while the exhaust ones only have four each. The small holders on the right-hand end are marked 'I' and 'E' for Intake and Exhaust respectively. If the marks are not visible, make your own before

disturbing them – it is essential that they are returned to their original locations on installation **(see illustration)**.

8 Unscrew the camshaft holder bolts for the camshaft being worked on, slackening them evenly and a little at a time in a criss-cross pattern, starting from the outside and working towards the centre. Slacken the bolts above any lobes that are pressing onto a valve last in the sequence so that the pressure from the open valves cannot cause the camshaft to bend.

Caution: A camshaft could break if the holder bolts are not slackened as described and the pressure from a depressed valve causes the shaft to bend. Also, if the holder does not come squarely away from the head, the holder is likely to break. If this happens the cylinder head *must be renewed; the holders are matched to the head and cannot be renewed separately.*

Remove the bolts, then lift off the camshaft holders, noting how they fit **(see illustration)**. Retrieve the dowels from either the holder or the cylinder head, if they are loose. Remove the camshafts, rotating them towards the centre of the engine as you do so **(see illustration)**. Keep all 'mated' parts together. While the camshafts are out, don't allow the cam chain to go slack and do not rotate the crankshaft – the chain may drop down and bind between the crankshaft and case, which could damage these components. Wire the chain to another component, or secure it using a rod of some sort to prevent it from dropping.

9 If the followers and shims are being

9.3d Exhaust camshaft alignment marks

9.7 Camshaft holder identification

9.8a Unscrew the bolts and lift off the holders...

9.8b ... then remove the camshafts

9.9a Lift out the follower...

9.9b ...and remove the shim from inside it

9.10 Inspect the bearing surfaces for scratches or wear

removed from the cylinder head, obtain a container which is divided into twenty compartments, and label each compartment with the location of its corresponding valve in the cylinder head and whether it belongs with an intake or an exhaust valve. If a container is not available, use labelled plastic bags (egg cartons also work very well!). Remove the cam follower of the valve in question, then retrieve the shim from the inside of the follower **(see illustrations)**. If it is not in the follower, pick it out of the top of the valve using either a magnet, a small screwdriver with a dab of grease on it (the shim will stick to the grease), or a screwdriver and a pair of pliers **(see illustration 9.21a)**. Do not allow the shim to fall into the engine.

Inspection

10 Inspect the bearing surfaces of the cylinder head and holders and the corresponding journals on the camshaft **(see illustration)**. Look for score marks, deep scratches and evidence of spalling (a pitted appearance). If damage is noted or wear is excessive, replace the cylinder head and holders as a set with new ones – individual holders are not available.

11 Check the camshaft lobes for heat discoloration (blue appearance), score marks, chipped areas, flat spots and spalling **(see illustration)**. Measure the height of each lobe with a micrometer **(see illustration)** and compare the results to the minimum lobe height listed in this Chapter's Specifications. If damage is noted or wear is excessive, the camshaft must be replaced with a new one. Also, be sure to check the condition of the followers.

12 Check the amount of camshaft runout by supporting each end of the camshaft on V-blocks, and measuring any runout using a dial gauge. If the runout exceeds the specified limit the camshaft must be replaced with a new one.

 Refer to Tools and Workshop Tips (Section 3) in the Reference section for details of how to read a micrometer and dial gauge.

9.11a Check the lobes of the camshaft for wear – here is an example of damage requiring camshaft repair or renewal

13 Next, check the camshaft journal oil clearances. Check each camshaft in turn rather than at the same time – the exhaust camshaft is identifiable by its two lobes per cylinder, and the intake camshaft by its three lobes per cylinder. Clean the camshaft, the bearing surfaces in the cylinder head and camshaft holders with a clean lint-free cloth, then lay the camshaft in place in the head.

14 Cut some strips of Plastigauge and lay one piece on each journal, parallel with the camshaft centreline **(see illustration)**. Make sure the camshaft holder dowels are installed. Lay the holders in their correct place in the case (see Step 7). Lubricate the threads of the holder bolts with engine oil, then install them in the holders. Tighten the bolts evenly and a little at a time in a criss-cross pattern to the

9.14 Lay a strip of Plastigauge across each bearing journal, parallel with the camshaft centreline

9.11b Measure the height of the camshaft lobes with a micrometer

torque setting specified at the beginning of the Chapter, working from the centre of the camshaft outwards, (i.e. starting with the bolts that are above any valves that may be opened when the camshaft is tightened down). Whilst tightening the bolts, make sure the holders are being pulled squarely down and are not binding on the dowels. Whilst doing this, don't let the camshaft rotate.

15 Now unscrew the bolts evenly and a little at a time in a criss-cross pattern, starting from the outside and working towards the centre, and carefully lift off the camshaft holders.

16 To determine the oil clearance, compare the crushed Plastigauge (at its widest point) on each journal to the scale printed on the Plastigauge container **(see illustration)**. Compare the results to this Chapter's

9.16a Compare the width of the crushed Plastigauge to the scale printed on the Plastigauge container

Engine, clutch and transmission 2•15

9.16b Measure the cam bearing journals with a micrometer

9.21a Fit the shim into the recess in the top of the valve . . .

9.21b . . . then install the follower

Specifications. If the oil clearance is greater than specified, measure the diameter of the camshaft journal with a micrometer **(see illustration)**. If the journal diameter is less than the specified limit, replace the camshaft with a new one and recheck the clearance. If the clearance is still too great, or if the camshaft journal is within its limit, replace the cylinder head and holders as a set with new ones – individual holders are not available.

 Before renewing the camshafts, cylinder head or holders because of damage, check with local machine shops specialising in motorcycle engine work. In the case of the camshafts, it may be possible for cam lobes to be welded, reground and hardened, at a cost far lower than that of a new camshaft.

17 Except in cases of oil starvation, the cam chain wears very little. If the chain has stretched excessively, which makes it difficult to maintain proper tension, or if it is stiff or the links are binding or kinking, replace it with a new one. Refer to Section 8 for replacement.
18 Check the sprockets for wear, cracks and other damage – if the sprocket teeth have worn by 1/4 their original size, they are worn. If the sprockets are worn, the cam chain is also worn, and so is the sprocket on the crankshaft. If severe wear is apparent, the entire engine should be disassembled for inspection.

19 Inspect the cam chain guide blade and tensioner blade (see Section 8).
20 Inspect the outer surfaces of the cam followers for evidence of scoring or other damage. If a follower is in poor condition, it is probable that the bore in which it works is also damaged. Check for clearance between the followers and their bores. Whilst no specifications are given, if slack is excessive, renew the followers. If the bores are seriously out-of-round or tapered, then replace the cylinder head and holders, and the followers, with new ones.

Installation

21 If removed, lubricate each shim and its follower with molybdenum disulphide oil (a 50/50 mixture of molybdenum disulphide grease and engine oil) and fit each shim into its recess in the top of the valve, with the size marking on each shim facing up **(see illustration)**. Make sure each shim is correctly seated in the top of the valve assembly, then install each follower, making sure it fits squarely in its bore **(see illustration)**. **Note:** *It is most important that the shims and followers are returned to their original valves, otherwise the valve clearances will be inaccurate.*
22 Make sure the bearing surfaces on the camshafts and in the cylinder head are clean, then apply molybdenum disulphide oil (a 50/50 mixture of molybdenum disulphide grease and engine oil) to each of them. Also apply it to the camshaft lobes.
23 Check that the 'T' mark on the rotor still aligns with the crankcase mating surfaces (see Step 3) **(see illustration 9.3a)**.

24 Fit the exhaust camshaft, identifiable by its two lobes per cylinder **(see illustration)**, onto the front of the head, making sure the No. 1 (left-hand) cylinder lobes are facing forwards and the punch mark on the camshaft is facing up **(see illustrations 9.3b and d)**. Fit the cam chain around the sprocket, aligning the marks between sprocket tooth and link if made (in which case, first make sure that the mark between the crankshaft sprocket and chain align). When fitting the chain, pull up on the front run to remove all slack from it.
25 Now fit the intake camshaft, identifiable by its three lobes per cylinder **(see illustration 9.8b)**, onto the back of the head, making sure the No. 1 cylinder lobes are facing back and the punch mark on the camshaft end is facing up **(see illustrations 9.3b and c)**. Fit the cam chain around the intake sprocket, aligning the marks between sprocket tooth and link, if made. When fitting the chain, pull it tight to make sure there is no slack between the two camshaft sprockets – any slack in the chain must lie in the rear run, so that it is taken up by the tensioner.
26 Fit the camshaft holder dowels into the holder or cylinder head. Make sure the bearing surfaces in the holders are clean, then apply molybdenum disulphide oil (a 50/50 mixture of molybdenum disulphide grease and engine oil) to them. Lay the holders in their correct place in the case (see Step 7) **(see illustration)**. Lubricate the threads of the holder bolts with engine oil, then install them in the holders **(see illustration)**. Tighten the bolts evenly and a little at a time in a criss-

9.24 Install the camshaft as described

9.26a Fit the holders . . .

9.26b . . . then install the bolts and tighten them as described

2•16 Engine, clutch and transmission

9.27 Using a wooden dowel in the tensioner orifice to take up the slack in the chain

9.31a Locate the new gasket onto the dowels (arrowed)

9.31b Locate the pivot pin (A) in the hole B)

cross pattern to the torque setting specified at the beginning of the Chapter, working from the centre of the camshaft outwards, (i.e. starting with the bolts that are above any valves that may be opened when the camshaft is tightened down). Whilst tightening the bolts, make sure the holders are being pulled squarely down and are not binding on the dowels.

Caution: The camshaft is likely to break if it is tightened down onto the closed valves before the open valves. The holders are likely to break if they are not tightened down evenly and squarely.

27 Using a piece of wooden dowel, press on the back of the cam chain tensioner blade via the tensioner bore in the crankcase to ensure that any slack in the cam chain between the crankshaft and the intake camshaft, and between the two camshafts, is taken up and transferred to the rear run of the chain (where it will later be taken up by the tensioner) **(see illustration)**. At this point, check that all the timing marks are still in **exact** alignment as described in Steps 3 and 4. Note that it is easy to be slightly out (one tooth on the sprocket) without the marks appearing drastically out of alignment. If it is necessary to turn the engine, keep the wooden dowel pressed onto the tensioner blade as the chain is likely to jump around on the sprocket. If the marks are out, verify which sprocket is misaligned, then, if there is enough slack in

the chain, turn the camshaft and slip the chain round on the sprocket as you do. If there is not enough slack, unscrew the sprocket bolts and slide it off the camshaft, then disengage it from the chain. Move the camshaft round as required, then fit the sprocket back into the chain and onto the camshaft, and check the marks again. With everything correctly aligned, tighten the sprocket bolts to the torque setting specified at the beginning of the Chapter.

Caution: If the marks are not aligned exactly as described, the valve timing will be incorrect and the valves may strike the pistons, causing extensive damage to the engine.

28 Install the cam chain guide blade (see Section 8).
29 Install the cam chain tensioner (see Section 8). Turn the engine anti-clockwise through two full turns and check again that all the timing marks still align (see Steps 3 and 4).
30 Check the valve clearances and adjust them if necessary (see Chapter 1). This is essential if new components have been fitted.
31 Install the timing rotor/pick-up coil cover using a new gasket and a smear of sealant on the pick-up coil wiring grommet, and do not forget the dowels if removed **(see illustration)**. Locate the cam chain tensioner blade pivot pin in the hole in the cover **(see illustration)**. Tighten the cover bolts to the torque setting specified at the beginning of

the Chapter, not forgetting the wiring clamp **(see illustration 9.2)**.
32 Install the valve cover (see Section 7).

10 Cylinder head removal and installation

Caution: The engine must be completely cool before beginning this procedure or the cylinder head may become warped.
Note: To remove the cylinder head the engine must be removed from the frame.

Removal

1 Remove the engine from the frame (see Section 4).
2 Remove the valve cover (see Section 7) and the camshafts and followers (see Section 9).
3 The cylinder head is secured by two bolts and ten nuts **(see illustration)**. First unscrew and remove the bolts on the right-hand end of the head. Now slacken the nuts evenly and a little at a time in a criss-cross pattern, starting from the outside and working inwards (see *Tools and Workshop Tips* (Section 4) in the *Reference* section), until they are all slack, then remove the nuts and their washers. Use either a magnet, a screwdriver, or a piece of wire hooked over at the end to lift them out where necessary. Note which nut fits where, as there are different types **(see illustration)**.

10.3a Cylinder head bolts (A), sleeve nuts (B), shouldered nuts (C) and domed nuts (D)

10.3b Cylinder head bolts (A), sleeve nuts (B), shouldered nuts (C) and domed nuts (D)

4 Pull the cylinder head up off the crankcase **(see illustration)**. If it is stuck, tap around the joint faces of the head with a soft-faced mallet to free it. Do not attempt to free the head by inserting a screwdriver between it and the crankcase – you will damage the sealing surfaces. Remove the old cylinder head gasket and discard it, as a new one must be used.
5 If they are loose, remove the dowels from the cylinder block **(see illustration 10.8)**. If they appear to be missing they are probably stuck in the underside of the cylinder head.
6 Check the cylinder head gasket and the mating surfaces on the cylinder head and block for signs of leakage, which could indicate warpage. Refer to Section 11 and check the flatness of the cylinder head.

Installation

7 Clean all traces of old gasket material from the cylinder head and block. If a scraper is used, take care not to scratch or gouge the soft aluminium. Be careful not to let any of the gasket material fall into the crankcase, the cylinder bores or the oil passages. Lubricate the cylinder bores with new engine oil.

 Refer to Tools and Workshop Tips (Section 7) for details of gasket removal methods.

8 Ensure both cylinder head and crankcase mating surfaces are clean. If removed, fit the dowels into the crankcase, then lay the new head gasket in place, making sure it locates correctly over the dowels, and all the holes are correctly aligned **(see illustration)**. Never re-use the old gasket.
9 Carefully fit the cylinder head onto the crankcase, making sure it locates correctly onto the dowels **(see illustration 10.4)**.
10 Lubricate the threads and seating surfaces of the cylinder head nuts with clean engine oil. Install the nuts with their washers, making sure they are correctly located, and tighten them finger-tight **(see illustrations 10.3b and a)**. Now tighten the nuts in a criss-cross pattern starting from the centre and moving outwards (see *Tools and Workshop Tips* (Section 4) in the *Reference*

10.4 Carefully lift the head up off the block

section), first to the first stage torque setting specified at the beginning of the Chapter, and then in the same sequence to the second stage torque setting.
11 Now install the bolts and tighten them to the specified torque setting.
12 Install the remaining components in a reverse of their removal sequence, referring to the relevant Sections or Chapters (see Steps 1 and 2).

11 Cylinder head and valve overhaul

1 Because of the complex nature of this job and the special tools and equipment required, most owners leave servicing of the valves, valve seats and valve guides to a professional.
2 With the correct tools (a valve spring compressor is essential – make sure it is suitable for motorcycle work), you can also remove the valves and associated components from the cylinder head, clean them and check them for wear to assess the extent of the work needed, and, unless seat cutting or guide replacement is required, grind in the valves and reassemble them in the head.
3 A dealer service department or specialist can replace the guides and re-cut the valve seats.
4 After the valve service has been performed, be sure to clean it very thoroughly before

10.8 Lay the new gasket over the dowels (arrowed) and onto the head

installation on the engine to remove any metal particles or abrasive grit that may still be present from the valve service operations. Use compressed air, if available, to blow out all the holes and passages.

Disassembly

5 Before proceeding, arrange to label and store the valves along with their related components in such a way that they can be returned to their original locations without getting mixed up. A good way to do this is to use the same container as the shims and followers are stored in (see Section 9), or to obtain a separate container which is divided into twenty compartments, and to label each compartment with the identity of the valve which will be stored in it (i.e. number of cylinder, intake or exhaust side, inner, centre or outer valve). Alternatively, labelled plastic bags will do just as well.
6 Clean all traces of old gasket material from the cylinder head. If a scraper is used, take care not to scratch or gouge the soft aluminium.

 Refer to Tools and Workshop Tips (Section 7) in the Reference section for details of gasket removal methods.

7 Compress the valve spring on the first valve with a spring compressor, making sure it is correctly located onto each end of the valve assembly **(see illustrations)**. On the

11.7a Compressing the valve springs using a valve spring compressor

11.7b Make sure the compressor is a good fit both on the top . . .

11.7c . . . and the bottom of the valve assembly

2•18 Engine, clutch and transmission

11.7d Remove the collets with needle-nose pliers, tweezers, a magnet or a screwdriver with a dab of grease on it

11.7e If the valve stem (2) won't pull through the guide, deburr the area above the collet groove (1)

underside of the head, make sure the plate on the compressor only contacts the valve and not the soft aluminium of the head – if the plate is too big for the valve, use a spacer between them. Do not compress the springs any more than is absolutely necessary. Remove the collets, using either needle-nose pliers, tweezers, a magnet or a screwdriver with a dab of grease on it **(see illustration)**. Carefully release the valve spring compressor and remove the spring retainer, noting which way up it fits, and the spring from the top of the head, and the valve from the underside of the head **(see illustrations 11.28c, b and a)**. If the valve binds in the guide (won't pull through), push it back into the head and deburr the area around the collet groove with a very fine file or whetstone **(see illustration)**.

8 Pull the valve stem seals off the top of the valve guides with pliers and discard them (the old seals should never be reused) **(see illustration)**. Remove the spring seat, noting which way up it fits – using a magnet is the easiest way to lift the seat off the head **(see illustration)**.

9 Repeat the procedure for the remaining valves. Remember to keep the parts for each valve together and in order so they can be reinstalled in the same location.

10 Next, clean the cylinder head with solvent and dry it thoroughly. Compressed air will speed the drying process and ensure that all holes and recessed areas are clean.

11 Clean all the valve springs, collets, retainers and spring seats with solvent and dry them thoroughly. Do the parts from one valve at a time so that no mixing of parts between valves occurs.

12 Scrape off any deposits that may have formed on the valve, then use a motorised wire brush to remove deposits from the valve heads and stems. Again, make sure the valves do not get mixed up.

Inspection

13 Inspect the head very carefully for cracks and other damage. If cracks are found, a new head will be required. Check the cam bearing surfaces for wear and evidence of seizure. Check the camshafts for wear as well (see Section 9).

14 Using a precision straight-edge and a feeler gauge set to the warpage limit listed in the specifications at the beginning of the Chapter, check the head gasket mating surface for warpage. Refer to *Tools and Workshop Tips* (Section 3) in the *Reference* section for details of how to use the straight-edge. If the head is warped beyond the limit, but not excessively so, it should be possible to resurface it using a 400 to 600 grade wet and dry paper on a large surface plate, moving the cylinder head in a figure of eight rotation, and turning it frequently to ensure an even coverage. Take the head to a specialist repair shop if you lack the necessary equipment.

15 Examine the valve seats in the combustion chamber. If they are pitted, cracked or burned, the head will require work beyond the scope of the home mechanic. Measure the valve seat width and compare it to this Chapter's Specifications **(see illustration)**. If it exceeds the service limit, or if it varies around its circumference, valve overhaul is required.

16 Measure the valve stem diameter **(see illustration)**. Clean the valve guides to remove any carbon build-up, then measure the inside diameters of the guides (at both ends and the centre of the guide) with a small hole gauge and micrometer **(see**

11.8a Pull the seal off the top of the guide . . .

11.8b . . . then remove the spring seat

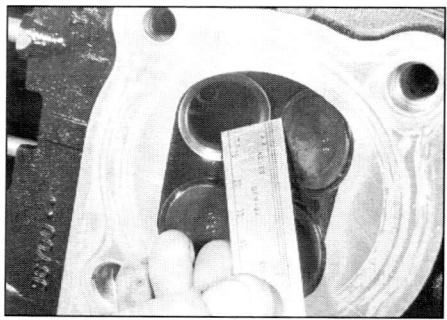

11.15 Measure the valve seat width with a ruler (or for greater precision use a vernier caliper)

11.16a Measure the valve stem diameter with a micrometer

Engine, clutch and transmission 2•19

11.16b Insert a small hole gauge into the valve guide and expand it so there's a slight drag when it's pulled out

11.16c Measure the small hole gauge with a micrometer

11.17a Check the valve face (A), stem (B) and collet groove (C) for signs of wear and damage

illustrations). The guides are measured at the ends and at the centre to determine if they are worn in a bell-mouth pattern (more wear at the ends). Subtract the stem diameter from the valve guide diameter to obtain the valve stem-to-guide clearance. If the stem-to-guide clearance is greater than listed in this Chapter's Specifications, renew whichever components are worn beyond their specification limits. If the valve guide is within specifications, but is worn unevenly, it should be renewed.

17 Carefully inspect each valve face, stem and collet groove area for cracks, pits and burned spots **(see illustration)**. Measure the valve margin thickness and compare it to the specifications **(see illustrations)**. If it is thinner than specified, replace the valve with a new one. The margin is the portion of the valve head which is below the valve seat.

18 Rotate the valve and check for any obvious indication that it is bent. Using V-blocks and a dial gauge if available, measure the valve stem runout and compare the results to the specifications **(see illustration)**. If the measurement exceeds the service limit specified, the valve must be replaced with a new one. Check the end of the stem for pitting and excessive wear. The presence of any of the above conditions indicates the need for valve servicing. The stem end can be ground down, provided that the amount of stem above the collet groove after grinding is sufficient.

19 Check the end of each valve spring for wear and pitting. Measure the spring free length and compare it to that listed in the specifications **(see illustration)**. If any spring is shorter than specified it has sagged and must be replaced with a new one. Also place the spring upright on a flat surface and check it for bend by placing a ruler against it **(see illustration)**. If the bend in any spring exceeds the specified limit, it must be replaced with a new one.

20 Check the spring retainers and collets for obvious wear and cracks. Any questionable parts should not be reused, as extensive damage will occur in the event of failure during engine operation.

21 If the inspection indicates that no overhaul work is required, the valve components can be reinstalled in the head. If any new valves are being installed, they can be identified as follows: the exhaust valves are marked '5LV', the outer intake valves are marked '4XV:', and the centre intake valve is marked '4XV.'.

Reassembly

22 Unless a valve service has been performed, before installing the valves in the head they should be ground in (lapped) to ensure a positive seal between the valves and seats. This procedure requires coarse and fine

A Head diameter
B Face width
C Margin thickness

11.17b Valve head measurement points

11.17c Measure the valve margin thickness as shown

11.18 Check the valve stem for runout using V-blocks and a dial gauge

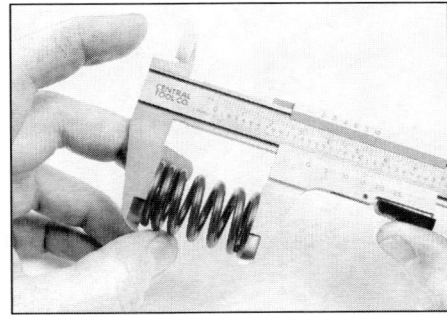

11.19a Measure the free length of the valve springs

11.19b Check the valve springs for squareness

2•20 Engine, clutch and transmission

11.23 Apply the lapping compound very sparingly, in small dabs, to the valve face only

11.24a Rotate the valve grinding tool back and forth between the palms of your hands

11.24b The valve face and seat should show a uniform unbroken ring . . .

valve grinding compound and a valve grinding tool (either hand-held or drill driven – note that some drill-driven tools specify using only a fine grinding compound). If a grinding tool is not available, a piece of rubber or plastic hose can be slipped over the valve stem (after the valve has been installed in the guide) and used to turn the valve.

23 Apply a small amount of coarse grinding compound to the valve face **(see illustration)**. Smear some molybdenum disulphide oil (a 50/50 mixture of molybdenum disulphide grease and engine oil) to the valve stem, then slip the valve into the guide **(see illustration 11.28a)**. **Note:** *Make sure each valve is installed in its correct guide and be careful not to get any grinding compound on the valve stem.* Attach the grinding tool to the valve.

24 If a hand tool is being used rotate the tool between the palms of your hands. Use a back-and-forth motion (as though rubbing your hands together) rather than a circular motion (i.e. so that the valve rotates alternately clockwise and anti-clockwise rather than in one direction only) **(see illustrations)**. If a motorised tool is being used, follow its instructions for use and take note of the correct drive speed for it – if your drill runs too fast and is not variable, use a hand tool instead. Lift the valve off the seat and turn it at regular intervals to distribute the grinding compound properly. Continue the grinding procedure until the valve face and seat contact area is of uniform width, and unbroken around the entire circumference.

25 Carefully remove the valve and wipe off all traces of grinding compound, making sure none gets in the guide. Use solvent to clean the valve and wipe the seat area thoroughly with a solvent soaked cloth.

26 Repeat the procedure with fine valve grinding compound, then use solvent to clean the valve and flush the guide, and wipe the seat area thoroughly with a solvent soaked cloth. Repeat the entire procedure for the remaining valves. On completion thoroughly clean the entire head again, then blow through all passages with compressed air. Make sure all traces of the grinding compound have been removed before assembling the head.

27 Working on one valve at a time, lay the spring seat in place in the cylinder head **(see illustration)**. Fit the intake valve seats with the dished side up so the spring sits in it. Fit the exhaust valve seats with the shouldered side up so the spring locates around it. Fit a new valve stem seal onto the guide **(see illustration)**. Use an appropriate size deep socket to push the seal over the end of the valve guide until it is felt to clip into place **(see illustration)**. Don't twist or cock the seal, or it will not seal properly against the valve stem. Also, don't remove it again or it will be damaged. Note that there are different size seals for the intake and exhaust valves – make sure you have the correct size for the valve being installed (the intake valve seals are slightly smaller).

28 Coat the valve stem with molybdenum disulphide oil (a 50/50 mixture of molybdenum disulphide grease and engine oil), then install it in its guide, rotating it slowly to avoid damaging the seal **(see illustration)**. Check

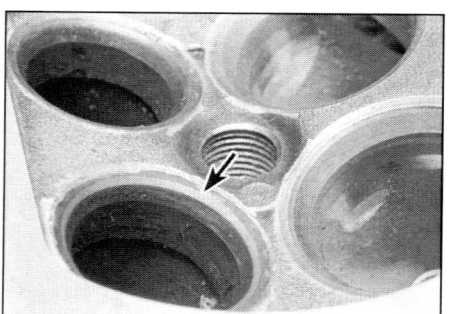

11.24c . . . and the seat (arrowed) should be the specified width all the way round

11.27a Fit the spring seat . . .

11.27b . . . followed by the valve stem seal

11.27c Press the seal into position using a suitable deep socket

11.28a Lubricate the stem and slide the valve into its correct location

Engine, clutch and transmission 2•21

11.28b Fit the valve spring with its closer wound coils facing down . . .

11.28c . . . then fit the spring retainer

that the valve moves up and down freely in the guide. Next, install the spring, with its closer-wound coils facing down into the cylinder head, followed by the spring retainer, with its shouldered side facing down so that it fits into the top of the spring **(see illustrations)**.

29 Apply a small amount of grease to the inside of the collets – this will help to hold them in place as the pressure is released from the spring **(see illustration)**. Compress the spring with the valve spring compressor and install the collets **(see illustration 11.7d)**. When compressing the spring, do so only as far as is necessary to slip the collets into place. Make certain that the collets are securely locked in the retaining groove **(see illustration)**.

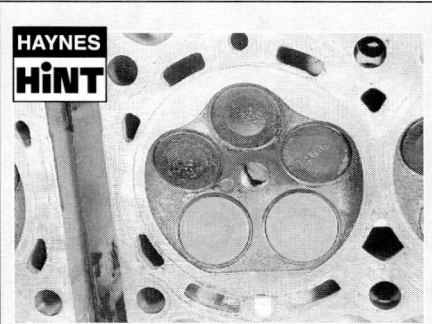

HAYNES HINT

Check for proper sealing of the valves by pouring a small amount of solvent into each of the valve ports. If the solvent leaks past any valve into the combustion chamber area the valve grinding operation on that valve should be repeated.

30 Support the cylinder head on blocks so the valves can't contact the workbench top, then very gently tap the top of the valve stem to help seat the collets in the groove **(see illustration)**.

31 Repeat the procedure for the remaining valves. Remember to keep the parts for each valve together and separate from the other valves so they can be reinstalled in the same location.

12 Clutch

Note: *The clutch can be removed with the engine in the frame. If the engine has been removed, ignore the steps which don't apply.*

Removal

1 Drain the engine oil (see Chapter 1).
2 Detach the clutch cable from the release mechanism arm (see Section 13).
3 Working evenly in a criss-cross pattern, unscrew the clutch cover bolts, noting the position of the wiring clamp and how the

11.29a A small dab of grease will help to keep the collets in place on the valve while the spring is released

11.29b Compress the springs and install the collets, making sure they locate in the groove

11.30 Tap the valve stem to help seat the collets in the groove

2•22 Engine, clutch and transmission

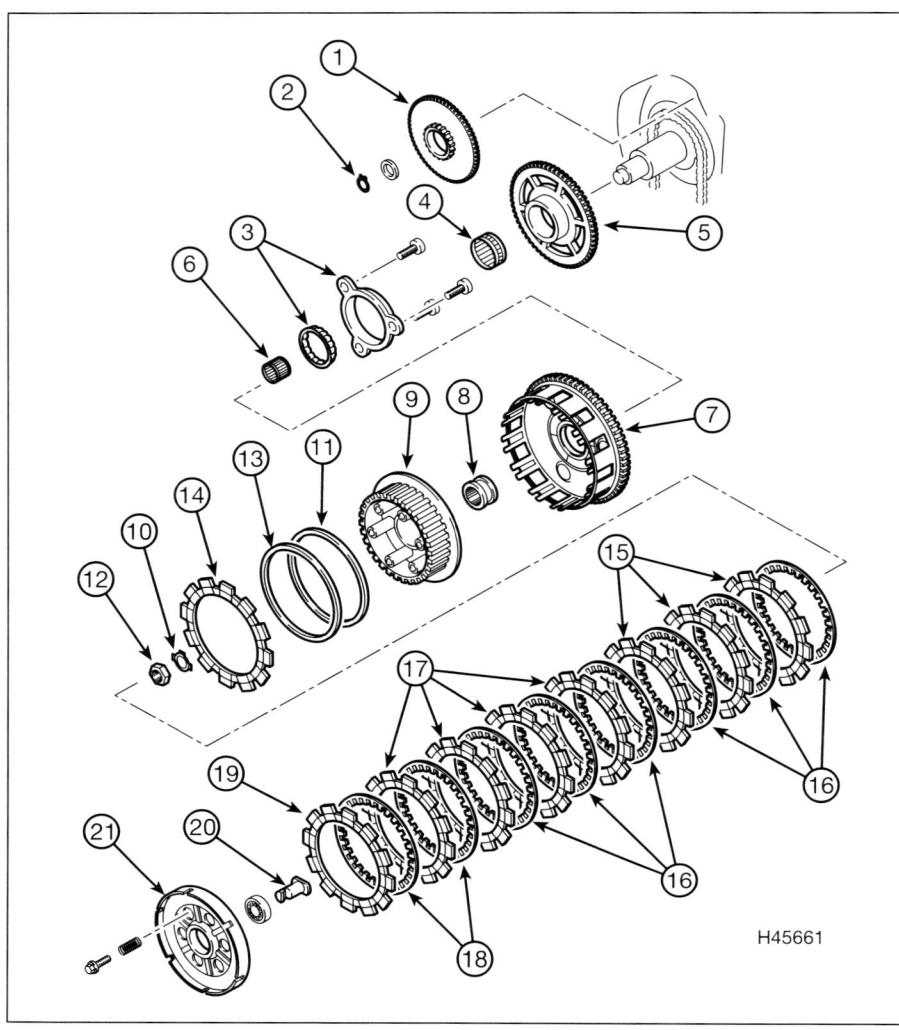

12.3a Clutch components

1 Idle/reduction gear
2 Circlip and washer
3 Starter clutch assembly
4 Needle bearing
5 Starter driven gear
6 Needle bearing
7 Clutch housing
8 Thrust washer
9 Clutch centre
10 Lockwasher
11 Spring seat
12 Clutch nut
13 Anti-judder spring
14 Friction plate – type B
15 Friction plates – blue-coded type A
16 Plain plates (standard thickness)
17 Friction plates – black coded type A
18 Plain plates (variable thickness – see text)
19 Friction plate – uncoded
20 Pull-rod
21 Pressure plate

12.3b Unscrew the bolts (arrowed) and remove the cover

cable bracket fits **(see illustrations)**. Remove the cover, being prepared to catch any residual oil.

4 Remove the gasket and discard it. Note the positions of the two locating dowels and remove them for safe-keeping if they are loose – they could be in either the cover or the crankcase.

5 Working in a criss-cross pattern, and holding the clutch housing to prevent it turning, gradually slacken the clutch pressure plate bolts until spring pressure is released, then remove the bolts, springs and the pressure plate **(see illustrations)**. Remove the pull-rod from the pressure plate, noting the bearing.

6 Grasp the complete set of clutch plates and remove them as a pack if possible, hooking them out individually if necessary. Keep the plates assembled in their original order, even if you are replacing them with new ones, as there are different types – the old ones can be used as a guide to installing the new ones **(see illustration)**. Also remove the anti-judder spring and spring seat, noting which way round they fit **(see illustration 12.27a)**.

7 Bend back the tabs on the clutch nut lockwasher **(see illustration)**. To remove the clutch nut, the transmission input shaft must be locked. This can be done in several ways. If the engine is in the frame, engage 1st gear and have an assistant hold the rear brake on hard with the rear tyre in firm contact with the ground. Alternatively, the Yamaha service tool – Pt. No. 90890-04086 (Europe models) or YM-91042 (US models) – or a similar

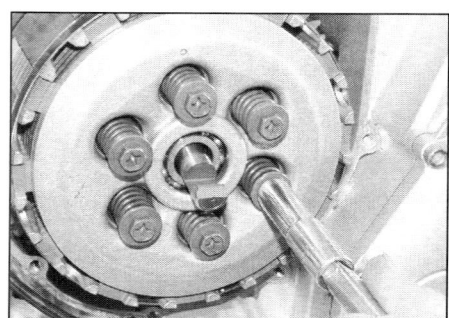

12.5a Unscrew the bolts and remove the springs . . .

12.5b . . . then remove the pressure plate with the pull rod

12.6 Draw the clutch plate pack out

Engine, clutch and transmission 2•23

12.7a Bend back the lockwasher tabs

12.7b Unscrew the clutch nut as described

12.9 Slide the clutch housing off the shaft

commercially available clutch holding tool, can be used to stop the clutch centre from turning whilst the nut is slackened. Unscrew the nut and remove the lockwasher from the input shaft, noting how it fits **(see illustration)**. Discard the lockwasher, as a new one must be used on installation.

8 Slide the clutch centre and the thrust washer off the shaft **(see illustrations 12.26a and 12.25)**.

9 Slide the clutch housing/starter clutch assembly off the shaft, noting how it engages with the primary drive gear, the starter driven gear and the oil pump drive sprocket **(see illustration)**. If the needle bearing did not come away with the housing, slide it off the shaft **(see illustration 12.24a)**. Otherwise, remove it from the housing. On 2003-on models remove the washer that fits between the clutch housing/starter clutch assembly and the oil pump drive sprocket.

10 If required (e.g. if the crankcase is being separated), refer to Section 17 and remove the oil pump drive sprocket and chain from the input shaft.

11 If required, separate the starter driven gear and starter clutch from the back of the clutch housing (see Section 14).

Inspection

12 After an extended period of service the clutch friction plates will wear and promote clutch slip. Measure the thickness of each friction plate (type A) using a vernier caliper, noting the thicker specification for the innermost (type B) plate **(see illustration)**. If any plate has worn to or beyond the service limit given in the Specifications at the beginning of the Chapter, all the friction plates must be replaced with a new set. Also, if any of the plates smell burnt or are glazed, they must be renewed as a set.

13 With the complete set of friction and plain plates together, and using the new plates if new ones are needed, measure the thickness of the complete pack using a Vernier caliper **(see illustration)**. If the thickness is less than the service limit given in the Specifications at the beginning of the Chapter, calculate by how much it is out of specification and replace either or both of the outermost plain plates with thinner or thicker ones as required to restore the assembled pack thickness. The standard plain plates fitted are 2.0 mm thick. Replacements are available in 1.6, 2.0 and 2.3 mm for the outermost plate and 2.0 and 2.3 mm for the second plate. If only one of the plain plates needs to be replaced, do so with the outermost one.

14 The plain plates should not show any signs of excess heating (bluing). Check for warpage using a flat surface and feeler gauges **(see illustration)**. If any plate exceeds the maximum permissible amount of warpage, or shows signs of bluing, all plain plates must be replaced with a new set. If that is done, repeat the pack thickness measurement detailed in Step 13.

15 Measure the free length of each clutch spring using a Vernier caliper **(see illustration)**. If any spring is below the service limit specified, replace all the springs with new ones as a set. Also place the spring upright on a flat surface and check it for bend by placing a ruler against it, or alternatively lay it against a set square **(see illustration 11.19b)**. If the bend in any spring is excessive, all springs must be replaced with new ones.

16 Inspect the edges of the tabs on the friction plates and the corresponding slots in the clutch housing for burrs and indentations. Similarly check for wear between the inner teeth of the plain plates and the slots in the clutch centre. Wear of this nature will cause clutch drag and slow disengagement during gear changes as the plates will snag when the

12.12 Measuring individual clutch friction plate thickness

12.13 Measuring clutch plate pack thickness

12.14 Check the plain plates for warpage

12.15 Measuring clutch spring free length

2•24 Engine, clutch and transmission

12.18 Check the pressure plate and its bearing (arrowed) as described

12.20a Remove the E-clip and washer . . .

12.20b . . . and draw the shaft out of the cover

12.20c Check the oil seal (A) and upper bearing (B) . . .

12.20d . . . and the lower bearing (arrowed)

12.20e Remove the circlip and washer from the top and draw the arm off the shaft, noting how the spring fits

pressure plate is lifted. With care a small amount of wear can be corrected by dressing with a fine file, but if wear is excessive new components should be installed.

17 Inspect the needle roller bearing in conjunction with the internal bearing surface of the clutch housing. If there are any signs of wear, pitting or other damage the affected parts must be replaced with new ones.

18 Check the pressure plate and its bearing for signs of wear or damage and roughness **(see illustration)**. Check the pull-rod for signs of roughness, wear or damage. Replace any parts, as necessary, with new ones.

19 Check the anti-judder spring and its seat for damage and distortion and replace them with new ones if necessary

20 Check the clutch release mechanism in the clutch cover for smooth operation. Check the pinion and pull-rod teeth for signs of damage. If necessary, prise off the E-clip and remove the washer securing the actuating shaft, and withdraw the shaft from the cover **(see illustrations)**. Check the condition of the oil seal and replace it with a new one, if necessary **(see illustration)**. Check the two bearings for roughness, wear or damage **(see illustration)**. If they need to be replaced with new ones, first remove the oil seal, then heat the cover in very hot water to ease removal and drift the bearings out. If required, note the alignment of the arm on the top of the shaft and make some marks to aid installation, then prise off the E-clip and remove the washer, then release the return spring ends, noting how they fit, and draw the arm, spring and washer off **(see illustration)**. Clean all components and lubricate the seal and bearings with grease. Installation is the reverse of removal. When installing the arm on the shaft, make sure it is the correct way up and correctly aligned, and do not forget to fit the return spring, locating it as shown **(see illustration)**.

Installation

21 Remove all traces of old gasket from the crankcase and clutch cover surfaces.
22 If removed, install the oil pump drive sprocket and chain (see Section 17).
23 If separated, fit the starter clutch and starter driven gear onto the back of the clutch housing (see Section 14).
24 Lubricate the needle roller bearing with clean engine oil and slide it onto the shaft **(see illustration)**. Install the housing, making sure the primary drive and driven gears, and the starter idle/reduction and driven gears engage correctly, and that the tabs on the oil pump drive sprocket locate into the slots in the back of the starter driven gear **(see illustration)**.

12.20f Locate the return spring ends as shown

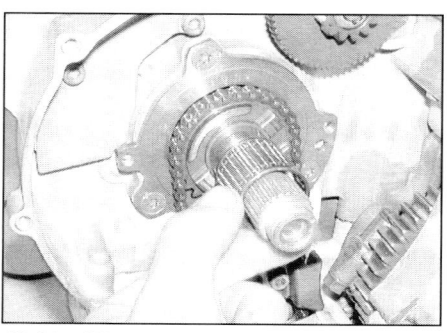

12.24a Slide the bearing onto the shaft . . .

12.24b . . . then install the housing as described

Engine, clutch and transmission 2•25

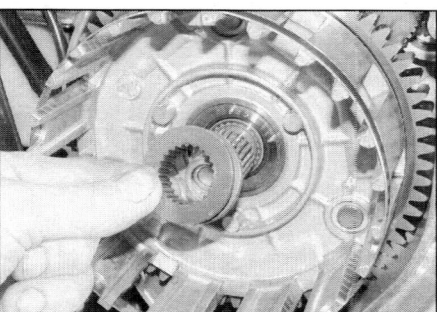

12.25 Fit the thrust washer . . .

12.26a . . . the clutch centre . . .

12.26b . . . the lockwasher . . .

The idle/reduction gear can be turned by hand to ease installation – remove the starter motor and turn the gear via the orifice if required, or use a screwdriver to turn the gear. To check that the housing has engaged correctly, turn it by hand – the oil pump drive chain should turn. If it doesn't, draw the housing away slightly and turn it, then press it in and continue to turn it until the housing is felt to engage with the sprocket and the chain starts to turn.

25 Lubricate the thrust washer with clean engine oil and fit it onto the shaft **(see illustration)**.

26 Slide the clutch centre onto the shaft splines, then fit the new lockwasher **(see illustrations)**. Install the clutch nut with the shouldered side on the inside, then tighten it to the torque setting specified at the beginning of the Chapter using the method employed on removal to lock the input shaft (see Step 7), **(see illustration)**. **Note:** *Check that the clutch centre rotates freely after tightening.* Bend up the tabs of the lockwasher to secure the nut **(see illustration)**.

27 Fit the anti-judder spring seat into the clutch centre, then fit the spring so that its outer edge is raised off the seat **(see illustrations)**.

28 Coat each clutch plate with engine oil prior to installation. Build up the plates as follows: first fit the type B friction plate, which is thicker and has the larger internal diameter so it fits over the anti-judder spring and seat

12.26c . . . and the clutch nut . . .

12.26d . . . then tighten the nut to the specified torque . . .

12.26e . . . and secure it by bending up the lockwasher tabs

(see illustration). Now fit a plain plate, followed by a blue colour-coded type A friction plate, then alternate plain and friction

12.27a Fit the spring seat and spring . . .

plates, fitting the two remaining blue-coded friction plates then the four black-coded type A friction plates, and fitting the different

12.27b . . . making sure the outer edge of the spring is raised off the seat

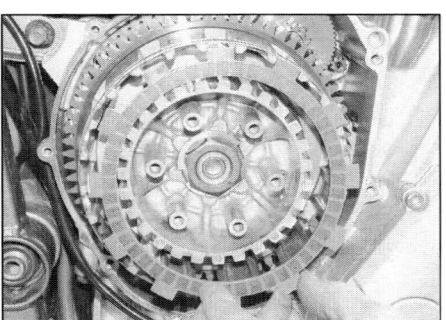

12.28a First fit the type B friction plate around the anti-judder spring and seat . . .

12.28b . . . then a plain plate

2•26 Engine, clutch and transmission

12.28c Identify the black (A) and blue (B) coded plates and fit them with the plain plates as described . . .

12.28d . . . finishing with the uncoded friction plate

12.29 Install the pressure plate, aligning the punch marks and making sure it locates correctly

thickness plain plates as described in Step 13 if necessary, and finishing with the uncoded friction plate **(see illustrations)**.

29 Lubricate the bearing in the pressure plate with some clean oil **(see illustration 12.18)**. Fit the pull-rod into the back of the pressure plate. Fit the pressure plate onto the clutch, aligning the punch marks, and making sure the castellations in the rim locate into the slots in the clutch centre (when it is properly located, there will be no freeplay between the plates) **(see illustration)**.

30 Fit the clutch springs and their bolts and tighten the bolts evenly and a little at a time in a criss-cross sequence to the specified torque setting **(see illustration 12.5a)**. Counter-hold the clutch housing to prevent it turning when tightening the bolts. Set the pull-rod so that the teeth point towards the front and are angled up slightly.

31 Insert the dowels in the crankcase if removed and fit the new gasket onto them **(see illustration)**. When installing the clutch cover, getting the release shaft to align correctly with the pull-rod can be tricky. Set the release arm so that it is pointing forwards but angled out a bit, then as the cover is installed and the shaft and pull rod engage, the arm should move in. Install the cover, making sure the end of the pull-rod locates in the bore in the cover and its cut-out engages correctly with the shaft so that when the shaft is turned into the engine it pulls the rod out, and tighten its bolts evenly in a criss-cross sequence to the specified torque setting, not forgetting the wiring clamp and the cable bracket **(see illustrations)**.

32 To check that the release mechanism is correctly aligned, push the release arm until all the freeplay in the release mechanism has been taken up. At this point the punch mark on the arm should align with the triangle mark on the cover **(see illustration)**. If the marks do not align (and this should only occur if the arm has been removed from the shaft and not

12.31a Locate the gasket onto the dowels (arrowed) . . .

12.31b . . . then install the cover as described, locating the pull-rod end (A) in the bore (B)

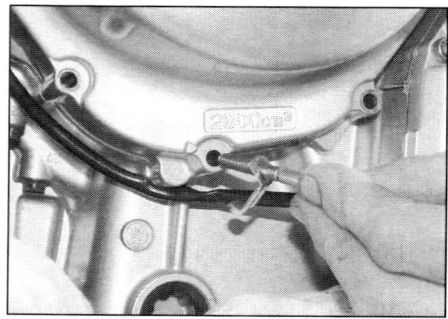

12.31c Do not forget the wiring clamp . . .

12.31d . . . and the cable bracket

12.32 The release mechanism is correctly set if the punch mark aligns with the triangle when the arm is pushed in

Engine, clutch and transmission 2•27

13.1 Slacken the locknuts and slip the cable out of the bracket

13.2 Bend back the tab on the retainer and slip the cable end out

13.3 Set the adjuster as described . . .

installed in the same position – the only other explanation is that the pull-rod and shaft have not engaged correctly), remove the E-clip and the arm, noting how the spring fits **(see illustrations 14.19b and c)**, and move the arm around on the splines of the shaft until they do. Make sure the spring is correctly set and install the E-clip.

33 Fit the clutch cable into the release arm (see Section 13).

34 Refill the engine with the correct quantity of oil (see Chapter 1).

13 Clutch cable

13.4a . . . then draw the cable out of the adjuster . . .

13.4b . . . and free it from the lever

5 Release the cable from its tie, the clip on the inside of the left-hand frame tube and its guide on the air filter housing **(see illustrations)**. Remove the cable from the machine, noting its routing.

clip and tie **(see illustrations 13.5b and a)**. Turn the adjuster on the lever bracket so that the slots are not aligned. On 2001 and 2002 models tighten the lockring against the adjuster. Bend in the retainer on the release mechanism arm to secure the cable end **(see illustration 13.2a)**. Check the clutch release mechanism for smooth operation and any signs of wear or damage. Remove it for cleaning and re-greasing if required (see Section 12).

7 Adjust the clutch lever freeplay (see Chapter 1).

Removal

1 Slacken the locknuts securing the cable in the bracket on the engine and slip the cable out of the bracket **(see illustration)**.

2 Bend out the tab in the cable retainer on the end of the release mechanism arm, then slip the cable end out of the retainer, noting how it fits **(see illustration)**.

3 On 2001 and 2002 models slacken the adjuster lockring at the handlebar end of the cable. On all models screw the adjuster at the handlebar end of the cable fully into the lever bracket, then turn it out to align the slot in the adjuster with that in the lever bracket **(see illustration)**.

4 Pull the outer cable end from the socket in the adjuster and release the inner cable from the lever **(see illustrations)**.

> **HAYNES HiNT** Before removing the cable from the bike, tape the lower end of the new cable to the upper end of the old cable. Slowly pull the lower end of the old cable out, guiding the new cable down into position. Using this method will ensure the cable is routed correctly.

Installation

6 Installation is the reverse of removal. Apply grease to the cable ends. Make sure the cable is correctly routed and secured in its guide,

14 Starter clutch and idle/reduction gear

Check

1 The operation of the starter clutch can be checked in situ. Remove the starter motor (see Chapter 9). Insert your finger into the starter motor orifice and turn the idle/reduction gear by hand – it should turn freely clockwise (as you look at it from the orifice), and lock when turned anti-clockwise. If not, remove it for inspection.

Removal

2 Remove the clutch – the starter clutch is mounted on the back of the clutch housing (see Section 12). If the starter driven gear does not come away with the starter clutch, slide it off the shaft.

3 If required, remove the circlip and washer

13.5a Note the routing of the cable through the clip (arrowed) . . .

13.5b . . . and in the guide (arrowed)

2•28 Engine, clutch and transmission

14.3 Remove the circlip (arrowed) and slide off the washer and gear

14.4 Check that the driven gear turns freely anti-clockwise

14.6a Check the condition of the sprags (A) and the hub (B)

14.6b Unscrew the bolts (arrowed) . . .

14.6c . . . and remove the retainer and sprag assembly

14.6d Apply a threadlock to the retainer bolts

securing the idle/reduction gear on its shaft and slide it off, noting which way round it fits (place some rag around the bottom of the clutch casing to prevent the circlip or washer falling into the sump) **(see illustration)**.

Inspection

4 If separated, fit the starter driven gear into the starter clutch, rotating it anti-clockwise as you do to spread the sprags and allow it to enter **(see illustration 14.10b)**. With the clutch housing face down on a workbench, check that the starter driven gear rotates freely in an anti-clockwise direction and locks against the sprag assembly in a clockwise direction **(see illustration)**.
5 If it doesn't, withdraw the starter driven gear from the starter clutch, rotating it anti-clockwise as you do. Withdraw the needle bearing from the centre of the clutch **(see illustration 14.10a)**.
6 Check the condition of the sprags inside the starter clutch and the corresponding surface on the driven gear hub **(see illustration)**. If they are damaged, marked or flattened at any point, the sprag assembly should be replaced with a new one. To remove it, hold the clutch housing and unscrew the retainer bolts, then remove the retainer and lift out the sprag assembly, noting how they fit **(see illustrations)**. Install the new starter clutch in a reverse sequence. Apply clean engine oil to the sprags. Apply a suitable non-permanent thread locking compound to the bolts and tighten them to the torque setting specified at the beginning of the Chapter **(see illustration)**.
7 Check the needle roller bearing and the bearing surfaces in the starter driven gear hub and on the crankshaft **(see illustration 16.10a)**. If the bearing surface shows signs of excessive wear or the bearing itself is worn or damaged, they should be replaced with new ones.

8 Check the teeth of the starter idle/reduction gear and the corresponding teeth of the starter driven gear and starter motor drive shaft. Replace the gears and/or starter motor armature with new ones if worn or chipped teeth are discovered on related gears. Also check the idle/reduction gear shaft for damage, and check that the gear is not a sloppy fit on the shaft. Replace the gear and/or shaft with a new one if necessary – the shaft is secured from the inside of the crankcase by a bolt.

Installation

9 Lubricate the idle/reduction gear shaft with clean engine oil. Slide the gear onto the shaft, making sure the smaller pinion faces outwards, and the teeth of the larger pinion mesh correctly with the teeth of the starter motor shaft **(see illustration)**. Fit the washer and secure the gear with the circlip, making sure it locates in the groove **(see illustrations)**.

14.9a Slide the gear onto the shaft . . .

14.9b . . . then fit the washer . . .

14.9c . . . and secure them with the circlip

10 Lubricate the needle roller bearing with clean engine oil and fit it into the starter clutch **(see illustration)**. Lubricate the outside of the starter driven gear hub with clean engine oil, then fit it into the starter clutch, rotating it anti-clockwise as you do so to spread the sprags and allow the hub to enter **(see illustration)**.
11 Install the clutch (see Section 12).

15 Gearchange mechanism

14.10a Fit the bearing into the clutch . . .

14.10b . . . then install the driven gear

Note: *The gearchange mechanism can be removed with the engine in the frame. If the engine has been removed, ignore the steps which don't apply.*

Removal

1 Make sure the transmission is in neutral.
2 Slacken the gearchange lever linkage rod locknuts, then unscrew the rod and separate it from the lever and the arm (the rod is reverse-threaded on one end, so will unscrew from both lever and arm simultaneously when turned in the one direction) **(see illustration 4.11a)**. Note how far the rod is threaded into the lever and arm, as this determines the height of the lever relative to the footrest. Withdraw the rod from the frame **(see illustration 4.11b)**. Unscrew the gearchange lever linkage arm pinch bolt and slide the arm off the shaft, noting how the punch mark on the shaft aligns with the slit in the arm **(see illustration 4.11c)**. If no mark is visible, make your own before removing the arm so that it can be correctly aligned with the shaft on installation.
3 Unscrew the bolts securing the front sprocket cover and remove it **(see illustration)**.
4 Unscrew the bolts securing the gearchange mechanism cover and remove it, noting how the bottom two bolts secure the carburettor vent hose holder **(see illustration)**. Discard the gasket, as a new one must be used. Remove the dowels from either the cover or the crankcase if they are loose.
5 Note how the gearchange shaft centralising spring ends fit on each side of the locating pin in the crankcase, and how the pawls on the selector arm locate onto the pins on the end of the selector drum **(see illustration 15.11)**. Grasp the end of the shaft and withdraw the shaft/arm assembly **(see illustration)**.
6 Note how the stopper arm spring ends locate and how the roller on the arm locates in the neutral detent on the selector drum **(see illustration 15.10b)**. Unhook the spring from its anchor, then lift the stopper arm off the drum and remove it **(see illustrations)**. Retrieve the washer from the rim of the shaft bore in the crankcase or from the end of the collar **(see illustration)**.

Inspection

7 Check the selector arm for cracks, distortion and wear of its pawls, and check for any corresponding wear on the selector pins

15.3 Unscrew the bolts (arrowed) and remove the cover. Note how the wiring and hoses are routed

15.4 Unscrew the bolts (arrowed) and remove the cover, noting the vent hose holder (A)

15.5 Withdraw the shaft/arm assembly, noting how it fits

15.6a Unhook the spring . . .

15.6b . . . then remove the stopper arm, noting how it fits . . .

15.6c . . . and retrieve the washer

2•30 Engine, clutch and transmission

15.7a Check the gearchange shaft/selector arm assembly . . .

15.7b . . . and the stopper arm assembly as described

15.9a Lever the old seal out

15.9b Check the bearing (arrowed) in the cover

15.10a Fit the washer over the collar

15.10b Installed stopper arm assembly

on the selector drum **(see illustration)**. Also check the stopper arm roller and the detents in the selector drum for any wear or damage, and make sure the roller turns freely **(see illustration)**. Replace any components that are worn or damaged with new ones.

8 Inspect the shaft centralising spring and the stopper arm return spring for fatigue, wear or damage. If any faults are found, replace them with new ones. Slide the centralising spring off the shaft, noting the spacer. Also check that the centralising spring locating pin in the crankcase is securely tightened. If it is loose, remove it and apply a non-permanent thread locking compound to its threads, then tighten it to the torque setting specified at the beginning of the Chapter.

9 Check the gearchange shaft/arm assembly for distortion and damage to the splines. If the assembly is bent you can attempt to straighten it, but if the splines are damaged it must be replaced with a new one. Also check the condition of the shaft oil seal and bearing in the cover. If the oil seal is damaged, deteriorated or shows signs of leakage it must be replaced with a new one. Lever out the old seal with a flat-bladed screwdriver **(see illustration)**. If the bearing is damaged or does not run smoothly and freely, it must be replaced with a new one – refer to Section 5 of *Tools and Workshop Tips* in the *Reference* section for information on bearing check, removal and installation methods **(see illustration)**. Drive the new seal squarely into place, with its lip facing inward, using a seal driver or suitable socket.

Installation

10 Lubricate the inside and outside of the stopper arm collar with clean engine oil. Fit the washer onto the end of the collar **(see illustration)**. Install the stopper arm assembly, locating the arm onto the neutral detent on the selector drum **(see illustration 15.6b)**. Fit the return spring **(see illustration 15.6a)**, making sure the spring ends are positioned correctly **(see illustration)**.

11 Make sure the centralising spring ends are correctly positioned on the selector arm **(see illustration 15.7a)**. Slide the shaft/arm assembly into place **(see illustration 15.5)**, locating the selector arm pawls onto the pins on the selector drum and the centralising spring ends onto each side of the locating pin **(see illustration)**.

12 If removed, fit the gearchange mechanism cover dowels into the crankcase. Smear the cover oil seal lips with grease. Install the cover using a new gasket, making sure they locate correctly onto the dowels, and tighten the cover bolts securely, not forgetting to secure the carburettor vent hose holder with the bottom bolts **(see illustrations)**.

15.11 Installed gearchange shaft/selector arm assembly

15.12a Fit the gasket over the dowels (arrowed) . . .

15.12b . . . then install the cover . . .

Engine, clutch and transmission 2•31

15.12c ... with the hose holder

13 Install the front sprocket cover, making sure the wiring and hoses are correctly routed, and tighten the bolts **(see illustration)**.
14 Slide the gearchange lever linkage arm onto the shaft, aligning the punch mark on the shaft with the slit in the arm **(see illustration 4.11c)**. Tighten the pinch bolt. Slide the linkage rod into the frame and thread it onto the lever and arm (the rod is reverse-threaded on one end, so will screw onto both lever and arm simultaneously when turned in the one direction) **(see illustration 4.11b)**. Set it as noted on removal to give the same gearchange lever height, then tighten the locknuts securely **(see illustration 4.11a)**. To adjust the lever height, slacken the locknuts and thread the rod in or out as required, then retighten the nuts.

16 Oil sump, oil strainer and pressure relief valve

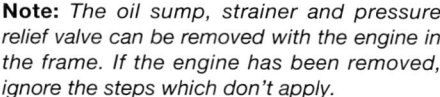

Note: *The oil sump, strainer and pressure relief valve can be removed with the engine in the frame. If the engine has been removed, ignore the steps which don't apply.*

Removal

1 Remove the exhaust system (see Chapter 4).
2 Drain the engine oil (see Chapter 1). Either remove the oil level sensor if required (see Chapter 9), or trace the wire from the switch and disconnect it at the connector. Feed the wiring down to the sensor, freeing it from any tied and noting its routing – you may have to remove the front sprocket cover (see Section 15, Steps 2 and 3).
3 Unscrew the sump bolts, slackening them evenly in a criss-cross sequence to prevent distortion, and remove the sump **(see illustration)**. Note the position of the oil level sensor wiring clamp. Discard the gasket, as a new one must be used. Note the positions of the dowels and remove them if they are loose. Note how the water pump drain pipe fits between the pump and sump and remove it if required **(see illustration)**.
4 Unscrew the oil strainer bolts and remove the strainer **(see illustration)**.
5 Pull the pressure relief valve out of the crankcase **(see illustration)**. Discard the O-ring, as a new one must be used.

Inspection

6 Remove all traces of gasket from the sump and crankcase mating surfaces, and clean the inside of the sump with solvent.
7 Clean the oil strainer in solvent and remove any debris caught in the strainer mesh. Inspect the strainer for any signs of wear or damage and replace it with a new one, if necessary – separate it from the housing by levering it off.
8 Push the relief valve plunger into the valve body and check that it moves smoothly and

15.13 Install the sprocket cover

16.3a Unscrew the bolts (arrowed) and remove the sump

16.3b Remove the drain pipe (arrowed) if required – it is a push fit

16.4 Unscrew the bolts (arrowed) and remove the strainer

16.5 Remove the pressure relief valve – it is a push fit

2•32 Engine, clutch and transmission

16.8a Check that the plunger is not seized in the valve body

16.8b Press down on the spring seat to remove the circlip

16.8c Circlip (A), spring seat (B), spring (C), plunger (D), O-ring (E)

freely against the spring pressure **(see illustration)**. If not, remove the circlip, noting that it is under spring pressure, and remove the spring seat, spring and plunger **(see illustrations)**. Clean all the components in solvent and check them for scoring, wear or damage. If any is found, replace the relief valve with a new one – individual components are not available. Otherwise, coat the inside of the valve body and the plunger with clean engine oil, then insert the plunger, spring and spring seat and secure them with the circlip. Check the action of the valve plunger again – if it is still suspect, replace the valve with a new one.

Installation

9 Fit a new O-ring onto the relief valve and smear it with grease **(see illustration)**. Push the valve into its socket in the crankcase **(see illustration 16.5)**.

10 Install the oil strainer, making sure the arrow points to the front of the engine **(see illustration)**. Apply a suitable non-permanent thread locking compound to the bolts and tighten them to the specified torque setting.

11 Check the condition of the water pump drain pipe O-rings and replace them with new ones if they are in any way damaged, deformed or deteriorated. Fit the pipe into the sump or water pump as required **(see illustration)**. If removed, fit the sump dowels into the crankcase. Lay a new gasket onto the sump (if the engine is in the frame) or onto the crankcase (if the engine has been removed and is positioned upside down on the work surface) **(see illustration)**. Make sure the holes in the gasket align correctly with the bolt holes.

12 Position the sump on the crankcase, making sure the water pump drain pipe locates correctly **(see illustrations)**. Apply a suitable non-permanent thread locking compound to the centre and front sump bolts **(see illustration)**. Install the bolts, not forgetting the oil level sensor wiring clamp (if the sensor was not removed, fit the wiring into

16.9 Install the relief valve using a new O-ring

16.10 The arrow on the strainer points to the front of the engine

16.11a Fit new O-rings onto the drain pipe if necessary

16.11b Fit the gasket onto the dowels (arrowed)

16.12a Install the sump . . .

16.12b . . . making sure the drain pipe locates correctly

16.12c Apply a threadlock to the front and centre bolts

Engine, clutch and transmission 2•33

the clamp, if it was, do not yet tighten the bolt holding the clamp), and tighten them evenly and a little at a time in a criss-cross pattern to the specified torque setting.

13 Either install the oil level sensor if removed (see Chapter 9), or connect the wire at the connector. Install the sprocket cover if removed (see Section 15, Steps 13 and 14).

14 Fill the engine with the correct type and quantity of oil (see Chapter 1).

15 Install the exhaust system (see Chapter 4). Start the engine and check that there are no leaks around the sump.

17 Oil pump

Note: *The oil pump and water pump come as an assembly and are removed as such. They can be removed with the engine in the frame. If the engine has been removed, ignore the steps which don't apply.*

Removal

1 Drain the engine oil and the coolant (see Chapter 1).

2 Remove the clutch (see Section 12), the sump and the oil strainer (see Section 16). If the water pump drain pipe does not come away with the sump, remove it from the pump **(see illustration 16.11a)**.

3 Slacken the clamps securing the coolant hoses to the water pump outlet pipe on the front of the engine and detach the hoses. Unscrew the bolt securing the pipe to the front of the engine and pull it out **(see illustrations)**. Discard the O-rings, as new ones must be used.

4 Unscrew the two bolts securing the large bore oil pipe and the single bolt securing the small bore pipe **(see illustrations)**. Remove the pipes, noting how they fit.

5 Unscrew the bolts securing the oil pump driven sprocket cover and remove the cover, noting how it fits **(see illustration)**. Unscrew the bolts securing the chain guide and remove it **(see illustration)**.

6 Unscrew the remaining bolt securing the pump assembly, then draw out the long dowel

17.3a Unscrew the bolt (arrowed) . . .

17.3b . . . and draw the pipe out of the engine

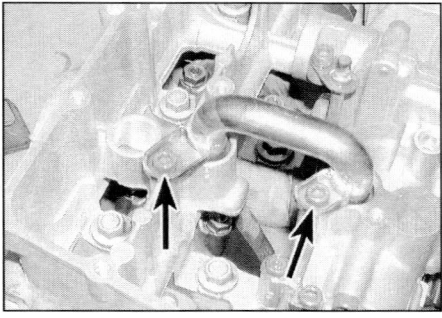

17.4a Unscrew the bolts (arrowed) and remove the large bore pipe . . .

17.4b . . . and the small bore pipe

17.5a Unscrew the bolts (arrowed) and remove the cover

17.5b Unscrew the bolts (arrowed) and remove the guide

using pliers **(see illustrations)**. Draw the pump out of the coolant inlet union in the crankcase, then tilt it to get some slack in the

chain and disengage the chain first from the drive sprocket, then from the driven sprocket on the pump, and remove it from the engine,

17.6a Unscrew the bolt . . .

17.6b . . . and withdraw the long dowel

17.6c Draw the pump out of the case and tilt it . . .

2•34 Engine, clutch and transmission

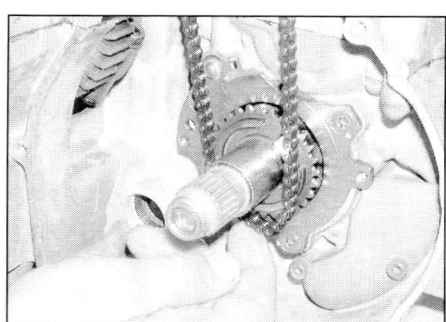

17.6d ... then disengage the chain from the drive sprocket to create slack

17.6e Slip the chain off the driven sprocket and remove the pump

17.7a Slide the drive sprocket off the shaft ...

being prepared to catch any residual oil and/or coolant **(see illustrations)**.

7 Remove the chain and slide the drive sprocket off the shaft, noting which way round it fits **(see illustration)**. Also slide the thrust washer off the shaft **(see illustration)**.

Inspection

8 If required, the pump can be disassembled for cleaning and inspection. Unscrew the driven sprocket bolt and remove the sprocket – use a screwdriver inserted through one of the holes in the sprocket and lodge it against the pump body to prevent the sprocket turning **(see illustration)**. Retrieve the washer from the end of the shaft or the back of the sprocket **(see illustration)**.

9 Unscrew the three bolts securing the oil pump housing **(see illustration)**. Remove the housing and its locating pins, then remove the

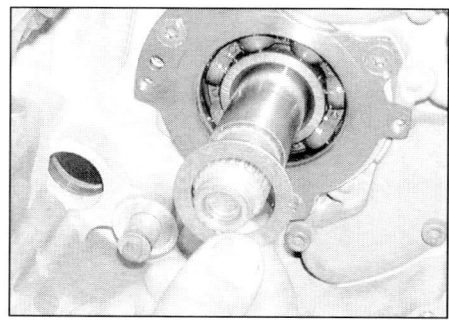

17.7b ... and remove the thrust washer

outer and inner rotors – they may come away with the housing or remain on the shaft **(see illustrations)**. Note which way round the rotors fit, as it is best to install them the same way round. Withdraw the drive pin from the

17.8a Unscrew the bolt and remove the sprocket ...

shaft, noting how it locates in the slots in the inner rotor **(see illustration)**.

10 Clean all components in solvent. Check that the oil pipes are clear by blowing them through with compressed air.

17.8b ... and the washer

17.9a Unscrew the bolts (arrowed) ...

17.9b ... and remove the housing ...

17.9c ... and its locating pins

17.9d Remove the outer and inner rotors ...

17.9e ... and the drive pin

Engine, clutch and transmission 2•35

17.12 Measure the outer rotor to body clearance as shown

17.13 Measure the inner rotor tip to outer rotor clearance as shown

17.15a Locate the slots in the inner rotor (A) over the drive pin ends (B) . . .

11 Inspect the pump housing and rotors for scoring and wear. If any damage, scoring or uneven or excessive wear is evident, replace them with new ones.

12 Fit the outer rotor into the pump housing, then fit the inner rotor into the outer rotor. Measure the clearance between the outer rotor and the pump housing with a feeler gauge and compare it to the specifications at the beginning of the Chapter **(see illustration)**. If the clearance measured is greater than the service limit, replace the housing and rotors with new ones.

13 Measure the clearance between the inner rotor tip and the outer rotor with a feeler gauge and compare it to the specifications at the beginning of the Chapter **(see illustration)**. If the clearance measured is greater than the service limit listed, replace the rotors with new ones. Lay a straight-edge across the face of the pump body and measure the end-float (the clearance between the rotor assembly and the straight-edge). Compare the result to the end-float clearance listed in the specifications at the beginning of the Chapter. If end-float is greater than the service, renew the pump body and rotor assembly.

14 Check the pump drive and driven sprockets and the chain for wear or damage, and replace them with new ones if necessary. Also check the bearing in the pump housing – refer to Section 5 of *Tools and Workshop Tips* in the *Reference* section for information on bearing checks and renewal.

15 If the pump is good, make sure all the

17.15b . . . then fit the outer rotor over the inner rotor

components are clean, then lubricate them with new engine oil. Fit the drive pin through the hole in the shaft – draw the shaft out a bit against the mechanical seal spring in the water pump to access the hole (or press the water pump impeller in if the cover has been removed) **(see illustration 17.9e)**. Slide the inner rotor onto the shaft, with the slots in the rotor facing down so that they locate over the drive pin **(see illustration)**. Fit the outer rotor onto the inner rotor **(see illustration)**. Fit the housing locating pins into the body, then fit the pump housing over the rotors **(see illustrations 17.9c and b)**. Install the bolts and tighten them to the torque setting specified at the beginning of the Chapter **(see illustration)**.

16 Fit the washer onto the end of the shaft **(see illustration 17.8c)**, then locate the driven sprocket, aligning the flats, and with the

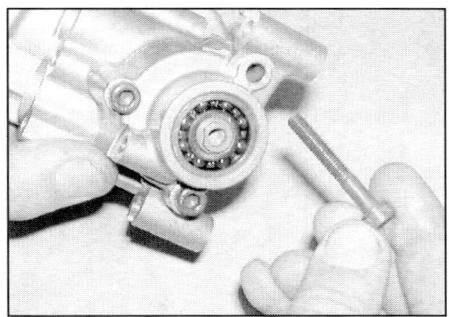

17.15c Install and tighten the housing bolts to the specified torque

marked side facing in **(see illustration)**. Apply a suitable non-permanent thread locking compound to the sprocket bolt and tighten it to the specified torque setting, using a screwdriver as on removal to prevent it turning **(see illustration)**.

17 Rotate the pump shaft by hand and check that the rotors turn smoothly and freely. If not, recheck the pump, then refer to Chapter 3 and disassemble the water pump for inspection.

Installation

18 If removed, slide the inner thrust washer onto the shaft, followed by the oil pump drive sprocket, making sure its drive tabs face out **(see illustrations 17.7b and a)**.

19 Before installing the pump, prime it by filling it with clean engine oil **(see illustration)**. Check the condition of the large bore oil pipe

17.16a Locate the sprocket over the flats on the shaft end . . .

17.16b . . . and tighten the bolt to the specified torque

17.19a Prime the pump with new oil

2•36 Engine, clutch and transmission

17.19b It is best to fit a new O-ring

17.20a Locate the chain as shown when installing the pump

17.20b Fit the long dowel into the pump and crankcase

17.20c Fit the sprocket cover

17.21a Install the pipe . . .

and coolant outlet pipe O-rings and replace them with new ones if they are in any way damaged, deformed or deteriorated. Similarly check the O-ring in the water pump inlet orifice **(see illustration)**. It is a good idea to use new O-rings whatever the condition of the old ones. Smear all the O-rings with lithium-based grease before installing them.

20 Locate the drive chain on the input shaft, but not on the drive sprocket – this gives it enough slack to engage with the driven sprocket on the pump **(see illustration)**. Install the pump, tilting it to engage the drive chain on the driven sprocket, then slip the chain onto the drive sprocket **(see illustrations 17.6e and d)**. Slide the pump into the crankcase, making sure the O-ring does not come out of its groove **(see illustration 17.6c)**. Fit the dowel into the pump and crankcase **(see illustration)**. Apply a suitable non-permanent thread locking

compound to the mounting bolt and sprocket cover bolts. Install the mounting bolt **(see illustration 17.6a)**, then locate the cover and tighten all the bolts to the torque setting specified at the beginning of the Chapter **(see illustration)**. Install the chain guide with the 'UP' marking facing up and out and tighten its bolts to the torque setting specified at the beginning of the Chapter **(see illustration 17.5b)**.

21 Install the small bore oil pipe, using a thread lock on its bolt and tightening it to the specified torque **(see illustrations)**. Fit the O-rings onto the large bore oil pipe and fit it into its sockets **(see illustrations)**. Apply a suitable non-permanent thread locking compound to the pipe bolts and tighten them to the torque setting specified at the beginning of the Chapter.

22 Fit the O-rings onto the coolant outlet pipe and fit it into its socket (see

illustration 17.3b). Apply a suitable non-permanent thread locking compound to the pipe bolt and tighten it to the torque setting specified at the beginning of the Chapter **(see illustration 17.3a)**. Attach the coolant hoses and secure them with the clamps.

23 Install the clutch (see Section 12), the oil strainer and the sump (see Section 16).

24 Fill the engine with the specified quantity and type of new engine oil and coolant (see Chapter 1).

18 Crankcase separation and reassembly

Note: *To separate the crankcase halves, the engine must be removed from the frame.*

Separation

1 To access the connecting rods, pistons and rings, crankshaft, bearings, transmission shafts, and selector drum and forks, the crankcase must be split into two parts.

2 To enable the crankcases to be separated, the engine must be removed from the frame (see Section 4). Before the crankcases can be separated the following components must be removed:

- Camshafts (Section 9).
- Cylinder head (Section 10).
- Oil sump (Section 16).
- Clutch (Section 12).
- Oil/water pump assembly and drive chain (Section 17).
- Alternator rotor and stator (Chapter 9).

17.21b . . . then threadlock the bolt and tighten it to the specified torque

17.21c Fit the O-rings . . .

17.21d . . . then install the pipe

Engine, clutch and transmission 2•37

18.4 Unscrew the bolts (arrowed) and remove the support plate

3 If the crankcases are being separated as part of a complete engine overhaul, remove the following components:
● Oil cooler (Section 6).
● Gearchange mechanism (Section 15).
● Starter motor (Chapter 9).
● Oil pressure relief valve (Section 16).
● Neutral switch, speed sensor and oil level sensor (Chapter 9).
● Pick-up coil (Chapter 5).

4 Unscrew the bolts securing the front sprocket cover support plate to the left-hand side of the engine and remove the plate (see illustration).

5 Turn the engine upside down so that it rests on the back of the upper crankcase and the cylinder head studs. The crankcases are joined by ten 9 mm bolts, two 8 mm bolts and sixteen 6 mm bolts. Make a cardboard template of the crankcase and punch a hole for each bolt location. This will ensure all bolts are installed in their correct locations on reassembly – this is important, as their lengths differ.

6 Unscrew the crankcase bolts evenly and a little at a time in a **reverse** of the numerical sequence shown and as marked on the crankcase (the number of each bolt is cast into the crankcase), until they are finger-tight, then remove them **(see illustrations)**. Note the washers fitted with some of the bolts.

18.6a Crankcase bolt location and TIGHTENING sequence – slacken them in REVERSE order

Note: *As each bolt is removed, store it in its relative position, with its washer where applicable, in the cardboard template of the crankcase halves.*

7 Carefully lift the lower crankcase half off the upper half, using a soft-faced hammer to tap around the joint to initially separate the halves, if necessary **(see illustration)**. **Note:** *If the halves do not separate easily, make sure all fasteners have been removed. Do not try and separate the halves by levering against the crankcase mating surfaces as they are easily scored and will leak oil. Tap around the joint faces with a soft-faced mallet.*

8 Remove the three locating dowels from the crankcase (they could be in either half) **(see illustration 18.14)**.

9 Refer to Sections 19 to 27 for the removal and installation of the components housed within the crankcases.

Reassembly

10 Remove all traces of sealant from the crankcase mating surfaces.

11 Ensure that all components and their bearings are in place in the upper and lower crankcase halves (see Section 21). If the transmission shafts have not been removed, check the condition of the oil seal on the left-hand end of the output shaft and replace it with a new one if it is damaged, deformed or deteriorated **(see illustration 25.7b)**. Check that the selector drum is in the neutral position (see Section 27).

12 Generously lubricate the crankshaft, transmission shafts and selector drum and

18.6b Each bolt number is cast into the crankcase

18.7 Lift the lower crankcase half off the upper half

18.13 Apply the sealant to the shaded area as shown

18.14 Fit the dowels (arrowed) into the crankcase

forks, particularly around the bearings, with clean engine oil, then use a rag soaked in high flash-point solvent to wipe over the mating surfaces of both crankcase halves to remove all traces of oil.

13 Apply a small amount of suitable sealant (such as Yamaha Bond 1215) to the mating surface of one crankcase half as shown **(see illustration)**.

Caution: *Do not apply an excessive amount of sealant as it will ooze out when the case halves are assembled and may obstruct oil passages. Do not apply the sealant on or too close (within 2 to 3 mm) to any of the bearing shells or surfaces.*

14 If removed, fit the three locating dowels into the crankcase **(see illustration)**.

15 Check again that all components are in position, particularly that the bearing shells are still correctly located in the lower crankcase half. If the timing rotor is still on the crankshaft, make sure the cam chain is installed with the crankshaft, otherwise the rotor will have to be removed. Carefully fit the lower crankcase half onto the upper crankcase half, making sure the dowels locate correctly **(see illustration 18.7)**.

16 Check that the lower crankcase half is correctly seated. **Note:** *The crankcase halves should fit together without being forced. If the casings are not correctly seated, remove the lower crankcase half and investigate the problem. Do not attempt to pull them together using the crankcase bolts as the casing will crack and be ruined.* Make sure the output shaft oil seal is correctly seated.

17 Clean the threads of the 9 mm lower crankcase bolts (Nos. 1 to 10) and apply new engine oil to their threads **(see illustration)**. Insert them with their washers in their original locations shown and as marked on the crankcase (the number of each bolt is cast into the crankcase) **(see illustrations 18.6a and b)**. Secure the bolts finger-tight at first, then tighten them evenly and a little at a time in the correct numerical sequence to the torque setting specified at the beginning of the Chapter **(see illustration)**. Go round the bolts once again to the same torque. Now tighten them by a further 45 to 50° (1/8 of a turn) using a degree disc (see Section 4 of *Tools and Workshop Tips* in the *Reference* section).

18 Clean the threads of the 8 and 6 mm crankcase bolts and apply new engine oil to their threads. Insert them in their original locations shown and as marked on the crankcase (the number of each bolt is cast into the crankcase) **(see illustrations 18.6a and b)**. Secure all bolts finger-tight at first, then tighten them evenly and a little at a time in the correct numerical sequence to the torque settings specified at the beginning of the Chapter. Be sure to distinguish correctly between the 8 and 6 mm bolts, and between the No. 16 and No. 24 6 mm bolts and the rest, as they have different settings (see Torque Wrench Settings under Specifications).

19 With all crankcase fasteners tightened, check that the crankshaft and transmission shafts rotate smoothly and easily. Check that the transmission shafts rotate freely and independently in neutral, then rotate the selector drum by hand and select each gear in turn whilst rotating the input shaft. Check that all gears can be selected and that the shafts rotate freely in every gear. If there are any signs of undue stiffness, tight or rough spots, or of any other problem, the fault must be rectified before proceeding further.

20 Apply a suitable non-permanent thread locking compound to the threads of the front sprocket cover support plate bolts, then fit the plate with the UP mark facing up and tighten the bolts to the specified torque setting **(see illustration)**.

21 Install all other removed assemblies in the reverse of the sequences given in Steps 2 and 3, according to your procedure.

18.17a Oil the bolt threads and do not forget the washers . . .

18.17b . . . and tighten them as described

18.20 Fit the plate with the UP mark at the top

Engine, clutch and transmission 2•39

19.2 Withdraw the oil pipe from the crankcase

19.8 Locate the tab in the cut-out in the crankcase (arrowed)

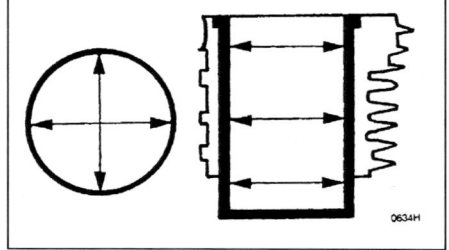

19.12 Measure the cylinder bore in the directions shown with a telescoping gauge, then measure the gauge with a micrometer

19 Crankcase and cylinder bore inspection and servicing

Crankcase halves

1 After the crankcases have been separated, remove the crankshaft and bearings, connecting rods and pistons, transmission shafts, selector drum and forks, and any other components or assemblies not already removed, referring to the relevant Sections of this and other Chapters (see Steps 2 and 3 of Section 18).

2 Withdraw the oil feed pipe from the upper crankcase – it is a push fit **(see illustration)**. Check the condition of the pipe O-rings and replace them with new ones if they are in any way damaged, deformed or deteriorated. If required, unscrew the bolts securing the two oil baffle plates in the upper crankcase half and remove them, noting how they fit. If required, unscrew the oil filter bolt from the front of the lower crankcase half.

3 Clean the crankcases thoroughly with new solvent and dry them with compressed air. Blow out all oil passages and pipes with compressed air.

4 Remove all traces of old gasket sealant from the mating surfaces. Minor damage to the surfaces can be cleaned up with a fine sharpening stone or grindstone.

Caution: Be very careful not to nick or gouge the crankcase mating surfaces, or oil leaks will result. Check both crankcase halves very carefully for cracks and other damage.

5 Small cracks or holes in aluminium castings can be repaired with an epoxy resin adhesive as a temporary measure. Permanent repairs can only be effected by argon-arc welding, and only a specialist in this process is in a position to advise on the economy or practical aspect of such a repair. If any damage is found that can't be repaired, renew the crankcase halves as a set.

6 Damaged threads can be economically reclaimed by using a diamond section wire insert, of the Heli-Coil type, which is easily fitted after drilling and re-tapping the affected thread.

7 Sheared studs or screws can be removed with stud or screw extractors, and they usually succeed in dislodging the most stubborn of them.

> **HAYNES HINT** *Refer to Tools and Workshop Tips (Section 2) in the Reference section for details of installing a thread insert and using screw extractors.*

8 Install the oil baffle plates, then apply a suitable non-permanent thread locking compound to the threads of the bolts and tighten them to the torque setting specified at the beginning of the Chapter. Apply a suitable sealant (such as Yamaha Bond 1215) to the groove in the edge of the seating side of the large baffle plate. Install the oil feed pipe using new O-rings if necessary and push it fully in, locating the tab on the outer end in the cut-out in the crankcase **(see illustration)**.

9 Install the crankshaft, pistons and bearings, cam chain, transmission shafts and selector drum and forks, before reassembling the crankcase halves.

Cylinder bores

Caution: Do not attempt to separate the liners from the cylinder block.

10 Clean any lime scale build-up out of the coolant jacket around the cylinder.

11 Check the bore walls carefully for scratches and score marks. Note that the bores are coated with a highly wear resistant material which should last the life of the engine – no attempt should be made to rebore or hone the bores.

12 Using telescoping gauges and a micrometer (see Section 3 of *Tools and Workshop Tips* in the *Reference* section), check the dimensions of each cylinder to assess the amount of wear, taper and ovality. Measure near the top (but below the level of the top piston ring at TDC), centre and bottom (but above the level of the oil ring at BDC) of the bore, both parallel to and across the crankshaft axis **(see illustration)**. Compare the results to the specifications at the beginning of the Chapter.

13 If the precision measuring tools are not available, take the crankcase to a Yamaha dealer or specialist motorcycle repair shop for assessment and advice.

14 If the cylinders are worn beyond the service limit, or badly scratched, scuffed or scored, replace the crankcases, pistons and rings with new components.

20 Main and connecting rod bearing information

1 Even though main and connecting rod bearings are generally replaced with new ones during the engine overhaul, the old bearings should be retained for close examination as they may reveal valuable information about the condition of the engine.

2 Bearing failure occurs mainly because of lack of lubrication, the presence of dirt or other foreign particles, overloading the engine and/or corrosion. Regardless of the cause of bearing failure, it must be corrected before the engine is reassembled to prevent it from happening again.

3 When examining the bearings, match them with their corresponding journal on the crankshaft to help identify the cause of any problem.

4 Dirt and other foreign particles get into the engine in a variety of ways. It may be left in the engine during assembly or it may pass through filters or breathers. It may get into the oil and from there into the bearings. Metal chips from machining operations and normal engine wear are often present. Abrasives are sometimes left in engine components after reconditioning operations, especially when parts are not thoroughly cleaned using the proper cleaning methods. Whatever the source, these foreign objects often end up imbedded in the soft bearing material and are easily recognised. Large particles will not imbed in the bearing and will score or gouge the bearing and journal. The best prevention for this cause of bearing failure is to clean all parts thoroughly and keep everything spotlessly clean during engine reassembly. Frequent and regular oil and filter changes are also essential to prevent contamination.

5 Lack of lubrication or lubrication

breakdown has a number of interrelated causes. Excessive heat (which thins the oil), overloading (which squeezes the oil from the bearing face) and oil leakage or throw off (from excessive bearing clearances, worn oil pump or high engine speeds) all contribute to lubrication breakdown. Blocked oil passages will also starve a bearing and destroy it. When lack of lubrication is the cause of bearing failure, the bearing material is wiped or extruded from the steel backing of the bearing. Temperatures may increase to the point where the steel backing and the journal turn blue from overheating.

 Refer to Tools and Workshop Tips (Section 5) in the Reference section for bearing fault finding.

6 Riding habits can have a definite effect on bearing life. Full throttle low speed operation, or labouring the engine, puts very high loads on bearings, which tend to squeeze out the oil film. These loads cause the bearings to flex, which produces fine cracks in the bearing face (fatigue failure). Eventually the bearing material will loosen in pieces and tear away from the steel backing. Short trip riding leads to corrosion of bearings, as insufficient engine heat is produced to drive off the condensed water and corrosive gases produced. These products collect in the engine oil, forming acid and sludge. As the oil is carried to the engine bearings, the acid attacks and corrodes the bearing material.

7 Incorrect bearing installation during engine assembly will lead to bearing failure as well. Tight fitting bearings which leave insufficient bearing oil clearances result in oil starvation. Dirt or foreign particles trapped behind a bearing insert result in high spots on the bearing which lead to failure.

8 To avoid bearing problems, clean all parts thoroughly before reassembly, double check all bearing clearance measurements and lubricate the new bearings with clean engine oil during installation.

21 Crankshaft and main bearings

Note: *To remove the crankshaft the engine must be removed from the frame and the crankcase halves separated.*

Removal

1 Remove the engine from the frame (see Section 4) and separate the crankcase halves (see Section 18).
2 Referring to Section 22, Steps 2, 3 and 4, unscrew the connecting rod cap nuts and separate the caps from the crankpin. Keep the caps in order and the correct way round, as they must be installed in their original location.

21.3 Carefully lift the crankshaft out of the crankcase

Note: *If no work is to be carried out on the piston/connecting rod assemblies there is no need to remove them from the bores, but push them up to the top of the bores so that the bottom ends are clear of the crankshaft.*

3 Lift the crankshaft out of the upper crankcase half, taking care not to dislodge the main bearing shells, then remove the cam chain **(see illustration)**.
4 If required, remove the bearing shells from the crankcase halves by pushing their centres to the side, then lifting them out **(see illustration)**. Keep the shells in order.

Inspection

5 Clean the crankshaft with solvent, using a rifle-cleaning brush to scrub out the oil passages. If available, blow the crank dry with compressed air, and also blow through the oil passages. Check the primary drive gear for wear or damage. If any of the teeth are excessively worn, chipped or broken, the crankshaft must be replaced with a new one. Check the primary driven gear on the back of the clutch housing for corresponding wear or damage. Also check the cam chain sprocket, the sprockets on the camshafts and the cam chain itself and replace them with new ones, if necessary.
6 Refer to Section 20 and examine the main bearing shells. If they are scored, badly scuffed or appear to have been seized, new bearings must be installed. Always replace the main bearings as a set. If they are badly damaged, check the corresponding crankshaft journals. Evidence of extreme heat, such as discoloration, indicates that lubrication failure has occurred. Be sure to thoroughly check the oil pump and pressure relief valve as well as all oil holes and passages before reassembling the engine.
7 Give the crankshaft journals a close visual examination, paying particular attention where damaged bearings have been discovered. If the journals are scored or pitted in any way, a new crankshaft will be required. Note that undersizes are not available, precluding the option of re-grinding the crankshaft.
8 Place the crankshaft on V-blocks and check the runout at the main bearing journals using a dial gauge. Compare the reading to the maximum specified at the beginning of the

21.4 To remove a main bearing shell, push it sideways and lift it out

Chapter. If the runout exceeds the limit, the crankshaft must be renewed.

Oil clearance check

9 Whether new bearing shells are being fitted or the original ones are being re-used, the main bearing oil clearance should be checked before the engine is reassembled. Main bearing oil clearance is measured with a product known as Plastigauge.
10 If not already done, remove the bearing shells from the crankcase halves (see Step 4). Clean the backs of the shells and the bearing housings in both crankcase halves, and the main bearing journals on the crankshaft.
11 Press the bearing shells into their cut-outs, ensuring that the tab on each shell engages in the notch in the crankcase **(see illustration 21.24)**. Make sure the bearings are fitted in the correct locations and take care not to touch any shell's bearing surface with your fingers.
12 Ensure the shells and crankshaft are clean and dry. Lay the crankshaft in position in the upper crankcase **(see illustration 21.3)**.
13 Cut several lengths of the appropriate size Plastigauge (they should be slightly shorter than the width of the crankshaft journals). Place a strand of Plastigauge on each journal, making sure it will be clear of the oil holes in the shells when the lower crankcase is installed **(see illustration)**. Make sure the crankshaft is not rotated.
14 If removed, fit the dowels into the crankcase **(see illustration 18.14)**. Carefully fit the lower crankcase half onto the upper

21.13 Place a strip of Plastigauge on each bearing journal

Engine, clutch and transmission 2•41

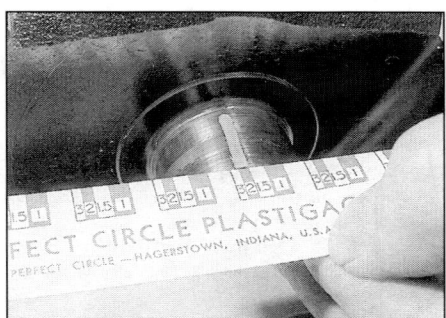

21.17 Measure the crushed Plastigauge using the scale on the pack – be sure to use the correct one as both metric and imperial are included

21.21a Main bearing journal numbers (A), big-end bearing journal numbers (B)

21.21b Main bearing housing numbers (arrowed)

21.21c If only one number is shown, all sizes are the same

21.24 Press each shell into place, locating the tab in the notch (arrowed)

half, making sure the dowels locate correctly and the Plastigauge is not disturbed (see illustration 18.7). Check that the lower crankcase half is correctly seated. Note: Do not tighten the crankcase bolts if the casing is not correctly seated.

15 Clean the threads of the 9 mm lower crankcase bolts (Nos. 1 to 10) and apply new engine oil to their threads (see illustration 18.17a). Insert them with their washers in their original locations shown and as marked on the crankcase (the number of each bolt is cast into the crankcase) (see illustrations 18.6a and b). Secure the bolts finger-tight at first, then tighten them evenly and a little at a time in the correct numerical sequence to the torque setting specified at the beginning of the Chapter (see illustration 18.17b). Go round the bolts once again to the same torque. Now tighten them by a further 45 to 50° (1/8 of a turn) using a degree disc (see Section 4 of Tools and Workshop Tips in the Reference section).

16 Now unscrew the bolts evenly and a little at a time in a reverse of the numerical sequence shown and as marked on the crankcase (the number of each bolt is cast into the crankcase), until they are finger-tight, then remove them with their washers (see illustrations 18.6a and b). Note: As each bolt is removed, store it in its relative position, with its washer, in the cardboard template of the crankcase halves. Carefully lift off the lower crankcase half, making sure the Plastigauge is not disturbed.

17 Compare the width of the crushed Plastigauge on each crankshaft journal to the scale printed on the Plastigauge envelope to obtain the main bearing oil clearance (see illustration). Compare the reading to the specifications at the beginning of the Chapter.

18 On completion carefully scrape away all traces of the Plastigauge material from the crankshaft journal and bearing shells; use a fingernail or other object which is unlikely to score them.

19 If the oil clearance falls into the specified range, new bearing shells are not required (provided they are in good condition). If the clearance is beyond the service limit, refer to the marks on the case and the marks on the crankshaft and select new bearing shells (see Steps 21 and 22). Install the new shells and check the oil clearance once again (the new shells may bring bearing clearance within the specified range). Always replace all of the shells at the same time.

20 If the clearance is still greater than the service limit listed in this Chapter's Specifications (even with replacement shells), the crankshaft journal is worn and the crankshaft should be replaced with a new one.

Main bearing shell selection

21 Replacement bearing shells for the main bearings are supplied on a selective fit basis. Code numbers are used to identify the correct replacement bearings. The crankshaft journal size numbers are stamped on the outside of the crankshaft web on the left-hand end (see illustration). The left-hand block of five numbers are for the main bearing journals (the right-hand block of four numbers are for the big-end bearing journals). The first number of the five is for the left-hand (No. 1) journal, and so on. The main bearing housing numbers are stamped into the back of the lower crankcase half (see illustration). The first number of the five is for the left-hand (No. 1) journal, and so on. Note that if there is only one number stamped into the crankcase, it means that all the journals are the same number (see illustration).

22 A range of bearing shells is available. To select the correct bearing for a particular journal, subtract the main bearing journal number (stamped on the crank web) from the main bearing housing number (stamped on the crankcase), and then subtract 2 from the result (i.e. crankcase number minus crank web number minus 2). Compare the bearing number calculated with the table below to find the colour coding of the replacement bearing required.

Number	Colour
-1	pink/violet
0	pink/white
1	pink/blue
2	pink/black
3	pink/brown

Installation

23 If not already done, remove the bearing shells from the crankcase halves (see Step 4). Clean the backs of the shells and the bearing cut-outs in both crankcase halves, and the main bearing journals on the crankshaft. If new shells are being fitted, ensure that all traces of the protective grease are cleaned off using paraffin (kerosene). Wipe the shells and crankcase halves dry with a lint-free cloth. Make sure all the oil passages and holes are clear, and blow them through with compressed air if it is available.

24 Press the bearing shells into their locations. Make sure the tab on each shell engages in the notch in the casing (see illustration). Make sure the bearings are fitted in the correct locations and take care not to touch any shell's bearing surface with your fingers. Lubricate each shell with clean engine oil.

25 If the timing rotor is still on the crankshaft, fit the cam chain onto its sprocket. If the rotor

2•42 Engine, clutch and transmission

has been removed, the cam chain can be installed later. Lower the crankshaft into position in the upper crankcase, feeding the cam chain into its tunnel if applicable, and making sure all bearings remain in place **(see illustration 21.3)**.

26 Refer to Section 22, Steps 30 to 32, and fit the connecting rods on to the crankshaft.

27 Check that the crankshaft rotates smoothly and freely. If there are any signs of roughness or tightness, detach the rods and recheck the assembly, and if that is good, the oil main and big-end clearances (see above and Section 22). Sometimes tapping the bottom of the connecting rod cap will relieve tightness.

28 Reassemble the crankcase halves (see Section 18).

22 Connecting rods

Note: *To remove the connecting rods the engine must be removed from the frame and the crankcases separated.*

Removal

1 Remove the engine from the frame (see Section 4) and separate the crankcase halves (see Section 18).

2 Before separating the rods from the crankshaft, measure the side clearance on each rod with a feeler gauge **(see illustration)**. If the clearance on any rod is greater than the service limit listed in this Chapter's Specifications, replace that rod with a new one.

3 Using paint or a felt marker pen, mark the relevant cylinder identity across the join between each connecting rod and cap. Note the 'Y' mark on each connecting rod which must face to the left-hand side of the engine, and the arrow on the piston which points to the front of the engine – these ensure that the cap and rod are fitted the correct way around on reassembly **(see illustration)**. Note that the number and letter already across the rod and cap indicate rod size and weight grade respectively, not cylinder number.

4 Unscrew the connecting rod cap nuts and separate the cap and rod from the crankpin **(see illustrations)**. If the cap appears stuck, tap it on one end with a hammer while pulling it. Lift the crankshaft out of the upper crankcase half, taking care not to dislodge the main bearing shells **(see illustration 21.3)**.

5 Turn the crankcase on its side. Push each piston/connecting rod assembly up and remove it from the top of the bore making

 HAYNES HiNT *To ease removal of the pistons, carefully remove any ridge of carbon built up on the top of each cylinder bore using a scraper. If there is a pronounced wear ridge, remove it using a ridge reamer.*

sure the connecting rod does not mark the cylinder bore walls **(see illustration)**.

Caution: *Do not try to remove the piston/connecting rod from the bottom of the cylinder bore. The piston will not pass the crankcase main bearing webs. If the piston is pulled right to the bottom of the bore the oil control ring will expand and lock the piston in position. If this happens it is likely the ring will be broken.*

6 Fit the relevant bearing shells (if removed), bearing cap, and bolts on each piston/connecting rod assembly so that they are all kept together as a matched set.

7 Separate the pistons from the connecting rods if required (see Section 23).

Inspection

8 Check the connecting rods for cracks and other obvious damage.

9 Apply clean engine oil to the piston pin, insert it into its connecting rod small-end and check for any freeplay between the two **(see illustration)**. If freeplay is excessive, measure the pin external diameter **(see illustration 23.13b)**. Compare the result to the specifications at the beginning of the Chapter. Replace the pin with a new one if it is worn beyond its specified limits. If the pin diameter is within specifications, replace the connecting rod with a new one. Repeat the measurements for all the rods.

10 Refer to Section 20 and examine the connecting rod bearing shells. If they are

22.2 Measure the connecting rod side clearance using a feeler gauge

22.3 The arrow on the piston (A) points to the front of the engine and the 'Y' mark on the connecting rod (B) faces the left-hand side

22.4a Unscrew the nuts (arrowed) . . .

22.4b . . . and pull the cap off the connecting rod

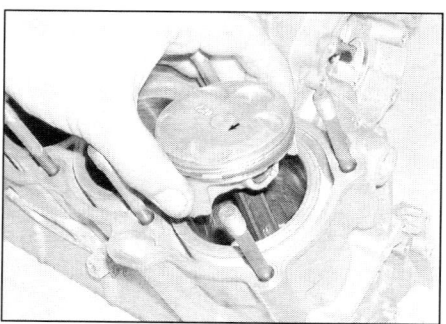

22.5 Remove the piston/rod assembly from the top of the bore

22.9 Slip the piston pin into the rod's small-end and rock it back and forth to check for looseness

22.13 To remove a big-end bearing shell, push it sideways and lift it out

22.14 Make sure the tab (A) locates in the notch (B)

22.24 Connecting rod size number

scored, badly scuffed or appear to have seized, new shells must be installed. Always replace the shells in the connecting rods as a set. If they are badly damaged, check the corresponding crankpin. Evidence of extreme heat, such as discoloration, indicates that lubrication failure has occurred. Be sure to thoroughly check the oil pump and pressure regulator as well as all oil holes and passages before reassembling the engine.

11 Have the rods checked for twist and bend by a Yamaha dealer if you are in doubt about their straightness.

Oil clearance check

12 Whether new bearing shells are being fitted or the original ones are being re-used, the connecting rod (big-end) bearing oil clearance should be checked prior to reassembly.

13 Work on one connecting rod at a time. Remove the bearing shells from the rod and cap, keeping them in order **(see illustration)**. Clean the backs of the shells and the bearing locations in both the connecting rod and cap, and the crankpin journal.

14 Press the bearing shells into their locations, ensuring that the tab on each shell engages the notch in the connecting rod/cap **(see illustration)**. Make sure the bearings are fitted in the correct locations and take care not to touch any shell's bearing surface with your fingers.

15 Cut a length of the appropriate size Plastigauge (it should be slightly shorter than the width of the crankpin). Place a strand of Plastigauge on the crankpin journal **(see illustration 21.13)**.

16 Apply molybdenum disulphide grease to the bolt shanks and threads and to the seats of the nuts. Fit the connecting rod and cap onto the crankshaft **(see illustrations 22.30a and b)**. Make sure the cap is fitted the correct way around so the previously made markings align, and that the rod is facing the right way (see Step 3). Fit the nuts and tighten them finger-tight, making sure the connecting rod does not rotate on the crankshaft.

17 Tighten the cap nuts to the initial torque setting specified at the beginning of the Chapter, making sure the connecting rod does not rotate on the crankshaft **(see illustration 22.32)**. Now tighten each nut in turn and in one continuous movement to the final torque setting specified. If tightening is paused between the initial and final settings, slacken the nut to below the initial setting and repeat the procedure.

18 Slacken the cap nuts and remove the cap and the rod, again taking great care not to rotate the rod or crankshaft.

19 Compare the width of the crushed Plastigauge on the crankpin to the scale printed on the Plastigauge envelope to obtain the connecting rod bearing oil clearance **(see illustration 21.19)**. Compare the reading to the specifications at the beginning of the Chapter.

20 On completion, carefully scrape away all traces of the Plastigauge material from the crankpin and bearing shells using a fingernail or other object which is unlikely to score the shells.

21 If the clearance is within the range listed in this Chapter's Specifications and the bearings are in perfect condition, they can be reused. If the clearance is beyond the service limit, replace the bearing shells with new ones (see Steps 24 and 25). Check the oil clearance once again (the new shells may be thick enough to bring bearing clearance within the specified range). Always replace all of the shells at the same time.

22 If the clearance is still greater than the service limit listed in this Chapter's Specifications, the big-end bearing journal is worn and the crankshaft should be replaced with a new one.

23 Repeat the procedure for the remaining connecting rods.

Bearing shell selection

24 Replacement bearing shells for the big-end bearings are supplied on a selected fit basis. Code numbers are used to identify the correct replacement bearings. The crankshaft journal size numbers are stamped on the outside of the crankshaft web on the left-hand end **(see illustration 21.23a)**. The right-hand block of four numbers are for the big-end bearing journals (the left-hand block of five numbers are for the main bearing journals). The first number of the four is for the left-hand (No. 1 cylinder) journal, and so on. Each connecting rod size number is marked in ink across the flat face of the connecting rod and cap **(see illustration)**.

25 A range of bearing shells is available. To select the correct bearing for a particular connecting rod, subtract the big-end bearing journal number (stamped on the crank web) from the connecting rod number (marked on the rod), and then subtract 2 from the result (i.e. connecting rod number minus crank web number minus 2). Compare the bearing number calculated with the table below to find the colour coding of the replacement bearing required. The colour code is marked on the side of each bearing.

Number	Colour
-1	violet
0	white
1	blue
2	black

Installation

26 If removed, fit the pistons onto the connecting rods (see Section 25).

27 Clean the backs of the bearing shells and the bearing locations in both cap and rod. If new shells are being fitted, ensure that all traces of the protective grease are cleaned off using paraffin (kerosene). Wipe the shells, cap and rod dry with a clean lint-free cloth. Install the bearing shells in the connecting rods and caps, making sure the tab on each shell locates in the notch in the connecting rod/cap **(see illustration 22.14)**. Make sure the bearings are fitted in their correct locations and take care not to touch any shell's bearing surface with your fingers. Lubricate the shells with clean engine oil.

28 Place the crankcase on blocks to prevent the connecting rod bolts hitting the bench before the piston is fully in the bore. Lubricate the pistons, rings and cylinder bore with clean engine oil. Insert the piston/connecting rod assembly into the top of its bore, taking care not to allow the connecting rod to mark the bore **(see illustration 22.5)**. Make sure the arrow marked on the piston crown points to the front of the bore and the 'Y' mark on the rod faces the left-hand side of the engine (see Step 3) **(see illustration 22.3)**, then carefully compress and feed each piston ring into the

22.28a Carefully feed each ring into the bore using a screwdriver and/or fingernails

22.28b Clamp the rings in position by tightening the bands on the compressor . . .

22.28c . . . then push the piston into its bore

22.30a Pull the rod onto the crankpin . . .

22.30b . . . then fit the cap

22.32 Tighten the nuts as described, first to the initial torque, then to the final torque

bore until the piston crown is flush with the top of the bore (see illustration). If available, a piston ring compressor makes installation a lot easier (see illustrations).
29 If the timing rotor is still on the crankshaft, fit the cam chain onto its sprocket. If the rotor has been removed, the cam chain can be installed later. Lower the crankshaft into position in the upper crankcase, feeding the cam chain into its tunnel if applicable, and making sure all bearings remain in place (see illustration 21.3).
30 Working on one connecting rod at a time, lubricate the crankpin and the shells in the connecting rod and cap with clean engine oil. Pull the rod onto the crankpin and fit the cap with its shell onto the rod (see illustrations). Make sure the cap is fitted the correct way around so the previously made markings align (see Step 3).
31 Apply molybdenum disulphide grease to the bolt shanks and threads and to the seats of the nuts. Fit the nuts and tighten them finger-tight. Check again to make sure all components have been returned to their original locations using the marks made on disassembly.
32 Tighten the cap nuts to the initial torque setting specified at the beginning of this Chapter (see illustration). Now tighten each nut in turn and in one continuous movement to the final torque setting specified. If tightening is paused between the initial and final settings, slacken the nut to below the initial setting and repeat the procedure. Fit the

remaining rods onto the crankshaft in the same way.
33 Check that the crankshaft rotates smoothly and freely. If there are any signs of roughness or tightness, detach the rods and recheck the assembly, and if that is good, the main and big-end oil clearances (see above and Section 23). Sometimes tapping the bottom of the connecting rod cap will relieve tightness.
34 Reassemble the crankcase halves (see Section 18).

23 Pistons

Note: *To remove the pistons the engine must be removed from the frame and the crankcase halves separated.*

Removal

1 Remove the connecting rods (see Section 22).
2 Before removing the piston from the connecting rod, use a sharp scriber or felt marker pen to write the cylinder identity on the crown of each piston (or on the inside of the skirt if the piston is dirty and going to be cleaned) as it must be installed in its original cylinder. Each piston also has an arrow on its crown which points to the exhaust (front) side of the bore (see illustration). If this is not visible, mark the piston accordingly so that it

can be installed the correct way round.
3 Carefully prise out the circlip on one side of the piston using needle-nose pliers or a small flat-bladed screwdriver inserted into the notch (see illustration). Push the piston pin out from the other side to free the piston from the connecting rod (see illustration). Remove the other circlip and discard them both as new ones must be used. When the piston has been removed, install its pin back into its bore so that related parts do not get mixed up.

> **HAYNES HINT** *To prevent the circlip from pinging away, pass a rod or screwdriver, whose diameter is greater than the gap between the circlip ends, through the piston pin. This will trap the circlip if it springs out.*

23.2 Note the arrow on the piston which must point forwards

Engine, clutch and transmission 2•45

23.3a Prise out the circlip . . .

23.3b . . . then push out the pin and remove the piston

23.5a Removing the piston rings using a ring removal and installation tool

HAYNES HiNT *If a piston pin is a tight fit in the piston bosses, soak a rag in boiling water then wring it out and wrap it around the piston – this will expand the alloy piston sufficiently to release its grip on the pin. If the piston pin is particularly stubborn, extract it using a drawbolt tool, but be careful to protect the piston's working surfaces.*

Inspection

4 Before the inspection process can be carried out, the pistons must be cleaned and the old piston rings removed.

5 Using your thumbs or a piston ring removal and installation tool, carefully remove the rings from the pistons **(see illustration)**. Do not nick or gouge the pistons in the process. Carefully note which way up each ring fits and in which groove, as they must be installed in their original positions if being re-used. The upper surface of each ring should have a manufacturer's mark or letter at one end – if the mark on each ring is different, note which mark is for the top ring and which is for the second. The rings can also be distinguished by their different profiles **(see illustration)**.

6 Scrape all traces of carbon from the tops of the pistons. A hand-held wire brush or a piece of fine emery cloth can be used once most of the deposits have been scraped away. Do not, under any circumstances, use a wire brush mounted in a drill motor to remove deposits from the pistons; the piston material is soft and will be eroded away by the wire brush.

7 Use a piston ring groove cleaning tool to remove any carbon deposits from the ring grooves. If a tool is not available, a piece broken off an old ring will do the job. Be very careful to remove only the carbon deposits. Do not remove any metal and do not nick or gouge the sides of the ring grooves.

8 Once the deposits have been removed, clean the pistons with solvent and dry them thoroughly. If the identification previously marked on the piston is cleaned off, be sure to re-mark it with the correct identity. Make sure the oil return holes below the oil ring groove are clear.

9 Carefully inspect each piston for cracks around the skirt, at the pin bosses and at the ring lands. Normal piston wear appears as even, vertical wear on the thrust surfaces of the piston and slight looseness of the top ring in its groove. If the skirt is scored or scuffed, the engine may have been suffering from overheating and/or abnormal combustion, resulting in excessively high operating temperatures. The oil pump should be checked thoroughly. Also check that the circlip grooves are not damaged.

10 A hole in the piston crown, although extreme, is an indication that abnormal combustion (pre-ignition) was occurring. Burned areas at the edge of the piston crown are usually evidence of spark knock (detonation). If any of the above problems exist, the causes must be corrected or the damage will occur again.

11 Measure the piston ring-to-groove clearance by laying each piston ring in its groove and slipping a feeler gauge in beside it **(see illustration)**. Make sure you have the correct ring for the groove (see Step 5). Check the clearance at three or four locations around the groove. If the clearance is greater than specified, renew both the piston and rings as a set. If new rings are being used, measure the clearance using the new rings. If the clearance is greater than that specified, the piston is worn and must be renewed.

12 Check the piston-to-bore clearance by measuring the bore (see Section 19) and the piston diameter. Make sure each piston is matched to its correct cylinder. Measure the piston 5 mm up from the bottom of the skirt and at 90° to the piston pin axis **(see illustration)**. Subtract the piston diameter from the bore diameter to obtain the clearance. If it is greater than the specified figure, check whether it is the bore or piston that is worn beyond its specified service limit. If the bores are good, install new pistons and rings. If the bores are worn, replace the crankcases with new ones and fit new rings onto the pistons. Yamaha recommend that the cases, pistons and rings should be replaced as a new set if the clearance is too great.

23.5b The top ring (A) and second ring (B) can be identified by their different profiles

23.11 Measure the piston ring-to-groove clearance with a feeler gauge

23.12 Measure the piston diameter with a micrometer at the specified distance from the bottom of the skirt

23.13a Slip the pin (A) into the piston (B) and try to rock it back and forth. If it is loose, renew the piston and pin

23.13b Measure the external diameter of the pin . . .

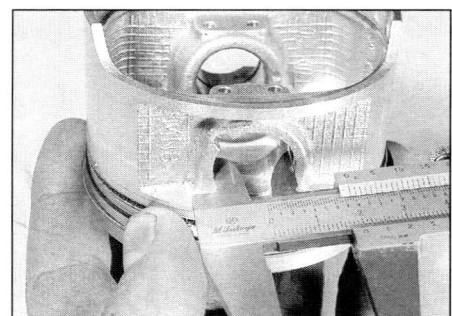

23.13c . . . and the internal diameter of the bore in the piston

23.16 Do not over-compress the circlips and make sure they seat in the groove

13 Apply clean engine oil to the piston pin, insert it into the piston and check for any freeplay between the two **(see illustration)**. Measure the pin external diameter, and the pin bore in the piston **(see illustrations)**. Subtract the bore diameter from the pin diameter to obtain the clearance. If it is greater than the specified figure, check whether it is the pin bore or pin that is worn beyond its specified service limit and replace with new ones as required.

Installation

14 Inspect and install the piston rings (see Section 24).
15 Lubricate the piston pin, the piston pin bore and the connecting rod small-end bore with clean engine oil.
16 Install a **new** circlip in one side of the piston (do not re-use old circlips). Line up the piston on its correct connecting rod so that the arrow on the piston crown will point to the front of the engine and the 'Y' mark will face the left-hand side of the engine when they are installed **(see illustration 22.3)**. Insert the piston pin from the side without the circlip **(see illustration 23.3b)**. Secure the pin with the other **new** circlip **(see illustration)**. When installing the circlips, compress them only just enough to fit them in the piston, and make sure they are properly seated in their grooves with the open end away from the removal notch.
17 Install the connecting rods (see Section 22).

24 Piston rings

1 It is good practice to fit new piston rings when an engine is overhauled. Before installing the rings (new or old), check the installed end gaps of the rings as follows.

Inspection

2 If new rings are being used, lay out each piston with a new ring set and keep them together so the rings will be matched with the same piston and bore during the end gap measurement procedure and engine assembly. If the old rings are being reused, make sure they are matched with their correct piston and cylinder.
3 Insert the ring into the top of its bore and square it up with the bore walls by pushing it in with the top of the piston. The ring should be about 20 mm below the top edge of the bore. Slip a feeler gauge between the ends of the ring and measure the gap **(see illustration)**. Compare the measurements to the specifications at the beginning of the Chapter.
4 If the gap is larger or smaller than specified, double check to make sure that you have the correct rings before proceeding.
5 If the gap is too small, the ring ends may come in contact with each other during engine operation, which can cause serious damage.
6 Excess end gap is not critical unless it exceeds the service limit. Again, double-check to make sure you have the correct rings for your engine and check that the bore is not worn (see Section 19).
7 Repeat the procedure for the other ring. Remember to keep the rings, pistons and bores matched up.

Installation

8 Once the ring end gaps have been checked/corrected, the rings can be installed on the pistons.
9 The oil control ring (lowest on the piston) is installed first. It is composed of three separate components, namely the expander and the upper and lower side rails. Slip the expander into the groove, then install the lower side rail **(see illustrations)**. Do not use a piston ring installation tool on the oil ring side rails as they may be damaged. Instead, place one end of the side rail into the groove between the expander and the ring land. Hold it firmly in place and slide a finger around the piston

24.3 Measuring piston ring installed end gap

24.9a Fit the oil ring expander in its groove . . .

24.9b . . . then fit the lower side rail . . .

Engine, clutch and transmission 2•47

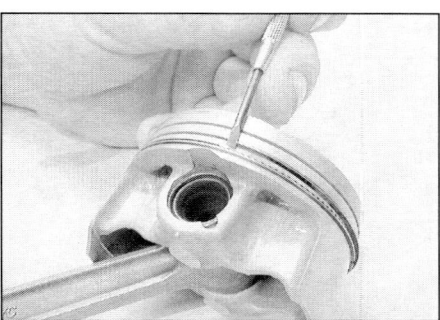

24.9c ... and the upper side rail each side of it. The oil ring components must be installed by hand

24.12a Carefully feed the second ring into its groove

24.12b Old pieces of feeler gauge blade can be used to guide the ring over the piston

24.13 Finally install the top ring

while pushing the rail into the groove. Next, install the upper side rail in the same manner (see illustration). Make sure the ends of the expander do not overlap.

10 After the three oil ring components have been installed, check to make sure that both the upper and lower side rails can be turned smoothly in the ring groove.

11 The upper surface of each compression ring should have a mark or letter at one end which must face up when the ring is installed on the piston. The rings can be distinguished by their different profiles (see illustration 23.5b).

12 Fit the second ring into the middle groove in the piston. Do not expand the ring any more than is necessary to slide it into place (see illustration). To avoid breaking the ring, use a piston ring installation tool (see

24.14 Stagger the ring end gaps as shown

1 Top compression ring
2 Oil ring lower rail
3 Oil ring upper rail
4 Second compression ring

illustration 23.5a), or pieces of old feeler gauge blades (see illustration).

13 Finally, install the top ring in the same manner into the top groove in the piston (see illustration).

14 Once the rings are correctly installed, check they move freely without snagging and stagger their end gaps as shown (see illustration).

25 Transmission shaft removal and installation

Note: *To remove the transmission shafts the engine must be removed from the frame and the crankcase halves separated.*

Removal

1 Remove the engine from the frame (see Section 4) and separate the crankcase halves (see Section 18).
2 Lift the output shaft out of the crankcase (see illustration). If it is stuck, use a soft-faced hammer and gently tap on the ends of the shaft to free it. Remove the bearing half-ring retainer from the crankcase or bearing, noting how it fits (see illustration 25.7a). Discard the oil seal from the left-hand end of the shaft and obtain a new seal for installation (see illustration 25.7b).
3 Remove the selector drum and forks (see Section 27).
4 Undo the Torx screws securing the input shaft bearing housing (see illustration). Obtain two 6 mm bolts, 30 mm long excluding the bolt head, and with a 1 mm thread pitch, and screw them into the two holes in the bearing housing as shown (see illustration). Tighten the bolts until they contact the surface of the crankcase, then continue tightening them evenly and a little at a time until the bearing housing is displaced. Withdraw the

25.2 Lift the output shaft out of the crankcase

25.4a Remove the Torx screws (arrowed)

25.4b Thread the specified bolts into the housing and tighten them as described to displace the housing . . .

2•48 Engine, clutch and transmission

25.4c ... then withdraw the input shaft from the crankcase

25.5a Slide the shaft into position ...

25.5b ... then install the new Torx screws and tighten them to the specified torque

25.5c Stake the edge of each screw into the housing

25.7a Fit the retainer into the slot in the bearing ...

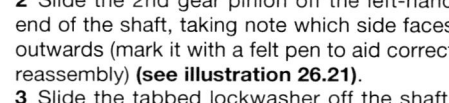

25.7b ... then slide on the new oil seal

input shaft from the crankcase (**see illustration**). Discard the Torx screws, as new ones should be used.

Installation

5 Slide the input shaft into the crankcase, locating the shaft end into its bore (**see illustration**). Make sure the bearing housing screw holes are correctly aligned, and tap the housing in with a soft-faced mallet if necessary. Install the **new** Torx screws and tighten them to the torque setting specified at the beginning of the Chapter (**see illustration**). Stake the edge of each screw into the indent in the housing using a suitable punch (**see illustration**).
6 Install the selector drum and forks (see Section 27).
7 Fit the output shaft bearing half-ring retainer into its slot in the bearing (**see illustration**). Smear the lips of the output shaft seal with grease. Slide the seal onto the left-hand end of the shaft (**see illustration**).
8 Lower the output shaft into position in the upper crankcase, making sure the groove in the bearing engages correctly with the half-ring retainer (**see illustration 25.2**).
9 Make sure both transmission shafts are correctly seated and their related pinions are correctly engaged.
Caution: If the half-ring retainer is not correctly engaged, the crankcase halves will not seat correctly.
10 Position the gears in the neutral position and check the shafts are free to rotate easily and independently (i.e. the input shaft can turn whilst the output shaft is held stationary) before proceeding further.

11 Reassemble the crankcase halves (see Section 18).

26 Transmission shaft disassembly, inspection and reassembly

1 Remove the transmission shafts from the crankcase (see Section 25). Always disassemble the transmission shafts separately to avoid mixing up the components.

Input shaft disassembly

> **HAYNES HiNT** When disassembling the transmission shafts, place the parts on a long rod or thread a wire through them to keep them in order and facing the proper direction.

26.5 The 1st gear pinion is integral with the shaft

2 Slide the 2nd gear pinion off the left-hand end of the shaft, taking note which side faces outwards (mark it with a felt pen to aid correct reassembly) (**see illustration 26.21**).
3 Slide the tabbed lockwasher off the shaft, then turn the slotted splined washer to offset the splines and slide it off the shaft, noting how they fit together (**see illustrations 26.20c and a**). Slide the sixth gear pinion and its bush off the shaft, followed by the splined washer (**see illustrations 26.19c, b and a**).
4 Remove the circlip securing the combined 3rd/4th gear pinion, then slide the pinion off the shaft (**see illustrations 26.18b and a**).
5 Remove the circlip securing the 5th gear pinion, then slide the splined washer, the pinion and its bush off the shaft (**see illustrations 26.17d, c, b and a**). The 1st gear pinion is integral with the shaft (**see illustration**).
6 If required, remove the bearing and its housing from the right-hand end of the shaft,

26.6 Remove the housing and bearing if required

Engine, clutch and transmission 2•49

26.17a Slide the 5th gear pinion bush . . .

26.17b . . . the 5th gear pinion . . .

26.17c . . . and the splined washer onto the shaft . . .

referring to *Tools and Workshop Tips* (Section 5) in the *Reference* section **(see illustration)**.

Input shaft inspection

7 Wash all of the components in clean solvent and dry them off.
8 Check the gear teeth for cracking, chipping, pitting and other obvious wear or damage. Any pinion that is damaged as such must be replaced.
9 Inspect the dogs and the dog holes in the gears for cracks, chips, and excessive wear especially in the form of rounded edges. Make sure mating gears engage properly. Renew the paired gears as a set if necessary.
10 Check for signs of scoring or bluing on the pinions, bushes and shaft. This could be caused by overheating due to inadequate lubrication. Check that all the oil holes and passages are clear. Replace any damaged pinions or bushes with new ones.
11 Check that each pinion moves freely on the shaft or bush but without undue freeplay. Check that each bush moves freely on the shaft but without undue freeplay.
12 The shaft is unlikely to sustain damage unless the engine has seized, placing an unusually high loading on the transmission, or the machine has covered a very high mileage. Check the surface of the shaft, especially where a pinion turns on it, and replace the shaft with a new one if it has scored or picked up, or if there are any cracks. Check the shaft runout using V-blocks and a dial gauge and replace the shaft with a new one if the runout

26.17d . . . and secure them with the circlip . . .

exceeds the limit specified at the beginning of the Chapter.
13 Check the washers and circlips and renew any that are bent or appear weakened or worn. Use new ones if in any doubt. Note that it is good practice to renew all circlips when overhauling gear shafts.
14 Referring to *Tools and Workshop Tips* (Section 5) in the *Reference* section, check the bearings and replace them with new ones, if necessary. Do not forget the input shaft left-hand bearing, which is housed in the crankcase.

Input shaft reassembly

15 During reassembly, apply engine oil or molybdenum disulphide oil (a 50/50 mixture of molybdenum disulphide grease and engine oil) to the mating surfaces of the shaft, pinions and bushes. When installing the circlips, do not expand their ends any further than is

26.17e . . . making sure it locates in the groove

necessary. Install the stamped circlips and washers so that their chamfered side faces the pinion it secures **(see illustration 26.1a)**.
16 If removed, fit the bearing and its housing onto the right-hand end of the shaft, referring to *Tools and Workshop Tips* (Section 5) in the *Reference* section **(see illustration 26.6)**.
17 Slide the 5th gear pinion bush onto the left-hand end of the shaft, aligning the oil hole in the bush with the hole in the shaft **(see illustration)**. Fit the 5th gear pinion with its dogs facing away from the integral 1st gear **(see illustration)**. Slide the splined washer onto the shaft, then fit the circlip, making sure that it locates correctly in the groove in the shaft **(see illustrations)**.
18 Slide the combined 3rd/4th gear pinion onto the shaft with the smaller 3rd gear pinion facing the 5th gear pinion **(see illustration)**. Fit the circlip, making sure it locates correctly in its groove in the shaft **(see illustrations)**.

26.18a Slide the 3rd/4th gear pinion onto the shaft . . .

26.18b . . . and secure it with the circlip . . .

26.18c . . . making sure it locates in the groove

2•50 Engine, clutch and transmission

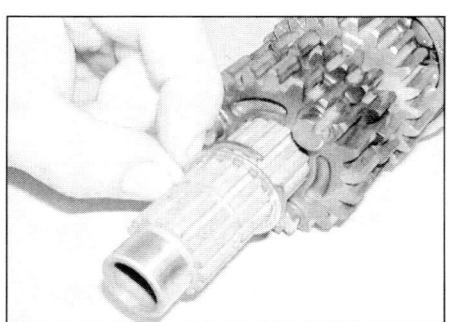

26.19a Slide the splined washer . . .

26.19b . . . the 6th gear pinion bush . . .

26.19c . . . and the 6th gear pinion onto the shaft

19 Slide the splined washer onto the shaft, followed by the 6th gear pinion bush, aligning the oil hole in the bush with the hole in the shaft, and the 6th gear pinion, making sure its dogs face the 3rd/4th gear pinion **(see illustrations)**.
20 Slide the slotted splined washer onto the shaft and locate it in its groove, then turn it in the groove, so that the splines on the washer align with the splines on the shaft and secure the washer in the groove **(see illustrations)**. Slide the tabbed lockwasher onto the shaft, so that the tabs locate into the slots in the outer rim of the splined washer **(see illustrations)**.
21 Slide the 2nd gear pinion onto the shaft, using any marks made on removal to identify its outer face **(see illustration)**.
22 Check that all components have been correctly installed **(see illustration)**.

Output shaft disassembly
23 Slide the bearing off the right-hand end of the shaft **(see illustration 26.38d)**.
24 Slide the thrust washer off the shaft, followed by the 1st gear pinion and its bush, and the 5th gear pinion **(see illustrations 26.38c, b and a, and 26.37)**.
25 Remove the circlip securing the 3rd gear pinion, then slide the splined washer, the pinion and its splined bush off the shaft **(see illustrations 26.36d, c, b and a)**.
26 Slide the tabbed lockwasher off the shaft, then turn the slotted splined washer to offset the splines and slide it off the shaft, noting how they fit together **(see illustrations 26.35c and a)**.
27 Slide the 4th gear pinion and its splined bush, followed by the splined washer, off the shaft **(see illustrations 26.34c, b and a)**.
28 Remove the circlip securing the 6th gear pinion, then slide the pinion off the shaft **(see illustrations 26.33b and a)**.
29 Remove the circlip securing the 2nd gear pinion, then slide the splined washer, the pinion and its bush off the shaft **(see illustrations 26.32d, c, b and a)**.

Output shaft inspection
30 Refer to Steps 7 to 13 above.

Output shaft reassembly
31 During reassembly, apply engine oil or molybdenum disulphide oil (a 50/50 mixture of molybdenum disulphide grease and engine oil) to the mating surfaces of the shaft, pinions and bushes. When installing the circlips, do not expand their ends any further than is necessary. Install the stamped circlips and washers so that their chamfered side faces the pinion it secures **(see illustration 26.1b)**.
32 Slide the 2nd gear pinion bush onto the

26.20a Slide the slotted splined washer onto the shaft . . .

26.20b . . . and position it as shown

26.20c Slide the tabbed lockwasher onto the shaft . . .

26.20d . . . and engage its tabs in the slots

26.21 Slide the 2nd gear pinion onto the end of the shaft

26.22 The assembled input shaft should be as shown

Engine, clutch and transmission 2•51

26.32a Slide the 2nd gear pinion bush . . .

26.32b . . . the 2nd gear pinion . . .

26.32c . . . and the splined washer onto the shaft . . .

shaft, aligning the oil hole in the bush with the hole in the shaft, then slide on the 2nd gear pinion (with its dog holes facing away from the bearing) and the splined washer **(see illustrations)**. Fit the circlip, making sure it is locates correctly in its groove in the shaft **(see illustrations)**.

33 Slide the 6th gear pinion onto the shaft with its selector fork groove facing away from the 2nd gear pinion, then fit the circlip, making sure it locates correctly in its groove in the shaft **(see illustrations)**.

34 Slide the splined washer and the 4th gear pinion bush onto the shaft, making sure the oil hole in the bush aligns with the hole in the shaft, then slide on the 4th gear pinion **(see illustrations)**.

26.32d . . . and secure them with the circlip . . .

26.32e . . . making sure it locates in the groove

26.33a Slide the 6th gear pinion onto the shaft . . .

26.33b . . . and secure it with the circlip . . .

26.33c . . . making sure it locates in the groove

26.34a Slide the splined washer . . .

26.34b . . . the 4th gear pinion bush . . .

26.34c . . . and the 4th gear pinion onto the shaft

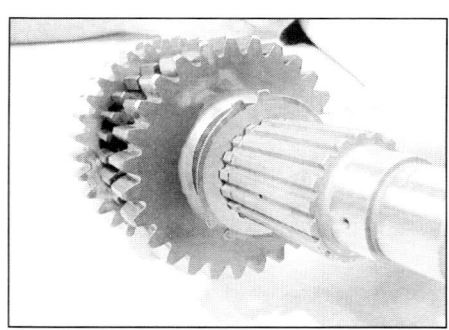

26.35a Slide the slotted splined washer onto the shaft . . .

26.35b . . . and position it as shown

26.35c Slide the tabbed lockwasher onto the shaft . . .

26.35d . . . and engage its tabs in the slots

26.36a Slide the 3rd gear pinion bush . . .

26.36b . . . the 3rd gear pinion . . .

35 Slide the slotted splined washer onto the shaft and locate it in its groove, then turn it in the groove so that the splines on the washer align with the splines on the shaft and secure the washer in the groove **(see illustrations)**. Slide the lockwasher onto the shaft, so that the tabs on the lockwasher locate into the slots in the outer rim of the splined washer **(see illustrations)**.

36 Slide the 3rd gear pinion bush onto the shaft, making sure the oil hole in the bush aligns with the hole in the shaft, followed by the 3rd gear pinion (with its recessed side facing away from the 4th gear pinion) and the splined washer. Fit the circlip, making sure it locates correctly in its groove in the shaft **(see illustrations)**.

37 Slide the 5th gear pinion onto the shaft with its selector fork groove facing the 3rd gear pinion **(see illustration)**.

38 Slide the 1st gear pinion bush onto the shaft, followed by the 1st gear pinion (with its recessed side facing the 5th gear pinion) and the thrust washer, then fit the bearing onto the end of the shaft **(see illustrations)**.

26.36c . . . and the splined washer onto the shaft . . .

26.36d . . . and secure them with the circlip . . .

26.36e . . . making sure it locates in the groove

26.37 Slide the 5th gear pinion onto the shaft

26.38a Slide the 1st gear pinion bush . . .

Engine, clutch and transmission 2•53

26.38b ... and the 1st gear pinion onto the shaft ...

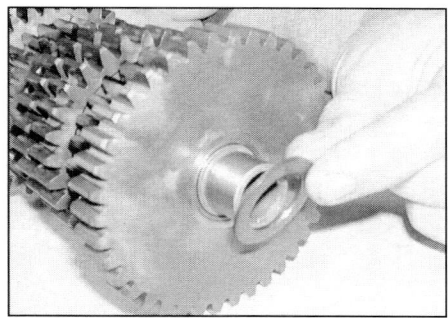
26.38c ... then fit the thrust washer ...

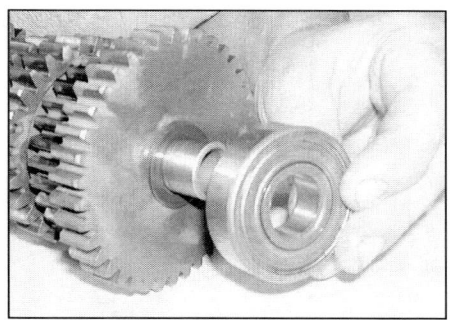
26.38d ... and the bearing

39 Check that all components have been correctly installed **(see illustration)**.

27 Selector drum and forks

Note: *To remove the selector drum and forks the engine must be removed from the frame and the crankcase halves separated.*

Removal

1 Position the transmission in neutral. Remove the engine from the frame (see Section 4) and separate the crankcase halves (see Section 18).
2 If not already done, remove the gearchange mechanism (see Section 15).
3 Remove the transmission output shaft (see Section 25).
4 Note the orientation of the selector drum as an aid for installation – the best way is to check which way the neutral detent in the end of the drum points, and to note how the neutral contact is located against the neutral switch contact **(see illustration)**. Unscrew the bolts securing the selector drum retainer plate and remove the plate, noting how it fits.
5 Before removing the selector forks, note that each fork is lettered for identification. The right-hand fork has an 'R', the centre fork a 'C', and the left-hand fork an 'L' **(see illustration)**. These letters face the right-hand side of the engine. If no letters are visible, mark them yourself using a felt pen.
6 Support the selector forks for the output shaft and withdraw the fork shaft from the crankcase, then remove the forks, noting how they fit **(see illustration)**. Slide the forks back onto the shaft in the correct order and the right way round. Note the springs in the ends of the shaft and remove them for safekeeping, if loose.
7 Support the selector fork for the input shaft and withdraw the shaft from the casing **(see illustration)**. Move the fork guide pin out of its track in the selector drum, then withdraw the selector drum from the left-hand side of the casing **(see illustration)**. Move the selector fork round in its groove in the pinion and remove it, noting how it fits **(see illustrations overleaf)**. Slide the fork back onto the shaft. Note the springs in the ends of the shaft and remove them for safekeeping, if loose.

Inspection

8 Inspect the selector forks for any signs of

26.39 The assembled output shaft should be as shown

27.4 Note the position of the neutral detent (A). Unscrew the bolts (B) and remove the plate

27.5 Note the letter on each fork denoting its position

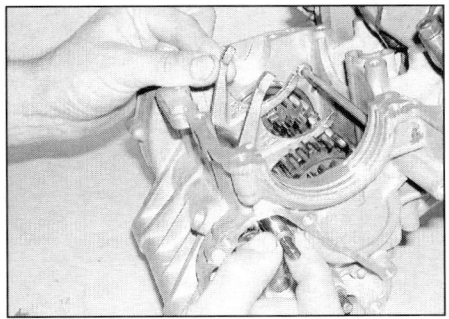
27.6 Withdraw the shaft and remove the forks

27.7a Withdraw the shaft ...

27.7b ... then displace the fork from its track and withdraw the selector drum

2•54 Engine, clutch and transmission

27.7c Slide the fork round . . .

27.7d . . . and remove it

27.14 Locate the forks as described and slide in the shaft

27.15 Install the retainer plate and tighten the bolts to the specified torque

wear or damage, especially around the fork ends where they engage with the groove in the pinion. Check that each fork fits correctly in its pinion groove. Check closely to see if the forks are bent. If the forks are in any way damaged they must be replaced with new ones.

9 Check that the forks fit correctly on their shaft. They should move freely with a light fit but no appreciable freeplay. Check that the fork shaft holes in the casing are not worn or damaged.

10 Check the selector fork shaft runout using V-blocks and a dial gauge and renew the shaft if the runout exceeds the limit specified at the beginning of the Chapter. A bent shaft will cause difficulty in selecting gears and make the gearchange action heavy. Replace the shafts with new ones if bent.

11 Inspect the selector drum grooves and selector fork guide pins for signs of wear or damage. If either show signs of wear or damage they must be replaced with new ones.

12 Check that the selector drum bearing rotates freely and has no signs of roughness or excessive freeplay between it and the drum or crankcase (when installed) (see *Tools and Workshop Tips* (Section 5) in the *Reference* section for more information on bearings). Replace the selector drum with a new one if necessary – the bearing is not available separately, though it would be worth checking with a bearing specialist before buying a new drum. Also check that the neutral switch contact in the drum is not damaged or worn away. If required, remove the contact and replace it with a new one.

Installation

13 Position the input shaft fork (marked C) in the crankcase, making sure the letter faces the right-hand side of the engine (see illustration 27.7d). Locate the fork in the groove in the combined 3rd/4th gear pinion, then slide it round and support it clear so that it does not get in the way when installing the selector drum (see illustration 27.7c). Align the selector drum so that the neutral detent points to the bottom of the engine and slide the drum into the crankcase (see illustration 27.7b). Make sure the drum end locates in its bore in the crankcase, and that the neutral contact locates against the neutral switch. Apply clean engine oil to the fork shaft, and fit the springs into the ends of the shaft if removed. Locate the selector fork guide pin into its track in the drum, then slide the shaft into the crankcase and through the fork (see illustration 27.7a).

14 Position the output shaft forks (marked 'R' and 'L') in the crankcase, making sure the letters face the right-hand side of the engine. Locate the fork marked 'R' in the groove in the 5th gear pinion, and the fork marked 'L' in the groove in the 6th gear pinion, and locate the fork guide pins in their tracks in the drum. Apply clean engine oil to the fork shaft, and fit the springs into the ends of the shaft if removed. Slide the shaft into the crankcase and through the forks (see illustration 27.7d).

15 Apply a suitable non-permanent thread locking compound to the selector drum retainer plate bolts. Install the plate and tighten the bolts to the torque setting specified at the beginning of the Chapter (see illustration).

16 Install the transmission output shaft (see Section 25).

28 Running-in procedure

1 Make sure the engine oil level and coolant level are correct (see *Daily (pre-ride) checks*).

2 Make sure there is fuel in the tank, then set the choke.

3 Start the engine in the normal way – set the choke lever enough to encourage the bike to start, but not so much as to allow it to race. Allow the engine to run at a moderately fast idle until it reaches operating temperature.

4 As no oil pressure warning light is fitted, an oil pressure check must be carried out (see Chapter 1). If a lubrication failure is suspected, stop the engine immediately and try to find the cause. If an engine is run without sufficient oil pressure, even for a short period of time, severe damage will occur.

5 Check carefully that there are no oil and coolant leaks and make sure the transmission and controls, especially the brakes, function properly before road testing the machine.

6 Treat the machine gently for the first few miles to make sure oil has circulated throughout the engine and any new parts installed have started to seat. Follow the recommended running-in procedure detailed below.

7 Even greater care is necessary if the engine has been extensively overhauled – the bike will have to be run in as when new. This means greater use of the transmission and a restraining hand on the throttle until at least 600 miles (1000 km) have been covered. There is no point in keeping to any set speed limit – the main idea is to keep from labouring the engine and to gradually increase performance up to the 600 mile (1000 km) mark. These recommendations apply less when only a partial overhaul has been done, though it does depend to an extent on the nature of the work carried out and which components have been renewed. Experience is the best guide, since it is easy to tell when an engine is running freely. If in any doubt, consult a Yamaha dealer. The following maximum engine speed limitations, which Yamaha provide for new motorcycles, can be used as a guide.

8 Upon completion of the road test, and after the engine has cooled down completely, recheck the valve clearances (see Chapter 1) and check the engine oil and coolant levels (see *Daily (pre-ride) checks*).

Up to 600 miles (1000 km)	5000 rpm max	Vary throttle position/speed. Do not use full throttle
600 to 1000 miles (1000 to 1600 km)	6000 rpm max	Vary throttle position/speed. Do not use full throttle
Over 1000 miles (1600 km)	Do not exceed tachometer red line	

Chapter 3
Cooling system

Contents

Coolant change and system checks . . . . .see Chapter 1	General information 1
Coolant hoses, pipes and unions 9	Oil cooler . . . . .see Chapter 2
Coolant level check . . . . .see Daily (pre-ride) checks	Radiator 7
Coolant reservoir 3	Radiator pressure cap 2
Coolant temperature warning LED and thermo unit 5	Thermostat and housing 6
Cooling fan and relay 4	Water pump 8

Degrees of difficulty

Easy, suitable for novice with little experience	Fairly easy, suitable for beginner with some experience	Fairly difficult, suitable for competent DIY mechanic	Difficult, suitable for experienced DIY mechanic	Very difficult, suitable for expert DIY or professional

Specifications

Coolant
Mixture type and capacity . . . . see Chapter 1

Radiator
Cap valve opening pressure . . . . 13.1 to 17.8 psi (0.95 to 1.25 Bar)

Thermo unit
Resistance
  @ 80°C . . . . 3.4 to 4.0 K-ohms
  @ 105°C . . . . 1.6 to 1.9 K-ohms

Thermostat
Opening temperature . . . . 71 to 85°C
Valve lift . . . . 8 mm (min) @ 85°C

Water pump
Impeller shaft tilt (max.) . . . . 0.15 mm

Torque wrench settings
Coolant inlet and outlet pipes to/from water pump . . . . 10 Nm
Coolant inlet union to cylinder block bolts . . . . 10 Nm
Coolant outlet pipes from valve cover . . . . 10 Nm
Thermo unit . . . . 15 Nm
Water pump cover bolts . . . . 10 Nm

3•2 Cooling system

1 General information

The cooling system uses a water/antifreeze coolant to carry away excess energy in the form of heat. The cylinders are surrounded by a water jacket, from which the heated coolant is circulated by thermo-syphonic action in conjunction with a water pump. The water pump is an integral assembly with the oil pump, and is driven by chain and sprockets off the clutch. The hot coolant passes upwards to the thermostat and through to the radiator. The coolant then flows across the radiator core, where it is cooled by the passing air, to the water pump and back to the engine, where the cycle is repeated.

A thermostat is fitted in the system to prevent the coolant flowing through the radiator when the engine is cold, therefore accelerating the speed at which the engine reaches normal operating temperature. An electric cooling fan is mounted on the back of the radiator to aid cooling in extreme conditions. A heat sensitive thermo unit that acts as a switch for both the warning LED in the instrument cluster and for the cooling fan is mounted in the thermostat housing. The cooling fan circuit is controlled by a relay.

The complete cooling system is partially sealed and pressurised, the pressure being controlled by a valve contained in the spring-loaded radiator cap. By pressurising the coolant the boiling point is raised, preventing premature boiling in adverse conditions. The overflow pipe from the system is connected to a reservoir, into which excess coolant is expelled under pressure. The discharged coolant automatically returns to the radiator when the engine cools.

The coolant is utilised to cool the engine oil via an oil cooler unit on the front of the crankcases; a spur from the water pump-to engine hose feeds coolant to the cooler unit and it is returned to the cooling system via a hose from the cooler body to the base of the radiator.

In certain markets, coolant is routed through passages in the carburettor bodies to prevent carburettor icing in extreme conditions. A check valve in the small-bore hose from the thermostat housing to the carburettor assembly allows coolant to flow under a pre-determined temperature. Coolant is returned via a hose at the other end of the carburettor bank via a small-bore hose to the top of the thermostat housing.

Warning: Do not remove the pressure cap from the radiator when the engine is hot. Scalding hot coolant and steam may be blown out under pressure and could cause serious injury. When the engine has cooled, place a thick rag such as a towel over the pressure cap; slowly rotate the cap anti-clockwise to the first stop. This procedure allows any residual pressure to escape. When any pressure has been released, press down on the cap while turning it anti-clockwise, and remove it. Do not allow antifreeze to come into contact with your skin, or painted surfaces of the motorcycle. Rinse off any spills immediately with plenty of water. Antifreeze is highly toxic if ingested. Never leave antifreeze lying around in an open container or in puddles on the floor; children and pets are attracted by its sweet smell and may drink it. Check with the local authorities about disposing of used antifreeze. Many communities will have collection centres which will see that antifreeze is disposed of safely.

Caution: At all times use the specified type of antifreeze, and always mix it with distilled water in the correct proportion. The antifreeze contains corrosion inhibitors which are essential to avoid damage to the cooling system. A lack of these inhibitors could lead to a build-up of corrosion which would block the coolant passages, resulting in overheating and severe engine damage. Distilled water must be used as opposed to tap water to avoid a build-up of scale which would also block the passages.

2 Radiator pressure cap

1 If problems such as overheating or loss of coolant occur, check the entire system as described in Chapter 1. The radiator cap opening pressure should be checked by a Yamaha dealer with the special tester required for the job. If the cap is defective, replace it with a new one.

3 Coolant reservoir

Removal

1 Remove the rear shock absorber (see Chapter 6).
2 Release the clamp securing the breather/overflow hose (coming out of the reservoir filler neck) and detach the hose (see illustration).
3 Place a suitable container underneath the reservoir. Unscrew the reservoir mounting bolts, then remove the reservoir cap and tip the coolant out of the reservoir into the container (see illustration 3.2). Disconnect the feed hose from the bottom of the reservoir and remove the reservoir.

Installation

4 Installation is the reverse of removal. Make sure the hoses are correctly installed and secured with their clamps (see illustration 3.2). On completion, refill the reservoir with fresh coolant as described in Chapter 1.

4 Cooling fan and relay

Cooling fan

Check

1 If the engine is overheating and the cooling fan isn't coming on, first check the fan fuse (see Chapter 9) and then the fan relay as described below.
2 If the fan still does not come on, the fault lies in either the cooling fan motor or the relevant wiring. Test all the wiring and connections as described under Fault Finding Equipment in the Reference Section at the end of the book and referring to the Wiring Diagrams at the end of Chapter 9.
3 To test the cooling fan motor, raise the fuel tank (see Chapter 4). Trace the wiring from the fan and disconnect it at the connector (see illustration). Using a 12 volt battery and two jumper wires, connect the positive (+ve) battery lead to the blue wire terminal on the fan wiring connector and the negative (–ve) lead to the black wire terminal. Once connected, the fan should operate. If it does not, and the wiring is all good, then the fan motor is faulty. Replace the fan assembly with a new one – individual components are not available.

Removal and installation

Warning: The engine must be completely cool before carrying out this procedure.

3.2 Breather/overflow hose (A), mounting bolts (B) and feed hose (C)

4.3 Fan motor wiring connector (arrowed)

Cooling system 3•3

4.5 Fan assembly mounting bolts (arrowed)

4.8a Cooling fan relay (arrowed)

4.8b Relay wire connector terminals

A Meter positive lead to brown
B Meter negative lead to blue
C Battery positive lead to brown
D Battery negative lead to green/black

4 Remove the radiator (see Section 7).
5 Unscrew the three bolts securing the fan assembly to the radiator and remove it **(see illustration)**.
6 Installation is the reverse of removal.

Cooling fan relay

Check

7 If the engine is overheating and the cooling fan isn't coming on, first check the fan fuse (see Chapter 9). If the fuse is blown, check the fan circuit for a short to earth (see the Wiring Diagrams at the end of this book).
8 If the fuse is good, disconnect the fan relay wiring connector **(see illustration)** – remove the left-hand side panel for access (see Chapter 8). Set a multimeter to the ohms x 1 scale and connect the positive (+) probe to the brown wire terminal on the relay and the negative (–ve) probe to the blue wire terminal **(see illustration)**. Using a fully-charged 12 volt battery and two insulated jumper wires, connect the positive (+ve) terminal of the battery to the brown wire terminal on the relay, and the negative (–) terminal to the green/black wire terminal on the relay. At this point the relay should be heard to click and the multimeter read 0 ohms (continuity). If this is the case the relay is proved good. If the relay does not click when battery voltage is applied and indicates no continuity (infinite resistance) across its terminals, it is faulty and must be replaced with a new one. If the relay is good, test the thermo unit (see Section 5). If the unit is good, test the fan motor (see Step 3).

5.6 Thermo unit (A) and its wiring connector (B)

9 If the fan motor and relay, and their associated wiring and fuse, are in good order, check the green/black wire from the relay to the instrument PCB for continuity, then check the thermo unit as described in Section 5.

Removal and installation

10 Remove the left-hand side panel (see Chapter 8). Release the relay from its mounting then disconnect the wiring connector and remove the relay **(see illustration 4.8a)**.
11 Installation is the reverse of removal.

5 Coolant temperature warning LED and thermo unit

Temperature warning LED

Check

1 The circuit consists of the thermo unit mounted in the thermostat housing and the warning LED in the instrument cluster.
2 The temperature warning LED should come on for a few seconds when the ignition is

5.9 Thermo unit testing set-up

switched on, then go out. This serves as a check that the circuit is good. If the LED does not come on, check that the battery is fully charged and that the fuses are all good.
3 Next test the circuit wiring and connections as described under Fault Finding Equipment in the Reference Section at the end of the book and referring to the Wiring Diagrams at the end of Chapter 9. If no problems are found, check the thermo unit as described below.
4 If the thermo unit is good, then it is likely that the fault lies in the instrument printed circuit board. The warning LED is integral with the instruments and the board. To test whether the LED has failed, refer to Chapter 9, section 17, Step 3. If necessary take the instrument cluster to a Yamaha dealer for further assessment, though it is likely that replacing the board with a new one is the only solution.

Removal and installation

5 See Chapter 9.

Thermo unit

Check

6 Remove the right-hand cockpit trim panel and raise the fuel tank (see Chapters 8 and 4). For improved access remove the fairing and the fuel tank, referring to the same Chapters. The thermo unit is mounted in the thermostat housing **(see illustration)**.
7 Disconnect the wiring connector. With the ignition switch ON, connect a jumper wire between the terminals in the connector. The warning LED should come on. If not, refer to Step 3 above.
8 If the display and warning light do come on, remove the thermo unit (see below).
9 Fill a small heatproof container with coolant and place it on a stove. Using an ohmmeter, connect the probes to the terminals on the unit **(see illustration)**. Using some wire or other support suspend the unit in the coolant so that just the sensing portion and the threads are submerged. Also place a thermometer capable of reading temperatures

3•4 Cooling system

6.4 Thermostat testing set-up

6.7 Pull the overflow hose off . . .

6.8a . . . then detach the cover, noting the O-ring . . .

of up to 130°C in the water so that its bulb is close to the unit. **Note:** *None of the components should be allowed to directly touch the container.* Heat the coolant, stirring it gently.

 Warning: This must be done very carefully to avoid the risk of personal injury.

10 When the temperature reaches around 80°C the meter reading should be as specified at the beginning of the Chapter. When the temperature reaches around 105°C the meter should again be as specified. If the meter readings obtained are different, or they are obtained at different temperatures, then the thermo unit is faulty and must be replaced with a new one.

Removal and installation

Warning: The engine must be completely cool before carrying out this procedure.

11 Remove the right-hand cockpit trim panel and raise the fuel tank (see Chapters 8 and 4). For improved access remove the fairing and the fuel tank, referring to the same Chapters. The thermo unit is mounted in the thermostat housing **(see illustration 5.6)**. Partially drain the cooling system so that the level is below that of the thermo unit, or fully drain it if preferred (see Chapter 1).
12 Disconnect the wiring connector. Unscrew the unit and remove it from the housing.
13 Apply a suitable sealant (Yamaha advise Three Bond Sealock 10) to the thermo unit threads, then install the unit and tighten it to the torque setting specified at the beginning of the Chapter. Take care not to overtighten the unit as it or the housing could be damaged. Connect the wiring connector.
14 Refill the cooling system (see Chapter 1). Install the fuel tank and fairing and/or trim panel as required.

6 Thermostat and housing

1 The thermostat is automatic in operation and should give many years' service without requiring attention. In the event of a failure, the valve will probably jam open, in which case the engine will take much longer than normal to warm up. Conversely, if the valve jams shut, the coolant will be unable to circulate and the engine will overheat. Neither condition is acceptable, and the fault must be investigated promptly.

Check

2 Remove the thermostat (see below).
3 Examine the thermostat visually before carrying out the test. If it remains in the open position at room temperature, replace it with a new one.
4 Suspend the thermostat by a piece of wire in a container of cold water. Place a thermometer in the water so that the bulb is close to the thermostat **(see illustration)**. Heat the water, noting the temperature when the thermostat opens, and compare the result with the specifications given at the beginning of the Chapter. Also check the amount the valve opens after it has been heated at 85°C for a few minutes and compare the measurement to the specifications. If the readings obtained differ from those given, the thermostat is faulty and must be replaced with a new one.
5 In the event of thermostat failure, as an emergency measure only, it can be removed from the housing and the machine used without it. **Note:** *Take care when starting the engine from cold, as it will take much longer than usual to warm up. Ensure that a new one is installed as soon as possible.*

Removal

 Warning: The engine must be completely cool before carrying out this procedure.

Thermostat

6 Remove the fairing (see Chapter 8). Partially drain the cooling system so that the level is below that of the thermostat housing, or fully drain it if preferred (see Chapter 1).
7 Pull the radiator overflow hose off its union on the filler neck **(see illustration)**.
8 Unscrew the bolts securing the thermostat housing cover and separate it from the housing, noting the O-ring **(see illustration)**. Withdraw the thermostat, noting how it fits **(see illustration)**.

Thermostat housing

9 Remove the fairing (see Chapter 8). Partially drain the cooling system so that the level is below that of the thermostat housing, or fully drain it if preferred (see Chapter 1).
10 Pull the radiator overflow hose off its union on the filler neck **(see illustration 6.7)**. Release the clamp securing the carburettor heater system hose to its union on the housing and pull it off **(see illustration)**.
11 Slacken the clamps securing the hoses to the thermostat housing and detach the hoses, noting which fits where. Disconnect the

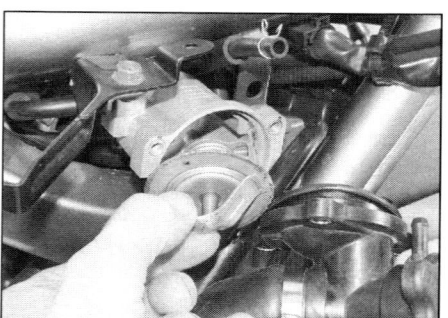

6.8b . . . and remove the thermostat

6.10 Detach the heater system hose (arrowed)

Cooling system 3•5

6.11 Disconnect the wiring connector as you remove the housing

6.12a Slacken the hose clamps . . .

6.12b . . . then unscrew the bolts (arrowed) . . .

6.12c . . . and manoeuvre the outlet pipe assembly away

6.18 Use new O-rings on the outlet pipes

Make sure the radiator overflow and carburettor heating system hoses are pushed fully onto their unions and secured by their clamps **(see illustrations 6.7 and 6.10)**. Connect the thermo unit wiring connector **(see illustration 6.11)**.

18 If the individual outlet pipes were removed, use new O-rings and smear them with grease **(see illustration)**. Tighten the outlet pipe bolts to the torque setting specified at the beginning of the Chapter. Make sure the hoses are pushed fully on to their unions and are secured by the clamps.

19 Refill the cooling system (see Chapter 1).

thermo unit wiring connector and remove the housing **(see illustration)**.

12 If required, for example when removing the valve cover, AIS system valve assembly, or the engine, remove the thermostat housing along with its hoses, detaching them from the outlet pipe joint piece and the radiator rather than the housing itself. Then slacken the clamps securing the outlet hoses to the individual outlet pipes, and unscrew the bolts securing the outlet pipe joint piece **(see illustrations)**. Manoeuvre the outlet pipe/hose assembly away **(see illustration)**. Now unscrew the bolt securing each individual outlet pipe to the valve cover and pull the pipes out. Discard the O-rings as new ones must be used.

Installation

Thermostat

13 Fit the thermostat into the housing, making sure that it seats correctly and that the hole is at the top **(see illustration 6.8b)**. Fit the cover onto the housing using a new O-ring, then install and tighten the bolts **(see illustrations 6.8a)**.

14 Fit the radiator overflow hose fully onto its union on the filler neck and secure it with the clamp **(see illustration 6.7)**.

15 Refill the cooling system (see Chapter 1).

16 Install the fairing (see Chapter 8).

Thermostat housing

17 Installation is the reverse of removal.

7 Radiator

Removal

Warning: The engine must be completely cool before carrying out this procedure.

1 Remove the fairing (see Chapter 8). Raise the fuel tank (see Chapter 4).

2 Drain the cooling system (see Chapter 1).

3 Trace the fan motor wiring and disconnect it at the connector **(see illustration 4.3)**.

4 Slacken the clamps securing all the radiator hoses and detach them from the radiator, noting which fits where **(see illustrations)**.

7.4a Release the clamps and detach the hoses (arrowed) from the right-hand side . . .

7.4b . . . and the left-hand side of the radiator

3•6 Cooling system

5 Unscrew the two bolts securing the radiator, noting the collars and washers, then carefully move the radiator to the left to free the other grommet from the lug, then remove the radiator **(see illustrations)**.

6 If necessary, separate the cooling fan from the radiator (see Section 4), and remove the side trim pieces and the front mesh.

7 Check the radiator for signs of damage and clear any dirt or debris that might obstruct air flow and inhibit cooling. If the radiator fins are badly damaged or broken the radiator must be replaced with a new one. Check the rubber mounting grommets for cracks and hardening and replace them with new ones if necessary.

Installation

8 Installation is the reverse of removal, noting the following.
- Make sure the grommets and collars are correctly installed with the mounting bolts **(see illustration 7.5c)**.
- Ensure the coolant hoses are in good condition (see Chapter 1), and are securely retained by their clamps, using new ones if necessary.
- Do not forget to connect the fan wiring connector.
- On completion refill the cooling system as described in Chapter 1.

7.5a Unscrew the bottom bolt (arrowed) . . .

7.5b . . . and the top bolt . . .

7.5c . . . noting the collars in the grommets . . .

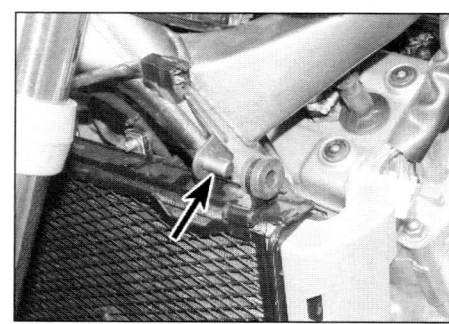

7.5d . . . then displace the radiator from the lug (arrowed) and remove it

8 Water pump

Check

1 The water pump is located inside the engine and is an integral assembly with the oil pump.

2 To prevent leakage of water from the cooling system to the lubrication system and vice versa, two seals are fitted on the pump shaft. The seal on the water pump side is of the mechanical type which bears on the rear face of the impeller. The second seal, which is mounted behind the mechanical seal, is of the normal feathered lip type. On the bottom of the sump there is a drain hole **(see illustration)**. If either seal fails, the drain allows the coolant or oil to escape and prevents them mixing. If on inspection there are signs of leakage, the seals must be removed and new ones installed (see below). If you are not sure about their condition, remove the pump (see below) and check them visually, looking for signs of damage and leakage.

3 Remove the pump, then remove the cover (see below). Wiggle the water pump impeller back-and-forth and in-and-out, and spin it by hand. If there is excessive movement, or the pump is noisy or rough when turned, the driveshaft bearing must be replaced with a

new one. If you are not sure about its condition, disassemble the pump (see below) and check the bearing visually and mechanically, referring to *Tools and Workshop Tips* (Section 5) in the *Reference* Section. See below for bearing renewal.

4 Check the pump housing and cover, and the impeller and shaft for cracks, deformation and any other damage. Check that the shaft is straight – if it tilts by more than the specified limit, replace it with a new one. Also check for corrosion or a build-up of scale in the pump body and clean or renew the pump as necessary.

5 Check the condition of the rubber damper and its holder on the rear face of the impeller. Do not remove them from the shaft unnecessarily, as they cannot be reused. If they are damaged or deteriorated, fit a new

8.2 Water pump drain hole (arrowed)

impeller – Yamaha do not list the damper and holder as being available separately, though it is worth checking first. If they are available separately, lever off the old ones with a flat-bladed screwdriver. Apply coolant to the new ones and press them squarely down the shaft on to the back of the impeller.

Removal

6 The water pump is located inside the engine and is an integral assembly with the oil pump. Refer to Chapter 2, Section 17 and remove the pump.

7 To disassemble the water pump, first disassemble the oil pump (see Chapter 2). Unscrew the bolts securing the pump cover and remove it **(see illustration)**. Note the two locating pins and remove them if loose. Discard the O-ring, as a new one must be

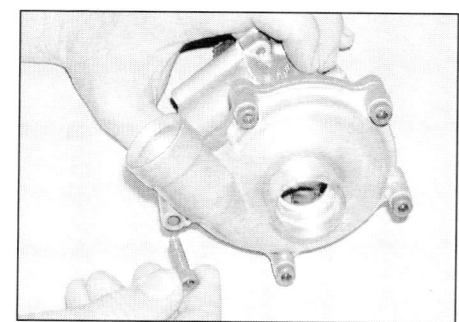

8.7a Unscrew the bolts and remove the cover

Cooling system 3•7

8.7b Withdraw the impeller from the pump

used. Withdraw the impeller from the housing **(see illustration)**.

Seal and bearing renewal

8 Remove the pump, then disassemble it (see above) **(see illustration)**.
9 To remove the mechanical seal, tap it out from the inside of the housing using a suitable punch, noting which way round it fits **(see illustration)**. Discard it, as a new one must be fitted.
10 To remove the oil seal, first remove the mechanical seal (see above). Tap the oil seal out from the inside of the housing using a

8.8 Water pump components

| 1 Cover | 3 O-ring | 5 Oil seal | 7 Locating pins |
| 2 Impeller/shaft | 4 Mechanical seal | 6 Bearing | |

suitable punch, noting which way round the seal fits. Discard it, as a new one must be fitted.
11 To remove the bearing, first remove the seals (see above). Tap the bearing out from the inside of the housing using a bearing driver or suitable socket.
12 Press or drive the bearing into the housing, using a suitable sized socket or bearing driver. Drive the bearing in until it is properly seated **(see illustration 8.9)**.
13 Apply a smear of coolant to the lips of the new oil seal. Press or carefully drive the new oil seal into the housing, with its marked side facing out, so that it fits against the bearing – use a suitable sized socket or seal driver and make sure the seal is the correct way round **(see illustration 8.9)**.
14 Smear Yamaha Bond 1215 or a suitable equivalent to the mechanical seal housing. Press or carefully drive the new mechanical seal into the front of the pump body using a suitable sized socket or seal driver, shaped so that it bears only on the outer rim of the seal and not on the centre **(see illustration 8.9)**. Yamaha produce a special tool, Part No. 90890-04078 (Europe models) or YM-33221 (US models) for installing the seal if required.

8.9 Mechanical seal (1), oil seal (2), bearing (3)

Installation

15 Slide the driveshaft and impeller into the housing **(see illustration 8.7b)**.
16 If removed, fit the locating pins into the pump housing **(see illustration)**. Fit the new cover O-ring into its groove **(see illustration)**. Fit the cover, making sure it locates onto the pins, and tighten the bolts to the torque setting specified at the beginning of the Chapter **(see illustration)**.
17 Refer to Chapter 2, Section 17 and install the pump.

9 Coolant hoses, pipes and unions

Removal

1 Before removing a hose, pipe or union, drain the coolant (see Chapter 1).
2 Use a screwdriver to slacken the larger-bore hose clamps, then slide them back along the hose and clear of the union spigot. The smaller-bore hoses are secured by spring clamps which can be expanded by squeezing their ears together with pliers.

8.16a Fit the locating pins . . .

8.16b . . . and a new O-ring . . .

8.16c . . . then install the cover

3•8 Cooling system

Caution: The radiator unions are fragile. Do not use excessive force when attempting to remove the hoses.

3 If a hose proves stubborn, release it by rotating it on its union before working it off. If all else fails, cut the hose with a sharp knife then slit it at each union so that it can be peeled off in two pieces. Whilst this means renewing the hose, it is preferable to buying a new radiator.

4 Remove the coolant pipes and the unions on the engine by detaching the hoses (see above), then unscrewing the retaining bolt(s).

Discard the O-rings, as new ones must be used.

Installation

5 Slide the clamp onto the hose and then work it on to its respective union.

 HAYNES HiNT *If the hose is difficult to push onto its union, it can be softened by soaking it in very hot water, or alternatively a little soapy water can be used as a lubricant.*

6 Rotate the hose on its union to settle it in position before sliding the clamp into place and tightening it securely.

7 If the water pipes or unions on the engine have been removed, fit new O-rings and smear them with grease, then install them and tighten their mounting bolts to the torque setting specified at the beginning of the Chapter. Apply a suitable non-permanent thread locking compound to the bolt for the water pump outlet pipe on the front of the engine.

Chapter 4
Fuel and exhaust systems

Contents

Air filter cleaning and renewal	see Chapter 1	EXUP system	13
Air filter housing	3	EXUP system check	see Chapter 1
Air induction system (AIS)	16	Fuel pump and relay	14
Air/fuel mixture adjustment	4	Fuel system check and hose renewal	see Chapter 1
Carburettor overhaul general information	5	Fuel tank and fuel tap	2
Carburettor synchronisation	see Chapter 1	Fuel gauge and level sensor	15
Carburettor disassembly and inspection	7	General information and precautions	1
Carburettor reassembly, float height and fuel level check	9	Idle speed check	see Chapter 1
Carburettor removal and installation	6	Throttle and choke cable check and adjustment	see Chapter 1
Carburettor separation and joining	8	Throttle cables	10
Choke cable	11	Throttle position sensor	see Chapter 5
Exhaust system	12		

Degrees of difficulty

| Easy, suitable for novice with little experience | | Fairly easy, suitable for beginner with some experience | | Fairly difficult, suitable for competent DIY mechanic | 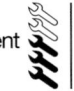 | Difficult, suitable for experienced DIY mechanic | | Very difficult, suitable for expert DIY or professional | |

Specifications

Fuel
Grade	Unleaded, minimum 91 RON (Research Octane Number)
Fuel tank capacity (including reserve)	21 litres
Reserve	approx. 4 litres

Carburettors
Type	4 x Mikuni BSR37
Carburettor numbering	1 to 4 from left to right
Float height	12.5 to 13.5 mm
Fuel level	3 to 4 mm above float chamber joint
Idle speed	1050 to 1150 rpm
Pilot screw setting (no. of turns out)	2
Main jet	
Carburettors 1 and 4	132.5
Carburettors 2 and 3	130
Main air jet	80
Jet needle (-clip position)	
Carburettors 1 and 4	5D129-3/5
Carburettors 2 and 3	5D130-3/5
Needle jet	P-OM
Pilot air jet	85
Pilot jet	15
Starter jet 1	42.5
Starter jet 2	0.8
Butterfly valve size	115

EXUP system
Servo motor variable resistance	zero to approx. 7.5 K-ohms

4•2 Fuel and exhaust systems

Fuel pump
Resistance .... 4 to 30 ohms @ 20°C

Fuel level sensor
Resistance
   At FULL position .... 4 to 10 ohms @ 20°C
   At EMPTY position .... 90 to 10 ohms @ 20°C

Torque wrench settings
Exhaust downpipe assembly nuts .... 20 Nm
Exhaust downpipe assembly rear bolt .... 20 Nm
Exhaust silencer clamp bolt .... 20 Nm
Exhaust silencer mounting bolt .... 48 Nm
EXUP valve cover bolts .... 10 Nm
EXUP pulley cover bolts .... 10 Nm
Fuel level sensor bolts .... 4 Nm
Fuel tank mounting bolts .... 10 Nm
Fuel tap screws .... 7 Nm

1 General information and precautions

General information

The fuel system consists of the fuel tank with internal level sensor, the fuel tap, in-line fuel filter, fuel pump, fuel hoses and carburettors. The fuel tap has an integral strainer, and the fuel pump is mounted externally with an in-line filter.

The carburettors used are CV types. There is a carburettor for each cylinder. For cold starting, a choke lever is connected to the carburettors by a cable; the lever is housed in the left-hand switch housing on the handlebar. Engine coolant is circulated around the carburettor bodies to prevent carburettor icing in extreme conditions.

Air is drawn into the carburettors via an air filter, which is housed under the fuel tank.

The exhaust is a four-into-one design, and incorporates Yamaha's EXUP system. An air induction system (AIS) reduces harmful emissions.

Many of the fuel system service procedures are considered routine maintenance items and for that reason are included in Chapter 1.

Precautions

 Warning: Petrol (gasoline) is extremely flammable, so take extra precautions when you work on any part of the fuel system. Don't smoke or allow open flames or bare light bulbs near the work area, and don't work in a garage where a natural gas-type appliance is present. If you spill any fuel on your skin, rinse it off immediately with soap and water. When you perform any kind of work on the fuel system, wear safety glasses and have a fire extinguisher suitable for a class B type fire (flammable liquids) on hand.

Always perform service procedures in a well-ventilated area to prevent a build-up of fumes.

Never work in a building containing a gas appliance with a pilot light, or any other form of naked flame. Ensure that there are no naked light bulbs or any sources of flame or sparks nearby.

Do not smoke (or allow anyone else to smoke) while in the vicinity of petrol (gasoline), or of components containing petrol. Remember the possible presence of vapour from these sources and move well clear before smoking.

Check all electrical equipment belonging to the house, garage or workshop where work is being undertaken (see the *Safety First!* section of this manual). Remember that certain electrical appliances such as drills, cutters etc. create sparks in the normal course of operation and must not be used near petrol (gasoline) or any component containing it. Again, remember the possible presence of fumes before using electrical equipment.

Always mop up any spilt fuel and safely dispose of the rag used.

Any stored fuel that is drained off during servicing work must be kept in sealed containers that are suitable for holding petrol (gasoline), and clearly marked as such; the containers themselves should be kept in a safe place. Note that this last point applies equally to the fuel tank if it is removed from the machine; also remember to keep its filler cap closed at all times.

Read the *Safety first!* section of this manual carefully before starting work.

2 Fuel tank and fuel tap

 Warning: Refer to the precautions given in Section 1 before starting work.

Fuel tank

Raise

1 Make sure the fuel filler cap is secure. Remove the seat (see Chapter 8).
2 Unscrew the fuel tank front mounting bolt and raise the tank up, then place a suitable support between it and the frame, protecting surfaces as required according to the support used **(see illustrations)**.

Caution: Do not raise the tank too high as the rear mounting rubber and bracket could be deformed.

2.2a Unscrew the bolt (arrowed) . . .

2.2b . . . then raise and support the tank

Fuel and exhaust systems 4•3

2.4 Turn the fuel tap to the 'OFF' position

2.5 Detach the overflow and breather hoses (arrowed)

2.6a Release the clamp . . .

2.6b . . . and pull the hose off the tap union

2.7 Disconnect the wiring connector

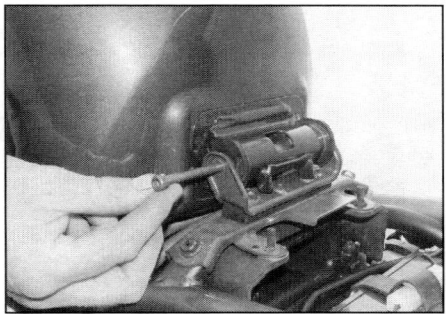

2.8a Unscrew the rear bolt . . .

Removal

3 Raise the tank (see Steps 1 and 2). Remove the left-hand side panel (see Chapter 8).
4 Turn the fuel tap off – it is located on the base of the tank **(see illustration)**.
5 Release the clamp securing the overflow hose, and on all except California models the breather hose, to their unions and detach the hoses, noting which fits where **(see illustration)**. On California models, detach the EVAP hose from its union.
6 Have a rag ready to catch any residual fuel from the hose and the fuel filter, then release the clamp securing the fuel hose to the fuel tap and detach the hose **(see illustrations)**.
7 Disconnect the fuel level sender wiring connector **(see illustration)**.
8 Remove the support and lower the tank. Unscrew and remove the bolt securing the rear of the tank **(see illustration)**. Carefully lift the tank off the frame and remove it **(see illustration)**.
9 Inspect the tank mounting rubbers for signs of damage or deterioration and replace them with new ones if necessary.

Draining

10 Remove the fuel tank as described above.
11 Connect a drain hose to the fuel outlet union on the tap and insert its end in a container suitable and large enough for storing the fuel. Turn the fuel tap to the 'ON' position and allow the tank to drain. When the tank has drained, turn the tap to the 'OFF' position.

Installation

12 Installation is the reverse of removal, noting the following:
● Make sure the hoses fully pushed onto their unions and secured by their clamps. Make sure the wiring connector is securely connected.
● Turn the fuel tap ON before lowering the tank.
● Tighten the mounting bolts to the torque settings specified at the beginning of the chapter.
● Start the engine and check that there is no sign of fuel leakage, then shut if off.

Fuel tap

Removal

13 Remove the fuel tank and drain it as described in Steps 3 to 11, then turn it over and rest it on some rag.
14 Undo the screws securing the tap to the tank and withdraw the tap **(see illustrations)**. Note the washers with the screws. Discard the O-ring as a new one must be used.
15 Clean the gauze strainer to remove all

2.8b . . . and carefully remove the tank

2.14a Undo the screws (arrowed) . . .

2.14b . . . and remove the tap

4•4 Fuel and exhaust systems

2.15 Clean and check the tap strainer (arrowed)

2.16a Install the tap using a new O-ring . . .

2.16b . . . and do not forget the washers

traces of dirt and fuel sediment **(see illustration)**. Check the gauze for holes. If any are found, a new tap must be fitted – the strainer is not available separately.

Installation

16 Fit a new O-ring into the groove on the base of the tap **(see illustration)**. Install the tap and secure it with its screws, not forgetting the washers **(see illustration)**. Tighten the screws to the torque setting specified at the beginning of the Chapter.
17 Install the fuel tank (see above).

Cleaning and repair

18 All repairs to the fuel tank should be carried out by a professional who has experience in this critical and potentially dangerous work. Even after cleaning and flushing of the fuel system, explosive fumes can remain and ignite during repair of the tank.
19 If the fuel tank is removed from the bike, it should not be placed in an area where sparks or open flames could ignite the fumes coming out of the tank. Be especially careful inside garages where a natural gas-type appliance is located, because the pilot light could cause an explosion.

3 Air filter housing

Removal

1 Remove the air filter (see Chapter 1).

4.1 Carburettor pilot screws (arrowed)

2 Remove the engine (see Chapter 2).
3 Release all hoses from their clips or unions on the housing.
4 Remove the three bolts securing the housing to the frame.
5 Draw the housing forward and remove it.

Installation

6 Installation is the reverse of removal. Check the condition of the various hoses and the air intake rubbers and replace them with new ones if necessary.

4 Air/fuel mixture adjustment

Note: *Due to the increased emphasis on controlling exhaust emissions in certain world markets, regulations have been formulated which prevent adjustment of the air/fuel mixture. On such models the pilot screw positions are pre-set at the factory and in some cases have a limiter cap fitted to prevent tampering. Where adjustment is possible, it can only be made in conjunction with an exhaust gas analyser to ensure that the machine does not exceed emissions regulations.*

1 If the engine runs extremely rough at idle or continually stalls, and if a carburettor overhaul does not cure the problem (and it definitely is a carburation problem – see Section 5), the pilot screws may require adjustment. It is worth noting at this point that unless you have the experience to carry this out it is best to entrust the task to a motorcycle dealer, tuner or fuel systems specialist. The pilot screws are located underneath the carburettors, between the float bowl and the intake duct on the cylinder head, and are best accessed using a purpose-made angled screwdriver with flexible drive, available from any good accessory dealer **(see illustration)**. Make sure the valve clearances are correct and the carburettors are synchronised before adjusting the pilot screws (see Chapter 1).
2 Before adjusting the pilot screws, warm the engine up to normal working temperature, then stop it. Screw in the pilot screw on each carburettor until it seats lightly, then back it out to the number of turns specified (see this Chapter's Specifications). This is the base position for adjustment.
3 Start the engine and reset the idle speed to the correct level (see Chapter 1). Working on one carburettor at a time, turn the pilot screw by a small amount either side of this position to find the point at which the highest consistent idle speed is obtained. When you've reached this position, reset the idle speed to the specified amount (see Chapter 1). Repeat on the other carburettors.

5 Carburettor overhaul

1 Poor engine performance, hesitation, hard starting, stalling, flooding and backfiring are all signs that major carburettor maintenance may be required.
2 Keep in mind that many so-called carburettor problems are really not carburettor problems at all, but mechanical problems within the engine, or ignition system malfunctions. Try to establish for certain that the carburettors are in need of maintenance before beginning a major overhaul.
3 Check the fuel tap, strainer and in-line filter, the fuel hoses, the fuel pump, the intake ducts on the cylinder head and their joint clamps, the air filter, the ignition system, the spark plugs and carburettor synchronisation before assuming that a carburettor overhaul is required.
4 Most carburettor problems are caused by dirt particles, varnish and other deposits which build up in and block the fuel and air passages. Also, in time, gaskets and O-rings shrink or deteriorate and cause fuel and air leaks which lead to poor performance.
5 When overhauling the carburettors, disassemble them completely and clean the parts thoroughly with a carburettor cleaning solvent and dry them with filtered, unlubricated compressed air. Blow through the fuel and air passages with compressed air to force out any dirt that may have been loosened but not removed by the solvent. Once the cleaning process is complete, reassemble the carburettor using new gaskets and O-rings.

Fuel and exhaust systems 4•5

6.2 Detach the hoses (arrowed) from their unions

6.3 Release the hoses from their clips (arrowed)

6.4a Detach the heater system hoses (arrowed) . . .

6.4b . . . on each side

6.5 Disconnect the throttle position sensor wiring connector

6.6 Detach the fuel supply hose

6 Before disassembling the carburettors, make sure you have all the necessary O-rings and other parts, some carburettor cleaner, a supply of clean rags, some means of blowing out the carburettor passages and a clean place to work. It is recommended that only one carburettor be overhauled at a time to avoid mixing up parts.

6 Carburettor removal and installation

Warning: *Refer to the precautions given in Section 1 before starting work.*

Removal

1 Remove the fuel tank (see Section 2).

Remove the side panels (see Chapter 8). Drain the coolant fully or partway, at least below the level of the carburettor warmer hoses which connect to the thermostat and radiator (see Chapter 1).
2 Detach the float chamber vent hoses from their unions on the holder **(see illustration)**.
3 Release the vacuum chamber vent hoses from their clips on the air filter housing **(see illustration)**.
4 Release the clamps securing the carburettor heater system inlet and outlet hoses and pull the hoses off their unions, being prepared with a rag to catch any residual coolant **(see illustrations)**.
5 Disconnect the throttle position sensor wiring connector **(see illustration)**.
6 Release the clamp securing the fuel supply hose to the carburettors and detach the hose,

being prepared with a rag to catch any residual fuel **(see illustration)**.
7 Detach the choke cable from the carburettors (see Section 11).
8 Detach the throttle cables from their bracket on the carburettors (see Section 10), but do not attempt to detach the cable ends from the throttle cam at this stage because access is restricted with the carburettors in place – do it after they have been displaced.
9 Displace the fuel pump from its mount. Slacken the three bolts securing the top and sides of the air filter housing to the frame **(see illustrations)**.
10 Fully slacken the clamp screws securing the air intake rubbers to the back of the carburettors – note the orientation of the clamps **(see illustration)**. Slide the air filter

6.9a Air filter housing top bolt (arrowed)

6.9b Displace the pump to access the bolt (arrowed) on the right-hand side

6.10a Slacken the clamp screws (arrowed) on each side . . .

4•6 Fuel and exhaust systems

6.10b ... and draw the housing back

6.11a Slacken the clamp bolts (arrowed) on each side ...

6.11b ... and draw the carburettors out to the left

housing back off the carburettors as far as it will go **(see illustration)**.

11 Fully slacken the clamp bolts securing the carburettors to the cylinder head intake rubbers, as above noting the orientation of the clamps **(see illustration)**. Ease the carburettors back out of the manifolds and draw them out from the left-hand side **(see illustration)**. *Note: Keep the carburettors level to prevent fuel spillage from the float chambers.*

12 Detach the throttle cable ends from the throttle cam, noting which fits where (see Section 10).

Caution: Stuff clean rag into each cylinder head intake after removing the carburettors, to prevent anything from falling in.

13 Place a suitable container below the float chambers, then slacken the drain bolt on each chamber in turn and drain all the fuel from the carburettors **(see illustration)**. Tighten the bolts once all the fuel has been drained.

Installation

14 Installation is the reverse of removal, noting the following.

- Check for cracks or splits in the air intake rubbers and the cylinder head intake rubbers, and replace them with new ones if necessary. The cylinder head rubbers are each secured by two bolts. Note the orientation of all the rubbers and which fits where before removing them as they must be installed the same way and in the same place.
- Make sure the carburettors are fully engaged with the cylinder head intake rubbers – they can be difficult to engage, so a squirt of WD40 or a smear of grease will ease entry. Make sure the clamps are positioned correctly.

6.13 Slacken the bolt (arrowed) on each float chamber to drain the carburettors

- Make sure all hoses are correctly routed and secured and not trapped or kinked.
- Refer to Section 10 for installation of the throttle cables, and Section 11 for the choke cable. Check the operation of the cables and adjust them as necessary (see Chapter 1).
- Do not forget to connect the throttle position sensor wiring connector.
- Check idle speed and carburettor synchronisation and adjust as necessary (see Chapter 1).

7 Carburettor disassembly and inspection

Warning: Refer to the precautions given in Section 1 before starting work.

Disassembly

1 Remove the carburettors from the machine as described in the previous Section. **Note:** *Do not separate the carburettors unless*

1 Top cover
2 Spring
3 Jet needle holder and O-ring
4 Spring, washer, E-clip, spacer and needle
5 O-ring
6 Diaphragm/piston
7 Synchronisation screw and springs
8 Pilot air jet
9 Needle valve seat, O-ring and strainer
10 Needle valve
11 Float pivot pin
12 Float
13 Choke plunger assembly
14 Main jet holder
15 Pilot screw, spring, washer and O-ring
16 Main jet
17 Pilot jet
18 Starter jet
19 Drain bolt

7.1 Carburettor components

Fuel and exhaust systems 4•7

7.2a Unhook the return spring . . .

7.2b . . . then undo the screws (arrowed) and lift off the linkage bar . . .

7.2c . . . and unscrew the choke plunger nut

7.3a Undo the screws (arrowed) and remove the top cover . . .

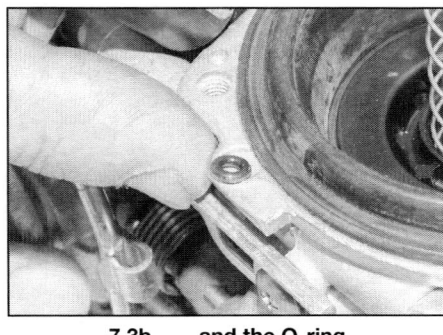

7.3b . . . and the O-ring

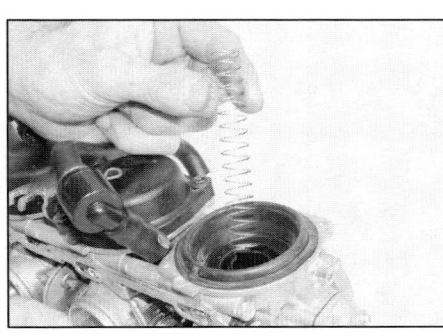

7.4a Remove the spring . . .

absolutely necessary; each carburettor can be dismantled sufficiently for all normal cleaning and adjustments while joined together. Dismantle the carburettors separately to avoid interchanging parts **(see illustration)**.

7.4b . . . and the piston/diaphragm assembly

7.4d . . . then push the needle up and remove it

2 Check the operation of the choke plungers by pulling on the linkage bar then letting it go. It should pull out smoothly and return home easily under spring pressure. If required unhook the choke linkage bar return spring,

7.4c Withdraw the needle holder using pliers . . .

7.5a On the No. 1 carb undo the screw (arrowed) to free the adjuster

noting how it fits **(see illustration)**. Remove the three screws securing the choke linkage bar to the carburettors, noting the plastic washers **(see illustration)**. Lift off the bar, noting how it fits **(see illustration 9.13b)**. Unscrew the choke plunger nut, using a pair of thin-nosed pliers if access is too restricted for a spanner, and withdraw the plunger assembly from each carburettor body **(see illustration)**.

3 Unscrew and remove the top cover retaining screws and remove the cover **(see illustration)**. Remove the small O-ring **(see illustration)**.

4 Remove the spring from inside the piston **(see illustration)**. Carefully peel the diaphragm away from its sealing groove in the carburettor and withdraw the diaphragm/piston assembly **(see illustration)**. Using a pair of thin-nosed pliers, carefully withdraw the jet needle holder from inside the piston – it is a press fit, held by an O-ring **(see illustration)**. Note the spring fitted into the bottom of the holder. Push the jet needle up from the bottom of the piston and withdraw it from the top, noting the washer on the top of the needle **(see illustration)**. If the E-clip, spacer and bottom washer are removed, note which notch the E-clip fits into.

Caution: Do not use a sharp instrument to displace the diaphragm, as it is easily damaged.

5 When dismantling the No.1 carburettor, undo the screw securing the idle speed adjuster holder to the float chamber and displace it **(see illustration)**. Undo the screws

4•8 Fuel and exhaust systems

7.5b Float chamber screws (arrowed)

7.6a Undo the pivot pin screw (arrowed) and remove the float assembly

7.6b Undo the screw (arrowed) and remove the needle valve seat

securing the float chamber to the base of the carburettor and remove it, noting how it fits **(see illustration)**. Remove the rubber gasket and discard it, as a new one must be used.

6 Undo the screw retaining the float pivot pin **(see illustration)**. Remove the float assembly, noting how it fits **(see illustration 9.7b)**. Unhook the needle valve from the tab on the float, noting how it fits **(see illustration 9.7a)**. Remove the screw securing the needle valve seat and draw out the seat **(see illustration)**. Discard its O-ring, as a new one must be used.

7 Unscrew and remove the pilot jet **(see illustration)**.

8 Unscrew and remove the starter jet, noting the collar **(see illustration)**.

9 Unscrew and remove the main jet **(see illustration)**.

10 Unscrew and remove the main jet holder, noting the O-ring **(see illustration)**.

11 Unscrew and remove the pilot air jet **(see illustration)**. The pilot screw can be removed from the carburettor, but note that its setting will be disturbed **(see Haynes Hint)**. Unscrew and remove the pilot screw along with its spring, washer and O-ring **(see illustration 4.1)**. Discard the O-ring, as a new one must be used.

> **HAYNES HiNT** To record the pilot screw's current setting, turn the screw in until it seats lightly, counting the number of turns necessary to achieve this, then fully unscrew it. On installation, the screw is simply backed out the number of turns you've recorded.

12 Undo the air cut-off valve cover screws and remove the spring and diaphragm, noting how they fit **(see illustration)**.

13 A throttle position sensor is mounted on the outside of the right-hand carburettor. Do not remove the sensor from the carburettor unless it is known to be faulty and is being replaced with a new one. Refer to Chapter 5 for checking and adjustment of the sensor.

Inspection

Caution: Use only a dedicated carburettor cleaner or petroleum-based solvent for carburettor cleaning. Do not use caustic cleaners.

14 Submerge the carburettor body and individual metal components in the solvent for

7.7 Remove the pilot jet (arrowed) . . .

7.8 . . . the starter jet (arrowed) with its collar . . .

7.9 . . . the main jet . . .

7.10 . . . and the main jet holder with its O-ring

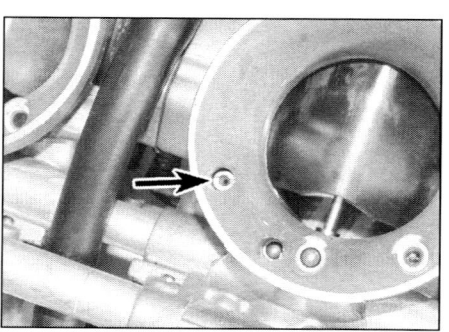

7.11 Pilot air jet (arrowed)

7.12 Undo the screws (arrowed) and remove the air cut-off valve components

Fuel and exhaust systems 4•9

7.17 Choke plunger assembly

7.18 Check the tapered portion of the pilot screw (arrowed) for wear

approximately thirty minutes (or longer, if the directions recommend it).

15 After the carburettor has soaked long enough for the cleaner to loosen and dissolve most of the varnish and other deposits, use a nylon-bristle brush to remove the stubborn deposits. Rinse it again, then dry it with compressed air.

16 Use a jet of compressed air to blow out all of the fuel and air passages in the main and upper body.

Caution: Never clean the jets or passages with a piece of wire or a drill bit, as they will be enlarged, causing the fuel and air metering rates to be upset.

17 Inspect the needle on the end of the choke plunger, the spring and the plunger linkage bar **(see illustration)**. Replace the assembly with a new one if any component is worn, damaged or bent – individual parts are not available.

18 If removed from the carburettor, check the tapered portion of the pilot screw and the spring and O-ring for wear or damage **(see illustration)**. Replace the assembly with a new one if necessary – individual parts are not available.

19 Check the carburettor body, float chamber and top cover for cracks, distorted sealing surfaces and other damage. If any defects are found, replace the faulty component with a new one, although replacement of the entire carburettor may be necessary (check with a Yamaha dealer on the availability of separate components).

20 Check the piston diaphragm for splits, holes, creases and general deterioration. Holding it up to a light will help to reveal problems of this nature. Replace it with a new one if necessary – it is available separately from the piston. Similarly check the air cut-off valve diaphragm. Check the spring for each diaphragm for distortion.

21 Insert the piston in the carburettor body and check that it moves up and down smoothly. Check the surface of the piston for wear. If it is worn excessively or doesn't move smoothly in the body, replace the components with new ones as necessary.

22 Check the jet needle is straight by rolling it on a flat surface such as a piece of glass. Replace it with a new one if it is bent, or if the tip is worn.

23 Check the tip of the float needle valve and the valve seat. If either has grooves or scratches in it, or is in any way worn, they must be replaced with a new set **(see illustration)**. Make sure the strainer is clean **(see illustration)**.

24 Operate the throttle shaft to make sure the throttle butterfly valve opens and closes smoothly. If it doesn't, clean the throttle linkage, and also check the butterfly for distortion, or for any debris caught between its edge and the carburettor. Also check that the butterfly is central on the shaft – if the screws securing it to the shaft have come loose it may be catching.

25 Check the float for damage. This will usually be apparent by the presence of fuel inside the float. If it is damaged, replace it with a new one.

26 Check the action of the sprung ball in the air cut-off valve housing passage by pushing it in with the tip of a small screwdriver **(see illustration)**. It should move in relatively easily and spring back to plug the passage when released. Check the tip of the peg in the centre of the inner face of the diaphragm for wear **(see illustration)**.

8 Carburettor separation and joining

Warning: Refer to the precautions given in Section 1 before proceeding.

Separation

1 The carburettors do not need to be separated for normal overhaul. If you need to

7.23a Check the valve's spring loaded rod (A) and tip (B) for wear or damage

7.23b Check the valve seat and the strainer on its base

7.26a Check the action of the ball . . .

7.26b . . . and the tip of the peg which acts on it

4•10 Fuel and exhaust systems

8.2 Carburettor assembly

1. Throttle position sensor
2. Gasket
3. Spacer
4. Fuel distribution pipe
5. Spacer
6. Spring
7. Heater system hoses
8. Spacer
9. Choke Linkage bar
10. Fuel inlet pipe
11. Joining bolt
12. Idle speed adjuster
13. Joining bolt
14. Float chamber air vent hose
15. Vacuum chamber air vent hose
16. Synchronisation screw and spring

separate them (to replace a carburettor body with a new one, for example), refer to the following procedure.

2 Remove the carburettors from the machine (see Section 6). Mark the body of each carburettor with its cylinder location to ensure that it is positioned correctly on reassembly **(see illustration)**.

3 Make a note of how the throttle return springs, linkage assembly and carburettor synchronisation springs are arranged, to ensure that they are fitted correctly on reassembly **(see illustration)**. Also note the arrangement of the various hoses, unions, joint pieces and collars, and of the cable brackets **(see illustrations)**.

4 Unhook the choke linkage bar return spring, noting how it fits **(see illustration 7.2a)**. Remove the screws securing the choke linkage bar to the carburettors, noting the plastic washers **(see illustration 7.2b)**. Lift off the bar, noting how it fits **(see illustration 9.13b)**.

5 The carburettors are joined by two long

8.3a Note how the throttle return springs and linkage assembly . . .

8.3b . . . the vent hose unions . . .

8.3c . . . and heater system hoses are arranged before separating the carburettors

Fuel and exhaust systems 4•11

8.5 Carburettor joining bolts (arrowed)

9.3 Screw the main jet into its holder

9.4a Make sure the collar is fitted on the starter jet . . .

bolts which pass through them **(see illustration)**. Remove the bolts, and remove the spacers from between the carburettors, noting which fits where, as they are of different lengths.

6 Mark the position of each carburettor and gently separate them. Note how the throttle linkage is connected and be careful not to lose any springs, or fuel and vent pipes and hose joints, that are present between the carburettors; note the O-rings fitted with them.

Joining

7 Fit new O-rings onto the fuel and vent pipes **(see illustration 8.2)**. Lubricate the O-rings with a light film of oil and install the fittings into their respective holes, making sure they seat completely. Also fit the hose joints.

8 Position the coil springs between the carburettors, gently push the carburettors together, then make sure the throttle linkages are correctly engaged **(see illustration 8.3a)**. Check the fuel and vent fittings and hose joints to make sure they engage properly also **(see illustrations 8.3b)**.

9 Install the two long through-bolts with their spacers, but do not tighten them yet. Make sure the spacers are correctly positioned, as they are of different lengths. Set the carburettors on a sheet of glass, then align them with a straight-edge placed along the edges of the bores. When the centrelines of the carburettors are all in horizontal and vertical alignment, tighten the bolts **(see illustration 8.5)**.

10 Fit the choke linkage bar onto the plungers, making sure the slots locate correctly behind the nipple on the end of each choke plunger **(see illustration 9.13b)**. Fit the plastic washers and secure the linkage bar in place with the screws **(see illustration 9.13c)**. Hook up the linkage bar return spring **(see illustration 7.2a)**. Make sure the choke linkage operates smoothly, and returns quickly under spring pressure.

11 Install the carburettor synchronisation springs, making sure they are correctly and squarely seated. Visually synchronise the throttle butterfly valves, turning the adjusting screws on the throttle linkage, if necessary, to equalise the clearance between the butterfly

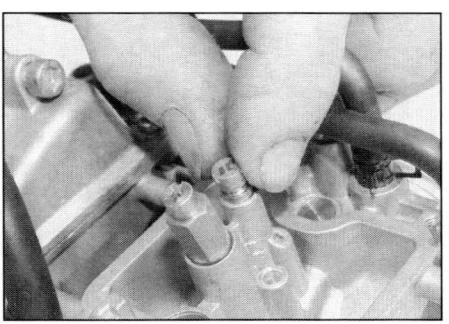

9.4b . . . then install the starter jet . . .

valve and throttle bore of each carburettor. Make sure the throttle operates smoothly, and returns quickly under spring pressure.

12 Install the carburettors (see Section 6) and check carburettor synchronisation and idle speed (see Chapter 1).

9 Carburettor reassembly, float height and fuel level check

⚠ **Warning:** *Refer to the precautions given in Section 1 before proceeding.*

Note: *When reassembling the carburettors, be sure to use the new O-rings, seals and other parts supplied in the rebuild kit. Do not overtighten the carburettor jets and screws, as they are easily damaged.*

9.6 Fit the valve seat using a new O-ring and secure it with the screw

9.5 . . . and then the pilot jet

Reassembly and float height

1 Install the pilot screw (if removed) along with its spring, washer and O-ring, turning it in until it seats lightly **(see illustration 4.1)**. Now, turn the screw out the number of turns previously recorded, or as specified at the beginning of the Chapter. Install the pilot air jet **(see illustration 7.11)**.

2 Install the main jet holder with its O-ring **(see illustration 7.10)**.

3 Install the main jet **(see illustration)**.

4 Install the starter jet with its collar **(see illustrations)**.

5 Install the pilot jet **(see illustration)**.

6 Fit a new O-ring onto the needle valve seat. Make sure the strainer is clean, then press the seat into place and secure it with the screw **(see illustration and 7.6b)**.

7 Hook the float needle valve onto the tab on the float assembly **(see illustration)**. Insert the

9.7a Hook the needle valve onto the tab on the float . . .

4•12 Fuel and exhaust systems

9.7b ... then install the float assembly, locating the valve in the seat

9.8 Measuring float height

9.9a Fit a new seal into the groove ...

9.9b ... and install the float chamber

9.10 Make sure the needle components are correctly fitted

9.11 Make sure the diaphragm rim is seated

pivot pin into the float pivot if removed. Position the float assembly onto the carburettor, making sure the needle valve locates in the seat **(see illustration)**. Install the pivot pin retaining screw **(see illustration 7.6a)**.

8 To check the float height, hold the carburettor so the float hangs down, then tilt it back until the needle valve is just seated, but not so far that the needle's spring-loaded tip is compressed. Measure the height of the float above the chamber mating surface with an accurate ruler **(see illustration)**. The height should be as specified at the beginning of the Chapter. If not, adjust the float height by carefully bending the float tab a little at a time until the correct height is obtained. **Note:** *With the float held the same way up as it is when installed, bending the tab up lowers the fuel level – bending it down raises the fuel level.*

9 Fit a new rubber seal onto the float chamber, making sure it is seated properly in its groove, then fit the chamber onto the carburettor and tighten its screws **(see illustrations)**. When assembling the No. 1 carburettor, fit the idle speed adjuster holder and secure it with its screw **(see illustration 7.5a)**.

10 If removed, fit the washer, spacer and E-clip onto the needle, making sure the clip is in the same groove from which it was removed, then fit the washer on top of the clip **(see illustration)**. Check that the spring and O-ring are fitted to the needle holder – use a new O-ring if necessary. Fit the jet needle into the piston, then fit the needle holder onto it and press it gently down until it is secure **(see illustrations 7.4d and c)**.

11 Fit the piston/diaphragm assembly into the carburettor and lightly push the piston down, making sure the needle is correctly aligned with the needle jet **(see illustration 7.4b)**. Press the rim of the diaphragm into its groove, making sure it is correctly seated **(see illustration)**. Fit the spring into the diaphragm assembly, making sure it locates correctly onto the needle holder **(see illustration 7.4a)**.

12 Fit the small O-ring into its cut-out **(see illustration 7.3b)**. Fit the top cover onto the carburettor making sure it is correctly orientated for the O-ring, locating the centre peg into the top of the spring and the outer pegs into the holes in the carburettor body, and tighten its screws **(see illustration)**. Check that the piston moves smoothly in the guide by pushing it up with your finger **(see illustration)**.

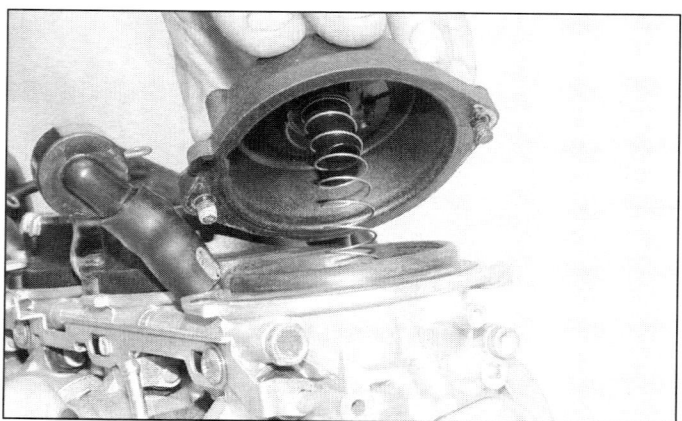

9.12a Insert the spring and fit the cover

9.12b Check the movement of the piston with your finger

Fuel and exhaust systems 4•13

9.13a Fit the choke plunger into the carburettor . . .

9.13b . . . and install the linkage bar, making sure the slots in the arms locate behind the nipples on the plungers (arrowed)

9.13c Fit the screws with their plastic washers

Note that the piston should descend slowly and smoothly as the diaphragm draws air into the chamber – it should not drop sharply under spring pressure.

13 Fit the choke plunger assembly into the carburettor body and tighten the nut to secure it **(see illustration)**. Fit the choke linkage bar onto the plungers, making sure the slots locate correctly behind the nipple on the end of each choke plunger **(see illustration)**. Fit the plastic washers and secure the linkage bar in place with the screws **(see illustration)**. Hook up the linkage bar return spring **(see illustration 7.2a)**.

14 Install the carburettors.

Fuel level check

Note: *The fuel level is checked with the carburettors installed.*

15 To check the fuel level, position the motorcycle on level ground and support it using the centrestand so that it is vertical. Raise the fuel tank (See Section 2).

16 Yamaha provide a fuel level gauge (part No. 90890-01312 in Europe or YU-01312-A in the US), or alternatively a length of suitable clear plastic tubing can be used. Attach the gauge or tubing to the drain hose union on the bottom of the float chamber on the first carburettor and position its open end vertically and above the level of the carburettors **(see illustration)**. Use tape to hold the hose in position – it is important that the hose position is not disturbed during the fuel level check.

17 Slacken the drain screw and allow the fuel to flow into the tube. The level at which the fuel stabilises in the tubing indicates the level of the fuel in the float chamber. Refer to the Specifications at the beginning of the Chapter and measure the level relative to the mating surface of the float chamber with the carburettor body. Tighten the drain screw, then detach the gauge or tubing, catching the residual fuel with a rag.

18 If the level was incorrect, remove the carburettors, then remove the float from the chamber (see Section 7), and adjust the float height by carefully bending the float tab a little at a time until the correct height is obtained. Repeat the procedure for the other carburettors. **Note:** *With the float held the same way up as it is when installed, bending the tab up lowers the fuel level – bending it down raises the fuel level.*

10 Throttle cables

Warning: *Refer to the precautions given in Section 1 before proceeding.*

Removal

1 Remove the fuel tank (see Section 2).
2 Mark each cable according to its location at both ends. If new cables are being fitted, match them to the old cables to ensure they are correctly installed.
3 Slacken the accelerator (opening) cable top locknut and thread it up the elbow **(see illustration)**.
4 Unscrew the decelerator (closing) cable hex, pulling up on it as you do so the lower nut remains captive against the lug on the bracket, thereby threading itself down **(see illustration 10.3)**.
5 Displace the carburettors (see Section 6), then slip the cables out of the bracket and detach the cable ends from the throttle cam

9.16 Fuel level check set-up

1 Gauge
2 Hose union
3 Drain bolt
4 Fuel level measurement

10.3 Slacken the nut (A) and the cable hex (B) as described

4•14 Fuel and exhaust systems

10.5a Slip the opening cable out of the bracket . . .

10.5b . . . detach its end from the cam . . .

10.5c . . . and draw it out

10.5d Slip the closing cable out of the bracket . . .

10.5e . . . detach its end from the cam

as they become accessible **(see illustrations)**.
6 Withdraw the cables from the machine noting their correct routing.
7 Unscrew the throttle opening cable elbow retaining plate bolt on the bottom of the right-hand switch housing **(see illustration)**. Unscrew the closing cable retaining ring **(see illustration)**. Separate the switch housing halves by undoing the bolts **(see illustrations)**. Detach the cable ends from the pulley in the housing, then remove the cable elbows from the housing **(see illustration)**.

Installation

8 Lubricate the cable nipples with multi-purpose grease and fit them into the throttle pulley at the handlebar, making sure they are the correct way round **(see illustration 10.7d)**. Fit the cable elbows into the housing, making sure they locate correctly. Join the housing halves, making sure the pin locates in the hole in the handlebar, and tighten the bolts **(see illustration and 10.7b)**. Tighten the closing cable retaining ring and fit the opening cable retaining plate and bolt **(see illustration 10.7a)**.
9 Feed the cables through to the carburettors, making sure they are correctly routed. The cables must not interfere with any other component and should not be kinked or bent sharply.
10 Fit the carburettors part-way between the engine and air filter housing (see Section 6). Lubricate the cable ends with multi-purpose grease.
11 Fit the decelerator cable end into the cam then locate the cable in the front of the bracket and draw it up so that the lower nut becomes captive against the small lug **(see illustrations 10.5e and d)**. Tighten the hex down onto the bracket **(see illustration 10.3)**.
12 Fit the accelerator cable end into the cam then locate the cable in the rear of the bracket **(see illustrations 10.5c, b and a)**.
13 Fully install the carburettors (see Section 6).

10.7a Unscrew the bolt (A) and the ring (B)

10.7b Unscrew the bolts (arrowed) . . .

10.7c . . . and separate the housing halves

10.7d Detach the cable ends from the pulley

10.8 Locate the pin (A) in the hole (B) in the handlebar

Fuel and exhaust systems

11.2a Slacken the clamp screw and free the outer cable from the clamp . . .

11.2b . . . and the cable end from the linkage bar

11.3a Remove the housing screws (arrowed) and separate the halves

11.3b Remove the choke lever and cable elbow from the housing . . .

11.3c . . . and free the cable end from the lever

11.5 Make sure the pin (A) in the housing locates in the hole (B) in the handlebar

Adjust the cable freeplay (see Chapter 1). Operate the throttle to check that it opens and closes freely. Turn the handlebars back and forth to make sure the cable doesn't cause the steering to bind.

14 Install the fuel tank (see Section 2).

15 Start the engine and check that the idle speed does not rise as the handlebars are turned. If it does, the throttle cable is routed incorrectly. Correct the problem before riding the motorcycle.

11 Choke cable

Removal

1 Remove the fuel tank (see Section 2).
2 Slacken the choke outer cable holder screw and free the cable from the holder, then detach the inner cable end from its socket **(see illustrations)**.
3 Unscrew the two handlebar switch/choke lever housing screws and separate the two halves **(see illustrations)**. Lift the cable elbow and lever out of the housing, noting how they fit, and detach the cable nipple from the lever **(see illustration)**. Withdraw the cable from the machine noting its correct routing.

Installation

4 Install the cable making sure it is correctly routed. The cable must not interfere with any other component and should not be kinked or bent sharply.
5 Lubricate the upper end of the cable with multi-purpose grease and attach it to the choke lever **(see illustration 11.3c)**. Fit the lever and cable elbow into the housing **(see illustration 11.3b)**, then fit the two halves of the housing onto the handlebar, making sure the lever fits correctly; the pin in the front half of the housing locates in the hole in the front of the handlebar **(see illustration)**. Install the screws and tighten them **(see illustration 11.3a)**.
6 Attach the lower end of the cable to its socket on the carburettor **(see illustration 11.2b)**. Fit the outer cable into its bracket, making sure there is a small amount of freeplay in the inner cable, and tighten the screw **(see illustrations 11.2a)**.
7 Check the operation of the choke cable (see Chapter 1).
8 Install the fuel tank (see Section 2).

12 Exhaust system

⚠ *Warning: If the engine has been running the exhaust system will be very hot. Allow the system to cool before carrying out any work.*

Silencer

Removal

1 Slacken the clamp bolt securing the silencer to the downpipe assembly.

2 Unscrew and remove the silencer mounting bolt and its washer, then release the silencer from the downpipe assembly **(see illustration)**. Note the collar fitted in the rubber mounting bush. Check the condition of the mounting rubber and replace it with a new one if it is damaged, deformed or deteriorated.
3 Check the condition of the sealing ring in the silencer and replace it with a new one if it is damaged or deformed. Care must be taken when installing a new sealing ring, not to damage it.

Installation

4 Fit the silencer onto the downpipe assembly, making sure it is pushed fully home. Align the silencer mounting bracket at the rear and install the bolt with its washer, but do not tighten it yet. Tighten the clamp bolt to the torque setting specified at the beginning of the Chapter, then the silencer mounting bolt.

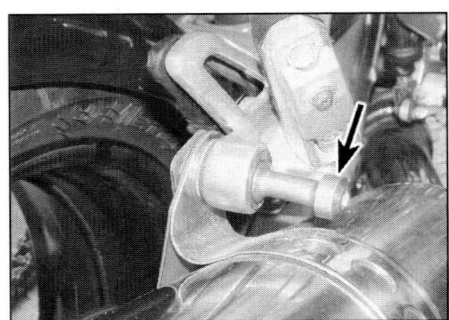

12.2 Silencer mounting bolt (arrowed)

4•16 Fuel and exhaust systems

12.7 Unscrew the bolt (arrowed) . . .

12.8 . . . and the downpipe flange nuts . . .

12.9 . . . and remove the exhaust system

12.11 Fit a new gasket into each port

rear bolt, but do not tighten them yet **(see illustrations 12.2 and 12.7)**.

13 Locate the downpipe flanges onto the studs, then fit the nuts and tighten them to the torque setting specified at the beginning of the Chapter **(see illustration 12.8)**. Now tighten the other bolts to the specified torque.

14 Attach the cables to the EXUP valve (see Section 13).

15 Run the engine and check that there are no exhaust gas leaks.

13 EXUP system

Cable renewal

1 Raise or remove the fuel tank (see Section 2).
2 Unscrew the bolts securing the EXUP pulley cover on the exhaust and remove the cover **(see illustration)**.
3 Unscrew the two bolts securing the cable bracket and displace it **(see illustration)**. Release the cable ends from the pulley and the elbows from the bracket, noting which fits where.
4 For best access to the cables at the servo end displace the servo from its mount, following the removal procedure below. Free the top ends of the outer cables from their holders on the servo housing, noting their location, and detach the cable nipples from the pulley **(see illustrations)**. Withdraw the cables from the machine, noting the correct routing of each cable.
5 Lubricate the cable nipples with multi-purpose grease and fit them into the servo pulley **(see illustration 13.4)**. Fit the outer cable ends into their holders, making sure they locate correctly.
6 Feed the cables through to the exhaust, making sure they are correctly routed. The cables must not interfere with any other component and should not be kinked or bent sharply.
7 Fit the outer cables into the bracket and locate the bracket behind the pulley on the valve cover, then fit the cable ends into the

5 Run the engine and check that there are no exhaust gas leaks.

Complete system

Removal

6 Detach the cables from the EXUP valve (see Section 13).
7 Slacken the silencer mounting bolt but do not remove it yet **(see illustration 12.2)**. Unscrew the bolt securing the rear of the downpipe assembly to the frame **(see illustration)**.
8 Unscrew the eight downpipe flange nuts and draw the flanges off the studs **(see illustration)**.
9 Supporting the system, remove the silencer mounting bolt, then detach the downpipes from the cylinder head and remove the system **(see illustration)**.

10 Remove the gasket from each port in the cylinder head and discard it, as a new one must be fitted.

Installation

11 Check the condition of the silencer mounting rubber and replace it with a new one if it is damaged, deformed or deteriorated. Check that the collar is fitted into the inside of the rubber. Fit a new gasket into each of the cylinder head ports **(see illustration)**. If necessary, apply a smear of grease to the gaskets to keep them in place whilst fitting the downpipe.
12 Manoeuvre the assembly into position so that the head of each downpipe is located in its port in the cylinder head **(see illustration 12.9)**, then install the silencer mounting bolt and the downpipe assembly

13.2 Unscrew the bolts (arrowed) and remove the cover

13.3 Unscrew the bracket bolts (arrowed) and detach the cables

13.4 Displace the servo housing then free the outer cables and detach the cable ends

Fuel and exhaust systems 4•17

pulley **(see illustrations)**. Align the bracket with the bolt holes and tighten the bolts to the torque setting specified at the beginning of the Chapter **(see illustration 13.3)**. Check and adjust cable freeplay (see Chapter 1), then install the cover and tighten the bolts to the specified torque setting **(see illustration 13.2)**.

Check

8 When the ignition is first switched ON, the EXUP system performs its own self-diagnosis. If a fault occurs, the tachometer will be seen to display zero rpm for 3 seconds, then 7000 rpm for 2.5 seconds, then the actual engine speed for 3 seconds, whereupon it will repeat the cycle until the engine is switched off. Note that the motorcycle can be ridden even though a fault has been diagnosed, though a difference in performance will be noticed.

9 Remove the servo (see below). Using a fully charged 12V battery and some jumper leads, connect the positive (+ve) terminal of the battery to the black/yellow wire terminal on the servo side of the connector, and the negative (–ve) terminal to the black/red wire terminal. When the battery is connected, the servo should operate. Disconnect the battery immediately after the test. If the servo does not operate, replace it with a new one.

Caution: Disconnect the battery immediately after the test to prevent possible damage to the servo motor.

10 If the servo now operates, yet did not beforehand, check for voltage at the wiring connector using a voltmeter – connect the positive (+ve) probe of the meter to the black/red wire terminal on the loom side of the connector, and the negative (–ve) terminal to the black/yellow wire terminal. Battery voltage should be present with the ignition ON. If not, check the connector for loose or corroded terminals, then check the fuse and the battery, and then the wiring between the connector and the ignition control unit, referring to the test procedures and *Wiring Diagrams* in Chapter 9.

11 Check the variable resistance between the blue wire terminal and the white/red wire terminal on the servo side of the connectors, while turning the servo pulley by hand.

13.7a Locate the bracket behind the pulley . . .

13.7b . . . then attach the cable ends

13.14a Displace the servo . . .

13.14b . . . and disconnect the wiring connector

Compare the reading range to that specified at the beginning of the Chapter. If the readings from either test are not within the range specified, replace the servo with a new one.

12 If the operation of the valve has been sticky, remove it as described below, then check the valve shaft, face, cover and housing for any corrosion or dirt which may be causing the problem. Also check the shaft bushes in which the valve turns – one in the housing and one in the cover. Clean off all dirt and corrosion and check the operation of the valve. If the shaft ends or bushes are worn, replace them with new ones.

Removal

13 To access the servo, raise or remove the fuel tank (see Section 2), then drain the coolant and displace the radiator forwards by detaching the hose from the top on the right-hand side and by unscrewing the mounting bolts (see Chapter 3) – there is no need to detach all the hoses. Before removing either the servo or the valve, detach the cables (see above). If only the servo is being removed, it may be necessary to detach the cables from the valve as well, to create enough slack.

14 To remove the servo, displace it from its mount, then disconnect the wiring connector **(see illustrations)**. Detach the cables as described above.

15 To remove the valve, detach the cables as described above. Using a suitable rod or pin located between the pulley tabs and the hole in the valve cover to prevent the pulley turning, unscrew the bolt and remove the pulley, spring, and washer, noting how they fit **(see illustrations)**. Unscrew the remaining

13.15a Unscrew the bolt (arrowed), securing the pulley as shown

13.15b Draw the pulley off the shaft . . .

13.15c . . . and remove the spring and washer

4•18 Fuel and exhaust systems

13.15d Unscrew the bolt . . .

13.15e . . . and remove the cover and valve

13.16a Lubricate all mated moving surfaces with copper grease

13.16b The shaft end locates in the bore (arrowed)

bolt securing the valve cover and remove the cover **(see illustrations)**. The valve may come away with the cover. If not, draw it out of the exhaust, noting how it fits. Note the bushes.

Installation

16 Installation is the reverse of removal. Lubricate the valve shaft ends, bushes and bolts with copper-based grease, as an anti-corrosion measure **(see illustration)**. Fit the inner bush onto the end of the shaft, then locate the shaft end into its bore in the exhaust **(see illustration)**. Fit the valve cover and attach the cables (see above), tightening the bolts to the torque setting specified at the beginning of the Chapter.

17 Check the operation of the system and the cable freeplay (see Chapter 1). Install the pulley cover and tighten the bolts to the specified torque **(see illustration 13.2)**.

14 Fuel pump and relay

⚠ *Warning: Refer to the precautions given in Section 1 before starting work.*

Check

1 The fuel pump is mounted behind the right-hand side panel – remove the panel for access (see Chapter 8) **(see illustration)**. The fuel pump relay is contained within the relay assembly, which is mounted behind the left-hand side panel – remove the panel for access (see Chapter 8) **(see illustration)**.

2 The fuel pump is controlled through the relay so that it runs whenever the ignition is switched ON and the ignition is operative (i.e. only when the engine is turning over). As soon as the ignition is killed, the relay will cut off the fuel pump's electrical supply (so that there is no risk of fuel being sprayed out under pressure in the event of an accident).

3 It should be possible to hear or feel the fuel pump running whenever the engine is turning over – either place your ear close beside the fuel pump or feel it with your fingertips. If you can't hear or feel anything, check that the battery is fully charged and the ignition circuit fuse is good (see Chapter 9) and that all the wiring is good. Then check the pump and relay for loose or corroded connections or physical damage, and rectify as necessary.

4 If the circuit is fine so far, switch the ignition OFF. Displace the relay assembly from its mount and unplug the wiring connector **(see illustration 14.1b)**. Using an ohmmeter or continuity tester, connect the positive (+ve) probe to the relay's red/black terminal, and the negative (–ve) probe to the relay's black/blue terminal. There should be no continuity. Leaving the meter connected, now connect a fully charged 12 volt battery and two insulated jumper wires, connect the positive (+ve) terminal of the battery to the relay's red/black terminal, and the negative (–ve) terminal of the battery to the relay's blue/red terminal. There should now be continuity. If the relay assembly does not behave as described, replace it with a new one.

5 If the pump still does not work, trace the wiring from the pump and disconnect it at the connector **(see illustration)**. Using an ohmmeter, connect the positive (+ve) probe to the pump's black/blue terminal, and the negative (–ve) probe to the black terminal, and measure the resistance. If the reading is not as specified at the beginning of the Chapter, replace the pump with a new one. A definitive check of the pump can be made by removing it (see below) and connecting a fully charged 12 volt battery and two insulated jumper wires, connecting the positive (+ve) terminal of the battery to the pump's black/blue terminal, and the negative (–ve) terminal of the battery to the pump's black terminal. The pump should work. If it doesn't, replace it with a new one.

Removal

6 Make sure the ignition is switched OFF.

14.1a Fuel pump (arrowed)

14.1b Relay assembly (arrowed)

14.5 Fuel pump wiring connector (arrowed)

Fuel and exhaust systems 4•19

14.8 Displace the pump from its mount

14.10 Make sure the hoses are connected as described

Raise the fuel tank (see Section 2) and turn the fuel tap to the OFF position.

7 The fuel pump is mounted behind the right-hand side panel – remove the panel for access (see Chapter 8) **(see illustration 14.1a)**. The fuel pump relay is contained within the relay assembly, which is mounted behind the left-hand side panel – remove the panel for access (see Chapter 8) **(see illustration 14.1b)**.

8 To remove the pump, trace the wiring and disconnect it at the connector **(see illustration 14.5)**. Release the wiring from its tie. Make a note or sketch of which fuel hose fits where, as an aid to installation **(see illustration 14.9)**. Using a rag to mop up any spilled fuel, disconnect the two fuel hoses from the fuel pump. Displace the pump from its bracket with its rubber mounting sleeve **(see illustration)**. Separate the pump from the sleeve.

9 To remove the relay assembly, displace it from its mounting and disconnect the wiring connector **(see illustration 14.1b)**.

Installation

10 Installation is a reverse of the removal procedure. Make sure the fuel hoses are correctly and securely fitted to the pump – the hose from the in-line filter attaches to the short straight union; the hose to the carburettors attaches to the longer curved union **(see illustration)**. Turn the fuel tap ON, lower the tank, then start the engine and check carefully that there are no leaks at the pipe connections.

15 Fuel gauge, warning light and sensor

Check

1 The circuit consists of the sensor mounted in the fuel tank and the gauge and warning light (which should come on when the volume of fuel drops to around 4 litres) mounted in the instrument panel. If the system malfunctions check first that the battery is fully charged and that the low fuel warning light bulb and fuses are good (see Chapter 9). If they are, remove the sensor (see below).

2 Connect the positive (+ve) probe of an ohmmeter to the green terminal on the sensor connector, and the negative (-ve) probe to the black terminal. Check the resistance of the sensor in both the FULL and EMPTY positions and compare the readings to those specified at the beginning of the Chapter **(see illustrations)**. If the readings are not as specified, replace the sensor with a new one.

3 If the readings are as specified, connect the sensor wiring connector and turn the ignition switch ON. With the sensor in the FULL position, the gauge should read FULL, and with the sensor in the empty position the gauge should read EMPTY (the gauge needle may not respond immediately – leave it in the position being tested for at least three minutes to accurately check the system).

4 If the gauge responds as described, remove the windshield (see Chapter 8) and disconnect the instrument cluster wiring connector **(see illustration)**. Check for voltage to the gauge by connecting the positive (+ve) probe of a voltmeter to the brown terminal on the loom side of the instrument cluster wiring connector, and the negative (-ve) probe to the black terminal, then turn the ignition switch ON. If no voltage is present, check for continuity to earth in the black wire, then if that is good check all the relevant wiring and wiring connectors in the

15.2a Check the resistance in the FULL position . . .

15.2b . . . and the EMPTY position

15.4 Disconnect the wiring connector from the back of the cluster

4•20 Fuel and exhaust systems

15.9a Free the wiring from its guides (arrowed) . . .

15.9b . . . then unscrew the bolts (arrowed) . . .

15.9c . . . and withdraw the sensor

15.10 Always use a new rubber seal and make sure it locates correctly

power circuit to the instrument cluster, and between the sensor and the gauge, referring to the Wiring Diagrams at the end of Chapter 9. If the wiring and connectors are good, there could be an internal fault in the instrument cluster wiring between the connector and the gauge. If not, replace the gauge with a new one (see Chapter 9).

5 Check that no fuel has entered the float due to a leak, and check that the arm moves up and down smoothly.

Replacement

 Warning: Refer to the precautions given in Section 1 before starting work.

6 See Chapter 9 for replacement of the fuel gauge and the low fuel warning light bulb.

7 To replace the sensor, remove the fuel tank (see Section 2).

8 Connect a drain hose to the fuel outlet union on the tap and insert its end in a container suitable and large enough for storing the petrol. Turn the fuel tap to the ON position and allow the tank to drain. When the tank has drained, turn the tap to the OFF position.

9 Free the wiring from its guides **(see illustration)**. Unscrew the bolts securing the sensor and carefully manoeuvre it out of the tank **(see illustrations)**. Discard the rubber seal as a new one must be used.

10 Fit a new seal onto the sensor then install then sensor in the tank with the wiring to the back **(see illustration)**. Tighten the bolts evenly and a little at a time in a criss-cross pattern to the torque setting specified at the

beginning of the Chapter. Fit the wiring into its guides.

11 Install the tank (see Section 2), and check carefully that there are no leaks from the sensor before using the bike.

16 Air induction system (AIS)

Function

1 The air induction system uses negative exhaust gas pulses to suck fresh air from the filter housing into the exhaust ports, where it mixes with hot combustion gases. The extra oxygen causes continued combustion, allowing unburnt hydrocarbons to burn off, thereby reducing emissions. An air cut-off valve controls the flow of fresh air into the unit and is actuated by vacuum taken from the intake duct to the No. 4 (right-hand) cylinder. Reed valves control the flow of air into the ports, opening when there is negative pressure, and preventing exhaust gases flowing back into the AIS. The air cut-off valve shuts off the flow of air during sudden deceleration (shutting the throttle causes a change in pressure in the duct which closes the valve), preventing after-burning or 'popping'.

2 Refer to Chapter 1, Section 6, for a check of the system.

Disassembly

3 Remove the thermostat housing along with its hoses, then remove the coolant outlet pipe assembly (see Chapter 3). Displace the ignition HT coil feeding cylinders 2 and 3 (see Chapter 5).

4 To remove the AIS valve assembly, slacken the clamps securing the Nos. 1 and 2 pipes to the valve assembly outlet hoses and the unions on the cylinder head and remove the pipes **(see illustrations)**. Release the clamps securing the Nos. 3 and 4 outlet hoses and push them back along the hoses. Pull the vacuum hose off its union on the No. 4 cylinder intake duct **(see illustration)**. Pull the air intake hose off its union on the unit **(see**

16.4a Release the clamps and detach the pipes from the valve . . .

16.4b . . . and from the head

16.4c Pull the vacuum hose off its union

Fuel and exhaust systems 4•21

16.4d Pull the intake hose off its union

16.4e Slacken the unit bolts (A) then unscrew the bracket bolts (B)

16.4f Manoeuvre the unit off the hoses . . .

16.4g . . . then unscrew the bolts (arrowed) . . .

16.4h . . . and remove the bracket . . .

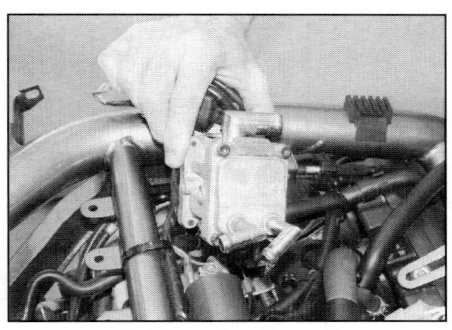
16.4i . . . then the unit

illustration). Slacken the bolts securing the unit to its bracket, then unscrew the bolts securing the bracket to the frame (see illustration). Manoeuvre the assembly out of the 3 and 4 outlet hoses and from under the frame cross-piece, then unscrew the unit-to-bracket bolts when accessible, noting the collars and grommets (see illustrations). Remove the bracket, then the unit (see illustrations). No individual internal components are available for the valve assembly, so if there are any faults in its function the assembly must be replaced with a new one.

5 To remove the Nos. 3 and 4 pipes, unscrew the bolt securing them to the valve cover, then proceed as in Step 4 for Nos. 1 and 2 pipes. Remove the sealing collars and replace them with new ones if they are deformed or damaged.

6 To access a reed valve, remove the valve assembly (see Step 4), then unscrew the reed valve cover bolts (see illustration). Remove the reed valve, noting how it fits (see illustration).

Reassembly

7 Reassemble the system, making sure all the hoses and pipes are securely connected at each end and held by their clamps, and are correctly routed.

16.6a Remove the cover . . .

16.6b . . . then lift the reed valve out

Notes

Chapter 5
Ignition system

Contents

General information 1	Pick-up coil 4
Ignition (main) switch . . . . .see Chapter 9	Relay assembly . . . . .see Chapter 9
Ignition control unit 5	Sidestand switch . . . . .see Chapter 9
Ignition HT coils 3	Spark plugs . . . . .see Chapter 1
Ignition system check 2	Throttle position sensor 7
Ignition timing 6	Tip-over sensor 8
Neutral switch . . . . .see Chapter 9	

Degrees of difficulty

| Easy, suitable for novice with little experience | Fairly easy, suitable for beginner with some experience | Fairly difficult, suitable for competent DIY mechanic | Difficult, suitable for experienced DIY mechanic | Very difficult, suitable for expert DIY or professional |

Specifications

General information
Cylinder numbering	1 to 4 from left to right
Spark plugs	see Chapter 1

Ignition timing
At idle	5° BTDC @ 1100 rpm
Full advance	55° BTDC @ 5000 rpm

Pick-up coil
Resistance	248 to 372 ohms @ 20°C

Ignition HT coils
Primary winding resistance	1.87 to 2.53 ohms @ 20°C
Secondary winding resistance (without plug caps)	12 to 18 K-ohms @ 20°C
Spark plug cap resistance	10 K-ohms @ 20°C
Minimum spark gap (see Section 2)	6 mm

Throttle position sensor
Maximum resistance	5.0 ± 1.0 K-ohms
Resistance range	Zero to 5.0 ± 1.0 K-ohms
Input voltage	4.95 to 5.05 V
Output voltage	0.65 to 0.75 V

Torque wrench settings
Pick-up coil bolts	10 Nm
Timing rotor/pick-up coil cover bolts	12 Nm

1 General information

All models are fitted with a fully transistorised electronic ignition system which, due to its lack of mechanical parts, is totally maintenance-free. The system comprises a trigger, pick-up coil, ignition control unit and ignition HT coils (refer to Wiring Diagrams at the end of Chapter 9 for details). All models are fitted with two HT coils. A throttle position sensor provides information on throttle opening for the ignition control unit.

The ignition trigger, which is on the rotor on the right-hand end of the crankshaft, magnetically operates the pick-up coil as the crankshaft rotates. The pick-up coil sends a signal to the ignition control unit, which then supplies the ignition HT coils with the power necessary to produce a spark at the plugs.

The ignition control unit incorporates an electronic advance system controlled by signals from the ignition triggers and pick-up coil and from the throttle position sensor.

The system also incorporates a safety interlock circuit which will cut the ignition if the sidestand is extended whilst the engine is running and in gear, or if a gear is selected whilst the engine is running and the sidestand is extended. It also prevents the engine from being started if the engine is in gear unless the clutch lever is pulled in. In a separate circuit a tip-over sensor cuts the ignition if the bike reaches an angle of lean in excess of that possible in normal riding (i.e. if the machine is dropped).

Because of their nature, the individual ignition system components can be checked but not repaired. If ignition system troubles occur, and the faulty component can be isolated, the only cure for the problem is to replace the part with a new one. Keep in mind that most electrical parts, once purchased, cannot be returned. To avoid unnecessary expense, make very sure the faulty component has been positively identified before buying a replacement part.

Note that there is no provision for adjusting the ignition timing on these models.

2 Ignition system check

⚠ **Warning: The energy levels in electronic systems can be very high. On no account should the ignition be switched on whilst the plugs or plug caps are being held. Shocks from the HT circuit can be most unpleasant. Secondly, it is vital that the engine is not turned over or run with any of the plug caps removed, and that the plugs are soundly earthed (grounded) when the system is checked for sparking. The ignition system components can be seriously damaged if the HT circuit becomes isolated.**

1 As no means of adjustment is available, any failure of the system can be traced to failure of a system component or a simple wiring fault. Of the two possibilities, the latter is by far the most likely. In the event of failure, check the system in a logical fashion, as described below.

2 Work on one cylinder at a time. Pull the cap off the spark plug. Fit a spare spark plug that is known to be good into the cap and lay the plug against the cylinder head with the threads contacting it. If necessary, hold the spark plug with an insulated tool.

⚠ **Warning: Do not remove any of the spark plugs from the engine to perform this check – atomised fuel being pumped out of the open spark plug hole could ignite, causing severe injury! Make sure the plugs are securely held against the engine – if they are not earthed when the engine is turned over, the ignition control unit could be damaged.**

3 Check that the kill switch is in the 'RUN' position and the transmission is in neutral, then turn the ignition switch ON, and turn the engine over on the starter motor. If the system is in good condition a regular, fat blue spark should be evident at the plug electrodes. If the spark appears thin or yellowish, or is non-existent, further investigation will be necessary. Turn the ignition off and repeat the test for the other spark plugs.

4 The ignition system must be able to produce a spark which is capable of jumping a particular size gap – Yamaha specify 6 mm. Simple ignition spark gap testing tools are commercially available, some of which are adjustable to enable you to set the spark gap at exactly 6 mm – follow the manufacturer's instructions, and check each spark plug.

5 If the test results are good the entire ignition system can be considered good. If the spark appears thin or yellowish, or is non-existent, further investigation is necessary.

6 Ignition faults can be divided into two categories, namely those where the ignition system has failed completely, and those which are due to a partial failure. The likely faults are listed below, starting with the most probable source of failure. Work through the list systematically, referring to the subsequent sections for full details of the necessary checks and tests, and to the Wiring Diagrams at the end of Chapter 9. **Note:** *Before checking the following items ensure that the battery is fully charged and that all fuses are in good condition.*

- Loose, corroded or damaged wiring connections, broken or shorted wiring between any of the component parts of the ignition system (see Chapter 9).
- Faulty HT lead or spark plug cap, faulty spark plug, dirty, worn or corroded plug electrodes, or incorrect gap between electrodes.
- Faulty ignition (main) switch or engine kill switch (see Chapter 9).
- Faulty neutral, clutch or sidestand switch, or starter circuit cut-off relay (see Chapter 9 under relay assembly).
- Faulty pick-up coil or damaged trigger.
- Faulty tip-over sensor.
- Faulty ignition HT coil(s).
- Faulty ignition control unit (ICU).

7 If the above checks don't reveal the cause of the problem, have the ignition system tested by a Yamaha dealer.

3 Ignition HT coils

Check

1 Raise the fuel tank (see Chapter 4). The coil for cylinders 1 and 4 is mounted across the frame and the coil for cylinders 2 and 3 is mounted in line with it **(see illustration)**.

2 Disconnect the battery negative (–ve) lead (see Chapter 9).

3 The coils can be tested in situ. Check each coil visually for cracks and other damage.

4 To measure the primary circuit resistance disconnect the primary circuit electrical connectors from the coil, noting which fits where **(see illustration)**. Set the meter to the ohms x 1 scale and measure the resistance

3.1 Nos. 1 and 4 cylinders coil (A), Nos. 2 and 3 cylinders coil (B)

3.4a Disconnect the primary circuit connectors (arrowed) from the coil

Ignition system 5•3

3.4b To test the coil primary resistance, connect the multimeter leads between the primary circuit terminals

3.5 To test the coil secondary resistance, connect the multimeter leads between the spark plug lead ends

3.6 Measuring the resistance of the spark plug cap

between the terminals on the coil **(see illustration)**. If the reading obtained is not within the range shown in the Specifications, it is likely that the coil is defective.

5 To measure the secondary circuit resistance pull the caps off the spark plugs then unscrew the caps from the HT leads. Set the meter to the K-ohm scale. Connect one meter probe to one HT lead end and the other probe to the other lead end **(see illustration)**. If the reading obtained is not within the range shown in the Specifications, it is likely that the coil is defective.

6 If the reading is as specified, measure the resistance of the spark plug cap by connecting the meter probes between the HT lead socket and the spark plug contact **(see illustration)**. If the reading obtained is not as specified, replace the spark plug cap with a new ones.

7 If either coil is confirmed to be faulty, it must be replaced with a new one: the coils are sealed units and cannot therefore be repaired.

Removal

8 Remove the seat (see Chapter 8). Disconnect the battery negative (–ve) lead.
9 The coils are mounted under the fuel tank – raise or remove the tank for access (see Chapter 4). The coil for cylinders 1 and 4 is mounted across the frame and the coil for cylinders 2 and 3 is mounted in line with it **(see illustration 3.1)**.
10 Mark the locations of all wires and leads before disconnecting them. Note the routing

of the HT leads. Disconnect the primary circuit wiring connectors **(see illustration 3.4a)**. Pull the caps off the spark plugs.
11 Unscrew the two bolts securing the coil, noting the nut fitted with the front bolt on the coil for cylinders 2 and 3 **(see illustration)**. Remove the coils, releasing the cable-tie around the coil for cylinders 2 and 3. If required unscrew the caps from the HT leads – new coils may not come with caps fitted.

Installation

12 Installation is the reverse of removal. Make sure the wiring connectors and HT leads are securely connected.

4 Pick-up coil

Check

1 Remove the seat (see Chapter 8). Disconnect the battery negative (–ve) lead.
2 Remove the right-hand side panel (see Chapter 8).
3 Trace the wiring from the pick-up coil cover on the right-hand side of the engine and disconnect it at the 2-pin connector inside the boot **(see illustration)**. Using a multimeter set to the ohms x 100 scale, measure the resistance between the terminals on the pick-up coil side of the connector.

4 Compare the reading obtained with that given in the Specifications at the beginning of this Chapter. The pick-up coil must be replaced with a new one if the reading obtained differs greatly from that given, particularly if the meter indicates a short circuit (no measurable resistance) or an open circuit (infinite, or very high resistance).
5 If the pick-up coil is thought to be faulty, first check that it is not due to a damaged or broken wire from the coil to the connector: pinched or broken wires can usually be repaired.

Removal and installation

6 Remove the seat (see Chapter 8). Disconnect the battery negative (–ve) lead.
7 Remove the right-hand side panel (see Chapter 8).
8 Trace the wiring from the pick-up coil on the right-hand side of the engine and disconnect it at the 2-pin connector inside the boot **(see illustration 4.3)**. Feed the wiring back to the coil, noting its routing and releasing it from any clips or ties.
9 Unscrew the bolts securing the timing rotor/pick-up coil cover on the right-hand side of the engine and remove the cover, noting the wiring clamp **(see illustration)**. Discard the gasket, as a new one must be used. Remove the dowels from either the crankcase or the cover if they are loose.
10 Unscrew the bolts securing the pick-up coil, then free its wiring grommet from the

3.11 Note the nut fitted with the front bolt

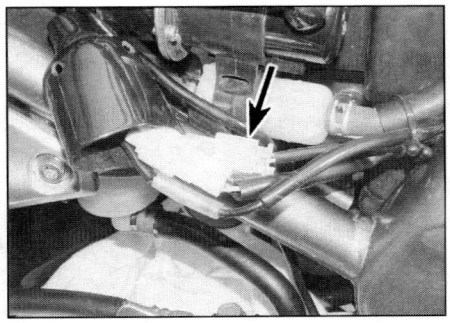

4.3 Disconnect the pick-up coil wiring connector (arrowed)

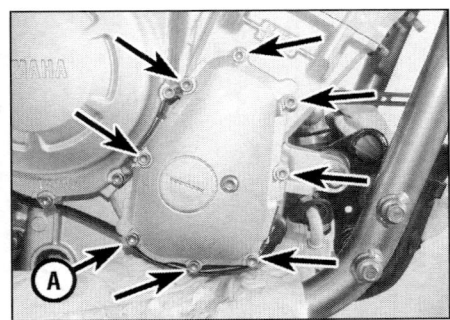

4.9 Unscrew the bolts (arrowed), noting the wiring clamp (A)

5•4 Ignition system

4.10a Unscrew the bolts and remove the pick-up coil . . .

4.10b . . . and free the wiring grommet

4.12a Fit the new gasket onto the dowels (arrowed) . . .

cutout and remove the coil from the engine **(see illustrations)**.

11 Smear some sealant onto the wiring grommet. Fit the coil onto the engine and the wiring grommet into its cutout. Apply a suitable non-permanent thread locking compound to the bolts and tighten them to the torque setting specified at the beginning of the chapter. Feed the wiring through to the connector, securing it with any clips or ties and making sure it is correctly routed, and reconnect it **(see illustration 4.3)**.

12 If removed, fit the timing rotor/pick-up coil cover dowels into the crankcase. Install the cover using a new gasket, making sure they locate correctly onto the dowels **(see illustration)**. Locate the cam chain tensioner blade pivot pin in the hole in the cover **(see illustration)**. Tighten the cover bolts to the torque setting specified at the beginning of the Chapter, not forgetting the wiring clamp **(see illustration 4.9)**.

13 Install the side panel (see Chapter 8). Reconnect the battery lead and install the seat.

5 Ignition control unit

Check

1 If the tests shown in the preceding or following Sections have failed to isolate the cause of an ignition fault, it is possible that the ignition control unit itself is faulty. No test details are available with which the unit can be tested. The best way to determine whether it is faulty is to substitute it with a known good one, if available. Otherwise, take the unit to a Yamaha dealer for assessment.

Removal

2 Remove the seat (see Chapter 8). Disconnect the battery negative (–ve) lead.
3 Disconnect the wiring connector from the ignition control unit **(see illustration)**.
4 Undo the screws securing the ignition control unit and remove the unit **(see illustration 5.3)**.

Installation

5 Installation is the reverse of removal. Make sure the wiring connector is securely connected.

6 Ignition timing

General information

1 Since no provision exists for adjusting the ignition timing and since no component is subject to mechanical wear, there is no need for regular checks: only if investigating a fault such as a loss of power or a misfire, should the ignition timing be checked.
2 The ignition timing is checked dynamically (engine running) using a stroboscopic lamp. The inexpensive neon lamps should be adequate in theory, but in practice may produce a pulse of such low intensity that the timing mark remains indistinct. If possible, one of the more precise xenon tube lamps should be used, powered by an external source of the appropriate voltage. **Note:** *Do not use the machine's own battery, as an incorrect reading may result from stray impulses within the machine's electrical system.*

Check

3 Warm the engine up to normal operating temperature, then stop it.
4 Unscrew the timing inspection bolt (the small bolt, not the large slotted plug) from the centre of the timing rotor/pick-up coil cover on the right-hand side of the engine **(see illustration 4.9)**.
5 The mark on the timing rotor which indicates the firing point at idle speed for the No. 1 cylinder is an 'H' mark on its side **(see illustration)**. The static timing marks with which this should align are the cutouts in the inspection hole.

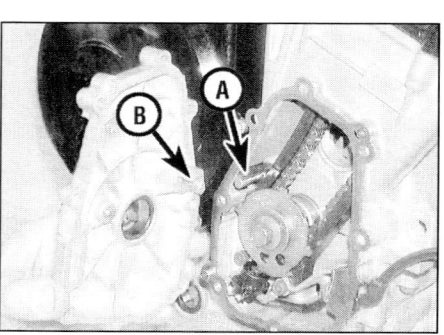

4.12b . . . then install the cover, locating the pin (A) in the hole (B)

5.3 Ignition control unit wiring connector (A) and mounting screws (B)

6.5 Timing mark

Ignition system 5•5

 HAYNES HiNT *The timing marks can be highlighted with a trace of white paint to make them more visible under the stroboscope light.*

6 Connect the timing light to the No. 1 cylinder HT lead as described in the manufacturer's instructions.

7 Start the engine and aim the light at the inspection hole.

8 With the machine idling at the specified speed, the static timing marks should point between the uprights of the 'H'.

9 Slowly increase the engine speed whilst observing the 'H' mark. The mark should move anti-clockwise, increasing in relation to the engine speed until it reaches full advance (no identification mark).

10 As already stated, there is no means of adjustment of the ignition timing on these machines. If the ignition timing is incorrect, or suspected of being incorrect, one of the ignition system components is at fault, and the system must be tested as described in the preceding Sections of this Chapter.

11 When the check is complete, install the timing inspection bolt, using a new sealing washer if the old one is damaged or deformed, and tighten it securely.

7 Throttle position sensor

1 The throttle position sensor (TPS) is mounted on the outside of the right-hand (No. 4) carburettor and is keyed to the throttle shaft. The sensor provides the ignition control unit with information on throttle position and rate of opening or closing.

2 When the ignition is first switched ON, or while the engine is running, the throttle position sensor performs its own self-diagnosis. If a fault occurs, the tachometer will be seen to display zero rpm for 3 seconds, then 3000 rpm for 2.5 seconds, then the actual engine speed for 3 seconds, whereupon it will repeat the cycle until the engine is switched off. Note that the motorcycle can be ridden even though a fault has been diagnosed, though a difference in performance will be noticed.

Check

3 The throttle sensor is mounted on the outside of the right-hand (No. 4) carburettor.

4 Raise the fuel tank (see Chapter 4). Make sure the ignition is switched OFF, then disconnect the sensor's wiring connector **(see illustration)**. Using an ohmmeter or multimeter set to the K-ohms range, measure the sensor maximum resistance by connecting the meter probes between the black/blue and blue wire terminals on the sensor. Now measure the resistance range by connecting the meter probes between the yellow and blue wire terminals on the sensor, and slowly opening the throttle from fully closed to fully open. If the readings obtained differ greatly from those specified at the beginning of the Chapter, replace the sensor with a new one. When checking the resistance range, it is more important that there is a smooth and constant change in the resistance as the throttle is opened, than that the figures themselves are exactly as specified. On 2003-on models turn the ignition ON, then check the input voltage to the sensor by inserting the positive probe of a voltmeter into the blue wire terminal on the connector (which must stay connected), and the negative probe to the black/blue wire terminal; it should be as specified at the beginning of the Chapter.

5 If the readings were as specified, remove the seat and disconnect the ignition control unit wiring connector. Using a multimeter set to resistance or a continuity tester, check for continuity between the terminals on the wiring loom side of the sensor wiring connector and the corresponding terminals on the ICU connector, referring to *Wiring Diagrams* at the end of Chapter 9. There should be continuity between each connected terminal. If not, this is probably due to a damaged or broken wire between the connectors: pinched or broken wires can usually be repaired. Also check the connectors for loose or corroded terminals, and check the sensor itself for cracks and other damage. If the wiring and connectors are good, check the adjustment of the sensor as described below.

6 If the sensor is suspected of being faulty, take it to a Yamaha dealer for further testing. If it is confirmed to be faulty, it must be replaced with a new one – the sensor is a sealed unit and cannot therefore be repaired.

Adjustment

7 Before adjusting the sensor, check the idle speed and carburettor synchronisation (see Chapter 1).

8 Raise the fuel tank (see Chapter 4).

9 On 2001 and 2002 models turn the ignition switch ON, then disconnect and reconnect the sensor wiring connector **(see illustration 7.4)**. This sets the tachometer to 'sensor adjustment mode'. Slacken the sensor Torx screws and rotate the sensor until the tachometer needle reads 5000 rpm **(see illustration)**. If the tachometer reads either 0 rpm or 10,000 rpm, the angle of the sensor is either too narrow or too wide. Adjust it as required until the reading is 5000 rpm, then tighten the screws evenly and a little at a time. If it cannot be adjusted to within the range, or if no reading is obtained, check it as described above. Start the engine or turn the ignition switch OFF to reset the tachometer mode.

10 On 2003-on models turn the ignition ON, then check the output voltage from the sensor by inserting the positive probe of a voltmeter into the yellow wire terminal on the connector (which must stay connected), and the negative probe to the black/blue wire terminal. It should be as specified at the beginning of the Chapter. If not, slacken the sensor Torx screws and rotate the sensor until

7.4 Disconnect the throttle position sensor wiring connector

7.9 Slacken the throttle position sensor screws (arrowed) and adjust as described

5•6 Ignition system

the reading is correct, then tighten the screws evenly and a little at a time, making sure the reading does not change. If it cannot be adjusted to within the range, or if no reading is obtained, check it as described above.

Removal and installation

11 Raise the fuel tank (see Chapter 4). The throttle sensor is mounted on the outside of the right-hand (no. 4) carburettor.
12 Disconnect the wiring connector and release it from its clip on the carburettor, then unscrew the sensor Torx screws and remove the sensor, noting how it fits **(see illustrations 7.4 and 7.9)**.
13 Install the sensor and lightly tighten the screws, then connect the wiring connector and adjust the sensor as described above until the correct reading is obtained. On completion, tighten the screws evenly and a little at a time.
14 Install the fuel tank (see Chapter 4).

8 Tip-over sensor

1 The tip-over sensor (TPS) is mounted under the seat **(see illustration)**. If the bike falls over it cuts off the ignition circuit to stop the engine.
2 When the ignition is first switched ON, or while the engine is running, the sensor performs its own self-diagnosis. If a fault

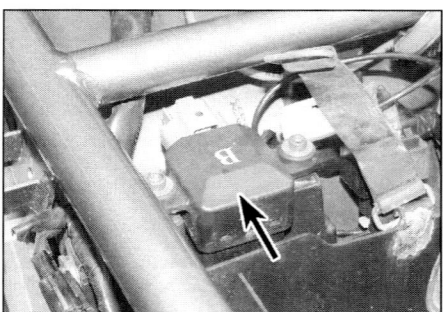

8.1 Tip over sensor (arrowed)

occurs, the tachometer will be seen to display zero rpm for 3 seconds, then 9000 rpm for 2.5 seconds, then the actual engine speed for 3 seconds, whereupon it will repeat the cycle until the engine is switched off. Note that the motorcycle can be ridden even though a fault has been diagnosed, though a difference in performance will be noticed.

Check

3 The tip-over sensor is mounted under the seat. No test details are provided for the sensor – the best way to determine whether it is faulty is to substitute it with one that is known to be good and see if the problem is solved.
4 Before doing that, remove the seat and using a multimeter set to measure resistance (ohms) or a continuity tester, check for continuity in the wiring to and from the sensor, referring to *Wiring Diagrams* at the end of

8.8 The arrow must point UP

Chapter 9 – pinched or broken wires can usually be repaired. Also check the connectors for loose or corroded terminals, and check the sensor itself for cracks and other damage. Using a voltmeter, also check that battery voltage is present at the red/white wire terminal with the ignition ON.
5 If the sensor is suspected of being faulty, take it to a Yamaha dealer for further testing. If it is confirmed to be faulty, it must be replaced with a new one – the sensor is a sealed unit and cannot therefore be repaired.

Removal and installation

6 Remove the seat (see Chapter 8).
7 Unscrew the sensor bolts, then displace the sensor and disconnect the wiring connector **(see illustration 8.1)**.
8 Installation is the reverse of removal – the sensor must be installed with the arrow pointing up **(see illustration)**.

Chapter 6
Frame, suspension and final drive

Contents

Drive chain removal and installation 16	Stand maintenance . . . . .see Chapter 1
Drive chain and sprocket check maintenance . . . . .see Chapter 1	Sidestand and centrestand removal and installation 4
Footrests, brake pedal and gearchange lever 3	Sidestand switch . . . . .see Chapter 9
Fork overhaul 8	Sprockets 17
Fork oil change 7	Steering head bearing maintenance . . . . .see Chapter 1
Fork removal and installation 6	Steering head bearing inspection 10
Frame inspection and repair 2	Steering stem and head bearings 9
General information 1	Suspension adjustments 13
Handlebar switches . . . . .see Chapter 9	Suspension check . . . . .see Chapter 1
Handlebars and levers 5	Swingarm bearings 15
Rear shock absorber 11	Swingarm removal and installation 14
Rear sprocket coupling/rubber dampers 18	Swingarm and suspension linkage maintenance . . . . . . .see Chapter 1
Rear suspension linkage 12	

Degrees of difficulty

Easy, suitable for novice with little experience	Fairly easy, suitable for beginner with some experience	Fairly difficult, suitable for competent DIY mechanic	Difficult, suitable for experienced DIY mechanic	Very difficult, suitable for expert DIY or professional

Specifications

Front forks
Fork oil type . . . . Yamaha suspension oil '01' or 5W fork oil
Fork oil capacity (per leg)
   Europe models
      2001 and 2002 models . . . . 440 cc
      2003-on models . . . . 435 cc
   US models . . . . 435 cc
Fork oil level* . . . . 140 mm
Fork spring free length . . . . 344 mm

*Oil level is measured from the top of the tube with the fork spring removed and the leg fully compressed.

Rear suspension
Shock absorber spring free length . . . . 182.5 mm
Shock absorber spring installed length . . . . 163 mm

Final drive

Chain type	DID 50VA8
No. of links	116 links
Chain freeplay and stretch limit	see Chapter 1

Torque wrench settings

Brake torque arm nuts	23 Nm
Footrest bolts (rider's)	55 Nm
Footrest bracket bolts (rider's)	30 Nm
Fork damper cartridge Allen bolts	35 Nm
Fork clamp bolts	
Top yoke	30 Nm
Bottom yoke	23 Nm
Fork top bolts	25 Nm
Front brake master cylinder clamp bolts	10 Nm
Front sprocket nut	85 Nm
Handlebar clamp bolts	23 Nm
Handlebar end-weights	26 Nm
Handlebar holder nuts	32 Nm
Rear shock absorber nuts	40 Nm
Rear suspension linkage nuts	
Linkage arm-to-frame	40 Nm
Linkage arm-to-shock absorber	40 Nm
Linkage arm-to-linkage rods	48 Nm
Linkage rods-to-swingarm	48 Nm
Steering head bearing adjuster nut using service tool	
Initial setting	52 Nm
Final setting	18 Nm
Steering stem nut	110 Nm
Swingarm pivot bolt nut	125 Nm
Rear sprocket nuts	69 Nm

1 General information

All models use a tubular steel cradle frame, with a removable right-hand cradle section.

Front suspension is by a pair of oil-damped telescopic forks, which use a cartridge-type damper. The forks are adjustable for spring pre-load and both rebound and compression damping.

At the rear, an aluminium alloy swingarm acts on a single shock absorber via a three-way linkage. The shock absorber is adjustable for spring pre-load and for both rebound and compression damping.

The drive to the rear wheel is by chain and sprockets.

2 Frame inspection and repair

1 The frame should not require attention unless accident damage has occurred. In most cases, a new frame is the only satisfactory remedy for such damage. A few frame specialists have the jigs and other equipment necessary for straightening the frame to the required standard of accuracy, but even then there is no simple way of assessing to what extent the frame may have been over-stressed.

2 After the machine has accumulated a lot of miles, examine the frame closely for signs of cracking or splitting at the welded joints. Loose engine mount bolts can cause ovaling or fracturing of the mounts themselves. Minor damage can often be repaired by welding, depending on the extent and nature of the damage, but this is a task for an expert.

3 Remember that a frame which is out of alignment will cause handling problems. If misalignment is suspected as the result of an accident, it will be necessary to strip the machine completely so that the frame can be thoroughly checked.

3 Footrests, brake pedal and gearchange lever

Brake pedal and rider's right-hand footrest

Removal

1 Remove the split pin and washer from the clevis pin securing the brake pedal to the master cylinder pushrod (see illustration). Remove the clevis pin and separate the pushrod from the pedal (see illustration). Unscrew the bolts securing the footrest bracket and displace it enough to provide

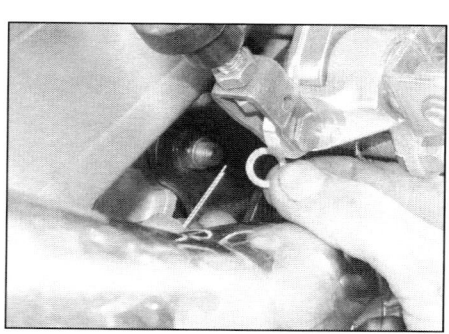

3.1a Remove the split pin and washer . . .

3.1b . . . and withdraw the clevis pin (B)

Frame, suspension and final drive 6•3

3.1c Unscrew the bolts (arrowed) and displace the bracket . . .

3.1d . . . then unhook the springs (A) from the lug and unscrew the footrest bolt (B)

3.3a Slacken the locknuts, then thread the rod off the lever and arm . . .

3.3b . . . and withdraw it from the frame

3.3c Unscrew the bolts (arrowed) and displace the bracket . . .

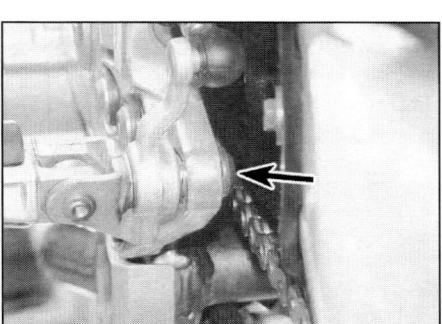

3.3d . . . then unscrew the bolt (arrowed) and remove the footrest and lever

access to the back (see illustration). Make sure no strain is placed on the brake switch wiring or brake hose. Unhook the pedal return spring and brake light switch spring from the lug on the pedal (see illustration). Unscrew the footrest bolt, then withdraw the footrest from the bracket and remove the pedal. Note the wave washer fitted between the pedal and the footrest bracket.

Installation

2 Installation is the reverse of removal. Apply grease to the brake pedal pivot. Use a new split pin on the clevis pin securing the brake pedal to the master cylinder pushrod. Tighten the footrest and footrest bracket bolts to the torque setting specified at the beginning of the Chapter. Check the rear brake pedal height and brake light switch setting (see Chapter 1, Section 9).

Gearchange lever and rider's left-hand footrest

Removal

3 Slacken the gearchange lever linkage rod locknuts, then unscrew the rod and separate it from the lever and the arm (the rod is reverse-threaded on one end, so will unscrew from both lever and arm simultaneously when turned in the one direction) (see illustration). Note how far the rod is threaded into the lever and arm, as this determines the height of the lever relative to the footrest. Withdraw the rod from the frame (see illustration). Unscrew the bolts securing the footrest bracket and displace it (see illustration). Unscrew the footrest bolt, then withdraw the footrest from the bracket and remove the lever (see illustration). Note the wave washer fitted between the lever and the footrest bracket.

Installation

4 Installation is the reverse of removal. Apply grease to the lever pivot. Tighten the footrest and footrest bracket bolts to the torque setting specified at the beginning of the Chapter. Slide the linkage rod into the frame and thread it onto the lever and arm (the rod is reverse-threaded on one end, so will screw onto both lever and arm simultaneously when turned in the one direction) (see illustration 3.3b). Set it as noted on removal to return to the same gearchange lever height, then tighten the locknuts securely (see illustration 3.3a).

Passenger footrests

5 Unscrew the nut from the bottom of the footrest pivot bolt, then withdraw the bolt and remove the footrest, noting the fitting of the detent plates, ball and spring – take care that they do not spring out when removing the footrest (see illustration). Also note the collar for the pivot bolt.
6 Installation is the reverse of removal.

4 Sidestand and centrestand removal and installation

Sidestand

Removal

1 The sidestand is bolted to the frame and held in either the retracted or extended positions by springs.
2 Place the bike on its centrestand. Unhook the sidestand springs (see illustration).

3.5 Unscrew the nut (A) then withdraw the bolt, noting the detent ball (B) and its spring

4.2 Unhook the springs (A) then unscrew the bolt (B)

6•4 Frame, suspension and final drive

4.7 Unhook the springs (A) then unscrew the nuts (B) and remove the bolts

5.2 Clutch switch (A), clutch lever bracket clamp bolt (B)

5.7a Remove the blanking caps . . .

3 Unscrew the pivot bolt and remove the washer and spring hook piece, then slide the sidestand off the pivot **(see illustration 4.2)**.

Installation

4 Installation is the reverse of removal. Apply grease to the pivot. Make sure the spring hook piece is correctly fitted.

5 Reconnect the springs and check that they hold the stand securely up when not in use – an accident is almost certain to occur if the stand extends while the machine is in motion **(see illustration 4.2)**. Make sure the stand locates against the sidestand switch plunger and actuates it correctly.

Centrestand

Removal

6 The centrestand is bolted to brackets on the frame and held in either the retracted or extended positions by springs.

7 Support the bike on its sidestand. Unhook the centrestand springs **(see illustration)**.

8 Unscrew the nut from each pivot bolt, then withdraw the bolts and remove the centrestand **(see illustration 4.7)**.

Installation

9 Installation is the reverse of removal. Apply grease to the pivot bolt shanks.

10 Reconnect the springs and check that they hold the stand securely up when not in use – an accident is almost certain to occur if the stand extends while the machine is in motion **(see illustration 4.7)**.

5 Handlebars and levers

Handlebar removal

Note: *If required, the handlebars can be displaced from the top yoke without having to remove the individual assemblies from them (see Step 7). If you do this, cover the instrument cluster with some rag and lay the handlebar assembly on it.*

1 Displace the front brake master (see Chapter 7).

2 Disconnect the wiring connector from the clutch switch **(see illustration)**. Remove the

5.7b . . . then unscrew the clamp bolts (arrowed)

clutch lever (see Step 10). Align the slot in the cable adjuster with that in the bracket and slip the cable out. Slacken the clutch lever bracket clamp bolt.

3 Refer to Chapter 4, Sections 10 and 11, and detach the throttle cables from the twistgrip and the choke cable from the lever. The procedures incorporate detaching the handlebar switch housings. Create slack in the throttle cables using the adjusters (see Chapter 1). If you can't get enough slack you can either leave the cables attached and slip the handlebar out of the pulley and grip after the clamps have been removed, or slip the cables out of the bracket on the carburettor, leaving them attached to the cam.

4 Unscrew the handlebar end-weight weight from the right-hand end of the handlebar and, if the cables have been detached, slide the throttle twistgrip off the end.

5 Unscrew the handlebar end-weight weight from the left-hand end of the handlebar and remove the grip. If the grip has been glued on, you will probably have to slit it with a knife to remove it. Slide the clutch lever bracket off the handlebar.

6 If the handlebar holders are being removed from the top yoke, slacken the nuts securing them on the underside of the yoke now.

7 Carefully prise the blanking caps out of the handlebar clamp bolts **(see illustration)**. Note how the punch mark on the handlebar aligns with the top mating surface of the holder. Support the handlebars, then unscrew the bolts and remove the clamps and the handlebars, noting the arrow on each clamp which points to the front **(see illustration)**. If

5.7c The handlebars can be displaced forwards and laid on some rag

you are just displacing the bars for top yoke removal, lay them on some protective rag across the instrument cluster **(see illustration)**.

8 If required, unscrew the nuts on the handlebar holder bolts, then draw the holders out of the top yoke, noting the washers and dampers.

Handlebar installation

9 Installation is the reverse of removal, noting the following.
● If removed, tighten the handlebar holder nuts after the handlebars are installed, and tighten them to the torque setting specified at the beginning of the Chapter.
● Fit the left-hand clamp first, with the arrow pointing to the front, then align the punch mark on the back of the handlebar with the mating surface of the left-hand holder **(see illustration)**. Make sure the handlebars are

5.9 Align the punch mark (arrowed) with the holder mating surface

Frame, suspension and final drive 6•5

5.10a Thread the adjuster in

5.10b Unscrew the nut (A) and remove the pivot screw (B)

5.12a Unscrew the nut . . .

5.12b . . . then unscrew the pivot . . .

5.12c . . . and remove the lever

bracket, and to the clutch cable nipple. Adjust the clutch cable freeplay (see Chapter 1).

Front brake lever

12 Unscrew the lever pivot bolt locknut, then unscrew the pivot bolt and remove the lever **(see illustrations)**.

13 Installation is the reverse of removal. Apply grease to the pivot bolt shaft and the contact areas between the lever and its bracket.

6 Fork removal and installation

Removal

1 Remove the front wheel (see Chapter 7). Tie the front brake calipers and hoses back so that they are out of the way.
2 Remove the front mudguard (see Chapter 8).
3 Measure and note the amount of protrusion (if any) of the fork tube above the top surface of the top yoke – measure up to the top rim of the tube itself, do not include the top bolt.
4 Working on one fork at a time, slacken the fork clamp bolt in the top yoke **(see illustration)**. If the fork is to be disassembled or if the fork oil is being changed, slacken the fork top bolt now while the fork is held by the bottom yoke **(see illustration 7.3)**.
5 Slacken the fork clamp bolts in the bottom yoke, and remove each fork by twisting it and pulling it downwards **(see illustrations)**.

central in the clamps – the roughened surface can be used to align them.
● Fit the right-hand clamp with the arrow pointing forwards, then tighten the front clamp bolts first, then the rear bolts, so that the gap between holders and clamps is at the back, and tighten them to the specified torque setting.
● Apply some grease to the throttle twistgrip section of the handlebar.
● Make sure the front brake master cylinder assembly clamp is installed with the UP mark facing up. Align the top mating surfaces of the clamp with the punch mark on the top of the handlebar, then tighten the top bolt first, then the bottom bolt, to the specified torque setting.
● Align the clutch lever bracket slit with the punch mark on the underside of the handlebar.
● Make sure the pin in each switch housing locates in its hole in the handlebar.

● Tighten the handlebar end-weights to the specified torque setting. If new grips are being fitted, secure them using a suitable adhesive.
● Do not forget to reconnect the front brake light switch and clutch switch wiring connectors.
● Check and adjust the throttle, choke and clutch lever freeplay (see Chapter 1).

Clutch lever

10 Thread the clutch cable adjuster fully into the bracket to provide maximum freeplay in the cable **(see illustration)**. Unscrew the lever pivot nut, then remove the pivot bolt shaft and slip the lever out, detaching the cable nipple as you do **(see illustration)**. Note the collar in the lever pivot bore.
11 Installation is the reverse of removal. Apply grease to the pivot bolt shaft and the contact areas between the lever and its

6.4 Slacken the clamp bolt (arrowed) in the top yoke

6.5a Slacken the clamp bolts (arrowed) in the bottom yoke . . .

6.5b . . . . then draw the fork down and out of the yokes – twisting it as you go eases removal

HAYNES HiNT *If the fork legs are seized in the yokes, spray the area with penetrating oil and allow time for it to soak in before trying again.*

Installation

6 Remove all traces of corrosion from the fork tube and the yokes. Slide the fork up through the bottom yoke and into the top yoke, making sure all cables, hoses and wiring are routed on the correct side of the fork **(see illustration 6.5b)**.

7 Set the amount of protrusion of the top of the fork tube (not the top of the fork top bolt) above the top yoke as noted on removal. Make sure it is the same on both sides. Yamaha state that the top of each fork tube must be flush with the upper surface of the top yoke.

8 Tighten the fork clamp bolts in the bottom yoke to the torque setting specified at the beginning of the Chapter **(see illustration 6.5a)**.

9 If the fork has been dismantled or if the fork oil was changed, and if not already done, tighten the fork top bolt to the specified torque setting – note that to apply a torque wrench it is necessary to displace the handlebars (see Section 5), so alternatively tighten the bolt securely using a ring spanner.

10 Tighten the fork clamp bolts in the top yoke to the specified torque **(see illustration 6.4)**.

11 Install the front mudguard (see Chapter 8), and the front wheel (see Chapter 7).

12 Check the operation of the front forks and brakes before taking the machine out on the road.

7 Fork oil change

1 Remove the forks (see Section 6). Always work on the fork legs separately to avoid interchanging parts and thus causing an accelerated rate of wear **(see illustration 8.1)**.

2 Note the current spring pre-load adjuster setting, then reset the adjuster to its minimum setting (see Section 13).

3 Unscrew the fork top bolt from the top of the fork tube **(see illustration)**. The bolt will remain threaded on the damper cartridge rod.

4 Using two spanners, one on the locknut and one on the pre-load adjuster flats, counter-hold the locknut and release the adjuster from it **(see illustration)**. Now hold the rod and thread the top bolt assembly off **(see illustration)**.

5 Withdraw the damping adjuster rod **(see illustration)**. Measure and note the position of the locknut on the damper rod threads, then unscrew the locknut **(see illustration)**. Remove the spacer and the washer **(see illustration)**. Withdraw the fork spring **(see illustration)**.

7.3 Unscrew the top bolt from the fork tube

7.4a Counter-hold the locknut and unscrew the pre-load adjuster . . .

7.4b . . . then thread the top bolt assembly off the rod

7.5a Withdraw the adjuster rod from inside the damper rod

7.5b Note the position of the locknut on the rod . . .

7.5c . . . then unscrew it . . .

7.5d . . . and remove the spacer . . .

7.5e . . . the washer . . .

7.5f . . . and the spring

Frame, suspension and final drive 6•7

7.6 Pump all the oil out of the fork as described

7.7a Pour in the specified quantity of the correct oil . . .

7.7b . . . and measure the oil level as described

6 Invert the fork over a suitable container and pump the fork tube and damper rod to expel as much oil as possible **(see illustration)**. Support the fork upside down in the container for a while to allow as much oil as possible to drain, and pump the fork and rod again.

7 Slowly pour in the specified quantity of the specified grade of fork oil, then pump the damper rod and fork tube slowly at least ten times to distribute it evenly – pump the damper rod through all its travel, but do not pump the tube over more than 150 mm or air can be drawn in **(see illustration)**. Allow the oil to settle and any air bubbles to disperse for about ten minutes with the fork supported upright. Fully compress the fork tube into the slider and measure the oil level, and make any adjustment by adding more or tipping some out until the oil is at the level specified at the beginning of the Chapter **(see illustration)**.

8 Pull the fork tube out of the slider as far as possible then install the spring with its closer-wound coils at the bottom **(see illustration 7.5f)**. Fit the spring and the spacer **(see illustrations 7.5e and d)**.

9 Thread the locknut onto the damper rod and set it at the position noted on removal **(see illustration 7.5c)**. Insert the damping adjuster rod **(see illustration 7.5a)**.

10 Check the condition of the top bolt O-ring and replace it with a new one if necessary. Smear the O-ring with fork oil. Thread the top bolt assembly onto the rod and against the locknut **(see illustration 7.4b)**. Counter-hold the locknut and tighten the pre-load adjuster tightly against it **(see illustration 7.4a)**.

11 Extend the fork tube and screw the top bolt into it, making sure it is not cross-threaded **(see illustration)**. Note: *The top bolt can be tightened to the specified torque setting at this stage if the tube is held between the padded jaws of a vice, but do not risk distorting the tube by doing so. A better method is to tighten the top bolt when the fork has been installed in the bike and is securely held in the bottom yoke.*

> **TOOL TIP** *Use a ratchet-type tool when installing the fork top bolt. This makes it unnecessary to remove the tool from the bolt whilst threading it in making it easier to maintain a downward pressure on the spring.*

12 Install the forks (see Section 6). Reset the spring pre-load adjuster to the original setting (see Section 13).

8 Fork overhaul

Disassembly

1 Remove the forks (see Section 6). Always work on each fork separately to avoid interchanging parts and thus causing an accelerated rate of wear **(see illustration 8.1)**.
2 Slacken the damper cartridge Allen bolt in the base of the fork slider **(see illustration)**. If

7.11 Thread the top bolt into the fork tube

1 Top bolt assembly
2 O-ring
3 Locknut
4 Spacer
5 Washer
6 Damping adjuster rod
7 Spring
8 Damper rod bolt
9 Sealing washer
10 Damper cartridge
11 Dust seal
12 Retaining clip
13 Fork tube and bottom bush
14 Oil seal
15 Washer
16 Top bush
17 Damper cartridge seat

8.1 Front fork components

6•8 Frame, suspension and final drive

8.2 Slacken the damper cartridge Allen bolt

8.4a Unscrew and remove the damper cartridge bolt . . .

8.4b . . . then withdraw the damper cartridge from the fork

an assistant is not available to hold the fork, clamp the brake caliper lugs between the padded jaws of a vice. If the bolt won't undo (usually because the damper cartridge turns with it), use an air wrench if available, or wait until the spring has been removed, then use a holding tool to prevent the damper cartridge turning with the bolt.
3 Set the spring pre-load adjuster to its minimum setting (see Section 13). Refer to Section 7, Steps 3 to 6, and drain the fork oil.
4 Remove the previously slackened damper cartridge bolt and its copper sealing washer from the bottom of the slider **(see illustration)**. Discard the sealing washer as a new one must be used on reassembly. Withdraw the damper cartridge from the top of the tube **(see illustration)**. If the damper cartridge bolt could not be slackened as described in Step 2, obtain the Yamaha service tool (pt no. 90890-01447 Europe models or YM-01447 US models) to pass down through the fork inner tube and engage the head of the cartridge whilst the bolt is slackened.
5 Carefully prise out the dust seal from the top of the slider to gain access to the oil seal retaining clip. Discard the dust seal as a new one must be used.
6 Carefully remove the retaining clip, taking care not to scratch the surface of the tube **(see illustration)**.
7 To separate the tube from the slider it is necessary to displace the oil seal and top bush. The bottom bush does not pass through the top bush, and this can be used to good effect. Push the tube gently inwards until it stops against the damper seat. Take care not to do this forcibly or the seat may be damaged. Now pull the tube sharply outwards until the bottom bush strikes the top bush **(see illustration)**. Repeat this operation until the top bush and seal are tapped out of the slider.
8 With the tube removed, slide off the oil seal, washer and top bush, noting which way up they fit **(see illustration)**. Discard the oil seal as a new one must be used.
Caution: Do not remove the bottom bush from the tube unless it is to be replaced.
9 Tip the damper rod seat out of the slider – you may have to push it from the bottom via the damper bolt hole.

Inspection

10 Clean all parts in solvent and blow them dry with compressed air, if available. Check the inner tube for score marks, scratches, flaking of the chrome finish and excessive or abnormal wear. Replace the inner tubes in both forks with new ones if any dents are found. Check the fork seal seat in the bottom of the tube for nicks, gouges and scratches. If damage is evident, leaks will occur. Also check the oil seal washer for damage or distortion, and replace it with a new one if necessary.
11 Check the fork tube for run-out (bending) using V-blocks and a dial gauge, or have it done by a Yamaha dealer or suspension specialist. Yamaha do not specify a run-out limit, but if the tube is bent beyond the generally accepted limit of 0.2 mm seek the advice of a suspension specialist.

> ⚠ **Warning: If the tube is bent, it should not be straightened; replace it with a new one.**

12 Check the spring for cracks and other damage. Measure the spring free length and compare the measurement to the specifications at the beginning of the Chapter **(see illustration)**. If it is defective or sagged below the service limit, replace the springs in both forks with new ones. Never replace only one spring.
13 Examine the working (sliding) surfaces of the two bushes; if worn or scuffed they must be replaced with new ones – they are worn if the grey Teflon coating has rubbed off to

8.6 Prise off the dust seal then lever out the retaining clip using a flat bladed screwdriver (arrow)

8.7 Slide the inner and outer tubes apart as described

8.8 Remove the oil seal (A), washer (B) and top bush (C)

8.12 Measure the spring free length

Frame, suspension and final drive 6•9

8.13 Prise the bush apart to release it from its seat

8.15 Fit the seat onto the bottom of the protruding damper cartridge

8.16a Slide the inner tube into the outer tube

reveal the copper surface. To remove the bottom bush from the fork tube, prise it apart at the slit using a flat-bladed screwdriver and slide it off **(see illustration)**. Make sure the new one seats properly. Note that Yamaha recommend using new bushes during a fork rebuild, whatever the condition of the old ones.

14 Check the damper cartridge assembly for damage and wear, and replace it with a new one if necessary. Holding the outside of the damper, pump the rod in and out. If the rod does not move smoothly in the damper, it must be replaced with a new one. Check that the damping adjuster rod is straight.

Reassembly

15 Insert the damper cartridge into the top of the fork tube and slide it down so that it projects fully from the bottom of the tube **(see illustration 8.4b)**. Fit the damper rod seat onto the bottom of the cartridge so that its bevelled edges faces downwards, then push them both up into the bottom of the tube **(see illustration)**.

16 Oil the fork tube and bottom bush with the specified fork oil and insert the assembly into the slider **(see illustration)**. Fit a new copper sealing washer onto the damper cartridge bolt and apply a few drops of a suitable non-permanent thread locking compound, then insert the bolt into the bottom of the slider and thread it into the cartridge **(see illustration)**. Tighten the bolt to the specified torque setting. If the damper cartridge rotates inside

the tube, wait until the fork is fully reassembled before tightening the bolt.

17 Push the fork tube fully into the slider, then oil the top bush and slide it down over the tube **(see illustration)**. Press the bush squarely into its recess in the slider as far as possible, then install the oil seal washer **(see illustration)**. Use either the Yamaha service tool (Pt. Nos. 90890-01367 and 90890-01374), or a suitable piece of plastic tubing to tap the bush fully into place; the tubing must be slightly larger in diameter than the fork tube and slightly smaller in diameter than the bush recess in the slider. Take care not to scratch the fork tube during this operation; if using a piece of metal tubing wind insulating tape around the exposed length of tube, and push the fork tube fully into the slider so that any accidental scratching is confined to the

8.16b Apply a threadlock to the bolt threads and fit a new washer

area above the oil seal. A drift or punch can be used, but this does not help the bush enter squarely, and the angle narrows as the bush gets deeper and makes it more difficult to make a good contact with a hammer **(see illustration)**. If using a drift or punch, wrap tape around it to prevent it scratching the tube.

18 Remove the washer to check the bush is seated fully and squarely in its recess in the slider, then wipe the recess clean and refit the washer.

19 Smear the new oil seal's lips with fork oil and slide it over the tube so that its markings face upwards **(see illustration)**. Press the seal into the slider, then drive it fully into place as described in Step 17 until the retaining clip groove is visible above it.

20 Once the seal is correctly seated, fit the

8.17a Fit the top bush . . .

8.17b . . . then slide the washer onto it . . .

8.17c . . . and drive it in as described

8.19 Drive the oil seal into place . . .

6•10 Frame, suspension and final drive

8.20 ... then fit the retaining clip into its groove ...

8.21 ... and press in the dust seal

9.3 Displace the hose splitter and remove the horn bracket

retaining clip, making sure it is correctly located in its groove **(see illustration)**.
21 Lubricate the lips of the new dust seal then slide it down the fork tube and press it into position **(see illustrations)**.
22 Refer to Section 7, Steps 7 to 11, and refill the fork with oil.
23 If necessary now tighten the damper cartridge bolt to the specified torque setting **(see illustration 8.2)**.
24 Install the forks (see Section 6). Reset the amount of spring pre-load (see Section 13).

9 Steering stem and head bearings

Removal
1 Remove the fairing and the fuel tank (see

Chapters 8 and 4). This will prevent the possibility of damage should a tool slip.
2 Remove the horn (see Chapter 9).
3 Unscrew the bolts securing the front brake hose splitter and horn bracket to the bottom yoke **(see illustration)**.
4 Unscrew the bolt securing the brake hose guide to the top yoke **(see illustration)**.
5 Remove the front forks (see Section 6).
6 Displace the handlebars and lay them on some rag across the frame, behind the steering head (see Section 5).
7 Unscrew the steering stem nut and remove the washer – the washer sits in a recess in the yoke and needs to be eased out with a small screwdriver or a magnet, or alternatively tip it out of the yoke after it has been lifted off **(see illustration)**.
8 Ease the top yoke up and off the steering stem and position it clear, using a rag

to protect other components **(see illustration)** – if you need to remove it completely disconnect the ignition switch wiring connector and free the wiring from any ties, noting its routing.
9 Remove the tabbed lockwasher, noting how it fits **(see illustration)**. Unscrew and remove the locknut, if required using either a C-spanner, a peg spanner or a drift located in one of the notches (though it should only be finger-tight), and remove the rubber washer **(see illustration)**.
10 Supporting the bottom yoke, unscrew the adjuster nut using either a C-spanner, a peg-spanner or a drift located in one of the notches, then remove the bearing cover and the inner race from the steering stem **(see illustrations)**.
11 Gently lower the bottom yoke and steering stem out of the frame **(see**

9.4 Unscrew the bolt (arrowed) and displace the guide

9.7 Unscrew the steering stem nut and remove the washer ...

9.8 ... then lift the yoke up off the steering stem

9.9a Remove the lockwasher ...

9.9b ... the locknut and the rubber washer

9.10a Unscrew the adjuster nut ...

Frame, suspension and final drive 6•11

9.10b ... then remove the bearing cover ...

9.10c ... and the inner race

9.11 Gently lower the steering stem out of the frame

illustration). Take care not to strain or knock the brake hoses.

12 Remove the bearing from the top of the steering head **(see illustration)**. Remove the rubber washer from half-way up the steering stem and the bearing and seal from the base **(see illustration 9.14)**.

13 Clean off all traces of old grease from the bearings and races and check them for wear or damage as described in Section 10. *Note: Do not attempt to remove the races from the steering head or the steering stem unless they are to be replaced with new ones.*

Installation

14 Smear a liberal quantity of multi-purpose grease onto the bearing races, and work some grease well into both the upper and lower bearings. Also smear the grease seal lip, using a new seal if necessary. Fit the seal and lower bearing onto the base of the steering stem **(see illustration)**. Fit the rubber washer onto its ledge on the stem.

15 Carefully lift the steering stem/bottom yoke up through the steering head **(see illustration 9.11)**. Fit the upper bearing and the inner race into the top of the steering head, then fit the bearing cover **(see illustrations 9.10c and b)**. Thread the adjuster nut onto the steering stem and tighten it finger-tight **(see illustration 9.10a)**.

16 If the Yamaha special service tool (Pt. No. 90890-01403 for Europe models, or YU-33975 for US models) and a torque wrench are available tighten the adjuster nut to the initial torque setting specified at the beginning of the Chapter with the torque

wrench set at 90° to the centreline of the tool as shown **(see illustration)**. Now slacken the nut so that it is loose, then tighten it to the final torque setting specified. Check that the steering is still able to move freely from side to side, but that all freeplay is eliminated.

17 If the Yamaha tool is not available, using either a C-spanner, a peg spanner or a drift located in one of the notches, tighten the adjuster nut until all freeplay is removed, then tighten it a little more **(see illustration)**. This pre-loads the bearings. Now slacken the nut, then tighten it again until all freeplay is removed, yet the steering is able to move freely. The object is to set the adjuster nut so that the bearings are under a very light loading, just enough to remove any freeplay, but not so much that the steering does not move freely from side to side as described in the checking procedure in Chapter 1.

Caution: Take great care not to over-tighten the bearings as this will cause premature failure.

18 Now install all remaining components except the top yoke and handlebars, fuel tank and fairing. Re-check and finely adjust the amount of freeplay as described in Chapter 1.

19 When the bearings are correctly adjusted install the rubber washer and the locknut **(see illustration 9.9)**. Tighten the locknut finger-tight, then tighten it further until its notches align with those in the adjuster nut, but make sure it is not so tight that the rubber washer starts to be squeezed out the side. Install the tabbed lockwasher so that the tabs fit into the notches in both the locknut and adjuster nut **(see illustration 9.9a)**.

20 Fit the top yoke onto the steering stem **(see illustration 9.8)**, then install the washer and steering stem nut and tighten it to the torque setting specified at the beginning of the Chapter **(see illustration 9.7)**.

21 Install the remaining components in a reverse of the removal procedure.

22 Carry out a final check of the steering head bearing freeplay as described in Chapter 1, and if necessary re-adjust.

10 Steering head bearing inspection

Inspection

1 Remove the steering stem (see Section 9).
2 Remove all traces of old grease from the bearings and races and check them for wear or damage.

9.12 Remove the upper bearing

9.14 Fit the dust seal (A), the lower bearing (B) and the rubber washer (C)

9.16 Make sure the torque wrench arm is at 90° to the tool as shown

9.17 If the tool is not available, adjust the bearings as described

6•12 Frame, suspension and final drive

10.4 Drive the races out with a brass drift, locating it as shown

3 The inner and outer races should be polished and free from indentations. Inspect the bearing balls for signs of wear, damage or discoloration, and examine the ball retainer cage for signs of cracks or splits. If there are any signs of wear on any of the above components both upper and lower bearing assemblies must be replaced with new ones as a set. Only remove the outer races in the steering head and the lower bearing inner race on the steering stem if new ones are needed – do not re-use them once they have been removed.

Removal and installation

4 The outer races are an interference fit in the steering head and can be tapped from position with a suitable drift **(see illustration)**. Tap firmly and evenly around each race to ensure that it is driven out squarely. It may

10.7a Remove the lower bearing inner race as described . . .

10.7b . . . you may have to use a puller

10.6 Drawbolt arrangement for fitting steering stem bearing races

1 Long bolt or threaded bar
2 Thick washer
3 Guide for lower race

prove advantageous to curve the end of the drift slightly to improve access.
5 Alternatively, the races can be removed using a slide-hammer type bearing extractor; these can often be hired from tool shops.
6 The new outer races can be pressed into the head using a drawbolt arrangement **(see illustration)**, or by using a large diameter tubular drift. Ensure that the drawbolt washer or drift (as applicable) bears only on the outer edge of the race and does not contact the working surface. Alternatively, have the races installed by a Yamaha dealer equipped with the bearing race installation tools.

 HAYNES HiNT *Installation of new bearing outer races is made much easier if the races are left overnight in the freezer. This causes them to contract slightly making them a looser fit. Alternatively, use a freeze spray.*

7 The lower bearing inner race should only be removed from the steering stem if a new one

10.9 Drive the new race on, using a suitable driver or a length of pipe or tubing

is being fitted. To remove the race, use two screwdrivers placed on opposite sides to work it free, using blocks of wood to improve leverage and protect the yoke, or tap under it using a cold chisel **(see illustration)**. If the steering stem is placed on its side on a hard surface, thread a suitable nut onto the top to prevent the threads being damaged. If the race is firmly in place it will be necessary to use a puller **(see illustration)**. Take the steering stem to a Yamaha dealer if required.
8 Remove the seal from the bottom of the stem and replace it with a new one. Smear the new one with grease.
9 Fit the new lower race onto the steering stem. A length of tubing with an internal diameter slightly larger than the steering stem will be needed to tap the new race into position – make sure the drift contacts the inner rim of the race only and not the bearing sliding surface **(see illustration)**.
10 Install the steering stem (see Section 9).

11 Rear shock absorber

 Warning: Do not attempt to disassemble this shock absorber. It is nitrogen-charged under high pressure. Improper disassembly could result in serious injury. Instead, take the shock to a Yamaha dealer or suspension specialist to do the job.

Removal

1 Support the motorcycle on its centrestand. Place a support under the rear wheel or swingarm so that it does not drop when the shock absorber is removed, but also making sure that the weight of the machine is off the rear suspension so that the shock is not compressed. Make a note of which side the bolts go in from, and which way round the shock absorber fits.
2 Remove the side panels (see Chapter 8). If you plan to remove the suspension linkage, do so first (see Section 11), then ignore Steps 3 and 4 of this section.
3 Unscrew the nut, remove the washer and withdraw the bolt securing the linkage rods to the swingarm **(see illustration)**.

11.3 Unscrew the nut and withdraw the bolt securing the rods to the swingarm

Frame, suspension and final drive 6•13

11.5a Withdraw the bolt (arrowed), noting how the head locates . . .

11.5b . . . and lower the shock out of the frame

11.7 Look for cracks, pitting and oil leakage on the damper rod (arrowed)

11.8 Check the upper mounting bush (arrowed) for wear

4 Unscrew the nut and withdraw the bolt securing the bottom of the shock absorber to the linkage arm, then swing the rods and the arm down to provide clearance for the shock **(see illustration 12.3)**.
5 Unscrew the nut on the shock absorber upper mounting bolt, using a universal socket drive and extension bar if available, and remove the washer. Support the shock absorber and withdraw the bolt, noting how the flats on its head are held by two plates **(see illustration)**. Lower the shock out of the frame **(see illustration)**.

Inspection

6 Inspect the shock absorber for obvious physical damage and the coil spring for looseness, cracks or signs of fatigue.
7 Inspect the damper rod for signs of bending, pitting and oil leakage **(see illustration)**.
8 Check the condition of the bush in the upper mounting and replace it with a new one if it is worn or deteriorated – refer to Tools and Workshop tips for details on how to remove and install the bush using a drawbolt or press **(see illustration)**.
9 Check the reservoir for damage, cracks or leakage.
10 Apart from the bush individual components are not available for the shock absorber. If it is worn or damaged, it must be replaced with a new one.

Installation

11 Installation is the reverse of removal. Apply molybdenum lithium-based grease to the shock absorber and linkage pivot points. Make sure the head of the shock absorber upper bolt locates correctly between the plates on the bracket **(see illustration 11.5b)**. Tighten the shock absorber bottom nut before fitting the linkage rods onto the swingarm as the rods obscure the nut. Tighten the nuts to the torque settings specified at the beginning of the Chapter.

12 Rear suspension linkage

Removal

1 Support the motorcycle on its centrestand. Place a support under the rear wheel or swingarm so that it does not drop when the shock absorber is removed, but also making sure that the weight of the machine is off the rear suspension so that the shock is not compressed. Make a note of which side the bolts go in from.
2 Unscrew the nut, remove the washer and withdraw the bolt securing the linkage rods to the swingarm **(see illustration 11.3)**. Unscrew the nut, remove the washer and withdraw the bolt securing the linkage rods to the linkage arm and remove the rods **(see illustration)**
3 Unscrew the nut, remove the washer and withdraw the bolt securing the linkage arm to the shock absorber **(see illustration)**.
4 Unscrew the nut, remove the washer and withdraw the bolt securing the linkage arm to the frame and remove the linkage arm, noting which way round it fits **(see illustration)**.

12.2 Unscrew the nut and withdraw the bolt securing the rods to the arm and remove the rods

12.3 Detach the linkage arm from the shock absorber . . .

12.4 . . . and the frame and remove it

6•14 Frame, suspension and final drive

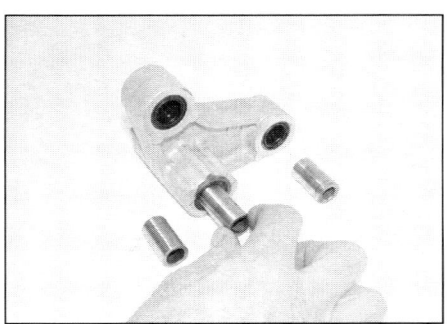

12.5a Remove the spacers from the linkage arm . . .

12.5b . . . and the swingarm . . .

12.5c . . . and lever out the grease seals

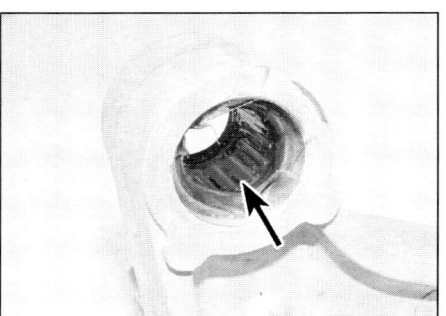

12.7 Check the needle bearings in the linkage arm and swingarm (arrow)

12.10 Press the new seals into place

Inspection

5 Withdraw the spacers from the linkage arm and swingarm, noting their different sizes **(see illustrations)**. Lever the grease seals out and discard them as new ones must be used **(see illustration)**. Thoroughly clean all components.

6 Inspect all components closely, looking for obvious signs of wear such as heavy scoring, or for damage such as cracks or distortion, and for corrosion that affects the action of the bearings. Slip each spacer back into its bearing and check that there is not an excessive amount of freeplay between the two components, and that they can rotate smoothly and freely. Replace corroded, worn or damaged components with new ones as required.

7 Check the condition of the needle roller bearings in the linkage arm and swingarm **(see illustration)**. Refer to *Tools and Workshop Tips* (Section 5) in the *Reference* section for more information on bearings.

8 Worn or corroded bearings can be drifted out of their bores, but note that removal will destroy them; new bearings should be obtained before work commences. The new bearings should be pressed or drawn into their bores rather than driven into position. In the absence of a press, a suitable drawbolt tool can be made up as described in *Tools and Workshop Tips* (Section 5) in the *Reference* section.

9 Lubricate the needle roller bearings and the spacers with lithium-based grease and install the spacers **(see illustrations 12.7 and 5a)**.

10 Pres the new grease seals squarely into place **(see illustration)**.

Installation

11 Installation is the reverse of removal. Apply lithium-based grease to the pivot points. Tighten the shock absorber bottom nut before fitting the linkage rods onto the swingarm as the rods obscure the nut. Tighten the nuts to the torque settings specified at the beginning of the Chapter.

13 Suspension adjustments

Note: *Refer to the Owner's Handbook supplied with the machine for recommended front and rear suspension settings to suit loading.*

Front forks

1 The front forks are adjustable for spring pre-load, rebound damping, and compression damping.

2 Spring pre-load is adjusted using a suitable spanner on the adjuster flats on the top of the forks **(see illustration)**. The amount of pre-load is indicated by lines on the adjuster. There are 5 lines. The standard position is with the 2nd line just visible above the top bolt hex. Turn the adjuster clockwise to increase pre-load, and anti-clockwise to decrease it. Always make sure both adjusters are set equally. Do not turn the adjuster out so the 5th line is above the top bolt hex.

3 Rebound damping is adjusted using a screwdriver in the slot in the adjuster protruding from the pre-load adjuster **(see illustration)**. The amount of damping is indicated by the number of clicks when turned anti-clockwise from the fully screwed-in (hardest) position. There are seventeen positions. The standard position is seven clicks out. Turn the adjuster clockwise to increase damping and anti-clockwise to decrease it. To establish the current setting, turn the adjuster in (clockwise) until it stops, counting the number of clicks, then reset it as required by turning it out. Always make sure both adjusters are set equally.

4 Compression damping is adjusted using a screwdriver in the slot in the adjuster on the

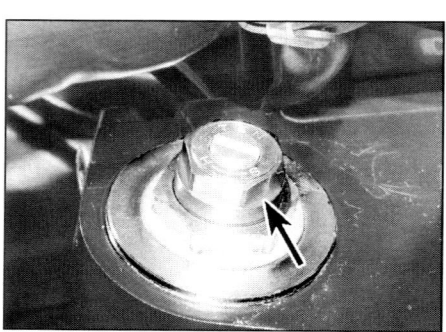

13.2 Spring pre-load adjuster (arrowed)

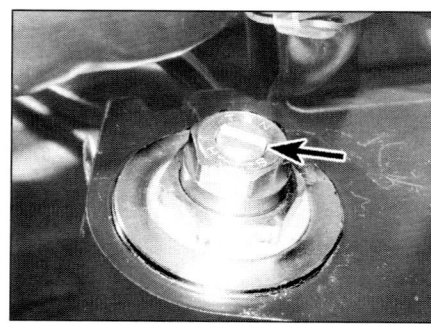

13.3 Rebound damping adjuster (arrowed)

Frame, suspension and final drive 6•15

base of each fork **(see illustration)**. The amount of damping is indicated by the number of clicks when turned anti-clockwise from the fully screwed-in (hardest) position. There are twenty one positions. The standard position is six clicks out. Turn the adjuster clockwise to increase damping and anti-clockwise to decrease it. To establish the current setting, turn the adjuster in (clockwise) until it stops, counting the number of clicks, then reset it as required by turning it out. Always make sure both adjusters are set equally.

Rear shock absorber

5 The rear shock absorber is adjustable for spring pre-load, rebound damping, and compression damping.

6 Spring pre-load is adjusted using a suitable C-spanner (one is provided in the toolkit) to turn the spring seat on the top of the shock absorber **(see illustration)**. There are eleven positions. The highest notch for the stopper is the softest setting, the 6th notch is the standard, the lowest notch is the hardest. Align the notch required with the adjustment stopper. Turn the spring seat anti-clockwise to increase pre-load and clockwise to decrease it.

7 Rebound damping is adjusted using by turning the adjuster ring on the base of the shock absorber **(see illustration)**. Turn the adjuster anti-clockwise to increase damping and clockwise to decrease it. There are twenty positions. The standard position is ten clicks out form the fully anti-clockwise (hardest) setting. To establish the current setting, turn the adjuster anti-clockwise until it stops, counting the number of clicks, then reset it as required by turning it clockwise.

8 Compression damping is adjusted using a screwdriver in the slot in the adjuster on the shock absorber reservoir **(see illustration)**. Turn the adjuster clockwise to increase damping and anti-clockwise to decrease it. There are twelve positions. The standard position is seven clicks in from the fully

13.4 Compression damping adjuster (arrowed)

13.7 Rebound damping adjuster (arrowed)

13.6 Spring pre-load adjuster (arrowed)

13.8 Compression damping adjuster (arrowed)

turned-out (softest) position. To establish the current setting, turn the adjuster out (anti-clockwise) until it stops, counting the number of clicks, then reset it as required by turning it in (clockwise).

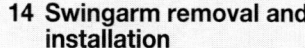

14 Swingarm removal and installation

Removal

Note: *Before removing the swingarm, it is advisable to perform the rear suspension* checks described in Chapter 1 to assess the extent of any wear.

1 Remove the rear wheel (see Chapter 7), and the rear shock absorber (see Section 11).

2 Unscrew the bolts securing the chainguard to the swingarm and remove it, noting how it fits **(see illustration)**.

3 Unscrew the bolts securing the pivot cover on each side of the frame and remove the covers **(see illustration)**.

4 Unscrew the nut and withdraw the bolt securing the brake torque arm to the swingarm. Unscrew the brake hose guide and clamp bolts. Loop the rear brake caliper assembly over the swingarm and secure it clear, making sure no strain is placed on the hose.

14.2 Unscrew the bolts (arrowed) and remove the guard

14.3 Unscrew the bolts (arrowed) and remove the cover on each side

6•16 Frame, suspension and final drive

14.6a Unscrew the nut (arrowed) and remove the washer . . .

14.6b . . . then withdraw the bolt and remove the swingarm

14.7a Unscrew the bolt, noting the collar . . .

14.7b . . . and remove the chain slider

14.10a Remove the dust cap . . .

14.10b . . . then withdraw the spacer

5 Before removing the swingarm it is advisable to re-check for play in the bearings (see Chapter 1). Any problems which may have been overlooked with the other suspension components attached to the frame are highlighted with them loose.

6 Unscrew the nut on the end of the swingarm pivot bolt and remove the washer **(see illustration)**. Support the swingarm, then withdraw the pivot bolt and remove the swingarm **(see illustration)**. Knock the pivot bolt through using a drift if required.

7 Remove the chain slider from the front of the swingarm if necessary – note the collar with the bolt **(see illustrations)**. If it is badly worn or damaged, it should be replaced with a new one.

8 Inspect all components for wear or damage as described in Section 15.

Installation

9 If removed, install the chain slider and tighten the bolt, not forgetting its collar **(see illustrations 14.7b and a)**.

10 Remove the dust cap from each side of the swingarm pivot, then withdraw the spacer **(see illustrations)**. Check the condition of the rubber seals fitted in each pivot cap and replace the caps with new ones if the rubber is damaged, deformed or deteriorated. Where water has found its way into the bearings there is likely to be corrosion on both the bearings and end sections of the spacer. Replace corroded or worn parts with new ones (see Section 15). Clean off all old grease, then lubricate the bearings, spacer, caps and the pivot bolt with lithium-based grease **(see illustration)**. Insert the spacer, then fit the dust caps.

11 Offer up the swingarm and have an assistant hold it in place. Make sure the drive chain is looped over the front of the swingarm. Slide the pivot bolt through from the right-hand side and push it all the way through, locating the flats on the head in the cut-out in the frame **(see illustrations)**.

14.10c Smear all components with new grease

14.11a Install the arm and slide the bolt through . . .

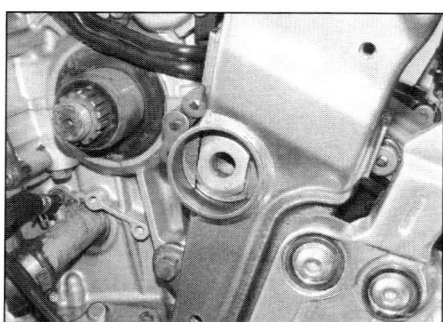

14.11b . . . locating its head as shown

Frame, suspension and final drive 6•17

14.12a Fit the washer and the nut . . .

14.12b . . . and tighten the nut to the specified torque

14.15 Fit the pivot covers

12 Install the nut with its washer, and tighten the nut to the torque setting specified at the beginning of the Chapter **(see illustrations)**. Move the swingarm up and down – it should move smoothly and freely. If it is tight, slacken the nut, then tighten it again to the specified torque.
13 Loop the brake caliper assembly over the swingarm so the hose is correctly routed around it. Locate the torque arm onto its mount, then fit the bolt and tighten the nut finger-tight only at this stage. Locate the brake hose guide and clamp and tighten their bolts.
14 Install the shock absorber (see Section 11), then the rear wheel (see Chapter 7). Check and adjust the drive chain slack (see Chapter 1). Now tighten the nut on the brake torque arm front bolt to the specified torque setting.
15 Install the chainguard, making sure it locates correctly **(see illustration 14.2)**. Fit the pivot cover onto each side of the frame **(see illustration)**.
16 Check the operation of the rear suspension before taking the machine on the road.

15 Swingarm and bearing inspection

Swingarm

1 Remove the swingarm (see Section 14).
2 Thoroughly clean the swingarm, removing all traces of dirt, corrosion and grease.
3 Inspect the swingarm closely, looking for obvious signs of wear such as heavy scoring, and cracks or distortion due to accident damage. Any damaged or worn component must be replaced with a new one.
4 Check the swingarm pivot bolt is straight by rolling it on a flat surface such as a piece of plate glass (first wipe off all old grease and remove any corrosion using wire wool). If it is bent replace it with a new one.

Bearings

5 Remove the dust cap from each side of the swingarm pivot, then withdraw the spacer **(see illustrations 14.10a and b)**.
6 Check the condition of the bearings – a needle roller bearing is fitted on each side **(see illustration)**. Where water has found its way into the bearings there is likely to be corrosion on both the bearings and end sections of the spacer. Replace corroded or worn parts with new ones. Slip the spacer back into its bearing and check that there is not an excessive amount of freeplay between the two components. If the bearings do not run smoothly and freely or if there is excessive freeplay, they must be replaced with new ones. Refer to *Tools and Workshop Tips* (Section 5) in the Reference section for more information on bearings.
7 Worn bearings can be drifted out of their bores, but note that removal will destroy them; new bearings should be obtained before work commences. The new bearings should be pressed or drawn into their bores rather than driven into position. In the absence of a press, a suitable drawbolt tool can be made up as described in *Tools and Workshop Tips* in the Reference section.
8 Check the condition of the rubber seals fitted in each pivot cap and replace the caps with new ones if the rubber is damaged, deformed or deteriorated. Clean off all old grease, then lubricate the bearings, spacer, caps and the pivot bolt with lithium-based grease. Insert the spacer, then fit the dust caps.

15.6 Check the needle bearing (arrowed) in each side as described

16 Drive chain removal and installation

Note: *The original equipment drive chain fitted is an endless chain, which means it doesn't have a split link and therefore cannot be split. Removal of an endless chain requires the removal of the swingarm. Note that the bike may have been subsequently fitted with a chain which uses a soft link (see below).*

Endless chain

1 Remove the front sprocket (see Section 17).
2 Remove the swingarm (see Section 14), then remove the chain.
3 If the chain is excessively dirty, soak it in kerosene (paraffin) for approximately five or six minutes, then clean it using a soft brush.
4 Refer to Chapter 1 to check the chain and determine its state of wear.
5 Installation is the reverse of removal. On completion adjust and lubricate the chain following the procedures described in Section 1.
Caution: *Don't use gasoline (petrol), solvent or other cleaning fluids which might damage its internal sealing properties. Don't use high-pressure water. Remove the chain, wipe it off, then blow dry it with compressed air immediately. The entire process shouldn't take longer than ten minutes – if it does, the O-rings in the chain rollers could be damaged.*

Split chain with soft link

6 Place the bike on its centrestand and rotate the chain through its full length to determine whether it has a soft link. The soft link sideplate is often of a slightly different colour to the other sideplates and the staked ends of the link's two pins which look as if they have been deeply centre-punched, instead of peened over as with all the other pins.
7 The chain can be separated at the soft link using a chain breaker tool and the soft link withdrawn to split the chain. Refer to Section 8 'Chains' of *Tools and Workshop Tips* in the Reference section at the end of this manual for details of how to use the tool and how to

6•18 Frame, suspension and final drive

17.3 Sprocket cover bolts (arrowed)

17.4a Bend back the lockwasher tabs...

17.4b ... then unscrew the nut and remove the washer

rivet the new soft link securely. Note that it is essential to use a new soft link when re-joining the chain. Never install a clip-type master link.

17 Sprockets

1 Refer to Chapter 1, Section 1 for sprocket checks.

Front sprocket

2 Slacken the gearchange lever linkage rod locknuts, then unscrew the rod and separate it from the lever and the arm (the rod is reverse-threaded on one end, so will unscrew from both lever and arm simultaneously when turned in the one direction) (see illustrations 3.3a). Note how far the rod is threaded into the lever and arm as this determines the height of the lever relative to the footrest. Withdraw the rod from the frame (see illustration 3.3b).
3 Unscrew the bolts securing the front sprocket cover and remove it (see illustration).
4 Bend down the tab(s) on the sprocket nut lockwasher (see illustration). Have an assistant apply the rear brake hard, then unscrew the nut and remove the washer (see illustration). Discard the washer, as a new one should be used. Refer to Chapter 1 and back off chain tension so that the chain is fully slack.
5 If the sprocket is not being replaced with a new one, mark the outside with a scratch or dab of paint, so that it can be installed the same way round. Slide the sprocket and chain off the shaft and slip the sprocket out of the chain (see illustration). If there is not enough slack on the chain to remove the sprocket, disengage the chain from the rear wheel.
6 Engage the new sprocket with the chain and slide it on the shaft (see illustration). Take up the slack in the chain (see Chapter 1).
7 Slide on the new lockwasher (see illustration). Fit the nut with the shouldered side facing in (see illustration 17.4b) and tighten it to the torque setting specified at the beginning of the Chapter, applying the rear brake to prevent the sprocket from turning (see illustration). Bend up the tabs of the lockwasher against the nut (see illustration).
8 Install the front sprocket cover, making sure the hoses and wiring are correctly routed, and tighten the bolts (see illustration).

17.5 Slide the sprocket off the shaft and remove it

17.6 Fit the sprocket into the chain and slide it onto the shaft

17.7a Fit the new lockwasher...

17.7b ... and tighten the nut to the specified torque

17.7c Bend the tabs up against the nut

17.8 Make sure everything is correctly routed when installing the cover

Frame, suspension and final drive

17.11 Unscrew the nuts (arrowed) and remove the sprocket

18.2 Lift the sprocket coupling out of the wheel...

9 Slide the linkage rod into the frame and thread it onto the lever and arm (the rod is reverse-threaded on one end, so will screw simultaneously onto both lever and arm when turned in the one direction) **(see illustration 3.3b)**. Set it as noted on removal to give the same gearchange lever height, then tighten the locknuts securely **(see illustration 3.3a)**.

Rear sprocket

10 Remove the rear wheel (see Chapter 7).
11 Unscrew the nuts securing the sprocket to the hub assembly **(see illustration)**. Remove the sprocket, noting which way round it fits.
12 Check the sprocket studs for wear or damage and make sure they are tight. If any are loose, remove them all, referring to Tools and Workshop Tips for information on removing and installing studs, and if necessary replace them with new ones. Apply a suitable thread locking compound on installation.
13 Install the sprocket onto the hub with the stamped mark facing out. Tighten the nuts evenly and a little at a time in a criss-cross sequence to the torque setting specified at the beginning of the Chapter.
14 Install the rear wheel (see Chapter 7).

18 Rear sprocket coupling/rubber dampers

1 Remove the rear wheel (see Chapter 7).
Caution: Do not lay the wheel down on the disc, as it could become warped. Lay the wheel on wooden blocks so that the disc is off the ground.
2 Lift the sprocket coupling away from the wheel, leaving the rubber dampers in position **(see illustration)**. Check the coupling for cracks or any obvious signs of damage.

18.3 ... and remove the rubber dampers

3 Lift the rubber damper segments from the wheel and check them for cracks, hardening and general deterioration **(see illustration)**. Replace them, with a new set if necessary.
4 Refer to Chapter 7 and check the sprocket coupling bearing.
5 Installation is the reverse of removal.

Notes

Chapter 7
Brakes, wheels and tyres

Contents

Brake fluid level check .... see *Daily (pre-ride) checks*	Rear brake caliper 7
Brake hoses and unions 10	Rear brake disc 8
Brake light switches .... see Chapter 9	Rear brake master cylinder 9
Brake system bleeding 11	Rear brake pads 6
Brake system check .... see Chapter 1	Rear wheel 15
Front brake calipers 3	Tyre fitting 17
Front brake discs 4	Tyre pressure, tread depth and condition .... see *Daily (pre-ride) checks*
Front brake master cylinder 5	Wheel bearing check .... see Chapter 1
Front brake pads 2	Wheel bearing replacement 16
Front wheel 14	Wheel alignment check 13
General information 1	Wheel inspection and repair 12

Degrees of difficulty

Easy, suitable for novice with little experience	Fairly easy, suitable for beginner with some experience	Fairly difficult, suitable for competent DIY mechanic	Difficult, suitable for experienced DIY mechanic	Very difficult, suitable for expert DIY or professional

Specifications

Brakes
Brake fluid type	DOT 4
Brake pad minimum thickness	0.5 mm
Front caliper bore ID	
Upper bore	30.20 mm
Lower bore	27.00 mm
Front disc thickness	
Standard	5.0 mm
Service limit	4.5 mm
Front disc maximum run-out	0.1 mm
Front master cylinder bore ID	14.0 mm
Rear caliper bore ID	42.9 mm
Rear disc thickness	
Standard	5.0 mm
Service limit	4.5 mm
Rear disc maximum run-out	0.1 mm
Rear master cylinder bore ID	12.7 mm

Wheels
Rim size	
Front	17 x MT3.50
Rear	17 x MT5.50
Wheel run-out (max)	
Axial (side-to-side)	0.5 mm
Radial (out-of-round)	1.0 mm

Tyres
Tyre pressures	see *Daily (pre-ride) checks*
Tyre sizes*	
Front	120/70-ZR17 (58W)
Rear	180/55-ZR17 (73W)

*Refer to the owners handbook, the tyre information label on the swingarm, or your dealer for approved tyre brands.

7•2 Brakes, wheels and tyres

Torque wrench settings

Bleed valves	6 Nm
Brake hose banjo bolts	30 Nm
Front axle	72 Nm
Front axle clamp bolt	23 Nm
Front brake caliper mounting bolts	40 Nm
Front brake disc bolts	18 Nm
Front brake master cylinder clamp bolts	10 Nm
Rear axle nut	150 Nm
Rear brake caliper mounting bolts	40 Nm
Rear brake disc bolts	18 Nm
Rear brake master cylinder mounting bolts	23 Nm
Rear brake torque arm nuts	23 Nm

1 General information

All models are fitted with cast alloy wheels designed for tubeless tyres only. Both front and rear brakes are hydraulically-operated disc brakes.

The front brakes are twin opposed-piston calipers. The rear brake is a single opposed-piston caliper.

Caution: *Disc brake components rarely require disassembly. Do not disassemble components unless absolutely necessary. If a hydraulic brake line is loosened, the entire system must be disassembled, drained, cleaned and then properly filled and bled upon reassembly. Do not use solvents on internal brake components. Solvents will cause the seals to swell and distort. Use only clean brake fluid or denatured alcohol for cleaning. Use care when working with brake fluid as it can injure your eyes and it will damage painted surfaces and plastic parts.*

2 Front brake pads

Warning: *The dust created by the brake system may contain asbestos, which is harmful to your health. Never blow it out with compressed air and don't inhale any of it. An approved filtering mask should be worn when working on the brakes. Do not, under any circumstances, use petroleum-based solvents to clean brake pads. Use a dedicated brake cleaner or denatured alcohol only.*

Note: *If the pad pins have not been previously greased and have not been removed for a while, they could well be very difficult to withdraw. If this is the case, they will have to be driven out using a suitable drift or punch. If you apply penetrating fluid this will help, but make sure none gets on the pads. Note that Yamaha recommend using a new pad spring, anti-chatter shims, pad pins and retaining clips when new pads are installed.*

1 Unscrew the bolt securing the brake hose holder to the front fork **(see illustration)**. Unscrew the caliper mounting bolts and slide the caliper off the disc **(see illustrations)** – there is no need to disconnect the hose.

2 Remove the retaining clip from each end of the pad pin **(see illustration)**. Withdraw the pad pin, noting how it fits through the pad spring **(see illustration)**. Remove the pad spring, noting which way round it fits **(see illustration 2.9c)**. Withdraw the pads from the top of the caliper, noting how they fit **(see illustration)**. If required, remove the anti-chatter shim from the back of each pad, noting how it fits **(see illustration 2.8)**.

3 Inspect the surface of each pad for

2.1a Unscrew the brake hose holder bolt

2.1b Unscrew the bolts (arrowed) . . .

2.1c . . . and slide the caliper off the disc

2.2a Remove the retaining clips . . .

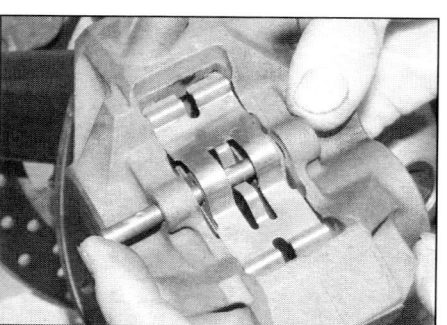

2.2b . . . then withdraw the pad pin

2.2c Remove the pad spring and lift the pads out of the caliper

Brakes, wheels and tyres

2.7a Push the pistons back into the caliper . . .

2.7b . . . using the proper tool if available

2.8 Make sure the shim is correctly fitted

contamination and check that the friction material has not worn beyond its service limit (see Chapter 1, Section 8). If either pad is worn down to or beyond the service limit wear indicator, is fouled with oil or grease, or is heavily scored or damaged by dirt and debris, both pads in each caliper must be replaced with new ones. Note that it is not possible to degrease the friction material; if the pads are contaminated in any way, new ones must be fitted.

4 If the pads are in good condition clean them carefully, using a fine wire brush which is completely free of oil and grease, to remove all traces of road dirt and corrosion. Using a pointed instrument, clean out the groove in the friction material and dig out any embedded particles of foreign matter. Spray the caliper area with a dedicated brake cleaner to remove any dust and remove and traces of corrosion which might cause sticking of the caliper/pad operation.

5 Check the condition of the brake disc (see Section 4).

6 Remove all traces of corrosion from the pad pin. Check it for signs of damage and replace it with a new one if necessary.

7 Clean around the exposed section of each piston to remove any dirt or debris that could cause the seals to be damaged. Now push the pistons back into the caliper – if new pads are being fitted you need to push them all the way in to create room for them; if the old pads are still serviceable push them in a little way, not only because it makes installation easier, but also because it serves as a check that none of the pistons are seized in their bores. To push the pistons back first block the pair of pistons not being pushed in to prevent them being pushed out, then use finger pressure or a piece of wood as leverage, or place the old pads back in the caliper and use a metal bar or a screwdriver inserted between them, or use grips and a piece of wood, rag or card to protect the caliper body, **(see illustration)**. Alternatively obtain a proper piston-pushing tool from a good tool supplier **(see illustration)**. It may be necessary to undo the master cylinder reservoir cover screws and remove the cover and diaphragm and siphon out some fluid (see *Daily (pre-ride) checks*). If the pistons are difficult to push back, remove the bleed valve cap, then attach a length of clear hose to the bleed valve and place the open end in a suitable container, then open the valve and try again **(see illustrations 11.5a and b)**. Take great care not to draw any air into the system. If in doubt, bleed the brakes afterwards (see Section 11). If any of the pistons appear seized, block the other pistons so all pressure is applied to the one being checked, then apply the brake lever and check whether the piston moves at all. If it moves out but can't be pushed back in the chances are there is some hidden corrosion stopping it. If it is completely seized you will have to overhaul the caliper (see Section 3).

8 Lightly smear the backs and sides of the pad backing material and the shank of the pad pin with copper-based grease, making sure that none gets on the front or sides of the pads. If removed, fit the shim onto the back of each pad **(see illustration)**.

9 Fit one pad into the caliper, making sure the friction material faces in, and locate it by inserting the pad pin part-way, turning it so the retaining clip holes face up **(see illustration)**. Fit the other pad, then locate the pad spring **(see illustrations)**. Slide the pin all the way through, making sure it passes under the outer leaves of the spring and over the inner leaf **(see illustration 2.2b)**. Fit the retaining clips **(see illustration 2.2a)**.

10 Slide the calipers onto the disc, making sure the pads locate correctly on each side **(see illustration 2.1c)**. Install the mounting bolts and tighten them to the torque setting specified at the beginning of the Chapter **(see illustration)**. Fit the brake hose holder onto the front fork and tighten the bolt **(see illustration 2.1a)**.

11 Top up the master cylinder reservoir if necessary (see *Daily (pre-ride) checks*), and refit the diaphragm, plate and reservoir cap. Operate the brake lever several times to bring the pads into contact with the disc. Check the operation of the brake before riding the motorcycle.

2.9a Fit one pad and secure it with the pin . . .

2.9b . . . then fit the other pad . . .

2.9c . . . and locate the pad spring

2.10 Fit the bolts and tighten them to the specified torque

3.3 Brake hose banjo bolt (arrowed)

3.8a Block the pistons on one side and use compressed air . . .

3.8b . . . to displace the pistons on the other side

3 Front brake calipers

Warning: *The dust created by the brake pads may contain asbestos, which is harmful to your health. Never blow it out with compressed air and don't inhale any of it. An approved filtering mask should be worn when working on the brakes. If a new caliper is being installed all old brake fluid should be flushed from the system. Do not, under any circumstances, use petroleum-based solvents to clean internal brake parts. Use new brake fluid only. Use care when working with brake fluid as it can injure your eyes and it will damage painted surfaces and plastic parts – cover these with rag.*

Note: *If the entire front brake system is being removed (i.e. master cylinder as well as calipers), or if you intend to change the brake fluid, drain the brake fluid completely from the system (see Section 11), as opposed to retaining the old fluid within it by blocking the hose as described (Step 3).*

1 If the caliper is leaking fluid, or if the brake pads are wearing unevenly, or the pistons do not move smoothly or are tight or stuck in their bores, then caliper overhaul is required – all the seals and a sachet of silicone grease come as a kit, but if new pistons are required they must be obtained separately.

2 If you are completely removing the caliper rather than just displacing it, you will need some new DOT 4 brake fluid and some clean rags.

Removal

3 If the caliper is just being displaced and not completely removed or overhauled, do not disconnect the brake hose. If the caliper is being completely removed or overhauled, unscrew the brake hose banjo bolt and detach the hose, noting its alignment with the caliper **(see illustration)**. Discard the sealing washers as new ones must be used on installation. Either clamp the hose, plug it using another suitable short piece of hose fitted through the eye of the banjo union (it must be a fairly tight fit to seal it properly), block it using a suitable bolt with sealing washers and a capped (domed) nut, or wrap some plastic foodwrap tightly around (a finger cut off a latex glove also works well), the object being to minimise fluid loss and prevent dirt entering the system. Whatever you do, also cover the end of the hose in rag, just in case. Similarly block or cover the caliper where the hose connects.

4 If the caliper is just being displaced unscrew the bolt securing the brake hose holder to the front fork **(see illustration 2.1a)**.

5 Unscrew the caliper mounting bolts and slide the caliper off the disc **(see illustrations 2.1b and c)**.

6 If the caliper is being overhauled, remove the brake pads (see Section 2).

Overhaul

7 Clean the exterior of the caliper with denatured alcohol or brake system cleaner.

8 Push the pistons on one side of the caliper all the way in, then block them using a flat piece of wood and grips. Displace the opposite pistons using compressed air directed into the banjo bolt bore **(see illustration)**. Use only low pressure to ease the pistons out and make sure both pistons on the side concerned are displaced at the same time **(see illustration)**. Remove the wood, then remove the pistons **(see illustration)**. Remove the seals (see Steps 9 and 10) from the bore of the displaced pistons, then reinstall the pistons and block them using the wood. Now displace the pistons from the other side using the same method. Remove the wood and all the pistons. Mark each piston head and caliper body with a felt marker to ensure that the pistons can be matched to their original bores on reassembly.

Warning: *Never place your fingers in front of the pistons in an attempt to catch or protect them when applying compressed air, as serious injury could result.*

Caution: *Do not try to remove the pistons by levering them out, or by using pliers or any other grips. Do not attempt to remove the caliper bore plugs on the outside of the caliper.*

9 Remove the dust seal from each caliper bore using a wooden or plastic tool **(see illustration)**. Discard them as new ones must be used on installation. If a metal tool is being used, take great care not to damage the bores.

10 Remove and discard the piston seals in the same way **(see illustration)**.

3.8c Remove the wood and lift the pistons out

3.9 Remove the dust seals . . .

3.10 . . . then the piston seals

Brakes, wheels and tyres 7•5

3.13a Lubricate the new piston seals . . .

3.13b . . . and fit them into their grooves

3.14 Lubricate and fit the new dust seals

11 Clean the pistons and bores with new DOT 4 brake fluid.
Caution: Do not, under any circumstances, use a petroleum-based solvent to clean brake parts.
12 Inspect the caliper bores and pistons for signs of corrosion, nicks and burrs and loss of plating. If surface defects are present, the caliper and/or pistons must be replaced with new ones. If the necessary measuring equipment is available, compare the dimensions of the caliper bores to those specified at the beginning of the Chapter, and install a new caliper if necessary. If the caliper is in bad shape the master cylinder should also be checked.
13 Lubricate the new piston seals with the silicone grease supplied in the kit or with clean brake fluid and fit them into their grooves in the caliper bores **(see illustrations)**. Note that two sizes of bore and piston are used (see Specifications), and care must therefore be taken to ensure that the correct size seals are fitted to the correct bores. The same applies when fitting the new dust seals and pistons.
14 Lubricate the new dust seals and fit them into their grooves in the caliper bores **(see illustration)**.
15 Lubricate the pistons and fit them closed-end first into the caliper bores **(see illustrations)**. Using your thumbs, push the pistons all the way in, making sure they enter the bore squarely **(see illustration)**.

Installation

16 If removed, install the brake pads (see Section 2).
17 Slide the caliper onto the disc, making sure the pads sit squarely on either side **(see illustration 2.1c)**. If the caliper doesn't slide on easily, push the pistons a little way back into the caliper using hand pressure on the pads or a piece of wood as leverage. Install the caliper mounting bolts and tighten them to the torque setting specified at the beginning of the Chapter **(see illustration 2.10)**.
18 Fit the brake hose holder onto the front fork and tighten the bolt **(see illustration 2.1a)**.
19 If removed, connect the brake hose to the caliper, using new sealing washers on each side of the fitting **(see illustration)**. Align the hose as

3.15a Lubricate the pistons . . .

3.15b . . . then fit them into their bores . . .

3.15c . . . and press them all the way down

noted on removal **(see illustration 3.3)**. Tighten the banjo bolt to the torque setting specified at the beginning of the Chapter. Top up the master cylinder reservoir with DOT 4 brake fluid (see *Daily (pre-ride) checks*) and bleed the hydraulic system as described in Section 11.
20 Check for leaks and thoroughly test the operation of the brake before riding the motorcycle.

4 Front brake discs

Inspection

1 Visually inspect the surface of the disc for score marks and other damage. Light scratches are normal after use and will not affect brake operation, but deep grooves and heavy score marks will reduce braking efficiency and accelerate pad wear. If a disc is badly grooved it must be machined, or a new one fitted.

3.19 Always use new sealing washers

2 To check disc run-out, position the bike on an auxiliary stand and support it so that the front wheel is raised off the ground. Mount a dial gauge to a fork leg, with the plunger on the gauge touching the surface of the disc about 10 mm (1/2 in) from the outer edge **(see illustration)**. Rotate the wheel and watch the

4.2 Set up a dial gauge with the probe contacting the brake disc, then rotate the wheel to check for run-out

7•6 Brakes, wheels and tyres

4.3 Using a micrometer to measure disc thickness

4.5 Unscrew the bolts (arrowed) and remove the disc

gauge needle, comparing the reading with the limit listed in the Specifications at the beginning of the Chapter. If the run-out is greater than the service limit, check the wheel bearings for play (see Chapter 1). If the bearings are worn, install new ones (see Section 16) and repeat this check. If the disc run-out is still excessive, a new pair of discs will have to be fitted, although machining by an engineer may be possible.

3 The disc must not be machined or allowed to wear down to a thickness less than the service limit as listed in this Chapter's Specifications. The thickness of the disc can be checked with a micrometer or any other measuring tool **(see illustration)**. If the thickness of the disc is less than the service limit, a new one must be fitted.

Removal

4 Remove the wheel (see Section 14).
Caution: Do not lay the wheel down and allow it to rest on the disc – the disc could become warped. Set the wheel on wood blocks so the disc does not support the weight of the wheel.

5 Mark the relationship of the disc to the wheel, so that it can be installed in the same position. Unscrew the disc retaining bolts, loosening them evenly and a little at a time in a criss-cross pattern to avoid distorting the disc, then remove the disc from the wheel **(see illustration)**.

Installation

6 Before installing the disc, make sure there is no dirt or corrosion where the disc seats on the hub, particularly right in the angle of the seat, as this will not allow the disc to sit flat when it is bolted down, and it will appear to be warped when checked or when using the front brake.

7 Mount the disc on the wheel, making sure any directional arrow is on the outside and pointing in the direction of normal (i.e. forward) rotation. Also note any R or L marking on the front discs that denotes on which side of the wheel it must be mounted. Align the previously applied match marks (if you're reinstalling the original disc).

8 Clean the threads of the disc mounting bolts, then apply a suitable non-permanent thread locking compound. Install the bolts and tighten them evenly and a little at a time in a criss-cross pattern to the torque setting specified at the beginning of the Chapter **(see illustration 4.5)**. Clean off all grease from the brake disc using acetone or brake system cleaner. If a new brake disc has been installed, remove any protective coating from its working surfaces.

9 Install the front wheel (see Section 14).

10 Operate the brake lever several times to bring the pads into contact with the disc. Check the operation of the brakes carefully before riding the bike.

5 Front brake master cylinder

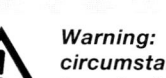

Warning: Do not, under any circumstances, use petroleum-based solvents to clean internal brake parts. Use new brake fluid only. Use care when working with brake fluid as it can injure your eyes and it will damage painted surfaces and plastic parts – cover these with rag.

Note: *If the entire front brake system is being disturbed (i.e. calipers as well as the master cylinder), or if you intend to change the brake fluid, drain the brake fluid completely from the system (see Section 11), as opposed to retaining the old fluid within it by blocking the hose as described (Step 6).*

1 If the master cylinder is leaking fluid, or if the lever does not produce a firm feel when the brake is applied, and bleeding the brakes does not help (see Section 11), and the hydraulic hoses and the brake calipers are all in good condition, then master cylinder overhaul is recommended.

2 Before disassembling the master cylinder, read through the entire procedure and make sure that you have the correct rebuild kit. Also, you will need some new DOT 4 brake fluid, some clean rags and internal circlip pliers. **Note:** *To prevent damage to the paint from spilled brake fluid, always cover the fuel tank when working on the master cylinder.*

Caution: Disassembly, overhaul and reassembly of the brake master cylinder must be done in a spotlessly clean work area to avoid contamination and possible failure of the brake hydraulic system components.

Removal

Note: *If the master cylinder is being displaced from the handlebar and not being removed completely or overhauled, follow Steps 5 and 7 only.*

3 Loosen, but do not remove, the screws holding the reservoir cover in place **(see illustration)**.

4 Remove the front brake lever (see Chapter 6).

5 Disconnect the electrical connectors from the brake light switch **(see illustration)**.

6 Unscrew the brake hose banjo bolt and separate the hose from the master cylinder, noting its alignment **(see illustration)**. Discard the sealing washers as they must be replaced with new ones. Either clamp the hose, plug it

5.3 Slacken the cover screws

5.5 Brake light switch wiring connectors (A) and mounting screw (B)

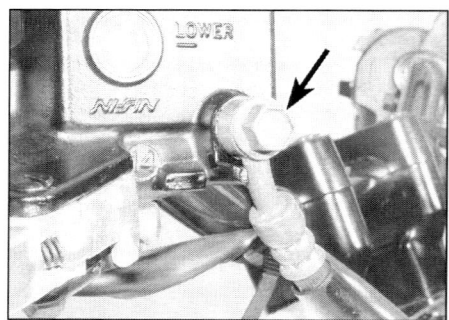

5.6 Brake hose banjo bolt (arrowed)

Brakes, wheels and tyres 7•7

5.7 Front brake master cylinder clamp bolts (arrowed)

5.10 Remove the rubber boot from the end of the master cylinder piston . . .

5.11a . . . then depress the piston and remove the circlip using a pair of internal circlip pliers . . .

using another suitable short piece of hose fitted through the eye of the banjo union (a fairly tight fit is necessary for a good seal), block it using a suitable bolt with sealing washers and a capped (domed) nut, or wrap some plastic foodwrap tightly around (a finger cut off a latex glove also works well), the object being to minimise fluid loss and prevent dirt entering the system. Whatever you do, also cover the end of the hose in rag, just in case.

7 Unscrew the master cylinder clamp bolts, then lift the master cylinder and reservoir away from the handlebar, noting how the mating surfaces of the clamp align with the punch mark on the top of the handlebar **(see illustration)**.

8 Remove the reservoir cover, diaphragm plate and rubber diaphragm. Drain the brake fluid from the reservoir into a suitable container. Wipe any remaining fluid out of the reservoir with a clean rag.

9 If required undo the brake light switch screw and remove the switch, noting how it fits **(see illustration 5.5)**.

Overhaul

10 Carefully remove the dust boot from the master cylinder **(see illustration)**.
11 Using circlip pliers, remove the circlip and slide out the piston assembly and the spring, noting how they fit **(see illustrations)**. Lay the

5.11b . . . and remove the piston . . .

parts out in the proper order to prevent confusion during reassembly.
12 Clean out the master cylinder bore with new brake fluid of the specified type.
Caution: Do not, under any circumstances, use a petroleum-based solvent to clean brake parts.
13 Check the master cylinder bore for corrosion, scratches, nicks and score marks. If the necessary measuring equipment is available, compare the diameter of the bore to that given in the Specifications Section of this Chapter. If damage or wear is evident, the master cylinder must be replaced with a new one. If the master cylinder is in poor condition, then the calipers should be checked as well.

5.11c . . . then the spring

Check that the fluid inlet and outlet ports in the master cylinder are clear.
14 The dust boot, circlip, piston, seal, cup and spring are included in the rebuild kit. Use all of the new parts, regardless of the apparent condition of the old ones. If the seal is not in place on the piston, lubricate it well with silicone grease or brake fluid and carefully fit it into its groove, making sure it is the correct way round – although at first it appears to be a tight fit and it seems likely the seal will split when getting it over the ridge, in fact it is quite flexible and fits fairly easily **(see illustrations)**. Fit the cup onto the end of the spring, locating the peg into the hole in the end of the spring **(see illustration)**.

5.14a Fit the seal onto the piston . . .

5.14b . . . making sure it locates correctly

5.14c Fit the cup onto the spring

7•8 Brakes, wheels and tyres

5.15a Lubricate the cup . . .

5.15b . . . then fit the spring . . .

5.15c . . . and push the cup into the bore

15 Lubricate the cup with silicone grease or brake fluid, then fit the spring into the master cylinder with the cup facing out **(see illustrations)**. Push the cup into the cylinder bore, making sure its lips do not turn inside out **(see illustration)**.
16 Lubricate the piston with clean brake fluid. Fit it into the master cylinder, making sure it is the correct way round **(see illustration)**. Make sure the lips on the seal do not turn inside out when they enter the bore. Depress the piston and install the new circlip, making sure that it locates in the groove – use circlip pliers to get it past the groove for the rubber boot, and thereafter it can be pushed into its own groove using a small screwdriver if your pliers are too big for the bore **(see illustrations)**.
17 Install the rubber dust boot, making sure the outer lip seats correctly in the groove in the master cylinder bore end, and the inner lip locates in the groove in the end of the piston **(see illustration)**.
18 Inspect the reservoir cap rubber diaphragm and replace it with a new one it if it is damaged or deteriorated.

Installation

19 If removed, install the brake light switch **(see illustration 5.5)**.
20 Attach the master cylinder to the handlebar and fit the clamp aligning the top mating surfaces of the clamp with the punch mark on the handlebar **(see illustration)**, and with its 'UP' mark facing up **(see illustration 5.7)**. Tighten the upper bolt first, then the lower bolt to the torque setting specified at the beginning of the Chapter.
21 If detached, connect the brake hose to the master cylinder, using new sealing washers on each side of the unions, and aligning the hoses as noted on removal **(see illustration and 5.6)**. Tighten the banjo bolt to the torque setting specified at the beginning of this Chapter.
22 If removed, install the brake lever (see Chapter 6).
23 Connect the brake light switch wiring connectors **(see illustration 5.5)**.
24 Fill the fluid reservoir with new DOT 4 brake fluid as described in *Daily (pre-ride) checks*. Refer to Section 11 of this Chapter and bleed the air from the system.
25 Fit the rubber diaphragm, making sure it is

5.16a Insert the piston . . .

5.16b . . . then push it in and fit the circlip . . .

5.16c . . . pressing it into place using a small screwdriver

5.17 Make sure the boot locates correctly in the bore and around the piston

5.20 Align the mating surfaces of the clamp with the punch mark (arrowed)

5.21 Always use new sealing washers

Brakes, wheels and tyres 7•9

correctly seated, the diaphragm plate and the cap onto the master cylinder reservoir, then fit the cover **(see illustrations)**.
26 Check the operation of the front brake before riding the motorcycle.

6 Rear brake pads

⚠ *Warning: The dust created by the brake system may contain asbestos, which is harmful to your health. Never blow it out with compressed air and don't inhale any of it. An approved filtering mask should be worn when working on the brakes. Do not, under any circumstances, use petroleum-based solvents to clean brake pads. Use a dedicated brake cleaner or denatured alcohol only.*

Note: *If the pad pins have not been previously greased and have not been removed for a while, they could well be very difficult to withdraw. If this is the case, they will have to be driven out using a suitable drift or punch. If you apply penetrating fluid this will help, but make sure none gets on the pads. Note that Yamaha recommend using a new pad spring, anti-chatter shims, pad pins and retaining clips when new pads are installed.*

1 Unscrew the caliper mounting bolts and slide the caliper off the disc **(see illustrations)** – there is no need to disconnect the hose.
2 Remove the pad pin retaining clips, then withdraw the pad pins from the caliper using a suitable pair of pliers and noting how they fit through the pad spring **(see illustrations)**. Remove the pad spring, noting how it fits. Withdraw the pads from the caliper body **(see illustration)**. If required, remove the anti-chatter shim from the back of each pad, noting how it fits **(see illustration 6.8)**.
3 Inspect the surface of each pad for contamination and check that the friction material has not worn beyond its service limit (see Chapter 1, Section 8). If either pad is worn down to or beyond the service limit wear indicator, is fouled with oil or grease, or is heavily scored or damaged by dirt and debris,

5.25a Wipe any moisture out of the diaphragm . . .

both pads must be changed as a set. Note that it is not possible to degrease the friction material; if the pads are contaminated in any way, new ones must be fitted.
4 If the pads are in good condition, clean them carefully using a fine wire brush which is completely free of oil and grease, to remove all traces of road dirt and corrosion. Using a pointed instrument, dig out any embedded particles of foreign matter. Spray with a dedicated brake cleaner to remove any dust.
5 Check the condition of the brake disc (see Section 8).
6 Remove all traces of corrosion from the pad pins. Check them for signs of damage and replace them with new ones, if necessary.
7 Clean around the exposed section of each piston to remove any dirt or debris that could cause the seals to be damaged. Now push the pistons back into the caliper – if new pads are being fitted you need to push them all the way

5.25b . . . then fit it and the plate and cover

in to create room for them; if the old pads are still serviceable push them in a little way, not only because it makes installation easier, but also because it serves as a check that neither of the pistons is seized in its bore. To push the pistons back use finger pressure or a piece of wood as leverage, or place the old pads back in the caliper and use a metal bar or a screwdriver inserted between them, or use grips and a piece of wood, rag or card to protect the caliper body, **(see illustration 2.7a)**. Alternatively obtain a proper piston-pushing tool from a good tool supplier **(see illustration 2.7b)**. It may be necessary to undo the master cylinder reservoir cap and remove the plate and diaphragm and siphon out some fluid (see *Daily (pre-ride) checks*). If the pistons are difficult to push back, remove the bleed valve cap, then attach a length of clear hose to the bleed valve and place the open end in a suitable container, then open the valve and try

6.1a Unscrew the bolts . . .

6.1b . . . and slide the caliper off the disc

6.2a Remove the retaining clips . . .

6.2b . . . then withdraw the pad pins

6.2c Remove the pad spring and lift the pads out of the caliper

7•10 Brakes, wheels and tyres

6.8 Fit the shim onto the back of the pad if removed

6.9b ... then insert the other pad

6.9a Insert one pad and retain it with the pad pins . . .

6.9c Fit the pad spring then slide the pins across it and through the other pad and into the caliper

again **(see illustrations 11.5a and b)**. Take great care not to draw any air into the system. If in doubt, bleed the brakes afterwards (see Section 11). If either of the pistons appear seized, block the other piston so all pressure is applied to the one being checked, then apply the brake pedal and check whether the piston moves at all. If it moves out but can't be pushed back in the chances are there is some hidden corrosion stopping it. If it is completely seized you will have to overhaul the caliper (see Section 7).

8 Lightly smear the backs and sides of the pad backing material and the shank of each pad pin with copper-based grease, making sure that none gets on the front or sides of the pads. If removed, fit the shim onto the back of each pad **(see illustration)**.

9 Fit one pad into the caliper, making sure the friction material faces in, and locate it by inserting the pad pins part-way, turning them so the retaining clip holes face up **(see illustration)**. Fit the other pad, then locate the pad spring and slide the pins all the way through, making sure they pass under the outer leaves of the spring and over the inner leaf **(see illustrations)**. Fit the retaining clips **(see illustration 6.2a)**.

10 Install the caliper (see Section 7). Top up the master cylinder reservoir if necessary (see *Daily (pre-ride) checks*).

11 Operate the brake pedal several times to bring the pads into contact with the disc. Check the operation of the brake before riding the motorcycle.

7 Rear brake caliper

> **Warning:** *The dust created by the brake pads may contain asbestos, which is harmful to your health. Never blow it out with compressed air and don't inhale any of it. An approved filtering mask should be worn when working on the brakes. If a new caliper is being installed all old brake fluid should be flushed from the system. Do not, under any circumstances, use petroleum-based solvents to clean internal brake parts. Use new brake fluid only. Use care when working with brake fluid as it can injure your eyes and it will damage painted surfaces and plastic parts – cover these with rag.*

7.3 Brake hose banjo bolt (arrowed)

Note: *If the entire rear brake system is being removed (i.e. master cylinder as well as caliper), or if you intend to change the brake fluid, drain the brake fluid completely from the system (see Section 11), as opposed to retaining the old fluid within it by blocking the hose as described (Step 3).*

1 If the caliper is leaking fluid, or if the brake pads are wearing unevenly, or the pistons do not move smoothly or are tight or stuck in their bores, then caliper overhaul is required – all the seals and a sachet of silicone grease come as a kit, but if new pistons are required they must be obtained separately.

2 If you are completely removing the caliper rather than just displacing it, you will need some new DOT 4 brake fluid and some clean rags.

Removal

3 If the caliper is just being displaced and not completely removed or overhauled, do not disconnect the brake hose. If the caliper is being completely removed or overhauled, unscrew the brake hose banjo bolt and detach the hose, noting its alignment with the caliper **(see illustration)**. Discard the sealing washers as new ones must be used on installation. Either clamp the hose, plug it using another suitable short piece of hose fitted through the eye of the banjo union (it must be a fairly tight fit to seal it properly), block it using a suitable bolt with sealing washers and a capped (domed) nut, or wrap some plastic foodwrap tightly around (a finger cut off a latex glove also works well), the object being to minimise fluid loss and prevent dirt entering the system. Whatever you do, also cover the end of the hose in rag, just in case. Similarly block or cover the caliper where the hose connects.

4 Unscrew the caliper mounting bolts and slide the caliper off the disc **(see illustrations 6.1a and b)**.

5 If the caliper is being overhauled, remove the brake pads (see Section 6).

Overhaul

6 Clean the exterior of the caliper with denatured alcohol or brake system cleaner.

7 Push the piston on one side of the caliper all the way in, then block it using a flat piece of wood and grips. Displace the opposite piston using compressed air directed into the banjo bolt bore **(see illustration)**. Use only low

7.7a Block the piston on one side and use compressed air . . .

Brakes, wheels and tyres 7•11

7.7b . . . to displace the piston on the other side

7.8 Remove the dust seals . . .

7.9 . . . then the piston seals

pressure to ease the piston out. Remove the wood, then remove the piston **(see illustration)**. Remove the seals (see Steps 8 and 9) from the bore of the displaced piston, then reinstall the piston and block it using the wood. Now displace the piston from the other side using the same method. Remove the wood and both the pistons. Mark each piston head and caliper body with a felt marker to ensure that the pistons can be matched to their original bores on reassembly.

⚠ **Warning: Never place your fingers in front of the pistons in an attempt to catch or protect them when applying compressed air, as serious injury could result.**

Caution: Do not try to remove the pistons by levering them out, or by using pliers or any other grips. Do not attempt to remove the caliper bore plugs on the outside of the caliper.

8 Remove the dust seal from each caliper bore using a wooden or plastic tool **(see illustration)**. Discard them as new ones must be used on installation. If a metal tool is being used, take great care not to damage the bores.

9 Remove and discard the piston seals in the same way **(see illustration)**.

10 Clean the pistons and bores with clean DOT 4 brake fluid.

Caution: Do not, under any circumstances, use a petroleum-based solvent to clean brake parts.

11 Inspect the caliper bores and pistons for signs of corrosion, nicks and burrs and loss of plating. If surface defects are present, the caliper and/or pistons must be replaced with new ones. If the necessary measuring equipment is available, compare the dimensions of the caliper bores to those specified at the beginning of the Chapter, and install a new caliper if necessary. If the caliper is in bad shape the master cylinder should also be checked.

12 Lubricate the new piston seals with the silicone grease supplied in the kit or with clean brake fluid and fit them into their grooves in the caliper bores **(see illustrations)**.

13 Lubricate the new dust seals and fit them into their grooves in the caliper bores **(see illustration)**.

14 Lubricate the pistons and fit them closed-end first into the caliper bores **(see illustrations)**. Using your thumbs, push the pistons all the way in, making sure they enter the bore squarely **(see illustration)**.

Installation

15 If removed, install the brake pads (see Section 6).

16 Slide the caliper onto the disc, making

7.12a Lubricate the new piston seals . . .

7.12b . . . and fit them into their grooves

7.13 Lubricate and fit the new dust seals

7.14a Lubricate the pistons . . .

7.14b . . . then fit them into their bores . . .

7.14c . . . and press them all the way down

7•12 Brakes, wheels and tyres

7.17 Always use new sealing washers

8.3 Rear brake disc bolts (arrowed)

sure the pads sit squarely on each side (see illustration 6.1b). If the caliper doesn't slide on easily, push the pistons a little way back into the caliper using hand pressure on the pads or a piece of wood as leverage. Install the caliper mounting bolts and tighten them to the torque setting specified at the beginning of the Chapter (see illustration 6.1a).

17 If removed, connect the brake hose to the caliper, using new sealing washers on each side of the fitting (see illustration). Align the hose as noted on removal (see illustration 7.3). Tighten the banjo bolt to the torque setting specified at the beginning of the Chapter. Top up the master cylinder reservoir with DOT 4 brake fluid (see *Daily (pre-ride) checks*) and bleed the hydraulic system as described in Section 11.

18 Check for leaks and thoroughly test the operation of the brake before riding the motorcycle.

8 Rear brake disc

Inspection

1 Refer to Section 4 of this Chapter, noting that the dial gauge should be attached to the swingarm.

Removal

2 Remove the rear wheel (see Section 15).
3 Mark the relationship of the disc to the wheel, so that it can be installed in the same position. Unscrew the disc retaining bolts, loosening them evenly and a little at a time in a criss-cross pattern to avoid distorting the disc, and remove the disc (see illustration).

Installation

4 Before installing the disc, make sure there is no dirt or corrosion where the disc seats on the hub, particularly right in the angle of the seat, as this will not allow the disc to sit flat when it is bolted down, and it will appear to be warped when checked or when using the rear brake.

5 Mount the disc on the wheel, making sure any directional arrow is on the outside and pointing in the direction of normal (i.e. forward) rotation. Align the previously applied match marks (if you're reinstalling the original disc).

6 Clean the threads of the disc mounting bolts, then apply a suitable non-permanent thread locking compound. Install the bolts and tighten them evenly and a little at a time in a criss-cross pattern to the torque setting specified at the beginning of the Chapter (see illustration 8.3). Clean off all grease from the brake disc, using acetone or brake system cleaner. If a new brake disc has been installed, remove any protective coating from its working surfaces.

7 Install the rear wheel (see Section 15).

8 Operate the brake pedal several times to bring the pads into contact with the disc. Check the operation of the brake carefully before riding the motorcycle.

9 Rear brake master cylinder

Warning: *Do not, under any circumstances, use petroleum-based solvents to clean internal brake parts. Use new brake fluid only. Use care when working with brake fluid as it can injure your eyes and it will damage painted surfaces and plastic parts – cover these with rag.*

Note: *If the entire rear brake system is being removed (i.e. caliper as well as the master cylinder), or if you intend to change the brake fluid, drain the brake fluid completely from the system (see Section 11), as opposed to retaining the old fluid within it by blocking the hose as described (Step 4).*

1 If the master cylinder is leaking fluid, or if the pedal does not produce a firm feel when the brake is applied, and bleeding the brakes does not help (see Section 11), and the hydraulic hose and brake caliper are in good condition, then master cylinder overhaul is recommended.

2 Before disassembling the master cylinder, read through the entire procedure and make sure that you have the correct rebuild kit. Also, you will need some new DOT 4 brake fluid, some clean rags and internal circlip pliers. **Note:** *To prevent damage to the paint from spilled brake fluid, always cover the surrounding components when working on the master cylinder.*

Caution: *Disassembly, overhaul and reassembly of the brake master cylinder must be done in a spotlessly clean work area to avoid contamination and possible failure of the brake hydraulic system components.*

Removal

3 Remove the screw securing the master cylinder fluid reservoir to the frame, then remove the reservoir cap, diaphragm plate and diaphragm, and pour the fluid into a container (see illustrations). Replace the cap assembly afterwards

4 Unscrew the brake hose banjo bolt and separate the hose from the master cylinder,

9.3a Remove the screw and displace the reservoir . . .

9.3b . . . then remove the cap, plate and diaphragm . . .

9.3c . . . and tip the brake fluid out

Brakes, wheels and tyres 7•13

9.4 Brake hose banjo bolt (arrowed)

9.5a Remove the split pin and washer...

9.5b ... then withdraw the clevis pin

noting its alignment **(see illustration)**. Discard the sealing washers as they must be replaced with new ones. Either clamp the hose, plug it using another suitable short piece of hose fitted through the eye of the banjo union (a fairly tight fit is necessary for a good seal), block it using a suitable bolt with sealing washers and a capped (domed) nut, or wrap some plastic foodwrap tightly around (a finger cut off a latex glove also works well), the object being to minimise fluid loss and prevent dirt entering the system. Whatever you do, also cover the end of the hose in rag, just in case.

5 Remove the split pin and washer from the clevis pin securing the brake pedal to the master cylinder pushrod **(see illustration)**. Withdraw the clevis pin and separate the pedal from the pushrod **(see illustration)**. Discard the split pin, as a new one must be used.

6 Unscrew the two bolts securing the master cylinder to the footrest bracket and remove the master cylinder and reservoir **(see illustrations)**.

Overhaul

7 If required, release the clamp securing the reservoir hose to the union on the master cylinder and detach the hose and reservoir, being prepared to catch any residual fluid **(see illustration)**.

8 Dislodge the rubber dust boot from the base of the master cylinder, then remove the circlip using circlip pliers **(see illustration)**.

9 Slide out the pushrod assembly, piston and spring **(see illustration)**. Lay the parts out in the proper order to prevent confusion during reassembly. Mark the position of the clevis locknut on the pushrod, then slacken the locknut and thread the clevis and its base nut,

followed by the locknut, off the pushrod **(see illustration)**.

10 Clean out the master cylinder bore with new brake fluid.

Caution: Do not, under any circumstances, use a petroleum-based solvent to clean brake parts.

11 Check the master cylinder bore for corrosion, scratches, nicks and score marks. If the necessary measuring equipment is available, compare the diameter of the bore to that given in the Specifications Section of this Chapter. If damage is evident, the master cylinder must be replaced with a new one. If the master cylinder is in poor condition, then the caliper should be checked as well.

12 Inspect the reservoir hose for cracks or splits and replace it with a new one, if necessary. If required, remove the union and its bush from the master cylinder.

9.6a Unscrew the bolts...

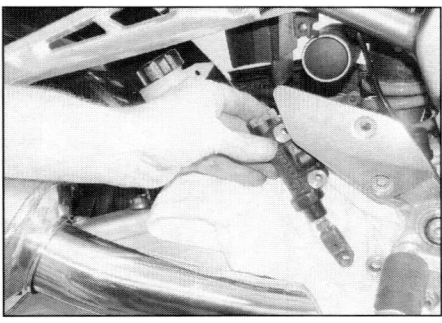

9.6b ... and remove the master cylinder and reservoir

9.7 Reservoir hose clamps (arrowed)

9.8 Displace the dust boot and remove the circlip...

9.9a ... and remove the pushrod, piston and spring

9.9b Clevis (A), its base nut (B) and locknut (C)

7•14 Brakes, wheels and tyres

9.13 Fit the seal (A) and cup (B) as shown

9.14 Clip the spring onto the end of the piston

9.15 Slide the spring and piston into the cylinder

13 The dust boot, circlip, pushrod, piston assembly (incorporating the cup and seal, which should already be fitted on the piston) and spring are included in the rebuild kit. Use all of the new parts, regardless of the apparent condition of the old ones. If the cup and seal are not on the piston, lubricate them with silicone grease or new brake fluid and fit them according to the layout of the old piston assembly **(see illustration)**. The dust boot should be on the pushrod, but if not fit it on, locating the inner lip in the groove.

14 Fit the spring onto the end of the piston, locating its end over the clips **(see illustration)**.

15 Lubricate the piston assembly with clean brake fluid. Fit the assembly spring first into the master cylinder, making sure the lips on the cup and seal do not turn inside out when they are slipped into the bore **(see illustration)**.

16 Thread the clevis locknut and the clevis with its base nut onto the master cylinder pushrod end **(see illustrations)**. Position the clevis as noted on removal, then tighten the locknut securely **(see illustration 9.9c)**.

17 Peel the rubber boot back, then fit the new circlip around the pushrod **(see illustration)**. Locate the pushrod end against the piston, then push the piston in until the washer on the pushrod is past the circlip groove, then fit the circlip into the groove, making sure it is properly seated **(see illustrations)**.

18 Fit the rubber dust boot, making sure the outer lip seats correctly in the groove in the master cylinder bore end, and the inner lip is located in the groove in the pushrod **(see illustration)**.

19 If removed, fit the reservoir hose union bush, then push the union into the bush. Fit the reservoir hose onto the union and secure it with the clamp. Check that the hose is secure and clamped at the reservoir end as well **(see illustration 9.7)**.

Installation

20 Fit the master cylinder onto the footrest bracket and tighten its mounting bolts to the torque setting specified at the beginning of the Chapter **(see illustrations 9.6b and a)**.

21 Align the brake pedal with the master cylinder pushrod clevis, then slide in the clevis pin and secure it using a new split pin, not forgetting the washer **(see illustrations 9.5b and a)**. Check the brake pedal height as described in Chapter 1, Section 9 and adjust it if necessary.

22 Connect the brake hose to the master cylinder, using a new sealing washer on each side of the banjo union **(see illustration)**. Ensure that the hose is positioned so that it butts against the rear lug and tighten the banjo bolt to the specified torque setting **(see illustration 9.4)**.

23 Make sure the reservoir hose is securely clamped at each end. Fill the fluid reservoir with new DOT 4 brake fluid (see *Daily (pre-*

9.16a Thread the locknut on first . . .

9.16b . . . then the clevis and its base nut

9.17a Fit the circlip onto the pushrod . . .

9.17b . . . then locate the pushrod tip in the end of the piston . . .

9.17c . . . push the piston in and locate the circlip in its groove

9.18 Locate the dust boot in its grooves

Brakes, wheels and tyres 7•15

9.22 Always use new sealing washers

ride) checks) and bleed the system following the procedure in Section 11. On completion install the reservoir and tighten the screw **(see illustration 9.3a)**.
24 Check the operation of the rear brake carefully before riding the motorcycle.

10 Brake hoses and unions

Inspection

1 Check brake hose condition regularly and replace the hoses at the specified four-yearly interval (see Chapter 1).
2 Twist and flex the hoses while looking for cracks, bulges and seeping fluid. Check extra carefully around the areas where the hoses connect with the banjo fittings, as these are common areas for hose failure.
3 Inspect the banjo union fittings connected to the brake hoses. If the fittings are rusted, scratched or cracked, replace them with new ones.

Replacement

4 The brake hoses have banjo union fittings on each end. Cover the surrounding area with plenty of rags and unscrew the banjo bolt at each end of the hose, noting its alignment **(see illustrations 3.3, 5.6, 7.3 and 9.4)**. Free the hoses from any clips or guides and remove them. Discard the sealing washers as new ones must be used.
5 Position the new hose, making sure it isn't twisted or otherwise strained, and abut the tab on the hose union with the lug on the component casting, where present. Otherwise align the hose as noted on removal. Install the hose banjo bolts using new sealing washers on both sides of the unions **(see illustrations 3.19, 5.21, 7.17 and 9.22)**. Tighten the banjo bolts to the torque setting specified at the beginning of this Chapter.
6 Make sure the hoses are correctly aligned and routed clear of all moving components. Flush the old brake fluid from the system, refill with new DOT 4 brake fluid (see *Daily (pre-ride) checks*) and bleed the air from the system (see Section 11). Check the operation of the brakes carefully before riding the motorcycle.

11 Brake system bleeding

Note: *If required use a commercially available vacuum-type brake bleeding tool **(see illustration)**. If bleeding the system using the conventional method does not work sufficiently well, it is advisable to obtain a bleeder and repeat the procedure detailed below, following the manufacturers instructions for using the tool.*

 Warning: Use care when working with brake fluid as it can injure your eyes and it will damage painted surfaces and plastic parts.

Bleeding

1 Bleeding the brakes is simply the process of removing all the air bubbles from the brake fluid reservoirs, the hoses and the brake calipers. Bleeding is necessary whenever a brake system hydraulic connection is loosened, when a component or hose is replaced, or when a master cylinder or caliper is overhauled. Leaks in the system may also allow air to enter, but leaking brake fluid will reveal their presence and warn you of the need for repair.
2 To bleed the brakes, you will need some new DOT 4 brake fluid, a length of clear vinyl or plastic tubing, a small container partially filled with clean brake fluid, some rags and a ring spanner to fit the brake caliper bleed valves.
3 Cover the body panels and other painted

11.5a Remove the cap from the valve – rear caliper outer valve shown

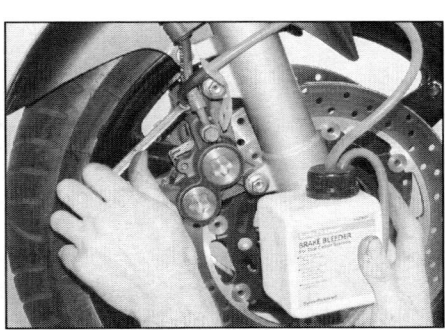

11.5c 'One-man' bleeding kit in use on the front caliper

11.0 Vacuum type brake bleeder

components as required to prevent damage in the event that brake fluid is spilled.
4 Remove the reservoir cover, diaphragm plate, and diaphragm (see *Daily (pre-ride) checks*) and slowly pump the brake lever or pedal a few times, until no air bubbles can be seen floating up from the holes in the bottom of the reservoir. Doing this bleeds the air from the master cylinder end of the line. Loosely refit the reservoir cover or cap.
5 Pull the dust cap off the bleed valve on the caliper **(see illustration)**. If you are using a ring spanner to slacken and tighten the valve (which is preferable to an open-ended spanner as it keeps itself in place) fit it over now – an open-ended spanner can be fitted later. Attach one end of the clear vinyl or plastic tubing to the bleed valve and submerge the other end in the brake fluid in the container **(see illustrations)**.
6 Check the fluid level in the reservoir – do

11.5b Fit the tubing over the valve – note the ring spanner

11.5d Note the twin hose set-up in use on the rear caliper which has two bleed valves

not allow it to drop below the lower mark during the bleeding process.
7 Carefully pump the brake lever or pedal three or four times and hold it in (front) or down (rear) while opening the caliper bleed valve. When the valve is opened, brake fluid will flow into the clear tubing and the lever will move toward the handlebar or the pedal will move down.
8 Retighten the bleed valve, then release the brake lever or pedal gradually. Repeat the process until no air bubbles are visible in the brake fluid leaving the caliper and the lever or pedal is firm when applied. On completion, disconnect the bleeding equipment, then tighten the bleed valve to the torque setting specified at the beginning of the chapter and install the dust cap. Note that there are two bleed valves on the rear caliper – some commercially available bleeding kits enable two valves to be bled simultaneously.
9 Install the diaphragm, plate, and cover. Wipe up any spilled brake fluid and check the entire system for leaks.

 If it's not possible to produce a firm feel to the lever or pedal the fluid may be aerated. Let the brake fluid in the system stabilise for a few hours and then repeat the procedure when the tiny bubbles in the system have settled out. Also check to make sure that there are no 'high-spots' in the brake hose in which an air bubble can become trapped – this will occur most often in an incorrectly mounted hose union, but can also arise through bleeding the brakes while some of the brake system components are at such an angle to encourage this. Reversing the angle or displacing and moving the offending component around will normally dislodge any trapped air.

Changing the fluid
10 Changing the brake fluid is a similar process to bleeding the brakes and requires the same materials, plus a suitable tool for siphoning the fluid out of the hydraulic reservoir (such as a syringe, though if one isn't available it is no problem to displace the reservoir and tip the fluid out as described in Section 5 or 9). Ensure that your container is large enough to take all the old fluid when it is flushed out of the system.
11 Follow Steps 3, 4 and 5, but after removing the reservoir cover, diaphragm plate, and diaphragm siphon or tip the old fluid out of the reservoir (if you want to tip the contents out of the front reservoir displace it from the handlebars). Fill the reservoir with new brake fluid, then follow Step 7.
12 Retighten the bleed valve, then release the brake lever or pedal gradually. Keep the reservoir topped-up with new fluid to above the LOWER level at all times or air may enter the system and greatly increase the length of the task. Repeat the process until new fluid can be seen emerging from the bleed valve.

 Old brake fluid is invariably much darker in colour than new fluid, making it easy to see when all old fluid has been expelled from the system.

13 Disconnect the hose, then tighten the bleed valve to the specified torque setting and install the dust cap.
14 Top-up the reservoir, install the diaphragm, plate, and cover. Wipe up any spilled brake fluid and check the entire system for leaks.
15 Check the operation of the brakes before riding the motorcycle.

Draining the system for overhaul
16 Draining the brake fluid is again a similar process to bleeding the brakes. The quickest and easiest way is to use a commercially available vacuum-type brake bleeding tool (see **Note** at the beginning of this Section) – follow the manufacturer's instructions. Otherwise follow the procedure described above for changing the fluid, but quite simply do not put any new fluid into the reservoir – the system fills itself with air instead.

12 Wheel inspection and repair

1 Position the motorcycle on its centrestand. When checking the front wheel support the bike so the wheel is raised off the ground. Clean the wheels thoroughly to remove mud and dirt that may interfere with the inspection procedure or mask defects. Make a general check of the wheels (see Chapter 1) and tyres (see *Daily (pre-ride) checks*).
2 To check axial (side-to-side) run-out, attach a dial gauge to the fork leg or the swingarm and position its stem against the side of the rim **(see illustration)**. Spin the wheel slowly

12.2 Check the wheel for radial (out-of-round) run-out (A) and axial (side-to-side) run-out (B)

and check the amount of run-out at the rim. To accurately check radial (out of round) run-out with the dial gauge, remove the wheel from the machine, and the tyre from the wheel. With the axle clamped in a vice and the dial gauge positioned on the top of the rim, rotate the wheel and check the run-out.
3 An easier, though slightly less accurate, method is to attach a stiff wire pointer to the fork slider or the swingarm and position the end a fraction of an inch from the wheel (where the wheel and tyre join). If the wheel is true, the distance from the pointer to the rim will be constant as the wheel is rotated. **Note:** *If wheel run-out is excessive, check the wheel bearings and axle very carefully before replacing.*
4 Visually inspect the wheels for cracks, flat spots on the rim, and other damage. Look very closely for dents in the area where the tyre bead contacts the rim. Dents in this area may prevent complete sealing of the tyre against the rim, which leads to deflation of the tyre over a period of time.
5 If damage is evident, or if run-out in either direction is excessive, the wheel will have to be replaced with a new one. Never attempt to repair a damaged cast alloy wheel.

13 Wheel alignment check

1 Misalignment of the wheels, which may be due to a cocked rear wheel or a bent frame or fork yokes, can cause strange and possibly serious handling problems. If the frame or yokes are at fault, repair by a frame specialist or replacement with new parts are the only alternatives.
2 To check the alignment you will need an assistant, a length of string or a perfectly straight piece of wood and a ruler. A plumb bob or other suitable weight will also be required.
3 Place the bike on its centrestand. Measure the width of both tyres at their widest points. Subtract the smaller measurement from the larger measurement, then divide the difference by two. The result is the amount of offset that should exist between the front and rear tyres on both sides.
4 If a string is used, have your assistant hold one end of it about halfway between the floor and the rear axle, touching the rear sidewall of the tyre.
5 Run the other end of the string forward and pull it tight so that it is roughly parallel to the floor **(see illustration)**. Slowly bring the string into contact with the rear sidewall of the rear tyre, then turn the front wheel until it is parallel with the string. Measure the distance from the front tyre sidewall to the string.
6 Repeat the procedure on the other side of the motorcycle. The distance from the front tyre sidewall to the string should be equal on both sides.

Brakes, wheels and tyres 7•17

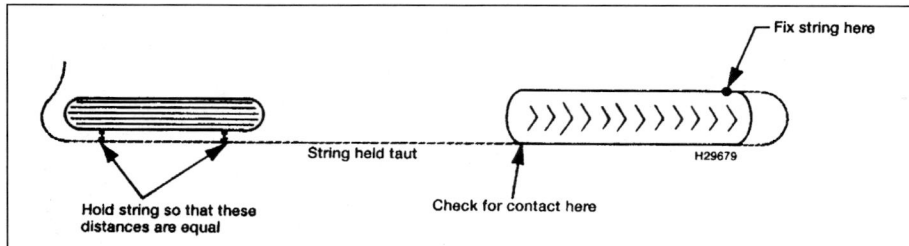

13.5 Wheel alignment check using string

13.7 Wheel alignment check using a straight-edge

7 As previously mentioned, a perfectly straight length of wood or metal bar may be substituted for the string **(see illustration)**. The procedure is the same.

8 If the distance between the string and tyre is greater on one side, or if the rear wheel appears to be cocked, refer to Chapter 1, Section 1 and check that the chain adjuster markings coincide on each side of the swingarm.

9 If the front-to-back alignment is correct, the wheels still may be out of alignment vertically.

10 Using a plumb bob, or other suitable weight, and a length of string, check the rear wheel to make sure it is vertical. To do this, hold the string against the tyre upper sidewall and allow the weight to settle just off the floor. When the string touches both the upper and lower tyre sidewalls and is perfectly straight, the wheel is vertical. If it is not, place thin spacers under one leg of the stand until it is.

11 Once the rear wheel is vertical, check the front wheel in the same manner. If both wheels are not perfectly vertical, the frame and/or major suspension components are bent.

Section 3). Support the calipers with a piece of wire or a bungee cord so that no strain is placed on the hydraulic hoses. There is no need to disconnect the hoses from the calipers. **Note**: *Do not operate the front brake lever with the calipers removed.*

3 Slacken the axle clamp bolt on the bottom of the right-hand fork, then unscrew the axle. If a large hex key is not available, you may be able to utilise an automotive sump plug tool or a bolt and nut arrangement, as shown **(see illustrations)**.

4 Support the wheel, then withdraw the axle from the right-hand side and remove the wheel **(see illustration)**. Use a drift to drive out the axle if required.

5 Remove the spacer from each side of the wheel **(see illustration)**.

Caution: Don't lay the wheel down and allow it to rest on either disc – the disc could become warped. Set the wheel on wood blocks so the disc does not support the weight of the wheel, or keep it upright.

14 Front wheel

Removal

1 Put the motorcycle on its centrestand and support it under the crankcase so that the front wheel is off the ground. Always make sure the motorcycle is properly supported.

2 Displace the front brake calipers (see

14.3a Slacken the clamp bolt (A) and unscrew the axle (B) . . .

14.3b . . . using either a hex key . . .

14.3c . . . or a nut and bolt arrangement as shown (use a spanner on the inner nut)

14.4 Withdraw the axle and remove the wheel

14.5 Remove the spacer from each side

7•18 Brakes, wheels and tyres

14.9 Make sure the directional arrows are pointing the correct way

14.10 Tighten the axle to the specified torque

6 Check the axle is straight by rolling it on a flat surface such as a piece of plate glass (first wipe off all old grease and remove any corrosion using wire wool). If the axle is bent, replace it with a new one.

7 Check the condition of the wheel bearings (see Section 16).

Installation

8 Apply lithium-based grease to the lips of the bearing seals. Fit the spacers into the wheel, with the shouldered end facing out **(see illustration 14.5)**.

9 Manoeuvre the wheel into position, making sure it is the correct way round with the arrows on both the wheel and the tyre pointing in the direction of forward rotation **(see illustration)**. Apply a thin coat of lithium-based grease to the axle.

10 Lift the wheel into place between the forks, making sure the spacers remain in position, and slide the axle in from the right-hand side **(see illustration 14.4)**. Tighten the axle to the torque setting specified at the beginning of the Chapter **(see illustration)**.

11 Install the brake calipers, making sure the pads sit squarely on each side of the discs (see Section 3).

12 Apply the front brake a few times to bring the pads back into contact with the discs. Take the bike off the stand, apply the front brake and pump the front forks a few times to settle all components in position. Now tighten the axle clamp bolt on the bottom of the right-hand fork to the specified torque setting **(see illustration 14.3a)**.

13 Check the operation of the front brake before riding the bike.

15 Rear wheel

Removal

1 Support the motorcycle on its centrestand.

2 Slacken the nuts on the brake caliper torque arm bolts **(see illustration)**.

3 Slacken the adjuster locknut on each side of the swingarm, then turn the adjusters in to provide some slack in the chain **(see illustration)**. Unscrew the axle nut and remove the washer and the adjustment position marker from the left-hand side of the swingarm **(see illustration)**.

4 Support the wheel then withdraw the axle along with the right-hand adjustment position marker and lower the wheel to the ground, allowing the caliper and bracket to drop with it **(see illustration)**. Note how the caliper bracket locates between the wheel and the swingarm.

5 Disengage the chain from the sprocket and remove the wheel from between the swingarm ends **(see illustration)**.

Caution: Do not lay the wheel down and allow it to rest on the disc or the sprocket – they could become warped. Set the wheel on wood blocks so the disc or the sprocket does not support the weight of the wheel. Do not operate the brake pedal with the wheel removed.

6 Remove the spacer from each side of the

15.2 Slacken the nuts on the torque arm bolts (arrowed)

15.3a Slacken the locknut (A) on each side and turn each adjuster (B) in

15.3b Unscrew the axle nut and remove the washer and the position marker (arrowed)

15.4 Withdraw the axle and lower the wheel to the ground

15.5 Disengage the chain and remove the wheel

Brakes, wheels and tyres 7•19

15.6a Remove the right-hand spacer . . .

15.6b . . . and the left-hand spacer, noting which fits where

15.11 Pivot the caliper up onto the disc

wheel, noting which fits where **(see illustrations)**.

7 Check the axle is straight by rolling it on a flat surface such as a piece of plate glass (first wipe off all old grease and remove any corrosion using wire wool). If the axle is bent, replace it with a new one.

8 Check the condition of the bearing seals and wheel bearings (see Section 16).

Installation

9 Apply a thin coat of lithium-based grease to the lips of each grease seal, and also to the spacers and the axle. Slide the left-hand adjustment position marker onto the axle, making sure it is the correct way around.

10 Fit the spacer into each side of the wheel **(see illustrations 15.6b and a)**.

11 Manoeuvre the wheel into place between the ends of the swingarm and engage the drive chain with the sprocket **(see illustration 15.5)**. Pivot the caliper and bracket up, making sure the pads locate on each side of the disc and the bracket fits between the wheel and the swingarm

12 Lift the wheel into position, making sure the spacers remain in place and the caliper bracket remains aligned, and slide the axle, with the adjustment marker, through from the right-hand side **(see illustration 15.4)**. Make sure it passes through the caliper bracket. Align the flats on the axle head between the raised sections on the adjustment marker, and make sure the raised sections are vertical, not horizontal **(see illustration)**. Check that everything is correctly aligned, then fit the left-hand adjustment position marker onto the axle, followed by the washer and the axle nut **(see illustration 15.3b)**.

13 Adjust the chain slack as described in Chapter 1, then tighten the axle nut to the torque setting specified at the beginning of the Chapter **(see illustration)**.

14 Tighten the brake torque arm nuts to the specified torque setting.

15 Operate the rear brake pedal several times to bring the pads into contact with the disc. Check the operation of the rear brake carefully before riding the bike.

16 Wheel bearing replacement

Note: *Before removing the bearings (but having removed the seals etc as required to access the bearings), refer to* Tools and Workshop Tips *in the Reference Section and check the bearings to determine if new ones are needed – however good their apparent condition, once the bearings have been removed from the wheel they should be replaced with new ones rather than being reused, as the impact on the inner race could damage them. Always replace the wheel bearings in sets. Never replace the bearings individually. Avoid using a high pressure cleaner on the wheel bearing area.*

Front wheel bearings

Note: *Always replace the wheel bearings in pairs, never individually. Avoid using a high pressure cleaner on the wheel bearing area.*

1 Remove the front wheel (see Section 14).

2 Set the wheel on blocks so as not to allow the weight of the wheel to rest on either brake disc.

15.12 Locate the flats on the axle head between the raised sections on the position marker

3 Lever out the grease seal on each side of the wheel using a large flat-bladed screwdriver, taking care not to damage the rim **(see illustration)**. Discard the seals.

> **HAYNES HiNT** *Position a piece of wood against the wheel to prevent the screwdriver shaft damaging it when levering the grease seal out.*

4 Refer to *Tools and Workshop Tips* (Section 5 in the Reference Section) and check the bearings as described. If worn, replace them with new ones as follows.

5 Remove the bearing on one side using a commercially available bearing puller, referring to Tools and Workshop tips in the reference Section for details on its use **(see illustration)**. Turn the wheel over to allow the bearing spacer to fall free, then remove the other bearing following the same procedure.

15.13 Tighten the axle nut to the specified torque

16.3 Lever out the grease seal on each side

16.5 Remove the bearings using a puller

16.6 A socket can be used to drive in the bearing

16.8 Press the grease seal into place

16.10a Lift the sprocket coupling out of the wheel . . .

16.10b . . . then remove the coupling spacer . . .

16.10c . . . and the bearing spacer

6 Thoroughly clean the hub area of the wheel. Install a new bearing into one side of the hub, with the marked or sealed side facing outwards. Using the old bearing, a bearing driver or a socket large enough to contact the outer race of the bearing only, drive it in until it's completely seated **(see illustration)**. Do not drive the bearing in against its inner race.

7 Turn the wheel over and install the bearing spacer. Drive the other bearing into place as described above.

8 Apply a smear of lithium based grease to the lips of the new seals, then press them into the wheel, using a seal or bearing driver or a suitable socket to drive it into place if necessary **(see illustration)**. As the seals sit flush with the top surface of their housing, using a piece of wood as shown will automatically set them flush without the risk of setting them too deep and having to lever them out again.

9 Clean off all grease from the brake discs using acetone or brake system cleaner then install the wheel (see Section 14).

Rear wheel bearings

10 Remove the wheel (see Section 15). Lift the sprocket coupling out of the wheel, noting how it fits **(see illustration)**. Remove the sprocket coupling spacer from inside the needle bearing, then withdraw the long bearing spacer **(see illustrations)**. A caged ball bearing is fitted in the right-hand side of the wheel and a needle bearing is fitted in the left-hand side.

11 Set the wheel on blocks with the disc facing up.

12 Lever out the grease seal on the right-hand side of the wheel using a large flat-bladed screwdriver, taking care not to damage the rim of the hub **(see Haynes Hint) (see illustration)**. Discard the seal.

13 Refer to *Tools and Workshop Tips* (Section 5 in the Reference Section) and check the bearings as described. If worn, replace them with new ones as follows.

14 Remove the circlip securing the caged ball bearing **(see illustration)**. Turn the wheel over so that the disc is facing down and rest it on the blocks so it is off the ground or bench. Using a metal rod (preferably a brass drift punch) inserted through the centre of the needle bearing, tap evenly around the inner race of the caged ball bearing to drive it from the hub **(see illustration)**.

15 Lay the wheel on its other side so that the needle bearing faces down. Drive the bearing out of the wheel using the same technique as above.

16 Thoroughly clean the hub area of the wheel. First install the new needle bearing into its recess in the left-hand side of the hub **(see illustration)**. Needle bearings should be pressed or drawn, rather than driven, into position. In the absence of a press, a suitable drawbolt arrangement can be made up as described in *Tools and Workshop Tips* (Section 5) in the *Reference* section.

17 Turn the wheel over. Drive the caged ball bearing squarely into its recess in the right-hand side of the hub, with the marked or sealed side facing outwards, using the old bearing, a bearing driver or a socket large enough to contact the outer race of the bearing, until it is completely seated **(see illustration)**. Fit the circlip, making sure it locates correctly in its groove **(see illustration 16.16a)**.

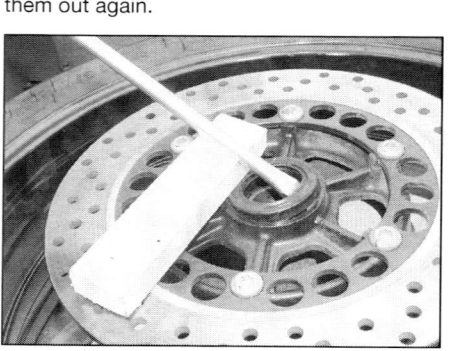

16.12 Lever out the grease seal

16.14a Remove the circlip (arrowed) . . .

16.14b . . . then turn the wheel over and drift the bearing out

Brakes, wheels and tyres 7•21

16.16 Fit the needle bearing (arrowed) into its housing

16.17 A socket can be used to drive in the ball bearing

18 Apply a smear of grease to the lips of the new grease seal, and press it into the right-hand side of the wheel, using a seal or bearing driver, a suitable socket or a flat piece of wood **(see illustration)**. Since the seals sit flush with the top surface of its housing, using a piece of wood, as shown, will automatically set it flush without the risk of setting it too deep and having to lever it out again.

19 Turn the wheel over and fit the bearing spacer into the hub, then fit the sprocket coupling spacer into the needle bearing **(see illustrations 16.10c and b)**.

20 Clean off all grease from the brake disc using acetone or brake system cleaner. Install the sprocket coupling assembly **(see illustration 16.10a)**. Install the wheel (see Section 15).

Sprocket coupling bearing

21 Remove the rear wheel (see Section 15). Lift the sprocket coupling out of the wheel, noting how it fits **(see illustration 16.10a)**.

22 Using a large flat-bladed screwdriver lever out the grease seal from the outside of the coupling, taking care not to damage the rim of the coupling **(see Haynes Hint) (see illustration)**. Discard the seal if it is damaged or deteriorated.

23 Refer to *Tools and Workshop Tips* (Section 5 in the Reference Section) and check the bearing as described. If worn, replace it with a new one as follows.

24 Support the coupling on blocks of wood and drive the bearing out from the inside using a bearing driver or socket **(see illustration)**.

25 Thoroughly clean the bearing recess in the coupling. Drive the bearing in from the outside of the coupling, with the marked or sealed side facing out, using the old bearing (if a new one is being fitted), a bearing driver or a socket large enough to contact the outer race of the bearing, until it is completely seated.

26 Apply a smear of grease to the lips of the new seal, and press it into the coupling, using a seal or bearing driver or a suitable socket if necessary **(see illustration)**.

16.18 Press the grease seal into place

16.22 Lever out the grease seal

16.24 Drive the bearing out from the inside

16.26 Press the grease seal into place

7•22 Brakes, wheels and tyres

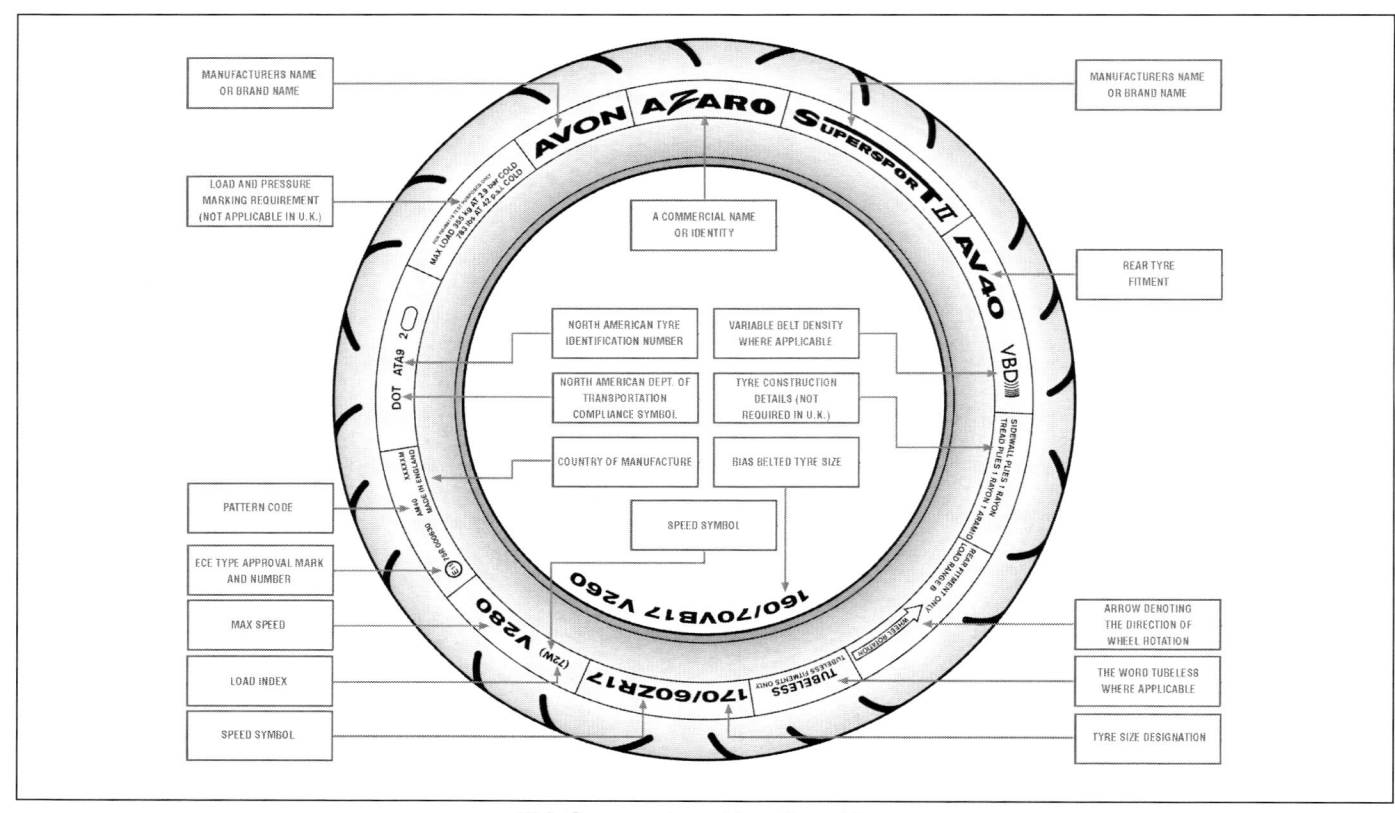

17.3 Common tyre sidewall markings

27 Check the sprocket coupling/rubber dampers (see Chapter 6, Section 18).
28 Fit the sprocket coupling into the wheel **(see illustration 16.10a)**, then install the wheel (see Section 15).

17 Tyre fitting

General information

1 The wheels fitted on all models are designed to take tubeless tyres only. Tyre sizes are given in the Specifications at the beginning of this chapter.
2 Refer to *Daily (pre-ride) checks* at the beginning of this manual for tyre maintenance.

Fitting new tyres

3 When selecting new tyres, refer to the tyre information label on the swingarm and the tyre options listed in the Owner's Handbook. Ensure that front and rear tyre types are compatible, and of the correct size and speed rating; if necessary, seek advice from a Yamaha dealer or tyre fitting specialist **(see illustration)**.
4 It is recommended that tyres are fitted by a motorcycle tyre specialist and that this is not attempted in the home workshop. This is particularly relevant in the case of tubeless tyres because the force required to break the seal between the wheel rim and tyre bead is substantial, and is usually beyond the capabilities of an individual working with normal tyre levers. Additionally, the specialist will be able to balance the wheels after tyre fitting.
5 Note that punctured tubeless tyres can in some cases be repaired. Seek the advice of a Yamaha dealer or a motorcycle tyre fitting specialist concerning tyre repairs.

Chapter 8
Bodywork

Contents

Fairing and body panels 3
Front mudguard 5
General information 1
Rear view mirrors 4
Seats 2

Degrees of difficulty

| Easy, suitable for novice with little experience | Fairly easy, suitable for beginner with some experience | Fairly difficult, suitable for competent DIY mechanic 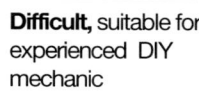 | Difficult, suitable for experienced DIY mechanic | Very difficult, suitable for expert DIY or professional 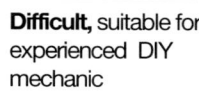 |

1 General information

1 This Chapter covers the procedures necessary to remove and install the body parts. Since many service and repair operations on these motorcycles require the removal of the body parts, the procedures are grouped here and referred to from other Chapters.

2 In the case of damage to the body parts, it is usually necessary to remove the broken component and replace it with a new (or used) one. There are, however, some companies that specialise in 'plastic welding' and there are a number of DIY repair kits now available.

3 When attempting to remove any body panel, first study it closely, noting any fasteners and associated fittings, to be sure of returning everything to its correct place on installation. In some cases the aid of an assistant will be required when removing panels, to help avoid the risk of damage to paintwork. Once the evident fasteners have been removed, try to withdraw the panel as described but DO NOT FORCE IT – if it will not release, check that all fasteners have been removed and try again. Where a panel engages another by means of tabs, be careful not to break the tab or its mating slot or to damage the paintwork. Remember that a few moments of patience at this stage will save you a lot of money in replacing broken fairing panels! To release trim clips, push the centre into the body, then draw the body out of the panel **(see illustration)**.

1.3 Trim clip removal and installation

To remove the trim clip, push its centre pin (A) inwards and withdraw the clip from the panel (B) To install the trim clip, depress the pawls and push the centre pin outwards so that the clip can be inserted in the panel (C), then press the centre pin in level with the head of the clip to lock it in place (D).

8•2 Bodywork

2.1 Turn the key and lift up the back of the seat then draw it back and remove it

2.2 The tab locates in the slot in the seat base

3.2 Remove the trim clips (arrowed) on each side

4 When installing a body panel, first study it closely, noting any fasteners and associated fittings removed with it, to be sure of returning everything to its correct place. Check that all fasteners are in good condition, including all trim nuts or clips and damping/rubber mounts; any of these must be replaced with new ones, if faulty, before the panel is reassembled. Check also that all mounting brackets are straight, and repair or renew them if necessary before attempting to install the panel. Where assistance was required to remove a panel, make sure your assistant is on hand to install it. To install trim clips, first push the centre back out so that it protrudes from the top of the body **(see illustration 1.3)**. Fit the body into its panel, then push the centre in so that it is flush with the top of the body. To install quick-release screws, turn them 90° clockwise.

5 Be careful not to overtighten any fasteners or the panel may break (not always immediately) due to the uneven stress.

2 Seat

1 To remove the seat, insert the ignition key into the seat lock located on the left-hand side of the bike, and turn it anti-clockwise to unlock the seat **(see illustration)**. Lift up the front of the seat and draw it forwards, noting how the tab at the front locates.

2 Position the seat, locating the tab in its socket **(see illustration)**. Push down on the back of the seat to engage the latch.

3 Fairing and body panels

Seat cowling

1 Remove the seat (see Section 2).
2 Release and remove the four trim clips on the underside of the seat cowling (two on each side) **(see illustration and 1.3)**.
3 Unscrew the passenger grab-rail bolts and remove each grab-rail, noting the rubber pads **(see illustrations)**.
4 Remove the bolt on each side at the front and the screw on the top at the back, noting the collar, then carefully draw the cowling back and off the bike **(see illustrations)**.
5 Installation is the reverse of removal.

Side panels

6 Remove the seat (see above).

3.3a Unscrew the bolts (arrowed) . . .

3.3b . . . and remove the grab-rail

3.4a Unscrew the bolts (A) and the screw (B) . . .

3.4b . . . and remove the cowling

Bodywork 8•3

3.7a Undo the screw (arrowed) . . .

3.7b . . . then release the cut-out (arrowed) . . .

3.7c . . . and the peg (arrowed)

7 Undo the screw securing the back of the panel **(see illustration)**. At the front of the panel draw the front away from the frame to release the cut-out from the grommet, then lift the bottom to release the peg from the grommet **(see illustrations)**.

8 Installation is the reverse of removal.

Cockpit trim panels

9 Undo the three screws securing the trim panel and manoeuvre it out it, noting how it fits **(see illustrations)**. Note the washer with the side screw.

10 Installation is the reverse of removal. Make sure the panel locates correctly with the fairing.

Windshield

11 Undo the six screws and remove the windshield, noting how it fits **(see illustrations)**. Do not disturb the rubber wellnuts set in the fairing.

12 Installation is the reverse of removal. Take care not to overtighten the screws.

Fairing

13 Remove the cockpit trim panels and the windshield (see above).

14 Remove the rear view mirrors (see Section 4).

15 Disconnect the instrument cluster wiring connector and displace the headlight relay(s) from its/their mount(s) **(see illustrations)**. Disconnect the fairing loom wiring connectors **(see illustration)**.

3.9a Undo the screws (arrowed) . . .

3.9b . . . and release the panel

3.11a Undo the screws (arrowed) . . .

3.11b . . . and remove the windshield

3.15a Disconnect the wiring connector . . .

3.15b . . . and displace the relays (arrowed)

3.15c Disconnect the wiring connectors (arrowed)

3.16 Two screws (arrowed) secure the fairing at the top

3.17a Undo the screws (arrowed) on each side . . .

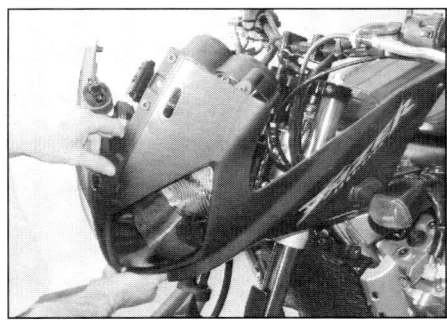

3.17b . . . then carefully remove the fairing

16 Undo the two screws securing the top of the fairing **(see illustration)**.

17 Undo the four screws securing the headlight and fairing assembly to the front sub-frame, supporting the fairing as you do **(see illustrations)**.

18 Carefully draw the fairing forwards, noting how the pegs locate in the grommets – the headlight comes away with the fairing. Separate them if required (see Chapter 9). Note the collars in the grommets. Remove the rubber pads that fit between the fairing and the mirror mounts on the sub-frame if required.

19 Installation is the reverse of removal **(see illustration)**. Make sure the grommets are in good condition and that the rubber pads for the mirror mounts are correctly located.

4 Rear view mirrors

1 Unscrew the nuts securing each mirror and remove the mirror **(see illustrations)**. Note the rubber pad that fits between the fairing and its sub-frame.

2 Installation is the reverse of removal.

5 Front mudguard

1 Unscrew the bolt securing the brake hose holder to the front fork **(see illustration)**.

2 Remove the two screws and the two bolts securing the mudguard and draw it forward **(see illustrations)**. Note the nuts fitted with the bolts, and the collars and grommets in the mudguard mounts.

3 Installation is the reverse of removal.

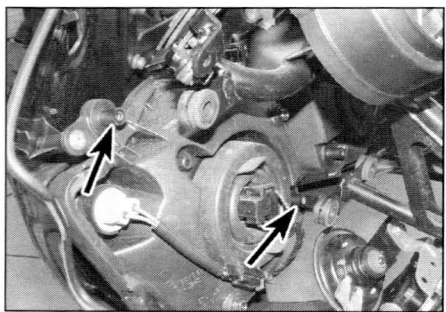

3.19 Make sure the pegs (arrowed) on each side locate in their grommets

4.1a Unscrew the two nuts (arrowed) . . .

4.1b . . . and remove the mirror

5.1 Release the brake hose holder . . .

5.2a . . . then undo the bolt, noting the nut, and the screw (arrowed) on each side . . .

5.2b . . . and remove the mudguard

Chapter 9
Electrical system

Contents

Alternator	31	Ignition (main) switch	18
Battery charging	4	Instrument and warning light bulbs	17
Battery removal and installation	3	Instrument cluster removal and installation	15
Brake light switches	14	Instrument check and disassembly	16
Brake/tail light bulbs	9	Lighting system check	6
Charging system	30	Neutral switch	21
Clutch switch	23	Oil level switch	26
Fault finding	2	Regulator/rectifier	32
Fuel pump and relay	see Chapter 4	Relay assembly	24
Fuses	5	Sidestand switch	22
General information	1	Starter motor overhaul	29
Handlebar switch check	19	Starter motor removal and installation	28
Handlebar switch housing removal and installation	20	Starter relay	27
Headlight aim check and adjustment	see Chapter 1	Tail light assembly	10
Headlight assembly	8	Turn signals	13
Headlight bulbs and sidelight bulbs	7	Turn signal bulbs	12
Horn	25	Turn signal circuit check	11

Degrees of difficulty

| Easy, suitable for novice with little experience | | Fairly easy, suitable for beginner with some experience | | Fairly difficult, suitable for competent DIY mechanic | | Difficult, suitable for experienced DIY mechanic | | Very difficult, suitable for expert DIY or professional | |

Specifications

Battery
Capacity	12V, 12Ah
Type	GT14B-4
Charge condition	
Fully charged	12.8V
Half-charged	12.4V
Discharged	12V or less
Charging time	Until fully charged (12.8V) (see Section 4)

Charging system
Current leakage	1 mA (max)
Alternator nominal output	14V, 26A @ 5000 rpm
Alternator stator coil resistance	0.27 to 0.33 ohms @ 20°C
Regulated voltage output (no load)	14.1 to 14.9V @ 5000 rpm

Starter relay
Resistance	4.18 to 4.62 ohms @ 20°C

Starter motor
Brush length	
Standard	12.5 mm
Service limit (min)	4 mm
Commutator diameter	
Standard	28 mm
Service limit (min)	27 mm
Mica depth	0.7 mm

Fuses

Main fuse (in starter relay)	30A
Circuit fuses – Europe models	
HEAD	20A
FAN	10A
IGNITION	20A
SIGNAL	20A
BACK-UP	10A
TURN	10A
Circuit fuses – US models	
HEAD	20A
FAN	10A
IGNITION	20A
SIGNAL	20A
BACK-UP	10A

Bulbs

Headlight	60/55W halogen x 2
Sidelight	5W x 2
Brake/tail light	21/5W x 2
Turn signal lights	
UK models	21W x 4
US models	27/8W x 2 (front with running light), 27W x 2 (rear)
Instrument illumination lights	2W x 3
Instrument warning light	
High beam, neutral, oil level, turn signal	1.4W x 5
Low fuel	2W x 1
Temperature	LED

Torque wrench settings

Alternator cover bolts	12 Nm
Alternator rotor bolt	65 Nm + 60°
Alternator stator bolts	14 Nm
Neutral switch	20 Nm
Oil level switch bolts	10 Nm
Starter motor long bolts	5 Nm

1 General information

All models have a 12 volt electrical system charged by a three-phase alternator with a separate regulator/rectifier.

The regulator maintains the charging system output within the specified range to prevent overcharging, and the rectifier converts the ac (alternating current) output of the alternator to dc (direct current) to power the lights and other components and to charge the battery. The alternator rotor is mounted on the left-hand end of the crankshaft.

The starter motor is mounted on the top of the crankcase. The starting system includes the motor, the battery, the relay and the various wires and switches. If the engine kill switch is in the 'RUN' position and the ignition (main) switch is ON, the starter relay allows the starter motor to operate only if the transmission is in neutral (neutral switch on) or, if the transmission is in gear, with the clutch lever pulled into the handlebar and the sidestand up.

Note: *Keep in mind that electrical parts, once purchased, cannot be returned. To avoid unnecessary expense, make very sure the faulty component has been positively identified before buying a replacement part.*

2 Fault finding

⚠ **Warning: To prevent the risk of short circuits, the ignition (main) switch must always be OFF and the battery negative (–) terminal should be disconnected before any of the bike's other electrical components are disturbed. Don't forget to reconnect the terminal securely once work is finished or if battery power is needed for circuit testing.**

1 A typical electrical circuit consists of an electrical component, the switches, relays, etc. related to that component and the wiring and connectors that link the component to the battery and the frame. To aid in locating a problem in any electrical circuit, and to guide you with the wiring colour codes and connectors, refer to the *Wiring Diagrams* at the end of this Chapter.

2 Before tackling any troublesome electrical circuit, first study the wiring diagram (see end of Chapter) thoroughly to get a complete picture of what makes up that individual circuit. Trouble spots, for instance, can often be narrowed down by noting if other components related to that circuit are operating properly or not. If several components or circuits fail at one time, chances are the fault lies in the fuse or earth (ground) connection, as several circuits often are routed through the same fuse and earth (ground) connections.

3 Electrical problems often stem from simple causes, such as loose or corroded connections or a blown fuse. Prior to any electrical fault finding, always visually check the condition of the fuse, wires and connections in the problem circuit. Intermittent failures can be especially frustrating, since you can't always duplicate the failure when it's convenient to test. In such situations, a good practice is to clean all connections in the affected circuit, whether or not they appear to be good. All of the connections and wires should also be wiggled to check for looseness which can cause intermittent failure.

4 If testing instruments are going to be utilised, use the wiring diagram to plan where you will make the necessary connections in order to accurately pinpoint the trouble spot.

Electrical system 9•3

5 The basic tools needed for electrical fault finding include a battery and bulb test circuit or a continuity tester, a test light, and a jumper wire. A multimeter capable of reading volts, ohms and amps is a very useful alternative and performs the functions of all of the above, and is necessary for performing more extensive tests and checks where specific voltage, current or resistance values are needed.

 Refer to Fault Finding Equipment in the Reference section for details of how to use electrical test equipment.

3 Battery removal and installation

Caution: Be extremely careful when handling or working around the battery. The electrolyte is very caustic and an explosive gas (hydrogen) is given off when the battery is charging.

Removal and installation

1 Remove the seat (see Chapter 8).
2 Lift up the insulating cover to access the negative (–) terminal, then unscrew the bolt and disconnect the lead **(see illustration)**.
3 Lift up the insulating cover to access the positive (+) terminal, then unscrew the bolt and disconnect the lead **(see illustration 3.2)**.
4 Disconnect the negative wire connector then release the battery strap **(see illustrations)**. Lift the battery out of its box **(see illustration)**.
5 Before installing the battery, clean the terminals and lead ends with a wire brush or knife, and emery paper.
6 Installation is the reverse of removal. When you reconnect the leads, connect the positive (+) terminal first. Note that the clock will need resetting – refer to the owners manual for details.

3.13 Measure the voltage to assess the condition of the battery from the chart

3.2 Disconnect the negative terminal (A) first, then the positive (B)

3.4b . . . then unhook the strap . . .

 Battery corrosion can be kept to a minimum by applying a layer of petroleum jelly to the terminals after the cables have been connected.

7 Install the seat (see Chapter 8).

Inspection and maintenance

8 All models are fitted with a sealed MF (maintenance free) battery. **Note:** *Do not attempt to remove the battery caps to check the electrolyte level or battery specific gravity. Removal will damage the caps, resulting in electrolyte leakage and battery damage.* However the following checks should be regularly performed – remove the battery first (see above).
9 Check that the battery terminals and leads are clean. If corrosion is evident, clean the terminals and lead ends with a wire brush or knife, and emery paper. On installation apply a thin coat of petroleum jelly or battery terminal grease to the connections to slow further corrosion.
10 Keep the battery case clean to prevent current leakage, which can discharge the battery over a period of time (especially when it sits unused). Wash the outside of the case with a solution of baking soda and water. Rinse the battery thoroughly, then dry it.
11 Look for cracks in the case and replace

3.4a Disconnect the wiring connector . . .

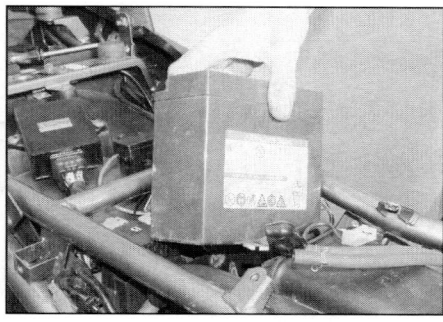

3.4c . . . and remove the battery

the battery with a new one if any are found. If acid has been spilled on the frame or battery box, neutralise it with a baking soda and water solution, dry it thoroughly, then touch up any damaged paint.
12 If the motorcycle sits unused for long periods of time, refer to Section 4 and charge the battery once every month to six weeks.
13 Assess the condition of the battery by measuring the voltage across the battery terminals – connect the voltmeter positive (+) probe to the battery positive (+) terminal, and the negative (–) probe to the battery negative (–) terminal. When fully charged there should be 12.8 volts (or more) present **(see illustration)**. If the voltage falls below 12.0 volts remove the battery (see above) and recharge it as described in Section 4.

4 Battery charging

Caution: Be extremely careful when handling or working around the battery. The electrolyte is very caustic and an explosive gas (hydrogen) is given off when the battery is charging.

1 The battery charger must be rated for 12 volts. Remove the battery (see Section 3). If not already done, refer to Section 3, Step 13, and check the open circuit voltage of the

9•4 Electrical system

4.1 Measure the voltage to determine the charging time required

4.2 If the charger doesn't have an ammeter built in, connect one in series as shown. DO NOT connect the ammeter between the battery terminals, or it will be ruined

battery. Refer to the chart **(see illustration)** and read off the charging time required according to the voltage reading taken.

2 Connect the charger to the battery, making sure that the positive (+) lead on the charger is connected to the positive (+) terminal on the battery, and the negative (–) lead is connected to the negative (–) terminal. The battery should be charged for the specified time, or until the voltage across the terminals reaches 12.8V (allow the battery to stabilise for 30 minutes after charging, before taking a voltage reading). Exceeding this can cause the battery to overheat, buckling the plates and rendering it useless. Few owners will have access to an expensive current controlled charger, so if a normal domestic charger is used check that after a possible initial peak, the charge rate falls to a safe level **(see illustration)**. If the battery becomes hot during charging **stop**. Further charging will cause damage. **Note:** *In emergencies the battery can be charged at a higher rate of around 3.0 amps for a period of 1 hour. However, this is not recommended and the low amp charge is by far the safer method of charging the battery.*

3 If the recharged battery discharges rapidly when left disconnected it is likely that an internal short caused by physical damage or sulphation has occurred. A new battery will be required. A sound item will tend to lose its charge at about 1% per day.

4 Install the battery (see Section 3).

5 If the motorcycle sits unused for long periods of time, charge the battery once every month to six weeks and leave it disconnected.

5 Fuses

1 The electrical system is protected by fuses of different ratings. All except the main fuse are housed in the fusebox, which is located under the seat **(see illustration)**. The main fuse is integral with the starter relay, which is also under the seat **(see illustration)**.

2 Remove the seat to access all fuses (see Chapter 8). Unclip the fusebox lid and note the fuse identification on the inside of the lid **(see illustration)**. To access the main fuse remove the fuse cover from the relay **(see illustration)**.

3 The fuses can checked visually. If you can't pull the fuse out with your fingertips, use a suitable pair of pliers **(see illustrations)**. A blown fuse is easily identified by a break in the element **(see illustration)**, or can be tested

5.1a Fusebox (arrowed)

5.1b Starter relay (arrowed)

5.2a Unclip the lid to access the fusebox fuses

5.2b Remove the cover to access the main fuse

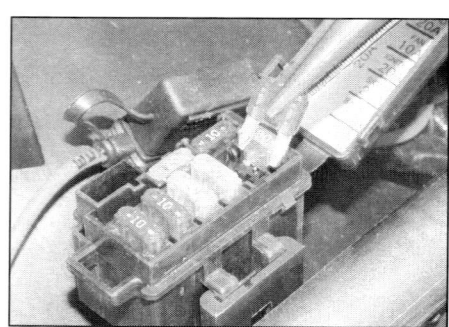

5.3a Use a pair of pliers . . .

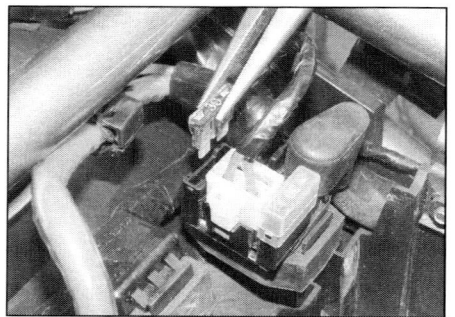

5.3b . . . to remove the fuses

5.3c A blown fuse can be identified by a break in its element

Electrical system 9•5

for continuity using an ohmmeter or continuity tester – if there is no continuity, it has blown. Each fuse is clearly marked with its rating and must only be replaced by a fuse of the same rating. Spare fuses are housed in the fusebox, and a spare main fuse is housed in the starter relay. If a spare fuse is used, always replace it with a new one so that a spare of each rating is carried on the bike at all times.

 Warning: Never put in a fuse of a higher rating or bridge the terminals with any other substitute, however temporary it may be. Serious damage may be done to the circuit, or a fire may start.

4 If a fuse blows, be sure to check the wiring circuit very carefully for evidence of a short-circuit. Look for bare wires and chafed, melted or burned insulation. If the fuse is renewed before the cause is located, the new fuse will blow immediately.

5 Occasionally a fuse will blow or cause an open-circuit for no obvious reason. Corrosion of the fuse ends and fusebox terminals may occur and cause poor fuse contact. If this happens, remove the corrosion with a wire brush or emery paper, then spray the fuse end and terminals with electrical contact cleaner.

6 Lighting system check

1 The battery provides power for operation of the headlight, tail light, brake light, turn signals and instrument cluster lights. If none of the lights operate, always check battery voltage before proceeding. Low battery voltage indicates either a faulty battery or a defective charging system. Refer to Section 3 for battery checks and Section 30 for charging system tests. Also, check the condition of the fuses (see Section 5). When checking for a blown filament in a bulb, it is advisable to back up a visual check with a continuity test of the filament as it is not always apparent that a bulb has blown. When testing for continuity, remember that on tail light and turn signal bulbs it is often the metal body of the bulb which is the ground or earth.

Headlights and relays

2 If the headlight fails to work, check the bulb, the terminals and the wiring connector first (see Section 7), then the fuse (see Section 5). If they are good check for battery voltage at the black/yellow (high beam) and/or black/green (low beam) wire terminal on the supply side of the headlight wiring connector, with the ignition switch, and where fitted the light switch ON, and with the dimmer switch set as required. If voltage is present, check for continuity between the black wire terminal and earth (ground). If there is no continuity, check the earth (ground) circuit for an open or poor connection.

3 If no voltage is indicated, check the wiring

6.4 Headlight relays (arrowed)

between the headlight, relays, lighting system switches, and the ignition switch, then check the switches themselves.

4 To check the headlight relay(s), remove the windshield (see Chapter 8), then disconnect the relevant relay wiring connector **(see illustration)**. Make the checks on the relay terminals. Use a continuity tester (or a multimeter set to the resistance range) and a 12V battery with insulated jumper wires according to the relevant procedure below to check the relays.

5 On Europe models the primary ON/OFF relay (4 wires) works in conjunction with the ignition switch, and the secondary HI/LO relay (5 wires) switches the current between the high beam and low beam circuits.

● Test the primary relay by connecting the meter probes between the red/yellow and black/blue wire terminals; no continuity should be shown. Now connect the battery positive (+) terminal to the blue/black wire terminal and the negative (-) terminal to the black wire terminal using the jumper wires; continuity should now be shown on the meter. Test the secondary relay low beam circuit by connecting the meter probes between the black/blue and black/green wires; continuity (0 ohms) should be shown.

● Test the secondary relay high beam circuit by connecting the meter probes between the black/blue and black/yellow wire terminals; no continuity should be shown. Leaving the meter in place, now connect the battery positive (+) terminal to the yellow wire terminal and the negative (-) terminal to the black wire terminal; continuity (0 ohms) should be shown on the meter.

6 On US models only one relay is fitted. To test the low beam circuit, connect the meter probes between the red/yellow and black/green wire terminals; continuity (0 ohms) should be shown. To test the high beam circuit, connect the meter probes between the red/yellow and black/yellow wire terminals; no continuity should be shown. Leaving the meter in place, now connect the positive (+) terminal of the battery to the yellow wire terminal and the negative (-) terminal to the black wire terminal using the jumper wires; continuity (0 ohms) should be shown on the meter.

Tail light

7 If a tail light fails to work, check the bulb, the terminals and the wiring connector first (see Section 9), then the fuse (see Section 5). If they are good check for battery voltage at the blue/red wire terminal on the supply side of the tail light wiring connector, with the ignition switch and where fitted the light switch ON. If voltage is present, check for continuity between the wiring connector terminals on the tail light side of the wiring connector and the corresponding terminals in the bulbholder. If voltage and continuity are present, check for continuity between the black wire terminal and earth (ground). If there is no continuity, check the earth (ground) circuit for an open or poor connection.

8 If no voltage is indicated, check the wiring between the tail light, the light switch (where fitted) and the ignition switch, then check the switches themselves.

Sidelight (Europe models)

9 If a sidelight fails to work, check the bulb and the bulb terminals and wiring connector first (see Section 7), then the fuse (see Section 5). If they are good check for battery voltage at the blue/red wire terminal on the supply side of the sidelight wiring connector, with the ignition switch and, where fitted, the light switch ON. If voltage is present, check for continuity between the wiring connector terminals on the sidelight side of the wiring connector and the corresponding terminals in the bulbholder. If voltage and continuity are present, check for continuity between the black wire terminal and earth (ground). If there is no continuity, check the earth (ground) circuit for an open or poor connection.

10 If no voltage is indicated, check the wiring between the sidelight, the light switch (where fitted) and the ignition switch, then check the switches themselves.

Brake light

11 If a brake light fails to work, check the bulb, the terminals and the wiring connector first (see Section 9), then the fuse (see Section 5). If they are good check for battery voltage at the yellow wire terminal on the supply side of the tail light wiring connector, with the ignition switch ON and the brake lever or pedal applied. If voltage is present, check for continuity between the black wire terminal and earth (ground). If there is no continuity, check the earth (ground) circuit for an open or poor connection.

12 If no voltage is indicated, check the brake light switches (see Section 14), then the wiring between the tail light and the switches.

Instrument and warning lights

13 See Section 17.

Turn signal lights

14 If one light fails to work, check the bulb and the bulb terminals first (see Section 12), then the wiring connectors. If none of the turn signals work, check the fuse.

15 If the fuse is good, see Section 11 for the turn signal circuit check.

9•6 Electrical system

7.2a Disconnect the wiring connector . . .

7.2b . . . and remove the dust cover

7.3a Release the clip . . .

7.3b . . . and remove the bulb

7.8a Release the bulbholder from the headlight . . .

7.8b . . . and remove the bulb from the holder

7 Headlight and sidelight bulbs

Note: *The headlight bulb is of the quartz-halogen type. Do not touch the bulb glass as skin acids will shorten the bulb's service life. If the bulb is accidentally touched, it should be wiped carefully when cold with a rag soaked in methylated spirit and dried before fitting.*

 Warning: Allow the bulb time to cool before removing it if the headlight has just been on.

Headlight bulbs

1 Remove the relevant cockpit trim panel (see Chapter 8).

8.2 Release the loom from the clip (A) and disconnect the wiring connectors (B) on each side

2 Disconnect the wiring connector from the back of the headlight and remove the rubber dust cover, noting how it fits **(see illustrations)**.
3 Release the bulb retaining clip, noting how it fits, then remove the bulb **(see illustrations)**.
4 Fit the new bulb, bearing in mind the information in the **Note** above. Make sure the tabs on the bulb fit correctly in the slots in the bulb housing, and secure it in position with the retaining clip.
5 Install the dust cover, making sure it is correctly seated and with the 'TOP' mark at the top, and connect the wiring connector **(see illustrations 7.2b and a)**.
6 Check the operation of the headlight. Install the cockpit trim panel (see Chapter 8).

8.3 Undo the screws (arrowed) and remove the headlight assembly

 Always use a paper towel or dry cloth when handling new bulbs to prevent injury if the bulb should break, and to increase bulb life.

Sidelight bulbs (Europe models)

7 Remove the relevant cockpit trim panel (see Chapter 8).
8 Release the bulbholder from the headlight by twisting it anti-clockwise **(see illustrations)**. Carefully pull the bulb out of the holder **(see illustration)**. Install the new bulb, then install the bulbholder.
9 Check the operation of the sidelight. Install the cockpit trim panel (see Chapter 8).

8 Headlight assembly

Removal

1 Remove the fairing (see Chapter 8).
2 As required, either remove the bulbholders and bulbs from the headlight (see Section 7), or release the wiring sub-loom from its clip and disconnect the turn signal wiring connectors so the loom can be removed with the headlight **(see illustration)**.
3 Remove the five screws securing the headlight assembly and lift it out of the fairing **(see illustration)**. Note the layout and routing of the sub-loom wiring.

Electrical system 9•7

9.1 Remove the cover

9.2a Release the bulbholder from the tail light . . .

9.2b . . . then release the bulb from the holder

Installation

4 Installation is the reverse of removal. Make sure all the wiring is correctly routed, connected and secured. Check the operation of the headlights and sidelights. Check the headlight aim (see Chapter 1).

9 Brake/tail light bulbs

1 Remove the seat (see Chapter 8). Remove the rubber bulbholder cover, noting how it fits **(see illustration)**.
2 Turn the bulbholder anti-clockwise and withdraw it from the tail light **(see illustration)**. Push the bulb into the holder and twist it anti-clockwise to remove it **(see illustration)**.
3 Check the socket terminals for corrosion and clean them if necessary. Line up the pins of the new bulb with the slots in the socket, then push the bulb in and turn it clockwise until it locks into place. **Note:** *The pins on the bulb are offset so it can only be installed one way. It is a good idea to use a paper towel or dry cloth when handling the new bulb to prevent injury if the bulb should break, and to increase bulb life.*
4 Fit the bulbholder into the tail light and turn it clockwise to secure it, then fit the rubber cover, with the 'UP' mark and arrow facing up **(see illustration 9.1)**. Install the seat (see Chapter 8).

10 Tail light assembly

1 Remove the seat cowling (see Chapter 8).
2 Disconnect the tail light assembly wiring connector **(see illustration)**.
3 Undo the three screws and remove the tail light, noting the routing of its and the turn signal's wiring **(see illustration)**.
4 Installation is the reverse of removal. Check the operation of the tail lights and the brake lights.

11 Turn signal circuit check

1 Most turn signal problems are the result of a burned-out bulb or corroded socket. This is especially true when the turn signals function properly in one direction, but fail to flash in the other direction. Check the bulbs and the sockets (see Section 12) and the wiring connectors. Also, check the fuse (see Section 5) and the switch (see Section 19).

10.2 Disconnect the tail light wiring connector (arrowed)

2 The battery provides power for operation of the turn signal lights, so if they do not operate, also check the battery voltage. Low battery voltage indicates either a faulty battery or a defective charging system. Refer to Section 3 for battery checks and Section 30 for charging system tests.
3 If the bulbs, sockets, connectors, fuse, switch and battery are good, check the turn signal relay, which is mounted under the seat **(see illustration)**. Remove the seat for access (see Chapter 8).
4 Displace the relay from its mount. Check for voltage at the brown wire terminal in the connector with the ignition ON. If no voltage is present, using the appropriate wiring diagram

10.3 Tail light mounting screws (arrowed)

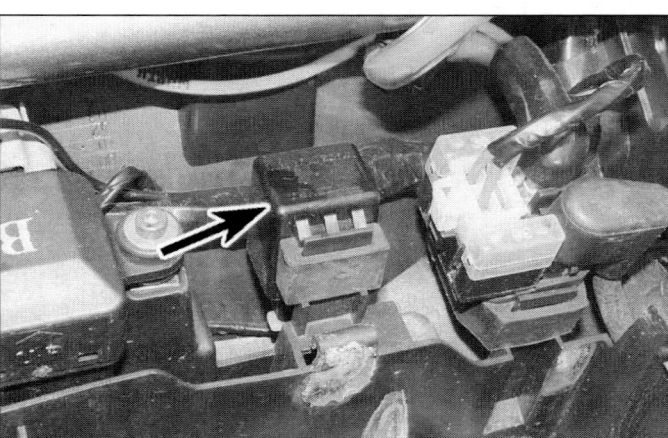

11.3 Turn signal relay (arrowed)

9•8 Electrical system

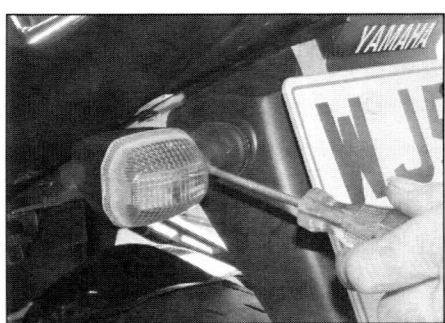

12.1 Remove the screw and detach the lens . . .

12.2 . . . and remove the bulb

12.3 Make sure the tab (arrowed) locates correctly when fitting the lens

at the end of this Chapter check the wiring between the relay and the ignition (main) switch. If voltage was present, check for voltage at the brown/white wire with the ignition ON, and with the switch turned to either LEFT or RIGHT. If no voltage is present, replace the relay with a new one. If voltage was present, check the wiring between the relay, turn signal switch and turn signal lights for continuity. Turn the ignition OFF when the check is complete.

12 Turn signal bulbs

1 Remove the screw securing the turn signal lens and remove the lens, noting how it fits **(see illustration)**.

13.3 Release the backing plate . . .

2 Push the bulb into the holder and twist it anti-clockwise to remove it **(see illustration)**. Check the socket terminals for corrosion and clean them, if necessary. Line up the pins of the new bulb with the slots in the socket, then push the bulb in and turn it clockwise until it locks into place.
3 Fit the lens onto the holder, making sure the tab locates correctly **(see illustration)**. Do not overtighten the screw as the lens or threads could be damaged.

13 Turn signals

Front

1 Remove the fairing (see Chapter 8).
2 Disconnect the turn signal wiring connectors and free the wiring from its clip **(see illustration 8.2)**.
3 Release the backing plate from the rubber mount and draw it off the wiring **(see illustration)**.
4 Unscrew the nut securing the turn signal to the inside of the fairing and remove the mounting plate **(see illustration)**. Remove the turn signal, noting how it fits. Take care not to snag the wiring as you pull it through.
5 Installation is the reverse of removal. Make sure the wiring is correctly routed and securely connected. Check the operation of the turn signals.

Rear

6 Remove the seat cowling (see Chapter 8).
7 Trace the wiring back from the turn signal and disconnect it at the connectors **(see illustration)**. Release the wiring from its clip and feed it through to the turn signal.
8 Release the backing plate from the rubber mount and draw it off the wiring **(see illustration and 13.3)**.
9 Unscrew the nut securing the turn signal to the inside of the fairing and remove the mounting plate **(see illustration 13.4)**. Remove the turn signal, noting how it fits. Take care not to snag the wiring as you pull it through.
10 Installation is the reverse of removal. Make sure the wiring is correctly routed and securely connected. Check the operation of the turn signals.

14 Brake light switches

Circuit check

1 Before checking the switches, check the brake light circuit (see Section 6).
2 The front brake light switch is mounted on the underside of the brake master cylinder. Disconnect the wiring connectors from the

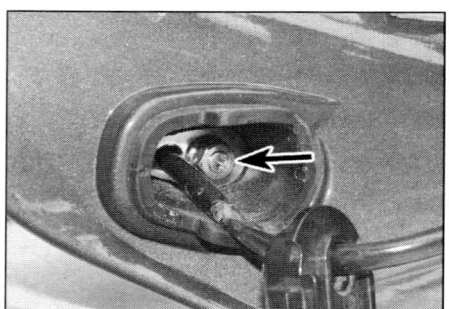

13.4 . . . then undo the nut (arrowed)

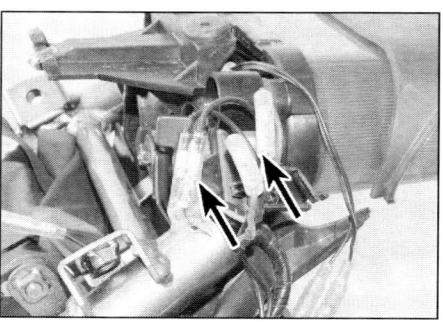

13.7 Disconnect the relevant turn signal wiring connectors (arrowed)

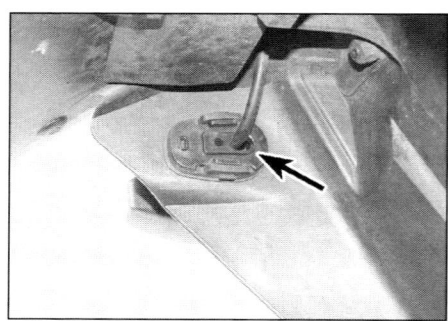

13.8 Release the backing plate (arrowed) to access the nut

Electrical system 9•9

14.2 Front brake switch wiring connectors (A) and mounting screw (B)

14.3a Rear brake light switch (A) and adjuster nut (B)

14.3b Rear brake light switch wiring connector

14.9 Unhook the spring (arrowed) from the lug

switch **(see illustration)**. Using a continuity tester, connect the probes to the terminals of the switch. With the brake lever at rest, there should be no continuity. With the brake lever applied, there should be continuity. If the switch does not behave as described, replace it with a new one.

3 The rear brake light switch is mounted on the right-hand side, above the brake pedal **(see illustration)**. Remove the right-hand side panel to access the wiring connector (see Chapter 8). Trace the wiring from the switch and disconnect it at the connector **(see illustration)**. Using a continuity tester, connect the probes to the terminals on the switch side of the wiring connector. With the brake pedal at rest, there should be no continuity. With the brake pedal applied, there should be continuity. If the switch does not behave as described, replace it with a new one.

4 If the switches are good, check for voltage at the brown wire terminal in the connector with the ignition switch ON – there should be battery voltage. If there is no voltage present, check the wiring between the switch and the ignition switch (see *Wiring Diagrams* at the end of this Chapter). If there is voltage check for continuity in the green/yellow or yellow wire (according to switch) between the connector and the tail light assembly.

Switch removal and installation

Front brake light switch

5 The switch is mounted on the underside of the brake master cylinder. Disconnect the wiring connectors from the switch **(see illustration 14.2)**.

6 Remove the single screw and washers securing the switch to the bottom of the master cylinder and remove the switch.

7 Installation is the reverse of removal. The switch is not adjustable.

Rear brake light switch

8 The switch is mounted on the right-hand side, above the brake pedal **(see illustration 14.3a)**. Remove the right-hand side panel to access the wiring connector (see Chapter 8). Trace the wiring from the switch and disconnect it at the connector **(see illustration 14.3b)**. Free the wiring from any clips or ties and feed it through to the switch.

9 Detach the lower end of the switch spring from the brake pedal **(see illustration)**. Unscrew and remove the switch from the adjuster nut in the bracket **(see illustration 14.3a)**.

10 Installation is the reverse of removal. Make sure the brake light is activated just before the rear brake pedal takes effect. If adjustment is necessary, hold the switch and turn the adjuster nut on the switch body until the brake light is activated when required.

15 Instrument cluster removal and installation

Removal

1 Remove the windshield (see Chapter 8). Pull back the rubber cover and disconnect the wiring connector from the instrument cluster **(see illustration)**.

2 You may be able to access the instrument cluster nuts with the fairing in place, depending on your dexterity and the tools available. If not, remove the fairing (see Chapter 8).

3 Unscrew the nuts and remove the washers securing the instrument cluster, then lift it off its mounts on the front sub-frame **(see illustrations)**.

Installation

4 Installation is the reverse of removal. Check all the rubber mounting grommets for cracks and deterioration and replace them with new ones if necessary.

15.1 Pull back the rubber cover then disconnect the wiring connector

15.3a Undo the nuts (arrowed) . . .

15.3b . . . and remove the instrument cluster

9•10 Electrical system

16.3a Speed sensor

16 Instrument check and disassembly

Check

1 Yamaha provide no specific test data for the instruments themselves. If after checking all other possibilities (see Steps 2 to 7) any of the instruments themselves are suspected of being faulty, take the instrument cluster to a Yamaha dealer for further assessment. The fuel gauge, the front and rear covers, and the warning light bulbs are available as individual components – the rest of the cluster, i.e. speedometer, tachometer, temperature warning LED, and printed circuit board (PCB), are all one component.
● The speedometer is controlled by the speed sensor, which is mounted in the back of the crankcase – see below.
● The tachometer is controlled by the ignition control unit – specific test details are not available.
● The coolant temperature LED is controlled by the thermo unit – refer to Chapter 3 for test details.
● The fuel gauge and warning light are controlled by the fuel level sensor – refer to Chapter 4 for test details.

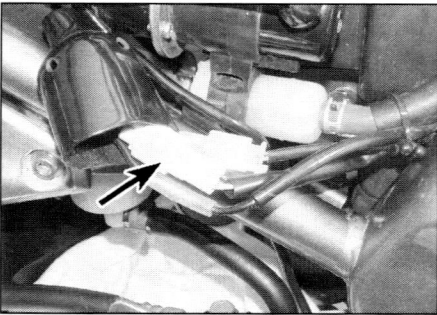

16.3b Speed sensor wiring connector (arrowed)

● The oil level warning light is controlled by the oil level switch – refer to Section 26 for test details.
● If any of the warning lights or instrument lights fail, refer to Section 17.

Speed sensor test

2 When the ignition is first switched ON, or while the engine is running, the speed sensor performs its own self-diagnosis in the event of failure or faulty wiring. If a fault occurs, the tachometer will be seen to display zero rpm for 3 seconds, then 4000 rpm for 2.5 seconds, then the actual engine speed for 3 seconds, whereupon it will repeat the cycle until the engine is switched off.
3 If a fault is indicated, check the speed sensor wiring circuit for shorts or breaks, and the connector (located in the boot behind the right-hand side panel) for loose, damaged or corroded terminals, referring to *Wiring Diagrams* at the end of the Chapter **(see illustrations)**.
4 To test the output from the sensor, place the motorcycle on its centrestand so the rear wheel is off the ground. Make sure the transmission is in neutral. Remove the right-hand side panel (see Chapter 8). Disconnect the sensor wiring connector, then connect the positive (+) probe of a voltmeter set to the DC20V scale to the white wire terminal on the sensor side of the connector, and connect the negative (–) probe to earth (ground). Turn the ignition (main) switch ON. Turn the rear wheel in its normal direction of rotation and check the readings on the meter – it should be seen to fluctuate between zero and 5 volts as the wheel is turned. If not, and the wiring to the connector is good, replace the sensor with a new one. Otherwise, assuming all the wiring and connectors are good, the ignition control unit could be faulty (see Chapter 5).
5 To fit a new sensor, release the wiring, then unscrew the bolt securing the old one and withdraw it from the crankcase **(see illustration 16.3a)**. Install the sensor, using a new O-ring if necessary. Smear the O-ring with oil.

Self diagnosis function

6 A fault diagnosis system monitors the circuits for the throttle position sensor, EXUP, speed sensor and tip-over sensor. Warning of a fault is displayed by the tachometer needle action. The tachometer will display zero rpm for 3 seconds, then the engine speed corresponding to the faulty circuit (see below) for 2.5 seconds, then the actual engine speed for 3 seconds, whereupon it will repeat the cycle until the engine is switched off. Note that the motorcycle can be ridden even though a fault has been diagnosed, though a difference in performance will be noticed. If more than one faulty circuit is being displayed, the tachometer will display one fault after the other.

TPS fault – 3000 rpm
EXUP fault – 7000 rpm
Speed sensor fault – 4000 rpm
Tip-over sensor fault – 9000 rpm

Disassembly

7 Remove the instrument cluster (see Section 15).
8 Place the instrument cluster face down on some card or rag. Undo the screws securing the rear cover and lift it off **(see illustrations)**.

16.8a Undo the screws . . .

16.8b . . . and lift off the back cover

Electrical system 9•11

16.9a Lift the instrument board out

16.9b Fuel gauge screws (arrowed)

9 Carefully lift the instrument board out of the front cover **(see illustration)**. If required separate the fuel gauge by undoing the three screws securing it to the PCB **(see illustration)**.
10 Reassemble the cluster in a reverse procedure. Do not overtighten the screws.

17 Instrument and warning light bulbs

1 With the exception of the temperature warning light, the instrument illumination and warning light bulbs are conventional and replaceable. The temperature warning light is an LED which is not available individually – if it fails, a new instrument board must be fitted.
2 To replace an instrument illumination bulb, first remove the instrument cluster (see Section 15). Place the instrument cluster face down on some card or rag. Undo the screws securing the rear cover and lift it off **(see illustrations 16.8a and b)**. Release the bulbholder by twisting it anti-clockwise and pulling it out **(see illustration)**. Pull the bulb out of the holder and fit the new one **(see illustration)**.
3 To test whether the LED has failed, remove the instrument cluster (see Section 15). Using a fully charged 12V battery and two suitable jump leads, and referring to *Wiring Diagrams* at the end of the Chapter, connect the jumper leads directly to the relevant terminals on the instrument cluster. If the LED comes on, the fault lies elsewhere in the circuit. If it doesn't, the LED has failed or there is a break in its circuit on the PCB – an electronics specialist might be able to effect a repair, but otherwise a new instrument board must be installed.

18 Ignition (main) switch

⚠ **Warning: To prevent the risk of short circuits, remove the seat and disconnect the battery negative (–) lead before making any ignition (main) switch checks.**

Check

1 Raise the fuel tank (see Chapter 4). Trace the ignition (main) switch wiring back from the base of the switch and disconnect it at the connectors **(see illustration)**. Make the checks on the switch side of the connector.
2 Using an ohmmeter or a continuity tester, check the continuity of the connector terminal pairs (see *Wiring Diagrams* at the end of this Chapter). Continuity should exist between the terminals connected by a solid line on the diagram when the switch key is turned to the indicated position.
3 If the switch fails any of the tests, replace it with a new one.

Removal

4 Raise the fuel tank (see Chapter 4). Trace the ignition (main) switch wiring back from the base of the switch and disconnect it at the connectors **(see illustration 18.1)**. Release it from any clips or ties and feed it through to the switch, noting its routing.
5 Remove the fairing (see Chapter 8). **Note:** *Although it is not strictly necessary to remove the fairing, doing so will prevent the possibility of damage should a tool slip.*
6 Unscrew the bolt securing the brake hose guide to the top yoke **(see illustration)**.

17.2a Release the relevant bulbholder . . .

17.2b . . . and install a new bulb

18.1 The ignition switch and handlebar switch wiring connectors are inside the boot above the carburettors

18.6 Unscrew the bolt (arrowed) and displace the guide

9•12 Electrical system

18.8a Slacken the clamp bolt (arrowed) on each side . . .

18.8b . . . then unscrew the steering stem nut and remove the washer

18.9 Ease the top yoke up off the steering stem and forks

7 Displace the handlebars and lay them on some rag across the frame behind the steering head (see Chapter 6).
8 Slacken the fork clamp bolt on each side of the top yoke **(see illustration)**. Unscrew the steering stem nut and remove the washer – the washer sits in a recess in the yoke and needs to be eased out with a small screwdriver or a magnet, or alternatively tip it out of the yoke after it has been lifted off **(see illustration)**.
9 Ease the top yoke up and off the steering stem and remove it **(see illustration)**.
10 Two shear-head bolts mount the ignition switch to the underside of the top yoke. The heads of the bolts must be tapped around using a suitable punch or drift, or drilled off, before the switch can be removed. To do this, mount the yoke in a vice equipped with soft jaws and padded out with rags. Remove the bolts and withdraw the switch from the top yoke.

Installation

11 Installation is the reverse of removal. Obtain new special shear-head bolts and tighten them until their heads shear off. Make sure wiring connectors are securely connected and correctly routed. Tighten the steering stem nut before the fork clamp bolts, and tighten them and the handlebar clamp bolts to the torque settings specified at the beginning of Chapter 6.

19 Handlebar switch check

1 Generally speaking, the switches are reliable and trouble-free. Most troubles, when they do occur, are caused by dirty or corroded contacts, but wear and breakage of internal parts is a possibility that should not be overlooked. If breakage does occur, the entire switch and related wiring harness will have to be replaced with a new one, as individual parts are not available.
2 The switches can be checked for continuity using an ohmmeter or a continuity test light.

3 Raise the fuel tank to access the switch wiring connectors (see Chapter 4). Trace the wiring harness of the switch in question back to its connectors and disconnect them **(see illustration 18.1)**.
4 Check for continuity between the terminals of the switch harness with the switch in the various positions (i.e. switch OFF – no continuity, switch ON – continuity) – see *Wiring Diagrams* at the end of this Chapter.
5 If the continuity check indicates a problem exists, refer to Section 20, separate the switch halves and spray the switch contacts with electrical contact cleaner. If they are accessible, the contacts can be scraped clean with a knife or polished with wire wool. If switch components are damaged or broken, it should be obvious when the switch is disassembled.

20 Handlebar switch housing removal and installation

Removal

1 If the switch is to be removed from the bike, rather than just displaced from the handlebar, raise the fuel tank (see Chapter 4) then trace the wiring of the switch in question back to its connectors and disconnect them **(see illustration 18.1)**. Work back along the harness, freeing it from all the relevant clips and ties, noting its correct routing.
2 Disconnect the wiring connector(s) from the brake light switch (if removing the right-hand switch) or the clutch switch (if removing the left-hand switch) **(see illustration 14.2 or 23.2)**.
3 To remove the right-hand switch refer to Chapter 4 and detach the throttle cables from the switch housing, then remove the housing.
4 To remove the left-hand switch refer to Chapter 4 and detach the choke cable from the switch housing, then remove the housing.

Installation

5 Installation is the reverse of removal. Refer to Chapter 4 for installation of the cables, if

required. Make sure the locating pin in the switch housing locates in the hole in the handlebar. Make sure the wiring connectors are correctly routed and securely connected.

21 Neutral switch

Check

1 Before checking the electrical circuit, check the fuse (see Section 5).
2 The switch is located on the back of the engine on the left-hand side. Make sure the transmission is in neutral. To access the neutral switch wiring connector, remove the right-hand side panel (see Chapter 8). Trace the wiring from the switch and disconnect it at the connector **(see illustration)**.
3 With the connector disconnected and the ignition switched ON, the neutral light should be out. If not, the wire between the connector and instrument cluster must be earthed (grounded) at some point.
4 Check for continuity between the light blue wire terminal on the switch side of the wiring connector, and the crankcase. With the transmission in neutral, there should be continuity. With the transmission in gear, there should be no continuity. If there is continuity when in gear, check that the wire is not earthed (grounded). If there is no continuity when in neutral, check for a break in the wire,

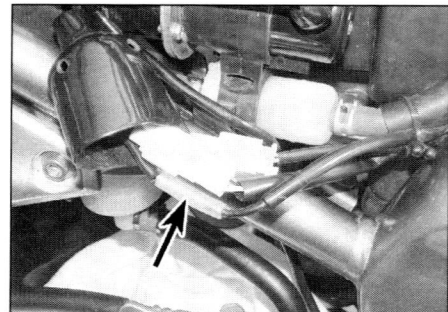

21.2 Disconnect the neutral switch wiring connector (arrowed)

21.4 Check the plunger in the end of the switch

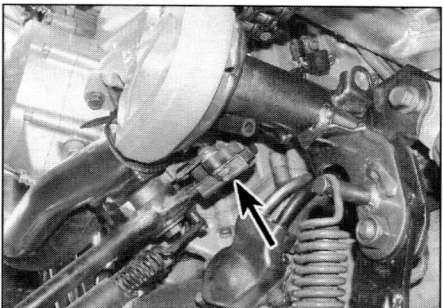

22.7 Sidestand switch (arrowed)

then remove the switch (see below), and check that the contact plunger is not damaged or seized in the switch body **(see illustration)**.

5 If the continuity tests prove the switch and wiring is good, check for voltage (ignition ON) at the brown terminal on the wiring loom side of the instrument cluster wiring connector – remove the windshield to access the connector (see Chapter 8). If there is no voltage present, check the wire between the connector and fuse (see *Wiring Diagrams* at the end of this Chapter). If the voltage is good, check the bulb in the instrument cluster (see Section 17), then check the starter circuit cut-off relay (Section 24) and other components in the starter circuit as described in the relevant Sections of this Chapter. If all components are good, check the wiring between the various components (see *Wiring Diagrams* at the end of this Chapter).

Removal

6 The switch is on the back of the engine on the left-hand side. Access to it is quite restricted, and could be impossible without the correct tools. For best access, remove the swingarm (see Chapter 6).
7 Detach the wire from the switch.
8 Unscrew the switch and withdraw it from the casing. Check the condition of the sealing washer and replace it with a new one if it is damaged or deformed.

Installation

9 Install the switch using a new sealing

23.2 Clutch switch wiring connector (arrowed)

washer if necessary, and tighten it to the torque setting specified at the beginning of the Chapter.
10 Connect the wire and check the operation of the neutral light.

22 Sidestand switch

Check

1 The sidestand switch is mounted on a bracket just behind the stand **(see illustration 22.7)**. The switch is part of the safety circuit which prevents or stops the engine running if the transmission is in gear whilst the sidestand is down, and prevents the engine from starting if the transmission is in gear unless the sidestand is up and the clutch lever is pulled in. Before checking the electrical circuit, check the fuse (see Section 5).
2 Trace the wiring from the switch and disconnect it at the connector.
3 Check the operation of the switch using an ohmmeter or continuity test light. Connect the meter probes to the terminals on the switch side of the connector. With the sidestand up there should be continuity (zero resistance) between the terminals, and with the stand down there should be no continuity (infinite resistance).
4 If the switch does not perform as expected,

23.5 Clutch switch mounting screw (arrowed)

it is defective and must be replaced with a new one.
5 If the switch is good, check the starter circuit cut-off relay (Section 24) and other components in the starter circuit as described in the relevant Sections of this Chapter. If all components are good, check the wiring between the various components (see *Wiring Diagrams* at the end of this Chapter).

Renewal

6 The sidestand switch is mounted on a bracket just behind the stand. Trace the wiring from the switch and disconnect it at the connector. Work back along the switch wiring, freeing it from any relevant retaining clips and ties, noting its correct routing.
7 Unscrew the nuts securing the switch to the bracket and remove it, noting how the plunger end locates against the stand boss **(see illustration)**.
8 Fit the new switch, making sure the plunger locates correctly, and tighten the nuts.
9 Make sure the wiring is correctly routed up to the connector and retained by all the necessary clips and ties. Reconnect the wiring connector and check the operation of the switch.

23 Clutch switch

Check

1 The clutch switch is mounted on the underside of the clutch lever bracket. The switch is part of the safety circuit which prevents or stops the engine running if the transmission is in gear whilst the sidestand is down, and prevents the engine from starting if the transmission is in gear unless the sidestand is up and the clutch lever is pulled in. The switch is not adjustable.
2 To check the switch, disconnect the wiring connector **(see illustration)**. Connect the probes of an ohmmeter or a continuity tester to the two switch terminals. With the clutch lever pulled in, continuity should be indicated. With the clutch lever out, no continuity (infinite resistance) should be indicated.
3 If the switch is good, check the starter circuit cut-off relay (Section 24) and other components in the starter circuit as described in the relevant Sections of this Chapter. If all components are good, check the wiring between the various components (see *Wiring Diagrams* at the end of this Chapter).

Removal and installation

4 The clutch switch is mounted on the underside of the clutch lever bracket.
5 Disconnect the wiring connector **(see illustration 23.2)**, then remove the screw and detach the switch **(see illustration)**.
6 Installation is the reverse of removal.

24.2 Relay assembly (arrowed)

25.3 Horn wiring connectors (arrowed)

25.6 Horn mounting bolt (arrowed)

24 Relay assembly

Starter circuit cut-off relay

Check

1 The starter circuit cut-off relay is part of the safety circuit which prevents or stops the engine running if the transmission is in gear whilst the sidestand is down, and prevents the engine from starting if the transmission is in gear unless the sidestand is up and the clutch lever is pulled in.
2 The starter circuit cut-off relay and its diodes are contained within the relay assembly, which is mounted behind the left-hand side panel **(see illustration)**. Remove the panel for access (see Chapter 8).
3 Displace the relay and disconnect the wiring connector. Refer to the wiring diagram (see end of chapter) and the following procedures:
4 To check the operation of the relay, connect a meter set to the ohms x 100 range, or a continuity tester, between the blue/white and black (Europe models) or blue (US models) wire terminals of the relay. No continuity should be shown. Now, using jumper wires, connect a fully charged 12V battery to the relay's red/black and black/yellow wire terminals (positive (+) lead to red/black and negative (–) lead to black/yellow). The meter should now show continuity with battery voltage applied. If it doesn't, replace the relay assembly with a new one.
5 The diodes contained within the relay assembly can be checked by performing a continuity test. Refer to the appropriate wiring diagram at the end of this Chapter and connect the meter (set to the ohms function) or continuity tester across the wire terminals for the diode being tested. The diodes should show continuity in one direction and no continuity when the meter or tester probes are reversed. If any diode shows the same condition in both directions it should be considered faulty, and the relay assembly must be replaced with a new one.

6 If the cut-off relay and diodes are proven good, but the starting system fault still exists, check all other components in the starting circuit (i.e. the neutral switch, sidestand switch, clutch switch, starter switch and starter relay) as described in the relevant Sections of this Chapter. If all components are good, check the wiring between the various components (see *Wiring Diagrams* at the end of this Chapter).

Removal and installation

7 The relay assembly is mounted behind the left-hand side panel **(see illustration 24.2)**. Remove the panel for access (see Chapter 8). Displace the relay and disconnect the wiring connector.
8 Installation is the reverse of removal.

Fuel pump relay

9 The fuel pump relay is housed within the relay assembly. Refer to Chapter 4, Section 14 for test details.

25 Horn

Check

1 If the horn, doesn't work, first check the fuse (see Section 5) and the battery (see Section 3).
2 The horn is mounted on the bottom yoke. Remove the fairing for best access to it (see Chapter 8).
3 Unplug the wiring connectors from the horn **(see illustration)**. Using two jumper wires, apply battery voltage directly to the terminals on the horn. If the horn sounds, check the switch (see Section 19) and the wiring between the switch and the horn (see *Wiring Diagrams* at the end of this Chapter).
4 If the horn doesn't sound, replace it with a new one.

Removal and installation

5 The horn is mounted on the bottom yoke. Remove the fairing for best access to it (see Chapter 8).

6 Unplug the wiring connectors from the horn **(see illustration 25.3)**. Unscrew the bolt securing the horn and remove it from the bike **(see illustration)**.
7 Install the horn and tighten the bolt. Connect the wiring connectors to the horn. Install the fairing (see Chapter 8).

26 Oil level switch

Check

1 With the ignition switch ON and the kill switch in the RUN position, the oil level warning light should not come on, indicating that the oil level is good. If the light does come on, check the oil level (see *Daily (pre-ride) checks*). If the oil level is good, check the switch (see Step 3).
2 Start the engine. The oil level warning light should come on, indicating that the oil level has dropped as it is being pumped round the engine. If the light does not come on, stop the engine and check the bulb (see Section 17). If the bulb is good, check for continuity in the wire between the switch bullet connector and the loom side of the instrument cluster wiring connector. Also check for continuity between the cluster side of the connector and the bulbholder.
3 To check the switch, remove it from the sump (see Steps 4 and 5 below). Connect one probe of an ohmmeter or continuity tester to the switch wire and the other probe to its base. With the switch in its normal installed position (wiring at the bottom), there should be continuity. Turn the switch upside down. There should be no continuity. If either condition does not occur, replace the switch with a new one.

Removal

4 Drain the engine oil (see Chapter 1).
5 Trace the wiring back from the switch and disconnect it at the single bullet connector. Free it from its clamp. Unscrew the two bolts securing the switch to the bottom of the sump and withdraw it from the sump, being

Electrical system 9•15

26.5 Free the wiring from its clamp (A) then unscrew the bolts (B) and remove the sensor

26.6 Smear the O-ring with grease before installing the sensor

27.2 Unscrew the bolt (arrowed) and detach the lead

prepared to catch any residual oil **(see illustration)**. Check the condition of the O-ring and replace it with a new one if it is damaged, deformed or deteriorated (but note that Yamaha do not actually list it as being available separately from the switch, so you will have to have it matched for size by them).

Installation

6 Fit a new O-ring onto the oil level switch if required. Smear the O-ring (old or new) with lithium grease, then fit the switch into the sump **(see illustration)**. Tighten its bolts to the torque setting specified at the beginning of the Chapter.
7 Connect the wiring at the connector and check the operation of the switch (see Steps 1 to 3 above). Secure the wiring in its clamp.
8 Fill the engine with the correct quantity of oil (see Chapter 1).

27 Starter relay

Check

1 If the starter circuit is faulty, first remove the seat (see Chapter 8) and check the main fuse on the starter relay and ignition fuse in the fusebox (see Section 5).
2 Lift the rubber terminal cover on the starter relay and unscrew the bolt securing the thick starter motor lead to the terminal marked 'M' **(see illustration)**; position the lead away from the relay terminal. With the ignition switch ON, the engine kill switch in the 'RUN' position, and the transmission in neutral, press the starter switch. The relay should be heard to click.
3 If the relay doesn't click, switch off the ignition and remove the relay as described below; test it as follows.
4 Set a multimeter to the ohms x 1 scale and connect it across the relay's starter motor and battery lead terminals (marked 'M' and 'B' respectively). Using a fully-charged 12 volt battery and two insulated jumper wires, connect the positive (+) terminal of the battery to the red/white wire terminal on the relay, and the negative (–) terminal to the blue/white wire terminal on the relay. At this point the relay should be heard to click and the multimeter read 0 ohms (continuity). If this is the case, the relay is proven good. If the relay does not click when battery voltage is applied and indicates no continuity (infinite resistance) across its terminals, it is faulty and must be replaced with a new one. The relay coil resistance can be measured by connecting an ohmmeter across the red/white and blue/white wire terminals of the relay.
5 If the relay is good, check for battery voltage at the red/white wire terminal on the loom side of the relay wiring connector with the ignition switch ON. If voltage is present, check the wiring, connectors and other components in the starter circuit as described in the relevant Sections of this Chapter, and referring to the *Wiring Diagrams* at the end of this Chapter. If no voltage was present, check the ignition switch and the wiring between it and the relay.

Removal and installation

6 Remove the seat (see Chapter 8). The starter relay is located behind the battery. Disconnect the battery negative (–) lead before removing the relay.
7 Disconnect the relay wiring connector **(see illustration)**. Lift the rubber terminal covers and unscrew the two bolts securing the starter motor and battery leads to the relay and detach the leads **(see illustration)**. Remove the relay with its rubber sleeve from its mounting lug on the frame.
8 Installation is the reverse of removal. The starter motor lead connects to the terminal marked 'M', and the battery lead to the terminal marked 'B' **(see illustration 27.7b)**. Make sure the terminal bolts are securely tightened. Connect the negative (–) lead last when reconnecting the battery.

28 Starter motor removal and installation

Removal

1 Remove the carburettors (see Chapter 4). The starter motor is mounted on the crankcase, behind the cylinder block.
2 Peel back the rubber terminal cover and unscrew the nut securing the lead to the starter motor **(see illustration)**. Detach the lead.
3 Unscrew the two bolts securing the starter

27.7a Disconnect the relay wiring connector . . .

27.7b . . . then unscrew the bolts (arrowed) and detach the leads

28.2 Pull back the rubber cover and unscrew the terminal nut

9•16 Electrical system

28.3a Unscrew the bolts, noting the earth lead . . .

28.3b . . . and remove the starter motor

28.5 Fit a new O-ring and smear it with grease

motor, noting the earth lead secured by the rear bolt **(see illustration)**. Draw the starter motor out of the crankcase and remove it from the machine **(see illustration)**.

4 Remove the O-ring on the end of the starter motor and discard it, as a new one must be used.

Installation

5 Fit a new O-ring onto the end of the starter motor, making sure it is seated in its groove, and smear it with grease **(see illustration)**.

6 Manoeuvre the motor into position and slide it into the crankcase **(see illustration 28.3b)**. Ensure that the starter motor teeth mesh correctly with those of the starter idle/reduction gear. Install the mounting bolts and tighten them, not forgetting to secure the earth lead with the rear bolt **(see illustration 28.3a)**.

7 Connect the lead to the starter motor and secure it with the nut **(see illustration 28.2)**. Make sure the rubber cover is correctly seated over the terminal.

8 Install the carburettors (see Chapter 4) and the seat (see Chapter 8).

29 Starter motor overhaul

Disassembly

1 Remove the starter motor (see Section 28).

2 Note the alignment marks between the main housing and the front and rear covers, or make your own if they are unclear **(see illustration)**.

3 Unscrew the two long bolts, then remove the front cover from the motor along with its sealing ring **(see illustrations)**. Discard the sealing ring, as a new one must be used. Remove the tabbed washer from the cover and slide the washer and shim(s) from the front end of the armature, noting their correct fitted order and the number of shims **(see illustrations)**.

4 Remove the rear cover from the motor, along with its sealing ring **(see illustration)**. Discard the sealing ring, as a new one must be used. Remove the shim(s) from the rear end of the armature, noting how

29.2 Note the alignment marks between the housing and the covers

29.3a Unscrew and remove the two bolts (arrowed) . . .

29.3b . . . then remove the front cover and sealing ring (arrowed)

29.3c Remove the tabbed washer . . .

29.3d . . . and the washer and shim(s) (arrowed)

29.4a Remove the rear cover and its sealing ring (arrowed) . . .

Electrical system 9•17

29.4b ... and remove the shims (arrowed)

29.5 Withdraw the armature from the housing

29.6 Slide the brushes out of the brush housings

many and their correct fitted positions **(see illustration)**.

5 Withdraw the armature from the main housing **(see illustration)**.

6 Slide the brushes out of their housings **(see illustration)**.

7 At this stage check for continuity between the terminal bolt and the two brushes with yellow insulation. There should be continuity (zero resistance). Check for continuity between the terminal bolt and the housing. There should be no continuity (infinite resistance). Also check for continuity between the brushes with uninsulated wires and the brushplate. There should be continuity (zero resistance). If there is no continuity when there should be or vice versa, identify the faulty component and replace it with a new one.

8 Remove the brushplate assembly, noting how it locates **(see illustration)**. Noting the correct fitted location of each component, unscrew the nut from the terminal bolt and remove the plain washer, the various insulating washers and the rubber O-ring **(see illustration)**. Remove the terminal bolt and the brush holder from the main housing, noting how they locate, then remove the insulator, and if required, the brushplate seat **(see illustrations)**.

29.8a Remove the brushplate assembly, noting how it locates (arrowed)

29.8b Remove the nut and washer (A), the insulating washers (B) and O-ring (C)

29.8c Remove the brush holder ...

29.8d ... and the insulator ...

29.8e ... and, if required, the brushplate seat

29.9 Check the length of each brush

29.11a Continuity should exist between the commutator bars

29.11b There should be no continuity between the commutator bars and the armature shaft

29.13 Check the oil seal and needle bearing in the front cover

Inspection

9 The parts of the starter motor that are most likely to require attention are the brushes. Measure the length of each brush and compare the results to the Specifications at the beginning of the Chapter **(see illustration)**. If any of the brushes are worn beyond the service limit, replace them with new ones. If the brushes are not worn excessively, nor cracked, chipped, or otherwise damaged, they may be re-used.

10 Inspect the commutator bars on the armature for scoring, scratches and discoloration. The commutator can be cleaned and polished with wire wool, but do not use sandpaper or emery paper. After cleaning, wipe away any residue with a cloth soaked in electrical system cleaner or denatured alcohol.

11 Using an ohmmeter or a continuity test light, check for continuity between the commutator bars **(see illustration)**. Continuity (0 ohms or a very small resistance (Yamaha specify 0.025 to 0.035 ohms) should exist between each bar and all of the others.

Also, check for continuity between the commutator bars and the armature shaft **(see illustration)**. There should be no continuity (infinite resistance) between the commutator and the shaft. If the checks indicate otherwise, the armature is defective. Also check the depth of the insulating Mica between the commutator bars – if it is less than the amount specified at the beginning of the Chapter, scrape it away using a pointed tool or suitable clean hacksaw blade until its is correct. Measure the diameter of the commutator and replace the starter motor with a new one if it has worn below the minimum diameter specified.

12 Check the starter pinion gear for worn, cracked, chipped and broken teeth. If the gear is damaged or worn, replace the starter motor with a new one.

13 Inspect the end covers for signs of cracks or wear. Check the oil seal and needle bearing in the front cover and the bush in the rear cover for wear and damage **(see illustration)**.

14 Inspect the insulating washers, the O-ring and insulator piece for signs of damage, and renew if necessary.

Reassembly

15 If removed, fit the brushplate seat **(see illustration 29.8e)**. Fit the insulator into the main housing **(see illustration 29.8d)**, then install the brush holder **(see illustration 29.8c)**. Insert the terminal bolt through the brush holder, insulator and the housing and fit the O-ring onto it **(see illustration)**. Slide the small insulating washer(s) onto the terminal bolt, followed by the large insulating

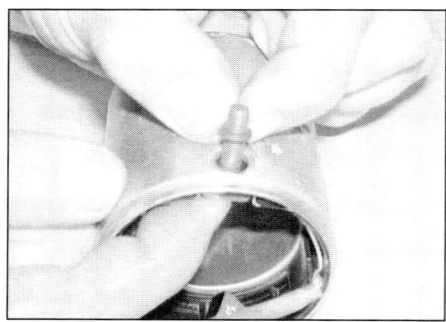

29.15 Insert the terminal bolt and fit the O-ring onto it

Electrical system 9•19

29.17 Retain each brush using its spring

29.18 Locate the spring ends onto the brushes

29.20 Fit a new sealing ring onto the rear of the housing

washer(s) and the plain washer **(see illustration 29.8b)**. Fit the nut onto the terminal bolt and tighten it securely.
16 Install the brushplate assembly, making sure its tab is correctly located in the housing slot, and that each of the insulated brush wires sits in its cut-out in the brushplate **(see illustration 29.8a)**.
17 Slide all the brushes back into position in their housings **(see illustration 29.6)**. Locate each brush spring against the top of its brush so that it holds the brush in place **(see illustration)**.

> **HAYNES HiNT**
> *Lifting the end of the brush spring so that it is against the top of the brush holder and not pressing the brush inwards, makes it much easier to install the armature.*

18 Insert the armature into the front of the housing and locate the brushes on the commutator bars **(see illustration 29.5)**. Slip each brush spring end off the top of the brush and against the brush end **(see illustration)**. Check that each brush is securely pressed against the commutator by its spring and is free to move easily in its housing.
19 Fit the shim(s) onto the rear of the armature shaft **(see illustration 29.4b)**. Apply a smear of grease to the end of the shaft.
20 Fit a new sealing ring onto the rear of the housing **(see illustration)**. Align the rear cover groove with the brushplate outer tab and install the cover – aligning the marks (See Step 2) between the cover and housing will help **(see illustrations 29.4a and 29.2)**.
21 Apply a smear of grease to the front cover oil seal lip. Fit the tabbed washer into the cover so that its teeth are correctly located with the cover ribs **(see illustration 29.3c)**.
22 Fit a new sealing ring onto the front of the housing **(see illustration)**. Slide the shim(s) onto the front end of the armature shaft then fit the washer **(see illustration 29.3d)**. Slide the front cover into position, aligning the marks made on removal **(see illustrations 29.3b and 29.2)**.
23 Check the marks made on removal are correctly aligned, then fit the long bolts and tighten them to the torque setting specified at the beginning of the Chapter **(see illustration)**.
24 Install the starter motor (see Section 28).

30 Charging system

General information and precautions

1 If the performance of the charging system is suspect, the system as a whole should be checked first, followed by testing of the individual components. **Note:** *Before beginning the checks, make sure the battery is fully charged and that all system connections are clean and tight.*
2 Checking the output of the charging system and the performance of the various components within the charging system requires the use of a multimeter (with voltage, current and resistance checking facilities).
3 When making the checks, follow the procedures carefully to prevent incorrect connections or short circuits, as irreparable damage to electrical system components may result if short circuits occur.
4 If a multimeter is not available, the job of checking the charging system should be left to a Yamaha dealer or automotive electrician.

29.22 Fit a new sealing ring onto the front of the housing

29.23 Fit the long bolts and tighten them to the specified torque

9•20 Electrical system

30.7 Checking the charging system leakage rate – connect the meter as shown

5 If the charging system of the machine is thought to be faulty, remove the seat (see Chapter 8) and perform the following checks.

Leakage test

Caution: Always connect an ammeter in series, never in parallel with the battery, otherwise it will be damaged. Do not turn the ignition ON or operate the starter motor when the ammeter is connected – a sudden surge in current will blow the meter's fuse.

6 Turn the ignition switch OFF and disconnect the lead from the battery negative (–) terminal.
7 Set the multimeter to the Amps function and connect its negative (–) probe to the battery negative (–) terminal, and positive (+) probe to the disconnected negative (–) lead **(see illustration)**. Always set the meter to a high amps range initially and then bring it down to the mA (milli Amps) range; if there is a high current flow in the circuit it may blow the meter's fuse.
8 No current flow should be indicated. If current leakage is indicated (generally greater than 0.1 mA), there is a short circuit in the wiring. Using the wiring diagrams at the end of this Chapter, systematically disconnect individual electrical components, checking the meter each time until the source is identified. Note that it an alarm is fitted, its current drawn should be taken into account when measuring current leakage.

31.6 Unscrew the bolts (arrowed) and remove the cover

31.2 Alternator wiring connector

9 If no leakage is indicated, disconnect the meter and connect the negative (–) lead to the battery, tightening it securely.

Output test

10 Start the engine and warm it up to normal operating temperature.
11 To check the regulated voltage output, allow the engine to idle and connect a multimeter set to the 0 to 20 volts DC scale (voltmeter) across the terminals of the battery (positive (+) lead to battery positive (+) terminal, negative (–) lead to battery negative (–) terminal). Slowly increase the engine speed briefly to 5000 rpm and note the reading obtained. The regulated voltage should be as specified at the beginning of the Chapter. If the voltage is outside these limits, check the alternator, then the regulator/rectifier (see Sections 31 and 32).

> **HAYNES HiNT** *Clues to a faulty regulator are constantly blowing bulbs, with brightness varying considerably with engine speed, and battery overheating.*

31 Alternator

Check

1 To access the wiring connector, remove the left-hand side panel (see Chapter 8).

31.7 Unscrewing the rotor bolt using a rotor holding strap

2 Trace the wiring back from the alternator cover on the left-hand side of the engine and disconnect it at the white connector containing the three white wires **(see illustration)**.
3 Using a multimeter set to the ohms x 1 (ohmmeter) scale, measure the resistance between each of the white wires on the alternator side of the connector, taking a total of three readings, then check for continuity between each terminal and ground (earth). If the stator coil windings are in good condition the three readings should be within the range shown in the Specifications at the start of this Chapter and there should be no continuity (infinite resistance) between any of the terminals and ground (earth). If not, check the fault is not due to damaged wiring between the connector and coils. If the wiring is good, the alternator stator coil assembly is at fault and should be replaced with a new one.

Removal

4 Drain the engine oil (see Chapter 1). To access the wiring connector, remove the left-hand side panel (see Chapter 8).
5 Trace the wiring back from the alternator cover on the left-hand side of the engine and disconnect it at the white connector containing the three white wires **(see illustration 31.2)**. Free the wiring from any clips or guides and feed it through to the alternator cover.
6 Working in a criss-cross pattern, unscrew the bolts securing the alternator cover and remove it **(see illustration)**. Note the position of the dowels and remove them if loose. Discard the gasket, as a new one must be used.
7 To remove the rotor bolt it is necessary to stop the rotor from turning. If a rotor holding strap or tool (Yamaha can provide a special tool Part No. 90890-01235 Europe models or YU-01235 US models) is not available, and if the engine is still in the fame, place the transmission in gear and have an assistant apply the rear brake, then unscrew the bolt **(see illustration)**. Discard the bolt as a new one must be used.
8 To remove the rotor from the shaft it is necessary to use a rotor puller. Yamaha can provide a special tool (Part No. 90890-01080 Europe models or YU-01080-A US models), or alternatively a similar tool can be obtained commercially **(see illustration)**.

31.8 Removing the rotor using a commercially available rotor puller

Electrical system 9•21

31.9a Unscrew the bolt (arrowed) and remove the wiring clamp . . .

31.9b . . . then unscrew the stator bolts (arrowed)

31.10a Install the stator . . .

31.10b . . . using a threadlock on the bolts

31.10c Fit the wiring grommet into the cut-out

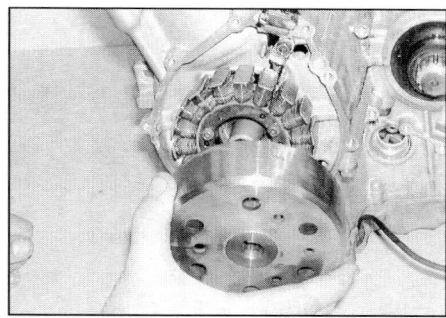

31.11 Slide the rotor onto the end of the crankshaft

9 To remove the stator, remove the bolt securing the wiring clamp and the three bolts securing the stator, then remove the assembly, noting how the rubber wiring grommet fits **(see illustrations)**.

Installation

10 Install the stator, aligning the rubber wiring grommet with the groove **(see illustration)**. Apply a suitable non-permanent thread locking compound to the stator bolt threads, then install the bolts and tighten them to the torque setting specified at the beginning of the Chapter **(see illustration)**. Apply a suitable sealant to the inner-facing portion of the wiring grommet, then press it into the cut-out **(see illustration)**. Secure the wiring with the clamp **(see illustration 31.9a)**.
11 Clean the tapered end of the crankshaft and the corresponding mating surface on the inside of the rotor with a suitable solvent. Make sure that no metal objects have attached themselves to the magnet on the inside of the rotor, then slide the rotor onto the shaft **(see illustration)**.
12 Apply some clean engine oil to the new rotor bolt threads and to the underside of the head, and to both sides of the washer **(see illustration)**. Tighten the bolt to the torque setting specified at the beginning of the Chapter, using the method employed on removal to prevent the rotor from turning **(see illustrations)**. Using a degree disc tighten the bolt further by turning it though 60°.

13 Apply a suitable sealant to the outer-facing portion of the wiring grommet. Fit the new gasket, making sure it locates onto the

31.12a Smear the bolt and washer with oil as described . . .

31.12c . . . and tighten the bolt to the specified torque

dowels **(see illustration)**. Install the cover and tighten the bolts evenly in a criss-cross pattern to the specified torque setting **(see**

31.12b . . . then install them . . .

31.13a Smear some sealant onto the grommet . . .

31.13b ... then locate the gasket onto the dowels (arrowed) ...

31.13c ... and install the cover

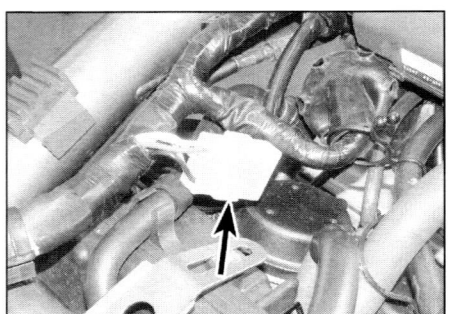

32.3 Regulator/rectifier wiring connector (arrowed)

32.4 Access the mounting bolts (arrowed) from the underside

illustration). Connect the alternator coil wiring connector, making sure it is correctly routed and secured by any clips or ties **(see illustration 31.2)**.

14 Install the left-hand side panel. Fill the engine with the correct quantity of oil (see Chapter 1).

32 Regulator/rectifier

Check

1 Yamaha provide no test specifications for the regulator/rectifier. If it is suspected of being faulty, first check all other components and the wiring and connectors in the charging circuit, referring to the relevant Sections in this Chapter and to the wiring diagrams at the end.

2 If all other components and the wiring are good, then the regulator/rectifier could be faulty. Remove the unit (see below) and take it to a Yamaha dealer for testing. Alternatively, substitute the suspect unit with a known good one and see if the fault is cured.

Removal and installation

3 The regulator/rectifier is mounted on a bracket on the left-hand side of the frame – remove the fairing and raise the fuel tank for access to it and its wiring connector (see Chapters 8 and 4). Disconnect the wiring connector **(see illustration)**.

4 Unscrew the two bolts securing the regulator/rectifier and remove it **(see illustration)**.

5 Install the new unit and tighten its bolts. Connect the wiring connector. Install the fuel tank and fairing (see Chapters 4 and 8).

Notes

Wiring diagrams

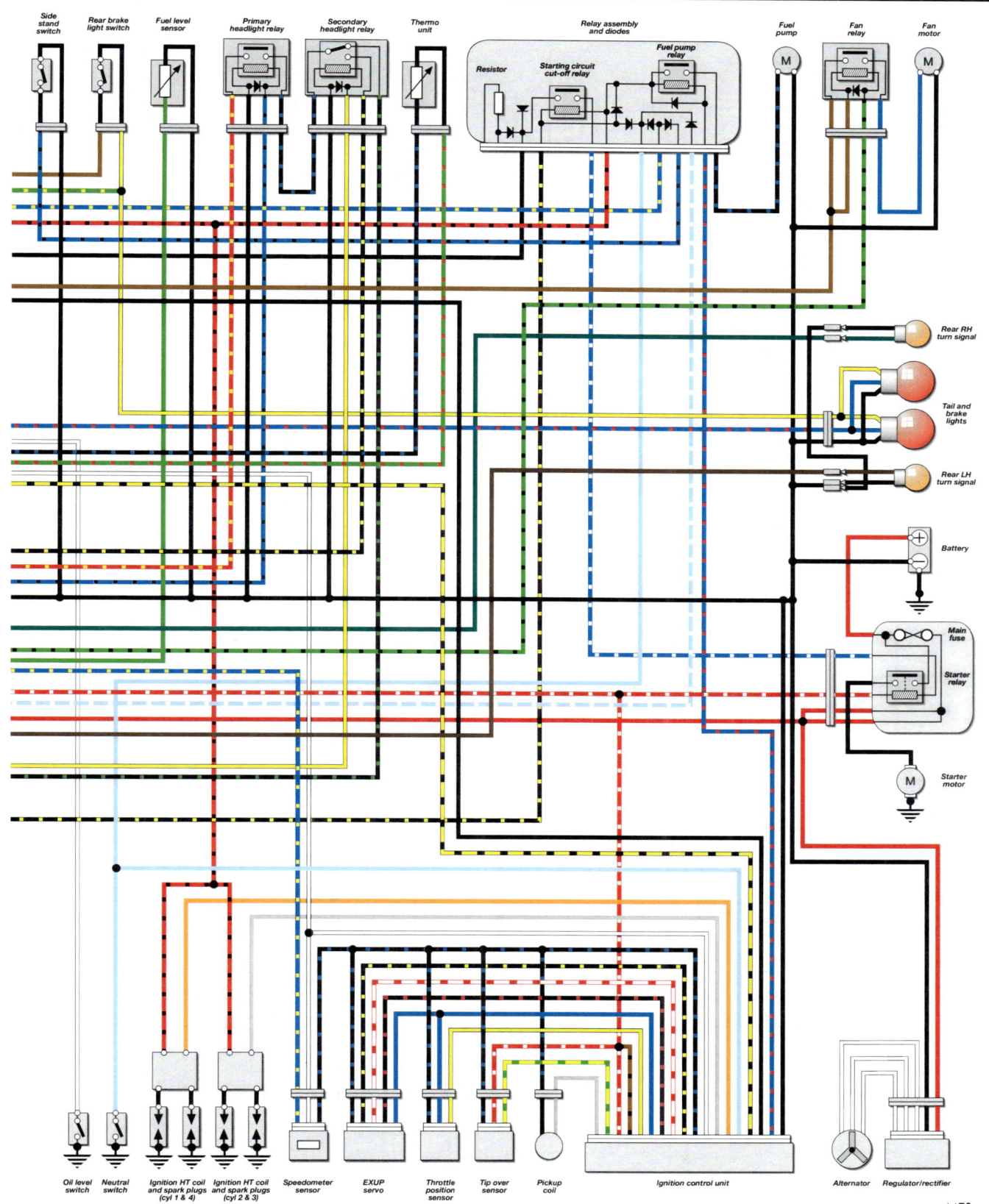

FZS1000 2001 and 2002 Europe models

9•26 Wiring diagrams

FZS1000 2003-on Europe models

Wiring diagrams 9•27

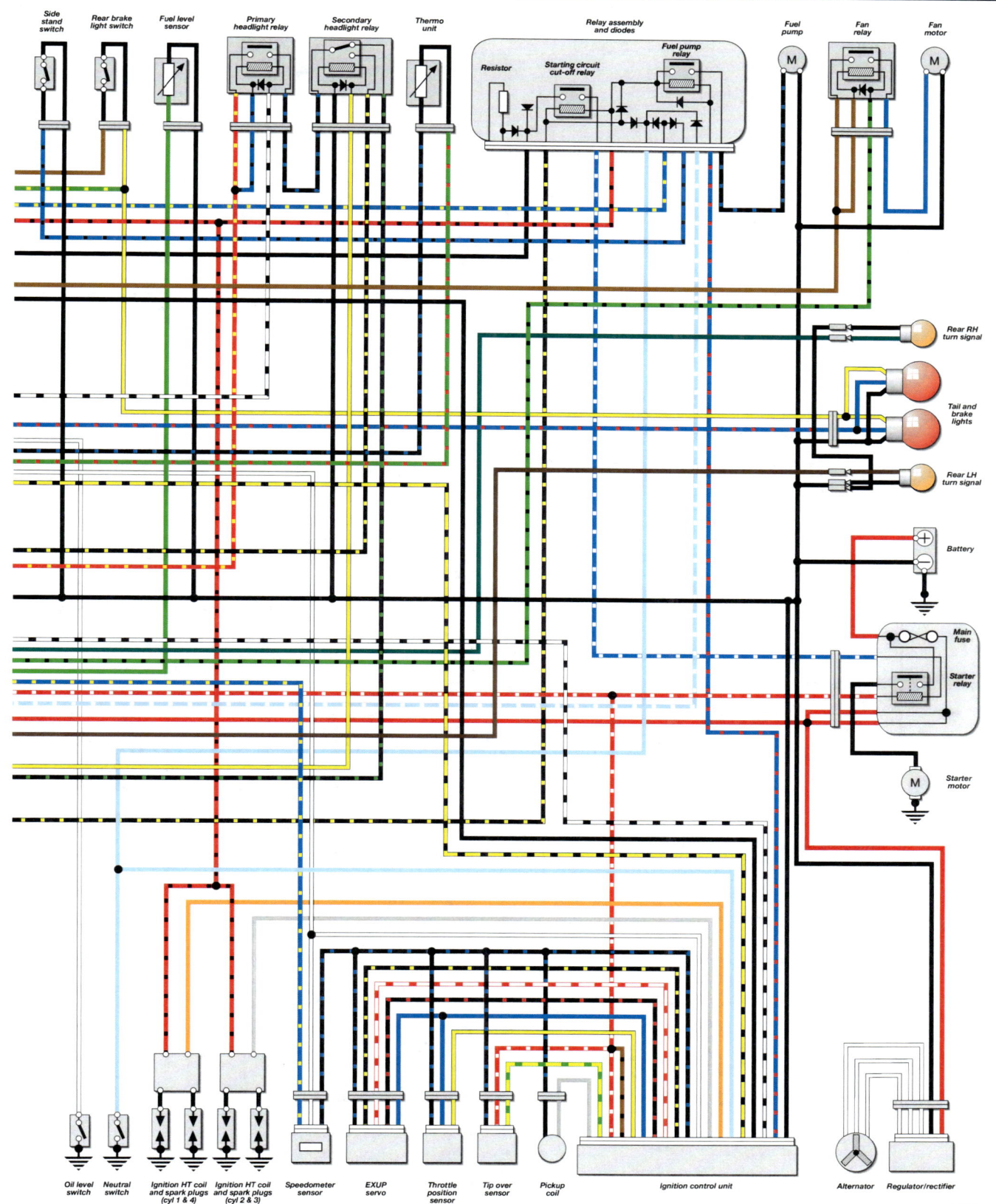

FZS1000 2003-on Europe models

9•28 Wiring diagrams

FZS1000 US models

Wiring diagrams 9•29

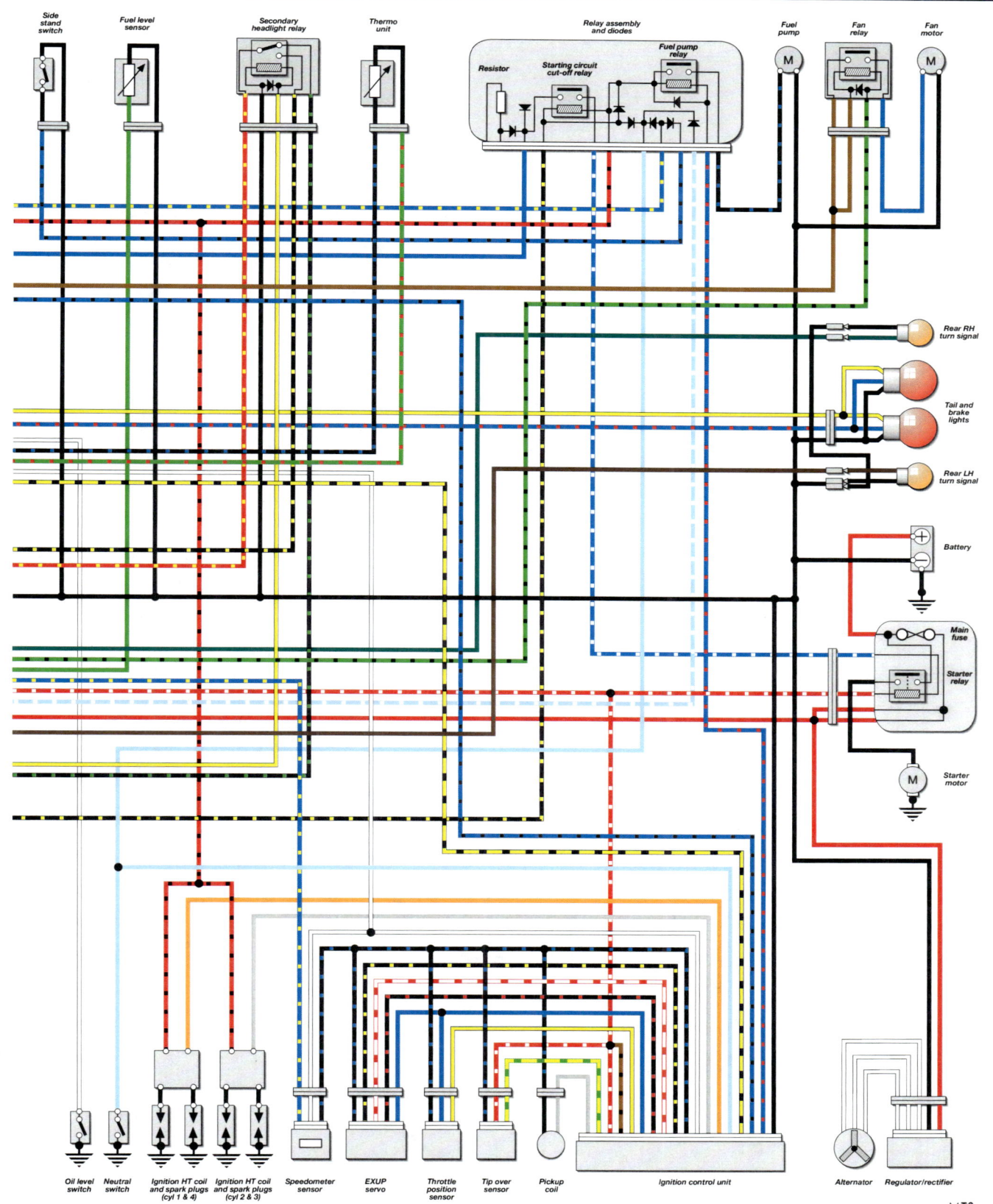

FZS1000 US models

Reference REF•1

Reference

Tools and Workshop Tips — REF•2

- Building up a tool kit and equipping your workshop ● Using tools
- Understanding bearing, seal, fastener and chain sizes and markings
- Repair techniques

Security — REF•20

- Locks and chains
- U-locks ● Disc locks
- Alarms and immobilisers
- Security marking systems ● Tips on how to prevent bike theft

Lubricants and fluids — REF•23

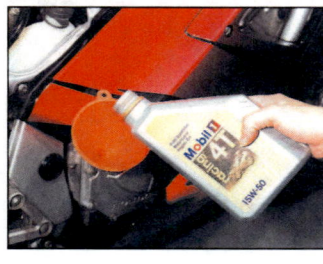

- Engine oils
- Transmission (gear) oils
- Coolant/anti-freeze
- Fork oils and suspension fluids ● Brake/clutch fluids
- Spray lubes, degreasers and solvents

Conversion Factors — REF•26

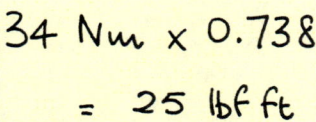

- Formulae for conversion of the metric (SI) units used throughout the manual into Imperial measures

MOT Test Checks — REF•27

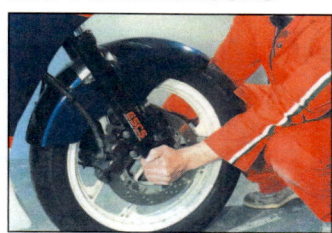

- A guide to the UK MOT test ● Which items are tested ● How to prepare your motorcycle for the test and perform a pre-test check

Storage — REF•32

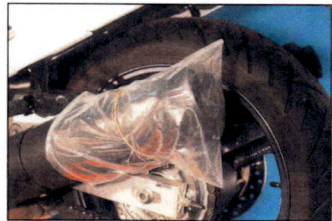

- How to prepare your motorcycle for going into storage and protect essential systems ● How to get the motorcycle back on the road

Fault Finding — REF•35

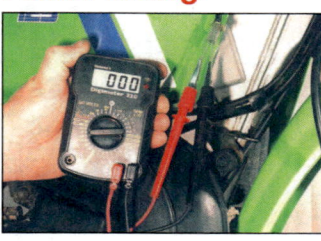

- Common faults and their likely causes ● How to check engine cylinder compression ● How to make electrical tests and use test meters

Technical Terms Explained — REF•48

- Component names, technical terms and common abbreviations explained

Index — REF•52

REF•2 Tools and Workshop Tips

Buying tools

A toolkit is a fundamental requirement for servicing and repairing a motorcycle. Although there will be an initial expense in building up enough tools for servicing, this will soon be offset by the savings made by doing the job yourself. As experience and confidence grow, additional tools can be added to enable the repair and overhaul of the motorcycle. Many of the specialist tools are expensive and not often used so it may be preferable to hire them, or for a group of friends or motorcycle club to join in the purchase.

As a rule, it is better to buy more expensive, good quality tools. Cheaper tools are likely to wear out faster and need to be renewed more often, nullifying the original saving.

> **Warning:** To avoid the risk of a poor quality tool breaking in use, causing injury or damage to the component being worked on, always aim to purchase tools which meet the relevant national safety standards.

The following lists of tools do not represent the manufacturer's service tools, but serve as a guide to help the owner decide which tools are needed for this level of work. In addition, items such as an electric drill, hacksaw, files, soldering iron and a workbench equipped with a vice, may be needed. Although not classed as tools, a selection of bolts, screws, nuts, washers and pieces of tubing always come in useful.

For more information about tools, refer to the Haynes *Motorcycle Workshop Practice TechBook* (Bk. No. 3470).

Manufacturer's service tools

Inevitably certain tasks require the use of a service tool. Where possible an alternative tool or method of approach is recommended, but sometimes there is no option if personal injury or damage to the component is to be avoided. Where required, service tools are referred to in the relevant procedure.

Service tools can usually only be purchased from a motorcycle dealer and are identified by a part number. Some of the commonly-used tools, such as rotor pullers, are available in aftermarket form from mail-order motorcycle tool and accessory suppliers.

Maintenance and minor repair tools

1 Set of flat-bladed screwdrivers
2 Set of Phillips head screwdrivers
3 Combination open-end and ring spanners
4 Socket set (3/8 inch or 1/2 inch drive)
5 Set of Allen keys or bits
6 Set of Torx keys or bits
7 Pliers, cutters and self-locking grips (Mole grips)
8 Adjustable spanners
9 C-spanners
10 Tread depth gauge and tyre pressure gauge
11 Cable oiler clamp
12 Feeler gauges
13 Spark plug gap measuring tool
14 Spark plug spanner or deep plug sockets
15 Wire brush and emery paper
16 Calibrated syringe, measuring vessel and funnel
17 Oil filter adapters
18 Oil drainer can or tray
19 Pump type oil can
20 Grease gun
21 Straight-edge and steel rule
22 Continuity tester
23 Battery charger
24 Hydrometer (for battery specific gravity check)
25 Anti-freeze tester (for liquid-cooled engines)

Tools and Workshop Tips

Repair and overhaul tools

1. Torque wrench (small and mid-ranges)
2. Conventional, plastic or soft-faced hammers
3. Impact driver set
4. Vernier gauge
5. Circlip pliers (internal and external, or combination)
6. Set of cold chisels and punches
7. Selection of pullers
8. Breaker bars
9. Chain breaking/riveting tool set
10. Wire stripper and crimper tool
11. Multimeter (measures amps, volts and ohms)
12. Stroboscope (for dynamic timing checks)
13. Hose clamp (wingnut type shown)
14. Clutch holding tool
15. One-man brake/clutch bleeder kit

Specialist tools

1. Micrometers (external type)
2. Telescoping gauges
3. Dial gauge
4. Cylinder compression gauge
5. Vacuum gauges (left) or manometer (right)
6. Oil pressure gauge
7. Plastigauge kit
8. Valve spring compressor (4-stroke engines)
9. Piston pin drawbolt tool
10. Piston ring removal and installation tool
11. Piston ring clamp
12. Cylinder bore hone (stone type shown)
13. Stud extractor
14. Screw extractor set
15. Bearing driver set

REF•4 Tools and Workshop Tips

1 Workshop equipment and facilities

The workbench

● Work is made much easier by raising the bike up on a ramp - components are much more accessible if raised to waist level. The hydraulic or pneumatic types seen in the dealer's workshop are a sound investment if you undertake a lot of repairs or overhauls **(see illustration 1.1)**.

1.1 Hydraulic motorcycle ramp

● If raised off ground level, the bike must be supported on the ramp to avoid it falling. Most ramps incorporate a front wheel locating clamp which can be adjusted to suit different diameter wheels. When tightening the clamp, take care not to mark the wheel rim or damage the tyre - use wood blocks on each side to prevent this.
● Secure the bike to the ramp using tie-downs **(see illustration 1.2)**. If the bike has only a sidestand, and hence leans at a dangerous angle when raised, support the bike on an auxiliary stand.

1.2 Tie-downs are used around the passenger footrests to secure the bike

● Auxiliary (paddock) stands are widely available from mail order companies or motorcycle dealers and attach either to the wheel axle or swingarm pivot **(see illustration 1.3)**. If the motorcycle has a centrestand, you can support it under the crankcase to prevent it toppling whilst either wheel is removed **(see illustration 1.4)**.

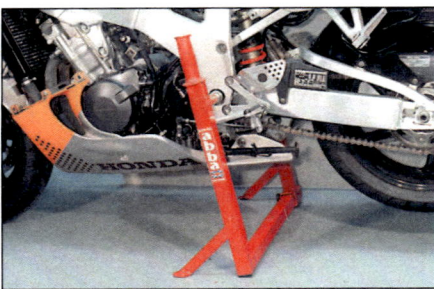

1.3 This auxiliary stand attaches to the swingarm pivot

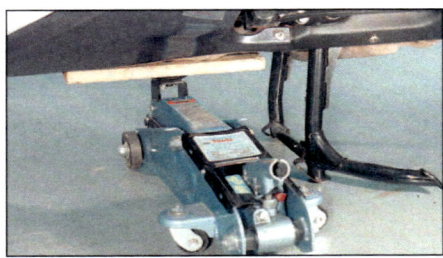

1.4 Always use a block of wood between the engine and jack head when supporting the engine in this way

Fumes and fire

● Refer to the Safety first! page at the beginning of the manual for full details. Make sure your workshop is equipped with a fire extinguisher suitable for fuel-related fires (Class B fire - flammable liquids) - it is not sufficient to have a water-filled extinguisher.
● Always ensure adequate ventilation is available. Unless an exhaust gas extraction system is available for use, ensure that the engine is run outside of the workshop.
● If working on the fuel system, make sure the workshop is ventilated to avoid a build-up of fumes. This applies equally to fume build-up when charging a battery. Do not smoke or allow anyone else to smoke in the workshop.

Fluids

● If you need to drain fuel from the tank, store it in an approved container marked as suitable for the storage of petrol (gasoline) **(see illustration 1.5)**. Do not store fuel in glass jars or bottles.

1.5 Use an approved can only for storing petrol (gasoline)

● Use proprietary engine degreasers or solvents which have a high flash-point, such as paraffin (kerosene), for cleaning off oil, grease and dirt - never use petrol (gasoline) for cleaning. Wear rubber gloves when handling solvent and engine degreaser. The fumes from certain solvents can be dangerous - always work in a well-ventilated area.

Dust, eye and hand protection

● Protect your lungs from inhalation of dust particles by wearing a filtering mask over the nose and mouth. Many frictional materials still contain asbestos which is dangerous to your health. Protect your eyes from spouts of liquid and sprung components by wearing a pair of protective goggles **(see illustration 1.6)**.

1.6 A fire extinguisher, goggles, mask and protective gloves should be at hand in the workshop

● Protect your hands from contact with solvents, fuel and oils by wearing rubber gloves. Alternatively apply a barrier cream to your hands before starting work. If handling hot components or fluids, wear suitable gloves to protect your hands from scalding and burns.

What to do with old fluids

● Old cleaning solvent, fuel, coolant and oils should not be poured down domestic drains or onto the ground. Package the fluid up in old oil containers, label it accordingly, and take it to a garage or disposal facility. Contact your local authority for location of such sites or ring the oil care hotline.

Note: It is antisocial and illegal to dump oil down the drain. To find the location of your local oil recycling bank, call this number free.

0800 66 33 66
www.oilbankline.org.uk

In the USA, note that any oil supplier must accept used oil for recycling.

Tools and Workshop Tips

2 Fasteners - screws, bolts and nuts

Fastener types and applications

Bolts and screws

● Fastener head types are either of hexagonal, Torx or splined design, with internal and external versions of each type **(see illustrations 2.1 and 2.2)**; splined head fasteners are not in common use on motorcycles. The conventional slotted or Phillips head design is used for certain screws. Bolt or screw length is always measured from the underside of the head to the end of the item **(see illustration 2.11)**.

2.1 Internal hexagon/Allen (A), Torx (B) and splined (C) fasteners, with corresponding bits

2.2 External Torx (A), splined (B) and hexagon (C) fasteners, with corresponding sockets

● Certain fasteners on the motorcycle have a tensile marking on their heads, the higher the marking the stronger the fastener. High tensile fasteners generally carry a 10 or higher marking. Never replace a high tensile fastener with one of a lower tensile strength.

Washers (see illustration 2.3)

● Plain washers are used between a fastener head and a component to prevent damage to the component or to spread the load when torque is applied. Plain washers can also be used as spacers or shims in certain assemblies. Copper or aluminium plain washers are often used as sealing washers on drain plugs.

2.3 Plain washer (A), penny washer (B), spring washer (C) and serrated washer (D)

● The split-ring spring washer works by applying axial tension between the fastener head and component. If flattened, it is fatigued and must be renewed. If a plain (flat) washer is used on the fastener, position the spring washer between the fastener and the plain washer.

● Serrated star type washers dig into the fastener and component faces, preventing loosening. They are often used on electrical earth (ground) connections to the frame.

● Cone type washers (sometimes called Belleville) are conical and when tightened apply axial tension between the fastener head and component. They must be installed with the dished side against the component and often carry an OUTSIDE marking on their outer face. If flattened, they are fatigued and must be renewed.

● Tab washers are used to lock plain nuts or bolts on a shaft. A portion of the tab washer is bent up hard against one flat of the nut or bolt to prevent it loosening. Due to the tab washer being deformed in use, a new tab washer should be used every time it is disturbed.

● Wave washers are used to take up endfloat on a shaft. They provide light springing and prevent excessive side-to-side play of a component. Can be found on rocker arm shafts.

Nuts and split pins

● Conventional plain nuts are usually six-sided **(see illustration 2.4)**. They are sized by thread diameter and pitch. High tensile nuts carry a number on one end to denote their tensile strength.

2.4 Plain nut (A), shouldered locknut (B), nylon insert nut (C) and castellated nut (D)

● Self-locking nuts either have a nylon insert, or two spring metal tabs, or a shoulder which is staked into a groove in the shaft - their advantage over conventional plain nuts is a resistance to loosening due to vibration. The nylon insert type can be used a number of times, but must be renewed when the friction of the nylon insert is reduced, ie when the nut spins freely on the shaft. The spring tab type can be reused unless the tabs are damaged. The shouldered type must be renewed every time it is disturbed.

● Split pins (cotter pins) are used to lock a castellated nut to a shaft or to prevent slackening of a plain nut. Common applications are wheel axles and brake torque arms. Because the split pin arms are deformed to lock around the nut a new split pin must always be used on installation - always fit the correct size split pin which will fit snugly in the shaft hole. Make sure the split pin arms are correctly located around the nut **(see illustrations 2.5 and 2.6)**.

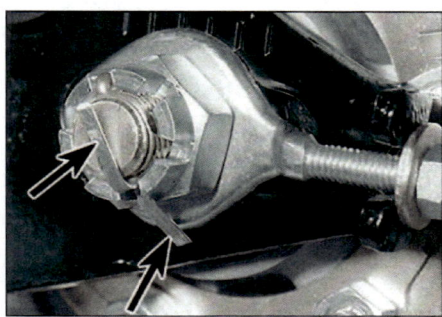

2.5 Bend split pin (cotter pin) arms as shown (arrows) to secure a castellated nut

2.6 Bend split pin (cotter pin) arms as shown to secure a plain nut

Caution: If the castellated nut slots do not align with the shaft hole after tightening to the torque setting, tighten the nut until the next slot aligns with the hole - never slacken the nut to align its slot.

● R-pins (shaped like the letter R), or slip pins as they are sometimes called, are sprung and can be reused if they are otherwise in good condition. Always install R-pins with their closed end facing forwards **(see illustration 2.7)**.

Tools and Workshop Tips

2.7 Correct fitting of R-pin. Arrow indicates forward direction

2.10 Align circlip opening with shaft channel

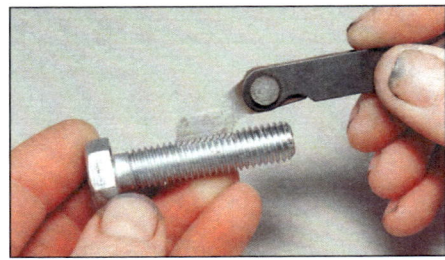

2.12 Using a thread gauge to measure pitch

Circlips (see illustration 2.8)

● Circlips (sometimes called snap-rings) are used to retain components on a shaft or in a housing and have corresponding external or internal ears to permit removal. Parallel-sided (machined) circlips can be installed either way round in their groove, whereas stamped circlips (which have a chamfered edge on one face) must be installed with the chamfer facing away from the direction of thrust load (see illustration 2.9).

2.8 External stamped circlip (A), internal stamped circlip (B), machined circlip (C) and wire circlip (D)

● Always use circlip pliers to remove and install circlips; expand or compress them just enough to remove them. After installation, rotate the circlip in its groove to ensure it is securely seated. If installing a circlip on a splined shaft, always align its opening with a shaft channel to ensure the circlip ends are well supported and unlikely to catch (see illustration 2.10).

2.9 Correct fitting of a stamped circlip

● Circlips can wear due to the thrust of components and become loose in their grooves, with the subsequent danger of becoming dislodged in operation. For this reason, renewal is advised every time a circlip is disturbed.

● Wire circlips are commonly used as piston pin retaining clips. If a removal tang is provided, long-nosed pliers can be used to dislodge them, otherwise careful use of a small flat-bladed screwdriver is necessary. Wire circlips should be renewed every time they are disturbed.

Thread diameter and pitch

● Diameter of a male thread (screw, bolt or stud) is the outside diameter of the threaded portion (see illustration 2.11). Most motorcycle manufacturers use the ISO (International Standards Organisation) metric system expressed in millimetres, eg M6 refers to a 6 mm diameter thread. Sizing is the same for nuts, except that the thread diameter is measured across the valleys of the nut.

● Pitch is the distance between the peaks of the thread (see illustration 2.11). It is expressed in millimetres, thus a common bolt size may be expressed as 6.0 x 1.0 mm (6 mm thread diameter and 1 mm pitch). Generally pitch increases in proportion to thread diameter, although there are always exceptions.

● Thread diameter and pitch are related for conventional fastener applications and the accompanying table can be used as a guide. Additionally, the AF (Across Flats), spanner or socket size dimension of the bolt or nut (see illustration 2.11) is linked to thread and pitch specification. Thread pitch can be measured with a thread gauge (see illustration 2.12).

2.11 Fastener length (L), thread diameter (D), thread pitch (P) and head size (AF)

AF size	Thread diameter x pitch (mm)
8 mm	M5 x 0.8
8 mm	M6 x 1.0
10 mm	M6 x 1.0
12 mm	M8 x 1.25
14 mm	M10 x 1.25
17 mm	M12 x 1.25

● The threads of most fasteners are of the right-hand type, ie they are turned clockwise to tighten and anti-clockwise to loosen. The reverse situation applies to left-hand thread fasteners, which are turned anti-clockwise to tighten and clockwise to loosen. Left-hand threads are used where rotation of a component might loosen a conventional right-hand thread fastener.

Seized fasteners

● Corrosion of external fasteners due to water or reaction between two dissimilar metals can occur over a period of time. It will build up sooner in wet conditions or in countries where salt is used on the roads during the winter. If a fastener is severely corroded it is likely that normal methods of removal will fail and result in its head being ruined. When you attempt removal, the fastener thread should be heard to crack free and unscrew easily - if it doesn't, stop there before damaging something.

● A smart tap on the head of the fastener will often succeed in breaking free corrosion which has occurred in the threads (see illustration 2.13).

● An aerosol penetrating fluid (such as WD-40) applied the night beforehand may work its way down into the thread and ease removal. Depending on the location, you may be able to make up a Plasticine well around the fastener head and fill it with penetrating fluid.

2.13 A sharp tap on the head of a fastener will often break free a corroded thread

Tools and Workshop Tips

- If you are working on an engine internal component, corrosion will most likely not be a problem due to the well lubricated environment. However, components can be very tight and an impact driver is a useful tool in freeing them **(see illustration 2.14)**.

2.14 Using an impact driver to free a fastener

- Where corrosion has occurred between dissimilar metals (eg steel and aluminium alloy), the application of heat to the fastener head will create a disproportionate expansion rate between the two metals and break the seizure caused by the corrosion. Whether heat can be applied depends on the location of the fastener - any surrounding components likely to be damaged must first be removed **(see illustration 2.15)**. Heat can be applied using a paint stripper heat gun or clothes iron, or by immersing the component in boiling water - wear protective gloves to prevent scalding or burns to the hands.

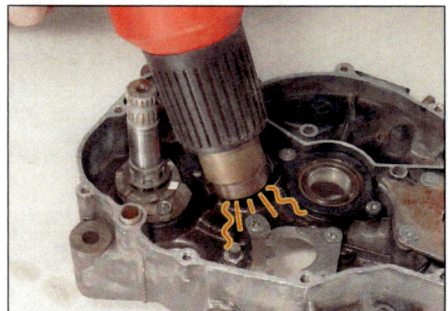

2.15 Using heat to free a seized fastener

- As a last resort, it is possible to use a hammer and cold chisel to work the fastener head unscrewed **(see illustration 2.16)**. This will damage the fastener, but more importantly extreme care must be taken not to damage the surrounding component.

Caution: Remember that the component being secured is generally of more value than the bolt, nut or screw - when the fastener is freed, do not unscrew it with force, instead work the fastener back and forth when resistance is felt to prevent thread damage.

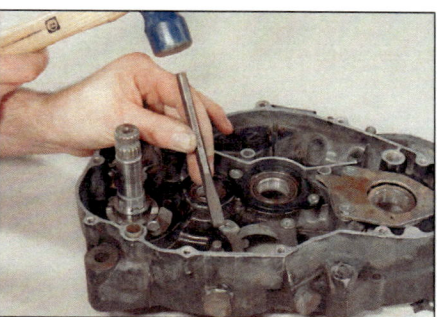

2.16 Using a hammer and chisel to free a seized fastener

Broken fasteners and damaged heads

- If the shank of a broken bolt or screw is accessible you can grip it with self-locking grips. The knurled wheel type stud extractor tool or self-gripping stud puller tool is particularly useful for removing the long studs which screw into the cylinder mouth surface of the crankcase or bolts and screws from which the head has broken off **(see illustration 2.17)**. Studs can also be removed by locking two nuts together on the threaded end of the stud and using a spanner on the lower nut **(see illustration 2.18)**.

2.17 Using a stud extractor tool to remove a broken crankcase stud

2.18 Two nuts can be locked together to unscrew a stud from a component

- A bolt or screw which has broken off below or level with the casing must be extracted using a screw extractor set. Centre punch the fastener to centralise the drill bit, then drill a hole in the fastener **(see illustration 2.19)**. Select a drill bit which is approximately half to three-quarters the

2.19 When using a screw extractor, first drill a hole in the fastener . . .

diameter of the fastener and drill to a depth which will accommodate the extractor. Use the largest size extractor possible, but avoid leaving too small a wall thickness otherwise the extractor will merely force the fastener walls outwards wedging it in the casing thread.

- If a spiral type extractor is used, thread it anti-clockwise into the fastener. As it is screwed in, it will grip the fastener and unscrew it from the casing **(see illustration 2.20)**.

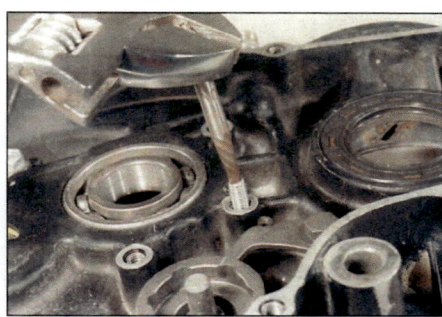

2.20 . . . then thread the extractor anti-clockwise into the fastener

- If a taper type extractor is used, tap it into the fastener so that it is firmly wedged in place. Unscrew the extractor (anti-clockwise) to draw the fastener out.

Warning: Stud extractors are very hard and may break off in the fastener if care is not taken - ask an engineer about spark erosion if this happens.

- Alternatively, the broken bolt/screw can be drilled out and the hole retapped for an oversize bolt/screw or a diamond-section thread insert. It is essential that the drilling is carried out squarely and to the correct depth, otherwise the casing may be ruined - if in doubt, entrust the work to an engineer.
- Bolts and nuts with rounded corners cause the correct size spanner or socket to slip when force is applied. Of the types of spanner/socket available always use a six-point type rather than an eight or twelve-point type - better grip

REF•8 Tools and Workshop Tips

2.21 Comparison of surface drive ring spanner (left) with 12-point type (right)

is obtained. Surface drive spanners grip the middle of the hex flats, rather than the corners, and are thus good in cases of damaged heads **(see illustration 2.21)**.

● Slotted-head or Phillips-head screws are often damaged by the use of the wrong size screwdriver. Allen-head and Torx-head screws are much less likely to sustain damage. If enough of the screw head is exposed you can use a hacksaw to cut a slot in its head and then use a conventional flat-bladed screwdriver to remove it. Alternatively use a hammer and cold chisel to tap the head of the fastener around to slacken it. Always replace damaged fasteners with new ones, preferably Torx or Allen-head type.

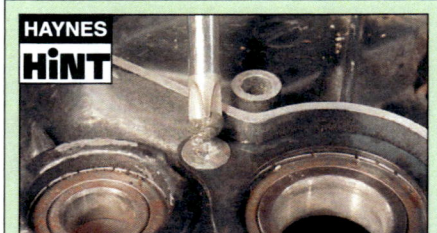

HAYNES HiNT

A dab of valve grinding compound between the screw head and screwdriver tip will often give a good grip.

Thread repair

● Threads (particularly those in aluminium alloy components) can be damaged by overtightening, being assembled with dirt in the threads, or from a component working loose and vibrating. Eventually the thread will fail completely, and it will be impossible to tighten the fastener.

● If a thread is damaged or clogged with old locking compound it can be renovated with a thread repair tool (thread chaser) **(see illustrations 2.22 and 2.23)**; special thread

2.22 A thread repair tool being used to correct an internal thread

2.23 A thread repair tool being used to correct an external thread

chasers are available for spark plug hole threads. The tool will not cut a new thread, but clean and true the original thread. Make sure that you use the correct diameter and pitch tool. Similarly, external threads can be cleaned up with a die or a thread restorer file **(see illustration 2.24)**.

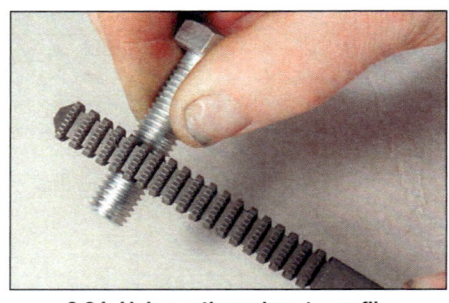

2.24 Using a thread restorer file

● It is possible to drill out the old thread and retap the component to the next thread size. This will work where there is enough surrounding material and a new bolt or screw can be obtained. Sometimes, however, this is not possible - such as where the bolt/screw passes through another component which must also be suitably modified, also in cases where a spark plug or oil drain plug cannot be obtained in a larger diameter thread size.

● The diamond-section thread insert (often known by its popular trade name of Heli-Coil) is a simple and effective method of renewing the thread and retaining the original size. A kit can be purchased which contains the tap, insert and installing tool **(see illustration 2.25)**. Drill out the damaged thread with the size drill specified **(see illustration 2.26)**. Carefully retap the thread **(see illustration 2.27)**. Install the

2.25 Obtain a thread insert kit to suit the thread diameter and pitch required

2.26 To install a thread insert, first drill out the original thread . . .

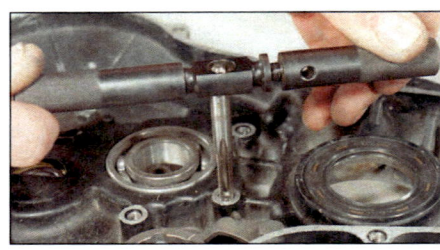

2.27 . . . tap a new thread . . .

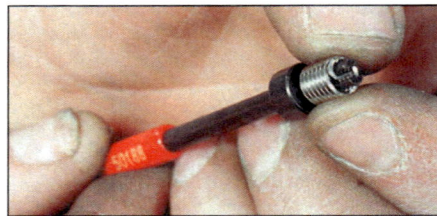

2.28 . . . fit insert on the installing tool . . .

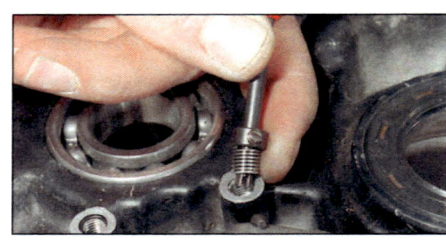

2.29 . . . and thread into the component . . .

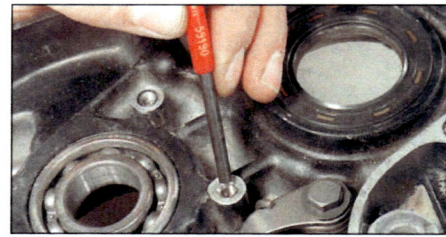

2.30 . . . break off the tang when complete

insert on the installing tool and thread it slowly into place using a light downward pressure **(see illustrations 2.28 and 2.29)**. When positioned between a 1/4 and 1/2 turn below the surface withdraw the installing tool and use the break-off tool to press down on the tang, breaking it off **(see illustration 2.30)**.

● There are epoxy thread repair kits on the market which can rebuild stripped internal threads, although this repair should not be used on high load-bearing components.

Tools and Workshop Tips

Thread locking and sealing compounds

- Locking compounds are used in locations where the fastener is prone to loosening due to vibration or on important safety-related items which might cause loss of control of the motorcycle if they fail. It is also used where important fasteners cannot be secured by other means such as lockwashers or split pins.
- Before applying locking compound, make sure that the threads (internal and external) are clean and dry with all old compound removed. Select a compound to suit the component being secured - a non-permanent general locking and sealing type is suitable for most applications, but a high strength type is needed for permanent fixing of studs in castings. Apply a drop or two of the compound to the first few threads of the fastener, then thread it into place and tighten to the specified torque. Do not apply excessive thread locking compound otherwise the thread may be damaged on subsequent removal.
- Certain fasteners are impregnated with a dry film type coating of locking compound on their threads. Always renew this type of fastener if disturbed.
- Anti-seize compounds, such as copper-based greases, can be applied to protect threads from seizure due to extreme heat and corrosion. A common instance is spark plug threads and exhaust system fasteners.

3 Measuring tools and gauges

Feeler gauges

- Feeler gauges (or blades) are used for measuring small gaps and clearances **(see illustration 3.1)**. They can also be used to measure endfloat (sideplay) of a component on a shaft where access is not possible with a dial gauge.
- Feeler gauge sets should be treated with care and not bent or damaged. They are etched with their size on one face. Keep them clean and very lightly oiled to prevent corrosion build-up.

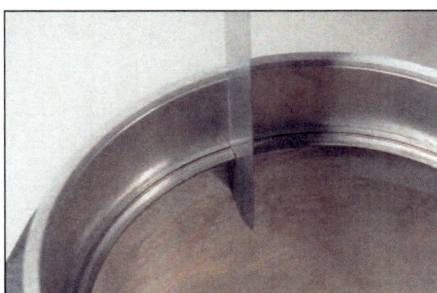

3.1 Feeler gauges are used for measuring small gaps and clearances - thickness is marked on one face of gauge

- When measuring a clearance, select a gauge which is a light sliding fit between the two components. You may need to use two gauges together to measure the clearance accurately.

Micrometers

- A micrometer is a precision tool capable of measuring to 0.01 or 0.001 of a millimetre. It should always be stored in its case and not in the general toolbox. It must be kept clean and never dropped, otherwise its frame or measuring anvils could be distorted resulting in inaccurate readings.
- External micrometers are used for measuring outside diameters of components and have many more applications than internal micrometers. Micrometers are available in different size ranges, eg 0 to 25 mm, 25 to 50 mm, and upwards in 25 mm steps; some large micrometers have interchangeable anvils to allow a range of measurements to be taken. Generally the largest precision measurement you are likely to take on a motorcycle is the piston diameter.
- Internal micrometers (or bore micrometers) are used for measuring inside diameters, such as valve guides and cylinder bores. Telescoping gauges and small hole gauges are used in conjunction with an external micrometer, whereas the more expensive internal micrometers have their own measuring device.

External micrometer

Note: *The conventional analogue type instrument is described. Although much easier to read, digital micrometers are considerably more expensive.*

- Always check the calibration of the micrometer before use. With the anvils closed (0 to 25 mm type) or set over a test gauge (for

3.2 Check micrometer calibration before use

the larger types) the scale should read zero **(see illustration 3.2)**; make sure that the anvils (and test piece) are clean first. Any discrepancy can be adjusted by referring to the instructions supplied with the tool. Remember that the micrometer is a precision measuring tool - don't force the anvils closed, use the ratchet (4) on the end of the micrometer to close it. In this way, a measured force is always applied.

- To use, first make sure that the item being measured is clean. Place the anvil of the micrometer (1) against the item and use the thimble (2) to bring the spindle (3) lightly into contact with the other side of the item **(see illustration 3.3)**. Don't tighten the thimble down because this will damage the micrometer - instead use the ratchet (4) on the end of the micrometer. The ratchet mechanism applies a measured force preventing damage to the instrument.
- The micrometer is read by referring to the linear scale on the sleeve and the annular scale on the thimble. Read off the sleeve first to obtain the base measurement, then add the fine measurement from the thimble to obtain the overall reading. The linear scale on the sleeve represents the measuring range of the micrometer (eg 0 to 25 mm). The annular scale

3.3 Micrometer component parts

| 1 Anvil | 3 Spindle | 5 Frame |
| 2 Thimble | 4 Ratchet | 6 Locking lever |

REF•10 Tools and Workshop Tips

on the thimble will be in graduations of 0.01 mm (or as marked on the frame) - one full revolution of the thimble will move 0.5 mm on the linear scale. Take the reading where the datum line on the sleeve intersects the thimble's scale. Always position the eye directly above the scale otherwise an inaccurate reading will result.

In the example shown the item measures 2.95 mm (see illustration 3.4):

Linear scale	2.00 mm
Linear scale	0.50 mm
Annular scale	0.45 mm
Total figure	**2.95 mm**

3.5 Micrometer reading of 46.99 mm on linear and annular scales . . .

3.7 Expand the telescoping gauge in the bore, lock its position . . .

3.4 Micrometer reading of 2.95 mm

3.6 . . . and 0.004 mm on vernier scale

3.8 . . . then measure the gauge with a micrometer

Most micrometers have a locking lever (6) on the frame to hold the setting in place, allowing the item to be removed from the micrometer.
● Some micrometers have a vernier scale on their sleeve, providing an even finer measurement to be taken, in 0.001 increments of a millimetre. Take the sleeve and thimble measurement as described above, then check which graduation on the vernier scale aligns with that of the annular scale on the thimble **Note:** *The eye must be perpendicular to the scale when taking the vernier reading - if necessary rotate the body of the micrometer to ensure this.* Multiply the vernier scale figure by 0.001 and add it to the base and fine measurement figures.

In the example shown the item measures 46.994 mm (see illustrations 3.5 and 3.6):

Linear scale (base)	46.000 mm
Linear scale (base)	00.500 mm
Annular scale (fine)	00.490 mm
Vernier scale	00.004 mm
Total figure	**46.994 mm**

Internal micrometer

● Internal micrometers are available for measuring bore diameters, but are expensive and unlikely to be available for home use. It is suggested that a set of telescoping gauges and small hole gauges, both of which must be used with an external micrometer, will suffice for taking internal measurements on a motorcycle.
● Telescoping gauges can be used to measure internal diameters of components. Select a gauge with the correct size range, make sure its ends are clean and insert it into the bore. Expand the gauge, then lock its position and withdraw it from the bore **(see illustration 3.7)**. Measure across the gauge ends with a micrometer **(see illustration 3.8)**.
● Very small diameter bores (such as valve guides) are measured with a small hole gauge. Once adjusted to a slip-fit inside the component, its position is locked and the gauge withdrawn for measurement with a micrometer **(see illustrations 3.9 and 3.10)**.

Vernier caliper

Note: *The conventional linear and dial gauge type instruments are described. Digital types are easier to read, but are far more expensive.*
● The vernier caliper does not provide the precision of a micrometer, but is versatile in being able to measure internal and external diameters. Some types also incorporate a depth gauge. It is ideal for measuring clutch plate friction material and spring free lengths.
● To use the conventional linear scale vernier, slacken off the vernier clamp screws (1) and set its jaws over (2), or inside (3), the item to be measured **(see illustration 3.11)**. Slide the jaw into contact, using the thumbwheel (4) for fine movement of the sliding scale (5) then tighten the clamp screws (1). Read off the main scale (6) where the zero on the sliding scale (5) intersects it, taking the whole number to the left of the zero; this provides the base measurement. View along the sliding scale and select the division which

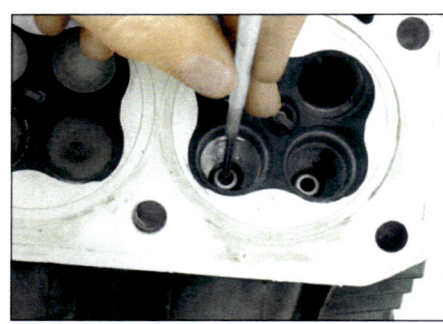

3.9 Expand the small hole gauge in the bore, lock its position . . .

3.10 . . . then measure the gauge with a micrometer

lines up exactly with any of the divisions on the main scale, noting that the divisions usually represents 0.02 of a millimetre. Add this fine measurement to the base measurement to obtain the total reading.

Tools and Workshop Tips REF•11

3.11 Vernier component parts (linear gauge)

1 Clamp screws
2 External jaws
3 Internal jaws
4 Thumbwheel
5 Sliding scale
6 Main scale
7 Depth gauge

In the example shown the item measures 55.92 mm **(see illustration 3.12)**:

3.12 Vernier gauge reading of 55.92 mm

Base measurement	55.00 mm
Fine measurement	00.92 mm
Total figure	**55.92 mm**

● Some vernier calipers are equipped with a dial gauge for fine measurement. Before use, check that the jaws are clean, then close them fully and check that the dial gauge reads zero. If necessary adjust the gauge ring accordingly. Slacken the vernier clamp screw (1) and set its jaws over (2), or inside (3), the item to be measured **(see illustration 3.13)**. Slide the jaws into contact, using the thumbwheel (4) for fine movement. Read off the main scale (5) where the edge of the sliding scale (6) intersects it, taking the whole number to the left of the zero; this provides the base measurement. Read off the needle position on the dial gauge (7) scale to provide the fine measurement; each division represents 0.05 of a millimetre. Add this fine measurement to the base measurement to obtain the total reading.

In the example shown the item measures 55.95 mm **(see illustration 3.14)**:

3.13 Vernier component parts (dial gauge)

1 Clamp screw
2 External jaws
3 Internal jaws
4 Thumbwheel
5 Main scale
6 Sliding scale
7 Dial gauge

Base measurement	55.00 mm
Fine measurement	00.95 mm
Total figure	**55.95 mm**

3.14 Vernier gauge reading of 55.95 mm

Plastigauge

● Plastigauge is a plastic material which can be compressed between two surfaces to measure the oil clearance between them. The width of the compressed Plastigauge is measured against a calibrated scale to determine the clearance.

● Common uses of Plastigauge are for measuring the clearance between crankshaft journal and main bearing inserts, between crankshaft journal and big-end bearing inserts, and between camshaft and bearing surfaces. The following example describes big-end oil clearance measurement.

● Handle the Plastigauge material carefully to prevent distortion. Using a sharp knife, cut a length which corresponds with the width of the bearing being measured and place it carefully across the journal so that it is parallel with the shaft **(see illustration 3.15)**. Carefully install both bearing shells and the connecting rod. Without rotating the rod on the journal tighten its bolts or nuts (as applicable) to the specified torque. The connecting rod and bearings are then disassembled and the crushed Plastigauge examined.

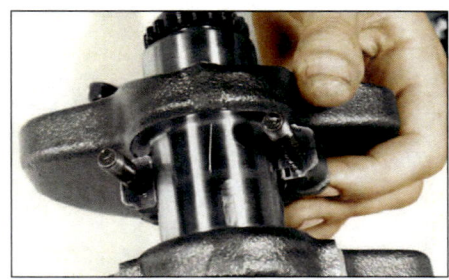

3.15 Plastigauge placed across shaft journal

● Using the scale provided in the Plastigauge kit, measure the width of the material to determine the oil clearance **(see illustration 3.16)**. Always remove all traces of Plastigauge after use using your fingernails.

Caution: Arriving at the correct clearance demands that the assembly is torqued correctly, according to the settings and sequence (where applicable) provided by the motorcycle manufacturer.

3.16 Measuring the width of the crushed Plastigauge

REF•12 Tools and Workshop Tips

Dial gauge or DTI (Dial Test Indicator)

● A dial gauge can be used to accurately measure small amounts of movement. Typical uses are measuring shaft runout or shaft endfloat (sideplay) and setting piston position for ignition timing on two-strokes. A dial gauge set usually comes with a range of different probes and adapters and mounting equipment.

● The gauge needle must point to zero when at rest. Rotate the ring around its periphery to zero the gauge.

● Check that the gauge is capable of reading the extent of movement in the work. Most gauges have a small dial set in the face which records whole millimetres of movement as well as the fine scale around the face periphery which is calibrated in 0.01 mm divisions. Read off the small dial first to obtain the base measurement, then add the measurement from the fine scale to obtain the total reading.

In the example shown the gauge reads 1.48 mm (see illustration 3.17):

Base measurement	1.00 mm
Fine measurement	0.48 mm
Total figure	**1.48 mm**

3.17 Dial gauge reading of 1.48 mm

● If measuring shaft runout, the shaft must be supported in vee-blocks and the gauge mounted on a stand perpendicular to the shaft. Rest the tip of the gauge against the centre of the shaft and rotate the shaft slowly whilst watching the gauge reading (see illustration 3.18). Take several measurements along the length of the shaft and record the maximum gauge reading as the amount of runout in the shaft. **Note:** *The reading obtained will be total runout at that point - some manufacturers specify that the runout figure is halved to compare with their specified runout limit.*

● Endfloat (sideplay) measurement requires that the gauge is mounted securely to the surrounding component with its probe touching the end of the shaft. Using hand pressure, push and pull on the shaft noting the maximum endfloat recorded on the gauge (see illustration 3.19).

3.19 Using a dial gauge to measure shaft endfloat

● A dial gauge with suitable adapters can be used to determine piston position BTDC on two-stroke engines for the purposes of ignition timing. The gauge, adapter and suitable length probe are installed in the place of the spark plug and the gauge zeroed at TDC. If the piston position is specified as 1.14 mm BTDC, rotate the engine back to 2.00 mm BTDC, then slowly forwards to 1.14 mm BTDC.

Cylinder compression gauges

● A compression gauge is used for measuring cylinder compression. Either the rubber-cone type or the threaded adapter type can be used. The latter is preferred to ensure a perfect seal against the cylinder head. A 0 to 300 psi (0 to 20 Bar) type gauge (for petrol/gasoline engines) will be suitable for motorcycles.

● The spark plug is removed and the gauge either held hard against the cylinder head (cone type) or the gauge adapter screwed into the cylinder head (threaded type) (see illustration 3.20). Cylinder compression is measured with the engine turning over, but not running - carry out the compression test as described in *Fault Finding Equipment*. The gauge will hold the reading until manually released.

Oil pressure gauge

● An oil pressure gauge is used for measuring engine oil pressure. Most gauges come with a set of adapters to fit the thread of the take-off point (see illustration 3.21). If the take-off point specified by the motorcycle manufacturer is an external oil pipe union, make sure that the specified replacement union is used to prevent oil starvation.

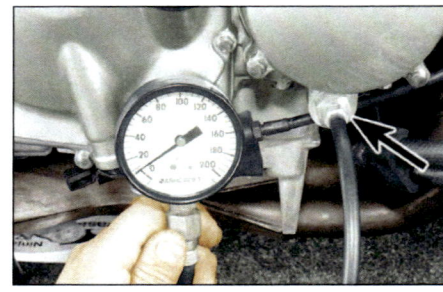

3.21 Oil pressure gauge and take-off point adapter (arrow)

● Oil pressure is measured with the engine running (at a specific rpm) and often the manufacturer will specify pressure limits for a cold and hot engine.

Straight-edge and surface plate

● If checking the gasket face of a component for warpage, place a steel rule or precision straight-edge across the gasket face and measure any gap between the straight-edge and component with feeler gauges (see illustration 3.22). Check diagonally across the component and between mounting holes (see illustration 3.23).

3.22 Use a straight-edge and feeler gauges to check for warpage

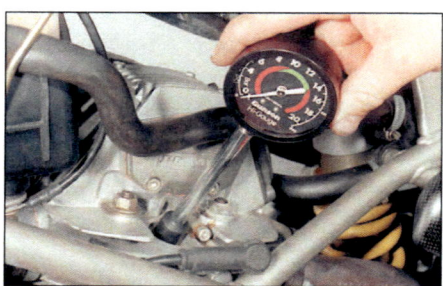

3.20 Using a rubber-cone type cylinder compression gauge

3.18 Using a dial gauge to measure shaft runout

3.23 Check for warpage in these directions

Tools and Workshop Tips

- Checking individual components for warpage, such as clutch plain (metal) plates, requires a perfectly flat plate or piece or plate glass and feeler gauges.

4 Torque and leverage

What is torque?

- Torque describes the twisting force about a shaft. The amount of torque applied is determined by the distance from the centre of the shaft to the end of the lever and the amount of force being applied to the end of the lever; distance multiplied by force equals torque.
- The manufacturer applies a measured torque to a bolt or nut to ensure that it will not slacken in use and to hold two components securely together without movement in the joint. The actual torque setting depends on the thread size, bolt or nut material and the composition of the components being held.
- Too little torque may cause the fastener to loosen due to vibration, whereas too much torque will distort the joint faces of the component or cause the fastener to shear off. Always stick to the specified torque setting.

Using a torque wrench

- Check the calibration of the torque wrench and make sure it has a suitable range for the job. Torque wrenches are available in Nm (Newton-metres), kgf m (kilograms-force metre), lbf ft (pounds-feet), lbf in (inch-pounds). Do not confuse lbf ft with lbf in.
- Adjust the tool to the desired torque on the scale **(see illustration 4.1)**. If your torque wrench is not calibrated in the units specified, carefully convert the figure (see *Conversion Factors*). A manufacturer sometimes gives a torque setting as a range (8 to 10 Nm) rather than a single figure - in this case set the tool midway between the two settings. The same torque may be expressed as 9 Nm ± 1 Nm. Some torque wrenches have a method of locking the setting so that it isn't inadvertently altered during use.

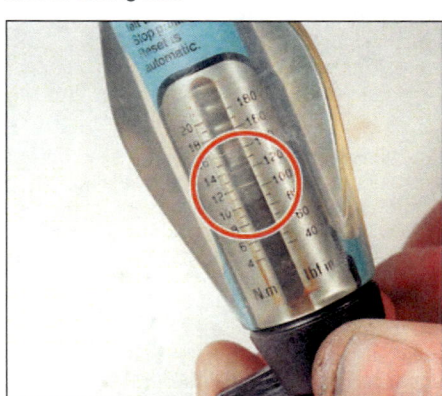

4.1 Set the torque wrench index mark to the setting required, in this case 12 Nm

- Install the bolts/nuts in their correct location and secure them lightly. Their threads must be clean and free of any old locking compound. Unless specified the threads and flange should be dry - oiled threads are necessary in certain circumstances and the manufacturer will take this into account in the specified torque figure. Similarly, the manufacturer may also specify the application of thread-locking compound.
- Tighten the fasteners in the specified sequence until the torque wrench clicks, indicating that the torque setting has been reached. Apply the torque again to double-check the setting. Where different thread diameter fasteners secure the component, as a rule tighten the larger diameter ones first.
- When the torque wrench has been finished with, release the lock (where applicable) and fully back off its setting to zero - do not leave the torque wrench tensioned. Also, do not use a torque wrench for slackening a fastener.

Angle-tightening

- Manufacturers often specify a figure in degrees for final tightening of a fastener. This usually follows tightening to a specific torque setting.
- A degree disc can be set and attached to the socket **(see illustration 4.2)** or a protractor can be used to mark the angle of movement on the bolt/nut head and the surrounding casting **(see illustration 4.3)**.

4.2 Angle tightening can be accomplished with a torque-angle gauge . . .

4.3 . . . or by marking the angle on the surrounding component

Loosening sequences

- Where more than one bolt/nut secures a component, loosen each fastener evenly a little at a time. In this way, not all the stress of the joint is held by one fastener and the components are not likely to distort.
- If a tightening sequence is provided, work in the REVERSE of this, but if not, work from the outside in, in a criss-cross sequence **(see illustration 4.4)**.

4.4 When slackening, work from the outside inwards

Tightening sequences

- If a component is held by more than one fastener it is important that the retaining bolts/nuts are tightened evenly to prevent uneven stress build-up and distortion of sealing faces. This is especially important on high-compression joints such as the cylinder head.
- A sequence is usually provided by the manufacturer, either in a diagram or actually marked in the casting. If not, always start in the centre and work outwards in a criss-cross pattern **(see illustration 4.5)**. Start off by securing all bolts/nuts finger-tight, then set the torque wrench and tighten each fastener by a small amount in sequence until the final torque is reached. By following this practice,

4.5 When tightening, work from the inside outwards

REF•14 Tools and Workshop Tips

the joint will be held evenly and will not be distorted. Important joints, such as the cylinder head and big-end fasteners often have two- or three-stage torque settings.

Applying leverage

● Use tools at the correct angle. Position a socket wrench or spanner on the bolt/nut so that you pull it towards you when loosening. If this can't be done, push the spanner without curling your fingers around it **(see illustration 4.6)** - the spanner may slip or the fastener loosen suddenly, resulting in your fingers being crushed against a component.

4.6 If you can't pull on the spanner to loosen a fastener, push with your hand open

● Additional leverage is gained by extending the length of the lever. The best way to do this is to use a breaker bar instead of the regular length tool, or to slip a length of tubing over the end of the spanner or socket wrench.
● If additional leverage will not work, the fastener head is either damaged or firmly corroded in place (see *Fasteners*).

5 Bearings

Bearing removal and installation

Drivers and sockets

● Before removing a bearing, always inspect the casing to see which way it must be driven out - some casings will have retaining plates or a cast step. Also check for any identifying markings on the bearing and if installed to a certain depth, measure this at this stage. Some roller bearings are sealed on one side - take note of the original fitted position.
● Bearings can be driven out of a casing using a bearing driver tool (with the correct size head) or a socket of the correct diameter. Select the driver head or socket so that it contacts the outer race of the bearing, not the balls/rollers or inner race. Always support the casing around the bearing housing with wood blocks, otherwise there is a risk of fracture. The bearing is driven out with a few blows on the driver or socket from a heavy mallet. Unless access is severely restricted (as with wheel bearings), a pin-punch is not recommended unless it is moved around the bearing to keep it square in its housing.

● The same equipment can be used to install bearings. Make sure the bearing housing is supported on wood blocks and line up the bearing in its housing. Fit the bearing as noted on removal - generally they are installed with their marked side facing outwards. Tap the bearing squarely into its housing using a driver or socket which bears only on the bearing's outer race - contact with the bearing balls/rollers or inner race will destroy it **(see illustrations 5.1 and 5.2)**.
● Check that the bearing inner race and balls/rollers rotate freely.

5.1 Using a bearing driver against the bearing's outer race

5.2 Using a large socket against the bearing's outer race

Pullers and slide-hammers

● Where a bearing is pressed on a shaft a puller will be required to extract it **(see illustration 5.3)**. Make sure that the puller clamp or legs fit securely behind the bearing and are unlikely to slip out. If pulling a bearing

5.3 This bearing puller clamps behind the bearing and pressure is applied to the shaft end to draw the bearing off

off a gear shaft for example, you may have to locate the puller behind a gear pinion if there is no access to the race and draw the gear pinion off the shaft as well **(see illustration 5.4)**.

> **Caution: Ensure that the puller's centre bolt locates securely against the end of the shaft and will not slip when pressure is applied. Also ensure that puller does not damage the shaft end.**

5.4 Where no access is available to the rear of the bearing, it is sometimes possible to draw off the adjacent component

● Operate the puller so that its centre bolt exerts pressure on the shaft end and draws the bearing off the shaft.
● When installing the bearing on the shaft, tap only on the bearing's inner race - contact with the balls/rollers or outer race with destroy the bearing. Use a socket or length of tubing as a drift which fits over the shaft end **(see illustration 5.5)**.

5.5 When installing a bearing on a shaft use a piece of tubing which bears only on the bearing's inner race

● Where a bearing locates in a blind hole in a casing, it cannot be driven or pulled out as described above. A slide-hammer with knife-edged bearing puller attachment will be required. The puller attachment passes through the bearing and when tightened expands to fit firmly behind the bearing **(see illustration 5.6)**. By operating the slide-hammer part of the tool the bearing is jarred out of its housing **(see illustration 5.7)**.
● It is possible, if the bearing is of reasonable weight, for it to drop out of its housing if the casing is heated as described opposite. If this

Tools and Workshop Tips

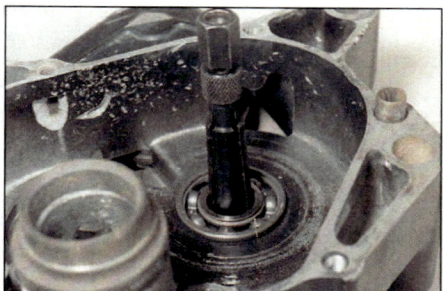

5.6 Expand the bearing puller so that it locks behind the bearing . . .

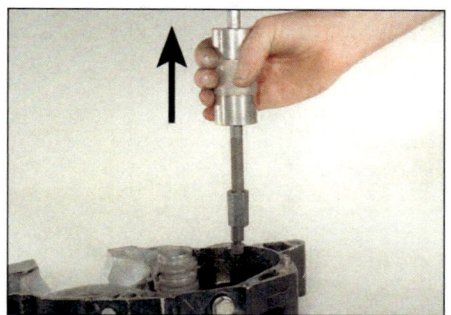

5.7 . . . attach the slide hammer to the bearing puller

method is attempted, first prepare a work surface which will enable the casing to be tapped face down to help dislodge the bearing - a wood surface is ideal since it will not damage the casing's gasket surface. Wearing protective gloves, tap the heated casing several times against the work surface to dislodge the bearing under its own weight (see illustration 5.8).

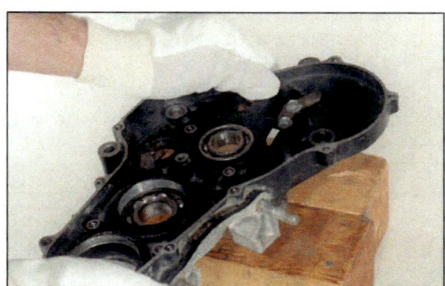

5.8 Tapping a casing face down on wood blocks can often dislodge a bearing

● Bearings can be installed in blind holes using the driver or socket method described above.

Drawbolts

● Where a bearing or bush is set in the eye of a component, such as a suspension linkage arm or connecting rod small-end, removal by drift may damage the component. Furthermore, a rubber bushing in a shock absorber eye cannot successfully be driven out of position. If access is available to a engineering press, the task is straightforward. If not, a drawbolt can be fabricated to extract the bearing or bush.

5.9 Drawbolt component parts assembled on a suspension arm

1 Bolt or length of threaded bar
2 Nuts
3 Washer (external diameter greater than tubing internal diameter)
4 Tubing (internal diameter sufficient to accommodate bearing)
5 Suspension arm with bearing
6 Tubing (external diameter slightly smaller than bearing)
7 Washer (external diameter slightly smaller than bearing)

5.10 Drawing the bearing out of the suspension arm

● To extract the bearing/bush you will need a long bolt with nut (or piece of threaded bar with two nuts), a piece of tubing which has an internal diameter larger than the bearing/bush, another piece of tubing which has an external diameter slightly smaller than the bearing/bush, and a selection of washers (see illustrations 5.9 and 5.10). Note that the pieces of tubing must be of the same length, or longer, than the bearing/bush.
● The same kit (without the pieces of tubing) can be used to draw the new bearing/bush back into place (see illustration 5.11).

5.11 Installing a new bearing (1) in the suspension arm

Temperature change

● If the bearing's outer race is a tight fit in the casing, the aluminium casing can be heated to release its grip on the bearing. Aluminium will expand at a greater rate than the steel bearing outer race. There are several ways to do this, but avoid any localised extreme heat (such as a blow torch) - aluminium alloy has a low melting point.
● Approved methods of heating a casing are using a domestic oven (heated to 100°C) or immersing the casing in boiling water (see illustration 5.12). Low temperature range localised heat sources such as a paint stripper heat gun or clothes iron can also be used (see illustration 5.13). Alternatively, soak a rag in boiling water, wring it out and wrap it around the bearing housing.

> **Warning:** All of these methods require care in use to prevent scalding and burns to the hands. Wear protective gloves when handling hot components.

5.12 A casing can be immersed in a sink of boiling water to aid bearing removal

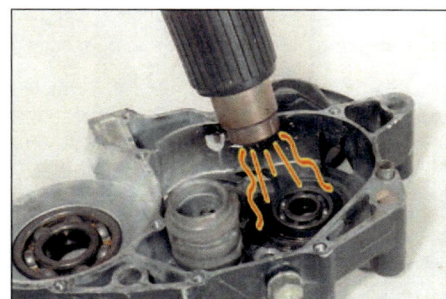

5.13 Using a localised heat source to aid bearing removal

● If heating the whole casing note that plastic components, such as the neutral switch, may suffer - remove them beforehand.
● After heating, remove the bearing as described above. You may find that the expansion is sufficient for the bearing to fall out of the casing under its own weight or with a light tap on the driver or socket.
● If necessary, the casing can be heated to aid bearing installation, and this is sometimes the recommended procedure if the motorcycle manufacturer has designed the housing and bearing fit with this intention.

Tools and Workshop Tips

- Installation of bearings can be eased by placing them in a freezer the night before installation. The steel bearing will contract slightly, allowing easy insertion in its housing. This is often useful when installing steering head outer races in the frame.

Bearing types and markings

- Plain shell bearings, ball bearings, needle roller bearings and tapered roller bearings will all be found on motorcycles **(see illustrations 5.14 and 5.15)**. The ball and roller types are usually caged between an inner and outer race, but uncaged variations may be found.

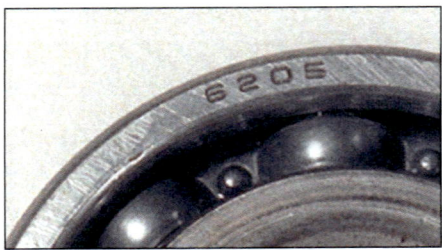

5.16 Typical bearing marking

Bearing fault finding

- If a bearing outer race has spun in its housing, the housing material will be damaged. You can use a bearing locking compound to bond the outer race in place if damage is not too severe.
- Shell bearings will fail due to damage of their working surface, as a result of lack of lubrication, corrosion or abrasive particles in the oil **(see illustration 5.17)**. Small particles of dirt in the oil may embed in the bearing material whereas larger particles will score the bearing and shaft journal. If a number of short journeys are made, insufficient heat will be generated to drive off condensation which has built up on the bearings.

5.14 Shell bearings are either plain or grooved. They are usually identified by colour code (arrow)

5.15 Tapered roller bearing (A), needle roller bearing (B) and ball journal bearing (C)

- Shell bearings (often called inserts) are usually found at the crankshaft main and connecting rod big-end where they are good at coping with high loads. They are made of a phosphor-bronze material and are impregnated with self-lubricating properties.
- Ball bearings and needle roller bearings consist of a steel inner and outer race with the balls or rollers between the races. They require constant lubrication by oil or grease and are good at coping with axial loads. Taper roller bearings consist of rollers set in a tapered cage set on the inner race; the outer race is separate. They are good at coping with axial loads and prevent movement along the shaft - a typical application is in the steering head.
- Bearing manufacturers produce bearings to ISO size standards and stamp one face of the bearing to indicate its internal and external diameter, load capacity and type **(see illustration 5.16)**.
- Metal bushes are usually of phosphor-bronze material. Rubber bushes are used in suspension mounting eyes. Fibre bushes have also been used in suspension pivots.

5.17 Typical bearing failures

- Ball and roller bearings will fail due to lack of lubrication or damage to the balls or rollers. Tapered-roller bearings can be damaged by overloading them. Unless the bearing is sealed on both sides, wash it in paraffin (kerosene) to remove all old grease then allow it to dry. Make a visual inspection looking to dented balls or rollers, damaged cages and worn or pitted races **(see illustration 5.18)**.
- A ball bearing can be checked for wear by listening to it when spun. Apply a film of light oil to the bearing and hold it close to the ear - hold the outer race with one hand and spin the inner race with the other hand **(see illustration 5.19)**. The bearing should be almost silent when spun; if it grates or rattles it is worn.

5.18 Example of ball journal bearing with damaged balls and cages

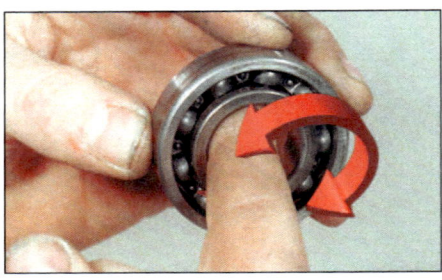

5.19 Hold outer race and listen to inner race when spun

6 Oil seals

Oil seal removal and installation

- Oil seals should be renewed every time a component is dismantled. This is because the seal lips will become set to the sealing surface and will not necessarily reseal.
- Oil seals can be prised out of position using a large flat-bladed screwdriver **(see illustration 6.1)**. In the case of crankcase seals, check first that the seal is not lipped on the inside, preventing its removal with the crankcases joined.

6.1 Prise out oil seals with a large flat-bladed screwdriver

- New seals are usually installed with their marked face (containing the seal reference code) outwards and the spring side towards the fluid being retained. In certain cases, such as a two-stroke engine crankshaft seal, a double lipped seal may be used due to there being fluid or gas on each side of the joint.

Tools and Workshop Tips

- Use a bearing driver or socket which bears only on the outer hard edge of the seal to install it in the casing - tapping on the inner edge will damage the sealing lip.

Oil seal types and markings

- Oil seals are usually of the single-lipped type. Double-lipped seals are found where a liquid or gas is on both sides of the joint.
- Oil seals can harden and lose their sealing ability if the motorcycle has been in storage for a long period - renewal is the only solution.
- Oil seal manufacturers also conform to the ISO markings for seal size - these are moulded into the outer face of the seal (see illustration 6.2).

6.2 These oil seal markings indicate inside diameter, outside diameter and seal thickness

7 Gaskets and sealants

Types of gasket and sealant

- Gaskets are used to seal the mating surfaces between components and keep lubricants, fluids, vacuum or pressure contained within the assembly. Aluminium gaskets are sometimes found at the cylinder joints, but most gaskets are paper-based. If the mating surfaces of the components being joined are undamaged the gasket can be installed dry, although a dab of sealant or grease will be useful to hold it in place during assembly.
- RTV (Room Temperature Vulcanising) silicone rubber sealants cure when exposed to moisture in the atmosphere. These sealants are good at filling pits or irregular gasket faces, but will tend to be forced out of the joint under very high torque. They can be used to replace a paper gasket, but first make sure that the width of the paper gasket is not essential to the shimming of internal components. RTV sealants should not be used on components containing petrol (gasoline).
- Non-hardening, semi-hardening and hard setting liquid gasket compounds can be used with a gasket or between a metal-to-metal joint. Select the sealant to suit the application: universal non-hardening sealant can be used on virtually all joints; semi-hardening on joint faces which are rough or damaged; hard setting sealant on joints which require a permanent bond and are subjected to high temperature and pressure. **Note:** *Check first if the paper gasket has a bead of sealant impregnated in its surface before applying additional sealant.*
- When choosing a sealant, make sure it is suitable for the application, particularly if being applied in a high-temperature area or in the vicinity of fuel. Certain manufacturers produce sealants in either clear, silver or black colours to match the finish of the engine. This has a particular application on motorcycles where much of the engine is exposed.
- Do not over-apply sealant. That which is squeezed out on the outside of the joint can be wiped off, whereas an excess of sealant on the inside can break off and clog oilways.

Breaking a sealed joint

- Age, heat, pressure and the use of hard setting sealant can cause two components to stick together so tightly that they are difficult to separate using finger pressure alone. Do not resort to using levers unless there is a pry point provided for this purpose (see illustration 7.1) or else the gasket surfaces will be damaged.
- Use a soft-faced hammer (see illustration 7.2) or a wood block and conventional hammer to strike the component near the mating surface. Avoid hammering against cast extremities since they may break off. If this method fails, try using a wood wedge between the two components.

Caution: If the joint will not separate, double-check that you have removed all the fasteners.

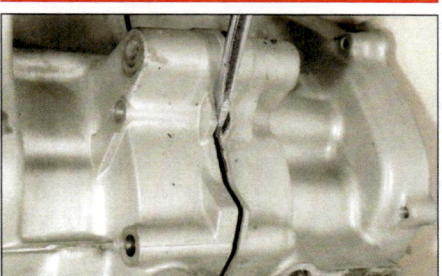

7.1 If a pry point is provided, apply gently pressure with a flat-bladed screwdriver

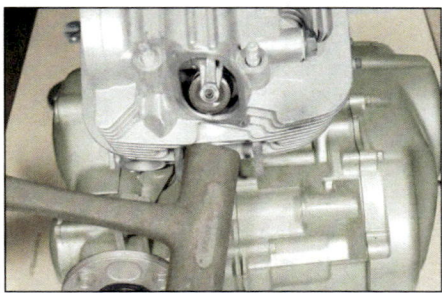

7.2 Tap around the joint with a soft-faced mallet if necessary - don't strike cooling fins

Removal of old gasket and sealant

- Paper gaskets will most likely come away complete, leaving only a few traces stuck on

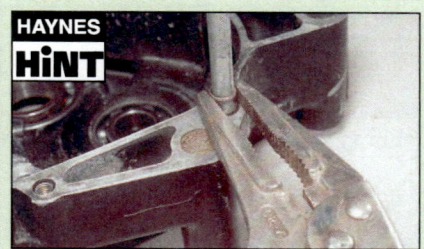

HAYNES HINT

Most components have one or two hollow locating dowels between the two gasket faces. If a dowel cannot be removed, do not resort to gripping it with pliers - it will almost certainly be distorted. Install a close-fitting socket or Phillips screwdriver into the dowel and then grip the outer edge of the dowel to free it.

the sealing faces of the components. It is imperative that all traces are removed to ensure correct sealing of the new gasket.
- Very carefully scrape all traces of gasket away making sure that the sealing surfaces are not gouged or scored by the scraper (see illustrations 7.3, 7.4 and 7.5). Stubborn deposits can be removed by spraying with an aerosol gasket remover. Final preparation of

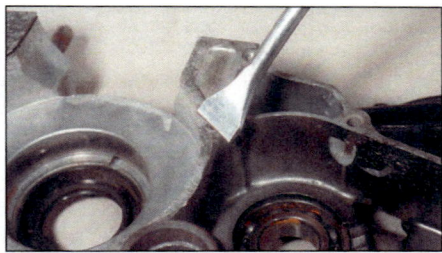

7.3 Paper gaskets can be scraped off with a gasket scraper tool . . .

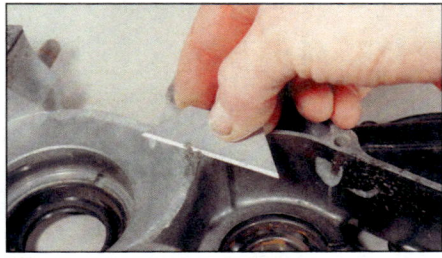

7.4 . . . a knife blade . . .

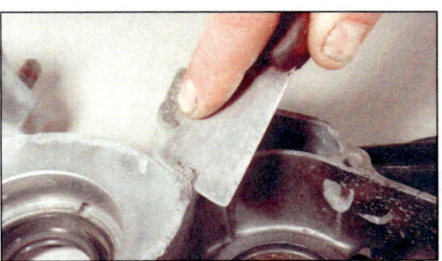

7.5 . . . or a household scraper

REF•18 Tools and Workshop Tips

7.6 Fine abrasive paper is wrapped around a flat file to clean up the gasket face

8.1 Tighten the chain breaker to push the pin out of the link . . .

8.4 Insert the new soft link, with O-rings, through the chain ends . . .

7.7 A kitchen scourer can be used on stubborn deposits

8.2 . . . withdraw the pin, remove the tool . . .

8.5 . . . install the O-rings over the pin ends . . .

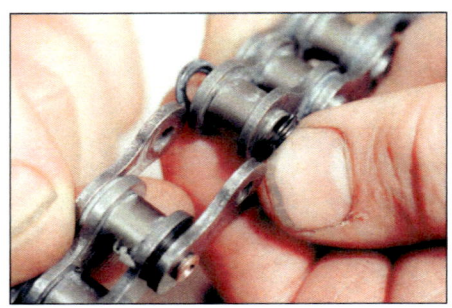

8.3 . . . and separate the chain link

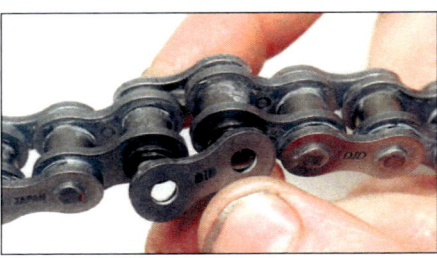

8.6 . . . followed by the sideplate

the gasket surface can be made with very fine abrasive paper or a plastic kitchen scourer **(see illustrations 7.6 and 7.7)**.

● Old sealant can be scraped or peeled off components, depending on the type originally used. Note that gasket removal compounds are available to avoid scraping the components clean; make sure the gasket remover suits the type of sealant used.

8 Chains

Breaking and joining final drive chains

● Drive chains for all but small bikes are continuous and do not have a clip-type connecting link. The chain must be broken using a chain breaker tool and the new chain securely riveted together using a new soft rivet-type link. Never use a clip-type connecting link instead of a rivet-type link, except in an emergency. Various chain breaking and riveting tools are available, either as separate tools or combined as illustrated in the accompanying photographs - read the instructions supplied with the tool carefully.

> ⚠ **Warning:** The need to rivet the new link pins correctly cannot be overstressed - loss of control of the motorcycle is very likely to result if the chain breaks in use.

● Rotate the chain and look for the soft link. The soft link pins look like they have been deeply centre-punched instead of peened over like all the other pins **(see illustration 8.9)** and its sideplate may be a different colour. Position the soft link midway between the sprockets and assemble the chain breaker tool over one of the soft link pins **(see illustration 8.1)**. Operate the tool to push the pin out through the chain **(see illustration 8.2)**. On an O-ring chain, remove the O-rings **(see illustration 8.3)**. Carry out the same procedure on the other soft link pin.

> **Caution:** Certain soft link pins (particularly on the larger chains) may require their ends to be filed or ground off before they can be pressed out using the tool.

● Check that you have the correct size and strength (standard or heavy duty) new soft link - do not reuse the old link. Look for the size marking on the chain sideplates **(see illustration 8.10)**.

● Position the chain ends so that they are engaged over the rear sprocket. On an O-ring chain, install a new O-ring over each pin of the link and insert the link through the two chain ends **(see illustration 8.4)**. Install a new O-ring over the end of each pin, followed by the sideplate (with the chain manufacturer's marking facing outwards) **(see illustrations 8.5 and 8.6)**. On an unsealed chain, insert the link through the two chain ends, then install the sideplate with the chain manufacturer's marking facing outwards.

● Note that it may not be possible to install the sideplate using finger pressure alone. If using a joining tool, assemble it so that the plates of the tool clamp the link and press the sideplate over the pins **(see illustration 8.7)**. Otherwise, use two small sockets placed over

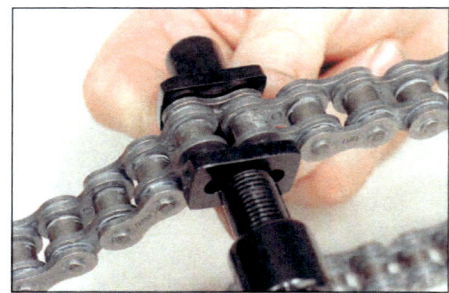

8.7 Push the sideplate into position using a clamp

Tools and Workshop Tips REF•19

8.8 Assemble the chain riveting tool over one pin at a time and tighten it fully

8.9 Pin end correctly riveted (A), pin end unriveted (B)

the rivet ends and two pieces of the wood between a G-clamp. Operate the clamp to press the sideplate over the pins.
● Assemble the joining tool over one pin (following the maker's instructions) and tighten the tool down to spread the pin end securely (see illustrations 8.8 and 8.9). Do the same on the other pin.

 Warning: Check that the pin ends are secure and that there is no danger of the sideplate coming loose. If the pin ends are cracked the soft link must be renewed.

Final drive chain sizing

● Chains are sized using a three digit number, followed by a suffix to denote the chain type (see illustration 8.10). Chain type is either standard or heavy duty (thicker sideplates), and also unsealed or O-ring/X-ring type.
● The first digit of the number relates to the pitch of the chain, ie the distance from the centre of one pin to the centre of the next pin (see illustration 8.11). Pitch is expressed in eighths of an inch, as follows:

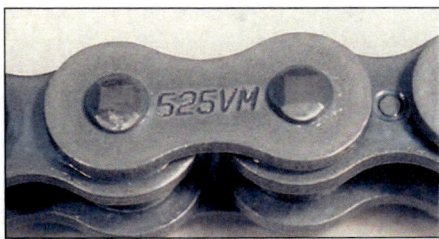

8.10 Typical chain size and type marking

8.11 Chain dimensions

Sizes commencing with a 4 (eg 428) have a pitch of 1/2 inch (12.7 mm)

Sizes commencing with a 5 (eg 520) have a pitch of 5/8 inch (15.9 mm)

Sizes commencing with a 6 (eg 630) have a pitch of 3/4 inch (19.1 mm)

● The second and third digits of the chain size relate to the width of the rollers, again in imperial units, eg the 525 shown has 5/16 inch (7.94 mm) rollers (see illustration 8.11).

9 Hoses

Clamping to prevent flow

● Small-bore flexible hoses can be clamped to prevent fluid flow whilst a component is worked on. Whichever method is used, ensure that the hose material is not permanently distorted or damaged by the clamp.
a) A brake hose clamp available from auto accessory shops (see illustration 9.1).
b) A wingnut type hose clamp (see illustration 9.2).

9.1 Hoses can be clamped with an automotive brake hose clamp . . .

9.2 . . . a wingnut type hose clamp . . .

c) Two sockets placed each side of the hose and held with straight-jawed self-locking grips (see illustration 9.3).
d) Thick card each side of the hose held between straight-jawed self-locking grips (see illustration 9.4).

9.3 . . . two sockets and a pair of self-locking grips . . .

9.4 . . . or thick card and self-locking grips

Freeing and fitting hoses

● Always make sure the hose clamp is moved well clear of the hose end. Grip the hose with your hand and rotate it whilst pulling it off the union. If the hose has hardened due to age and will not move, slit it with a sharp knife and peel its ends off the union (see illustration 9.5).
● Resist the temptation to use grease or soap on the unions to aid installation; although it helps the hose slip over the union it will equally aid the escape of fluid from the joint. It is preferable to soften the hose ends in hot water and wet the inside surface of the hose with water or a fluid which will evaporate.

9.5 Cutting a coolant hose free with a sharp knife

Security

Introduction

In less time than it takes to read this introduction, a thief could steal your motorcycle. Returning only to find your bike has gone is one of the worst feelings in the world. Even if the motorcycle is insured against theft, once you've got over the initial shock, you will have the inconvenience of dealing with the police and your insurance company.

The motorcycle is an easy target for the professional thief and the joyrider alike and the official figures on motorcycle theft make for depressing reading; on average a motorcycle is stolen every 16 minutes in the UK!

Motorcycle thefts fall into two categories, those stolen 'to order' and those taken by opportunists. The thief stealing to order will be on the look out for a specific make and model and will go to extraordinary lengths to obtain that motorcycle. The opportunist thief on the other hand will look for easy targets which can be stolen with the minimum of effort and risk.

Whilst it is never going to be possible to make your machine 100% secure, it is estimated that around half of all stolen motorcycles are taken by opportunist thieves. Remember that the opportunist thief is always on the look out for the easy option: if there are two similar motorcycles parked side-by-side, they will target the one with the lowest level of security. By taking a few precautions, you can reduce the chances of your motorcycle being stolen.

Security equipment

There are many specialised motorcycle security devices available and the following text summarises their applications and their good and bad points.

Once you have decided on the type of security equipment which best suits your needs, we recommended that you read one of the many equipment tests regularly carried out by the motorcycle press. These tests compare the products from all the major manufacturers and give impartial ratings on their effectiveness, value-for-money and ease of use.

No one item of security equipment can provide complete protection. It is highly recommended that two or more of the items described below are combined to increase the security of your motorcycle (a lock and chain plus an alarm system is just about ideal). The more security measures fitted to the bike, the less likely it is to be stolen.

Lock and chain

Pros: *Very flexible to use; can be used to secure the motorcycle to almost any immovable object. On some locks and chains, the lock can be used on its own as a disc lock (see below).*

Cons: *Can be very heavy and awkward to carry on the motorcycle, although some types will be supplied with a carry bag which can be strapped to the pillion seat.*

● Heavy-duty chains and locks are an excellent security measure **(see illustration 1)**. Whenever the motorcycle is parked, use the lock and chain to secure the machine to a solid, immovable object such as a post or railings. This will prevent the machine from being ridden away or being lifted into the back of a van.

● When fitting the chain, always ensure the chain is routed around the motorcycle frame or swingarm **(see illustrations 2 and 3)**. Never merely pass the chain around one of the wheel rims; a thief may unbolt the wheel and lift the rest of the machine into a van, leaving you with just the wheel! Try to avoid having excess chain free, thus making it difficult to use cutting tools, and keep the chain and lock off the ground to prevent thieves attacking it with a cold chisel. Position the lock so that its lock barrel is facing downwards; this will make it harder for the thief to attack the lock mechanism.

Ensure the lock and chain you buy is of good quality and long enough to shackle your bike to a solid object

Pass the chain through the bike's frame, rather than just through a wheel . . .

. . . and loop it around a solid object

Security REF•21

U-locks

Pros: *Highly effective deterrent which can be used to secure the bike to a post or railings. Most U-locks come with a carrier which allows the lock to be easily carried on the bike.*

Cons: *Not as flexible to use as a lock and chain.*

● These are solid locks which are similar in use to a lock and chain. U-locks are lighter than a lock and chain but not so flexible to use. The length and shape of the lock shackle limit the objects to which the bike can be secured **(see illustration 4)**.

Disc locks

Pros: *Small, light and very easy to carry; most can be stored underneath the seat.*

Cons: *Does not prevent the motorcycle being lifted into a van. Can be very embarrassing if you forget to remove the lock before attempting to ride off!*

U-locks can be used to secure the bike to a solid object – ensure you purchase one which is long enough

● Disc locks are designed to be attached to the front brake disc. The lock passes through one of the holes in the disc and prevents the wheel rotating by jamming against the fork/brake caliper **(see illustration 5)**. Some are equipped with an alarm siren which sounds if the disc lock is moved; this not only acts as a theft deterrent but also as a handy reminder if you try to move the bike with the lock still fitted.

● Combining the disc lock with a length of cable which can be looped around a post or railings provides an additional measure of security **(see illustration 6)**.

Alarms and immobilisers

Pros: *Once installed it is completely hassle-free to use. If the system is 'Thatcham' or 'Sold Secure-approved', insurance companies may give you a discount.*

Cons: *Can be expensive to buy and complex to install. No system will prevent the motorcycle from being lifted into a van and taken away.*

● Electronic alarms and immobilisers are available to suit a variety of budgets. There are three different types of system available: pure alarms, pure immobilisers, and the more expensive systems which are combined alarm/immobilisers **(see illustration 7)**.

● An alarm system is designed to emit an audible warning if the motorcycle is being tampered with.

● An immobiliser prevents the motorcycle being started and ridden away by disabling its electrical systems.

● When purchasing an alarm/immobiliser system, check the cost of installing the system unless you are able to do it yourself. If the motorcycle is not used regularly, another consideration is the current drain of the system. All alarm/immobiliser systems are powered by the motorcycle's battery; purchasing a system with a very low current drain could prevent the battery losing its charge whilst the motorcycle is not being used.

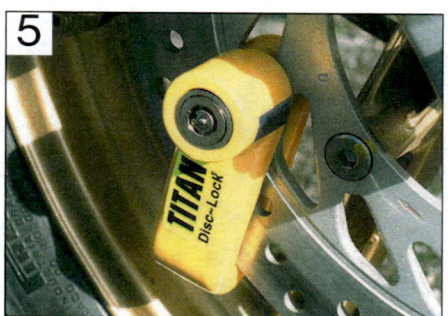
A typical disc lock attached through one of the holes in the disc

A disc lock combined with a security cable provides additional protection

A typical alarm/immobiliser system

REF•22 Security

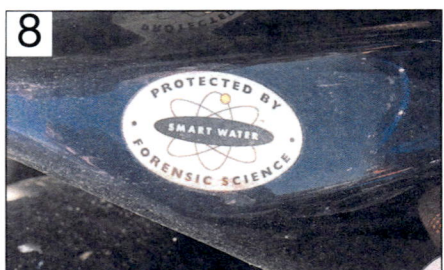

Indelible markings can be applied to most areas of the bike – always apply the manufacturer's sticker to warn off thieves

Chemically-etched code numbers can be applied to main body panels . . .

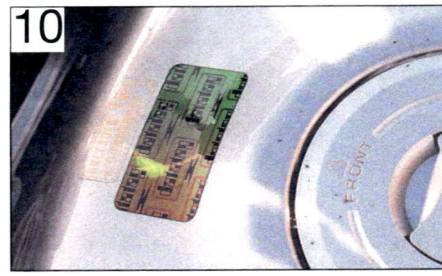

. . . again, always ensure that the kit manufacturer's sticker is applied in a prominent position

Security marking kits

Pros: *Very cheap and effective deterrent. Many insurance companies will give you a discount on your insurance premium if a recognised security marking kit is used on your motorcycle.*

Cons: *Does not prevent the motorcycle being stolen by joyriders.*

● There are many different types of security marking kits available. The idea is to mark as many parts of the motorcycle as possible with a unique security number **(see illustrations 8, 9 and 10)**. A form will be included with the kit to register your personal details and those of the motorcycle with the kit manufacturer. This register is made available to the police to help them trace the rightful owner of any motorcycle or components which they recover should all other forms of identification have been removed. Always apply the warning stickers provided with the kit to deter thieves.

Ground anchors, wheel clamps and security posts

Pros: *An excellent form of security which will deter all but the most determined of thieves.*

Cons: *Awkward to install and can be expensive.*

● Whilst the motorcycle is at home, it is a good idea to attach it securely to the floor or a solid wall, even if it is kept in a securely locked garage. Various types of ground anchors, security posts and wheel clamps are available for this purpose **(see illustration 11)**. These security devices are either bolted to a solid concrete or brick structure or can be cemented into the ground.

Permanent ground anchors provide an excellent level of security when the bike is at home

Security at home

A high percentage of motorcycle thefts are from the owner's home. Here are some things to consider whenever your motorcycle is at home:

✔ Where possible, always keep the motorcycle in a securely locked garage. Never rely solely on the standard lock on the garage door, these are usual hopelessly inadequate. Fit an additional locking mechanism to the door and consider having the garage alarmed. A security light, activated by a movement sensor, is also a good investment.

✔ Always secure the motorcycle to the ground or a wall, even if it is inside a securely locked garage.

✔ Do not regularly leave the motorcycle outside your home, try to keep it out of sight wherever possible. If a garage is not available, fit a motorcycle cover over the bike to disguise its true identity.

✔ It is not uncommon for thieves to follow a motorcyclist home to find out where the bike is kept. They will then return at a later date. Be aware of this whenever you are returning home on your motorcycle. If you suspect you are being followed, do not return home, instead ride to a garage or shop and stop as a precaution.

✔ When selling a motorcycle, do not provide your home address or the location where the bike is normally kept. Arrange to meet the buyer at a location away from your home. Thieves have been known to pose as potential buyers to find out where motorcycles are kept and then return later to steal them.

Security away from the home

As well as fitting security equipment to your motorcycle here are a few general rules to follow whenever you park your motorcycle.
✔ Park in a busy, public place.
✔ Use car parks which incorporate security features, such as CCTV.

✔ At night, park in a well-lit area, preferably directly underneath a street light.
✔ Engage the steering lock.
✔ Secure the motorcycle to a solid, immovable object such as a post or railings with an additional lock. If this is not possible, secure the bike to a friend's motorcycle. Some public parking places provide security loops for motorcycles.
✔ Never leave your helmet or luggage attached to the motorcycle. Take them with you at all times.

Lubricants and fluids

A wide range of lubricants, fluids and cleaning agents is available for motor-cycles. This is a guide as to what is available, its applications and properties.

Four-stroke engine oil

● Engine oil is without doubt the most important component of any four-stroke engine. Modern motorcycle engines place a lot of demands on their oil and choosing the right type is essential. Using an unsuitable oil will lead to an increased rate of engine wear and could result in serious engine damage. Before purchasing oil, always check the recommended oil specification given by the manufacturer. The manufacturer will state a recommended 'type or classification' and also a specific 'viscosity' range for engine oil.

● The oil 'type or classification' is identified by its API (American Petroleum Institute) rating. The API rating will be in the form of two letters, e.g. SG. The S identifies the oil as being suitable for use in a petrol (gasoline) engine (S stands for spark ignition) and the second letter, ranging from A to J, identifies the oil's performance rating. The later this letter, the higher the specification of the oil; for example API SG oil exceeds the requirements of API SF oil. **Note:** *On some oils there may also be a second rating consisting of another two letters, the first letter being C, e.g. API SF/CD. This rating indicates the oil is also suitable for use in a diesel engines (the C stands for compression ignition) and is thus of no relevance for motorcycle use.*

● The 'viscosity' of the oil is identified by its SAE (Society of Automotive Engineers) rating. All modern engines require multigrade oils and the SAE rating will consist of two numbers, the first followed by a W, e.g. 10W/40. The first number indicates the viscosity rating of the oil at low temperatures (W stands for winter – tested at –20°C) and the second number represents the viscosity of the oil at high temperatures (tested at 100°C). The lower the number, the thinner the oil. For example an oil with an SAE 10W/40 rating will give better cold starting and running than an SAE 15W/40 oil.

● As well as ensuring the 'type' and 'viscosity' of the oil match the recommendations, another consideration to make when buying engine oil is whether to purchase a standard mineral-based oil, a semi-synthetic oil (also known as a synthetic blend or synthetic-based oil) or a fully-synthetic oil. Although all oils will have a similar rating and viscosity, their cost will vary considerably; mineral-based oils are the cheapest, the fully-synthetic oils the most expensive with the semi-synthetic oils falling somewhere in-between. This decision is very much up to the owner, but it should be noted that modern synthetic oils have far better lubricating and cleaning qualities than traditional mineral-based oils and tend to retain these properties for far longer. Bearing in mind the operating conditions inside a modern, high-revving motorcycle engine it is highly recommended that a fully synthetic oil is used. The extra expense at each service could save you money in the long term by preventing premature engine wear.

● As a final note always ensure that the oil is specifically designed for use in motorcycle engines. Engine oils designed primarily for use in car engines sometimes contain additives or friction modifiers which could cause clutch slip on a motorcycle fitted with a wet-clutch.

Two-stroke engine oil

● Modern two-stroke engines, with their high power outputs, place high demands on their oil. If engine seizure is to be avoided it is essential that a high-quality oil is used. Two-stroke oils differ hugely from four-stroke oils. The oil lubricates only the crankshaft and piston(s) (the transmission has its own lubricating oil) and is used on a total-loss basis where it is burnt completely during the combustion process.

● The Japanese have recently introduced a classification system for two-stroke oils, the JASO rating. This rating is in the form of two letters, either FA, FB or FC – FA is the lowest classification and FC the highest. Ensure the oil being used meets or exceeds the recommended rating specified by the manufacturer.

● As well as ensuring the oil rating matches the recommendation, another consideration to make when buying engine oil is whether to purchase a standard mineral-based oil, a semi-synthetic oil (also known as a synthetic blend or synthetic-based oil) or a fully-synthetic oil. The cost of each type of oil varies considerably; mineral-based oils are the cheapest, the fully-synthetic oils the most expensive with the semi-synthetic oils falling somewhere in-between. This decision is very much up to the owner, but it should be noted that modern synthetic oils have far better lubricating properties and burn cleaner than traditional mineral-based oils. It is therefore recommended that a fully synthetic oil is used. The extra expense could save you money in the long term by preventing premature engine wear, engine performance will be improved, carbon deposits and exhaust smoke will be reduced.

REF•24 Lubricants and fluids

- Always ensure that the oil is specifically designed for use in an injector system. Many high quality two-stroke oils are designed for competition use and need to be pre-mixed with fuel. These oils are of a much higher viscosity and are not designed to flow through the injector pumps used on road-going two-stroke motorcycles.

Transmission (gear) oil

- On a two-stroke engine, the transmission and clutch are lubricated by their own separate oil bath which must be changed in accordance with the Maintenance Schedule.
- Although the engine and transmission units of most four-strokes use a common lubrication supply, there are some exceptions where the engine and gearbox have separate oil reservoirs and a dry clutch is used.
- Motorcycle manufacturers will either recommend a monograde transmission oil or a four-stroke multigrade engine oil to lubricate the transmission.
- Transmission oils, or gear oils as they are often called, are designed specifically for use in transmission systems. The viscosity of these oils is represented by an SAE number, but the scale of measurement applied is different to that used to grade engine oils. As a rough guide a SAE90 gear oil will be of the same viscosity as an SAE50 engine oil.

Shaft drive oil

- On models equipped with shaft final drive, the shaft drive gears are will have their own oil supply. The manufacturer will state a recommended 'type or classification' and also a specific 'viscosity' range in the same manner as for four-stroke engine oil.
- Gear oil classification is given by the number which follows the API GL (GL standing for gear lubricant) rating, the higher the number, the higher the specification of the oil, e.g. API GL5 oil is a higher specification than API GL4 oil. Ensure the oil meets or exceeds the classification specified and is of the correct viscosity. The viscosity of gear oils is also represented by an SAE number but the scale of measurement used is different to that used to grade engine oils. As a rough guide an SAE90 gear oil will be of the same viscosity as an SAE50 engine oil.
- If the use of an EP (Extreme Pressure) gear oil is specified, ensure the oil purchased is suitable.

Fork oil and suspension fluid

- Conventional telescopic front forks are hydraulic and require fork oil to work. To ensure the forks function correctly, the fork oil must be changed in accordance with the Maintenance Schedule.
- Fork oil is available in a variety of viscosities, identified by their SAE rating; fork oil ratings vary from light (SAE 5) to heavy (SAE 30). When purchasing fork oil, ensure the viscosity rating matches that specified by the manufacturer.
- Some lubricant manufacturers also produce a range of high-quality suspension fluids which are very similar to fork oil but are designed mainly for competition use. These fluids may have a different viscosity rating system which is not to be confused with the SAE rating of normal fork oil. Refer to the manufacturer's instructions if in any doubt.

Brake and clutch fluid

- All disc brake systems and some clutch systems are hydraulically operated. To ensure correct operation, the hydraulic fluid must be changed in accordance with the Maintenance Schedule.
- Brake and clutch fluid is classified by its DOT rating with most motorcycle manufacturers specifying DOT 3 or 4 fluid. Both fluid types are glycol-based and can be mixed together without adverse effect; DOT 4 fluid exceeds the requirements of DOT 3 fluid. Although it is safe to use DOT 4 fluid in a system designed for use with DOT 3 fluid, never use DOT 3 fluid in a system which specifies the use of DOT 4 as this will adversely affect the system's performance. The type required for the system will be marked on the fluid reservoir cap.
- Some manufacturers also produce a DOT 5 hydraulic fluid. DOT 5 hydraulic fluid is silicone-based and is not compatible with the glycol-based DOT 3 and 4 fluids. Never mix DOT 5 fluid with DOT 3 or 4 fluid as this will seriously affect the performance of the hydraulic system.

Coolant/antifreeze

- When purchasing coolant/antifreeze, always ensure it is suitable for use in an aluminium engine and contains corrosion inhibitors to prevent possible blockages of the internal coolant passages of the system. As a general rule, most coolants are designed to be used neat and should not be diluted whereas antifreeze can be mixed with distilled water to provide a coolant solution of the required strength. Refer to the manufacturer's instructions on the bottle.
- Ensure the coolant is changed in accordance with the Maintenance Schedule.

Chain lube

- Chain lube is an aerosol-type spray lubricant specifically designed for use on motorcycle final drive chains. Chain lube has two functions, to minimise friction between the final drive chain and sprockets and to prevent corrosion of the chain. Regular use of a good-quality chain lube will extend the life of the drive chain and sprockets and thus maximise the power being transmitted from the transmission to the rear wheel.
- When using chain lube, always allow some time for the solvents in the lube to evaporate before riding the motorcycle. This will minimise the amount of lube which will

Lubricants and fluids

'fling' off from the chain when the motorcycle is used. If the motorcycle is equipped with an 'O-ring' chain, ensure the chain lube is labelled as being suitable for use on 'O-ring' chains.

Degreasers and solvents

● There are many different types of solvents and degreasers available to remove the grime and grease which accumulate around the motorcycle during normal use. Degreasers and solvents are usually available as an aerosol-type spray or as a liquid which you apply with a brush. Always closely follow the manufacturer's instructions and wear eye protection during use. Be aware that many solvents are flammable and may give off noxious fumes; take adequate precautions when using them (see Safety First!).

● For general cleaning, use one of the many solvents or degreasers available from most motorcycle accessory shops. These solvents are usually applied then left for a certain time before being washed off with water.

Brake cleaner is a solvent specifically designed to remove all traces of oil, grease and dust from braking system components. Brake cleaner is designed to evaporate quickly and leaves behind no residue.

Carburettor cleaner is an aerosol-type solvent specifically designed to clear carburettor blockages and break down the hard deposits and gum often found inside carburettors during overhaul.

Contact cleaner is an aerosol-type solvent designed for cleaning electrical components. The cleaner will remove all traces of oil and dirt from components such as switch contacts or fouled spark plugs and then dry, leaving behind no residue.

Gasket remover is an aerosol-type solvent designed for removing stubborn gaskets from engine components during overhaul. Gasket remover will minimise the amount of scraping required to remove the gasket and therefore reduce the risk of damage to the mating surface.

Spray lubricants

● Aerosol-based spray lubricants are widely available and are excellent for lubricating lever pivots and exposed cables and switches. Try to use a lubricant which is of the dry-film type as the fluid evaporates, leaving behind a dry-film of lubricant. Lubricants which leave behind an oily residue will attract dust and dirt which will increase the rate of wear of the cable/lever.

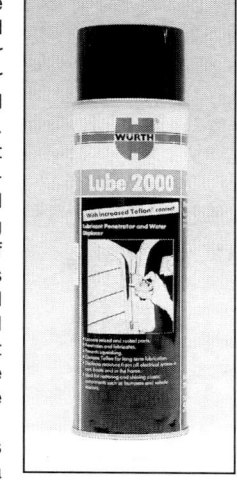

● Most lubricants also act as a moisture dispersant and a penetrating fluid. This means they can also be used to 'dry out' electrical components such as wiring connectors or switches as well as helping to free seized fasteners.

Greases

● Grease is used to lubricate many of the pivot-points. A good-quality multi-purpose grease is suitable for most applications but some manufacturers will specify the use of specialist greases for use on components such as swingarm and suspension linkage bushes. These specialist greases can be purchased from most motorcycle (or car) accessory shops; commonly specified types include molybdenum disulphide grease, lithium-based grease, graphite-based grease, silicone-based grease and high-temperature copper-based grease.

Gasket sealing compounds

● Gasket sealing compounds can be used in conjunction with gaskets, to improve their sealing capabilities, or on their own to seal metal-to-metal joints. Depending on their type, sealing compounds either set hard or stay relatively soft and pliable.

● When purchasing a gasket sealing compound, ensure that it is designed specifically for use on an internal combustion engine. General multi-purpose sealants available from DIY stores may appear visibly similar but they are not designed to withstand the extreme heat or contact with fuel and oil encountered when used on an engine (see 'Tools and Workshop Tips' for further information).

Thread locking compound

● Thread locking compounds are used to secure certain threaded fasteners in position to prevent them from loosening due to vibration. Thread locking compounds can be purchased from most motorcycle (and car) accessory shops. Ensure the threads of the both components are completely clean and dry before sparingly applying the locking compound (see 'Tools and Workshop Tips' for further information).

Fuel additives

● Fuel additives which protect and clean the fuel system components are widely available. These additives are designed to remove all traces of deposits that build up on the carburettors/injectors and prevent wear, helping the fuel system to operate more efficiently. If a fuel additive is being used, check that it is suitable for use with your motorcycle, especially if your motorcycle is equipped with a catalytic converter.

● Octane boosters are also available. These additives are designed to improve the performance of highly-tuned engines being run on normal pump-fuel and are of no real use on standard motorcycles.

Conversion Factors

Length (distance)
Inches (in)	x 25.4	= Millimetres (mm)	x 0.0394	=	Inches (in)
Feet (ft)	x 0.305	= Metres (m)	x 3.281	=	Feet (ft)
Miles	x 1.609	= Kilometres (km)	x 0.621	=	Miles

Volume (capacity)
Cubic inches (cu in; in^3)	x 16.387	= Cubic centimetres (cc; cm^3)	x 0.061	=	Cubic inches (cu in; in^3)
Imperial pints (Imp pt)	x 0.568	= Litres (l)	x 1.76	=	Imperial pints (Imp pt)
Imperial quarts (Imp qt)	x 1.137	= Litres (l)	x 0.88	=	Imperial quarts (Imp qt)
Imperial quarts (Imp qt)	x 1.201	= US quarts (US qt)	x 0.833	=	Imperial quarts (Imp qt)
US quarts (US qt)	x 0.946	= Litres (l)	x 1.057	=	US quarts (US qt)
Imperial gallons (Imp gal)	x 4.546	= Litres (l)	x 0.22	=	Imperial gallons (Imp gal)
Imperial gallons (Imp gal)	x 1.201	= US gallons (US gal)	x 0.833	=	Imperial gallons (Imp gal)
US gallons (US gal)	x 3.785	= Litres (l)	x 0.264	=	US gallons (US gal)

Mass (weight)
Ounces (oz)	x 28.35	= Grams (g)	x 0.035	=	Ounces (oz)
Pounds (lb)	x 0.454	= Kilograms (kg)	x 2.205	=	Pounds (lb)

Force
Ounces-force (ozf; oz)	x 0.278	= Newtons (N)	x 3.6	=	Ounces-force (ozf; oz)
Pounds-force (lbf; lb)	x 4.448	= Newtons (N)	x 0.225	=	Pounds-force (lbf; lb)
Newtons (N)	x 0.1	= Kilograms-force (kgf; kg)	x 9.81	=	Newtons (N)

Pressure
Pounds-force per square inch (psi; lbf/in^2; lb/in^2)	x 0.070	= Kilograms-force per square centimetre (kgf/cm^2; kg/cm^2)	x 14.223	=	Pounds-force per square inch (psi; lbf/in^2; lb/in^2)
Pounds-force per square inch (psi; lbf/in^2; lb/in^2)	x 0.068	= Atmospheres (atm)	x 14.696	=	Pounds-force per square inch (psi; lbf/in^2; lb/in^2)
Pounds-force per square inch (psi; lbf/in^2; lb/in^2)	x 0.069	= Bars	x 14.5	=	Pounds-force per square inch (psi; lbf/in^2; lb/in^2)
Pounds-force per square inch (psi; lbf/in^2; lb/in^2)	x 6.895	= Kilopascals (kPa)	x 0.145	=	Pounds-force per square inch (psi; lbf/in^2; lb/in^2)
Kilopascals (kPa)	x 0.01	= Kilograms-force per square centimetre (kgf/cm^2; kg/cm^2)	x 98.1	=	Kilopascals (kPa)
Millibar (mbar)	x 100	= Pascals (Pa)	x 0.01	=	Millibar (mbar)
Millibar (mbar)	x 0.0145	= Pounds-force per square inch (psi; lbf/in^2; lb/in^2)	x 68.947	=	Millibar (mbar)
Millibar (mbar)	x 0.75	= Millimetres of mercury (mmHg)	x 1.333	=	Millibar (mbar)
Millibar (mbar)	x 0.401	= Inches of water (inH$_2$O)	x 2.491	=	Millibar (mbar)
Millimetres of mercury (mmHg)	x 0.535	= Inches of water (inH$_2$O)	x 1.868	=	Millimetres of mercury (mmHg)
Inches of water (inH$_2$O)	x 0.036	= Pounds-force per square inch (psi; lbf/in^2; lb/in^2)	x 27.68	=	Inches of water (inH$_2$O)

Torque (moment of force)
Pounds-force inches (lbf in; lb in)	x 1.152	= Kilograms-force centimetre (kgf cm; kg cm)	x 0.868	=	Pounds-force inches (lbf in; lb in)
Pounds-force inches (lbf in; lb in)	x 0.113	= Newton metres (Nm)	x 8.85	=	Pounds-force inches (lbf in; lb in)
Pounds-force inches (lbf in; lb in)	x 0.083	= Pounds-force feet (lbf ft; lb ft)	x 12	=	Pounds-force inches (lbf in; lb in)
Pounds-force feet (lbf ft; lb ft)	x 0.138	= Kilograms-force metres (kgf m; kg m)	x 7.233	=	Pounds-force feet (lbf ft; lb ft)
Pounds-force feet (lbf ft; lb ft)	x 1.356	= Newton metres (Nm)	x 0.738	=	Pounds-force feet (lbf ft; lb ft)
Newton metres (Nm)	x 0.102	= Kilograms-force metres (kgf m; kg m)	x 9.804	=	Newton metres (Nm)

Power
Horsepower (hp)	x 745.7	= Watts (W)	x 0.0013	=	Horsepower (hp)

Velocity (speed)
Miles per hour (miles/hr; mph)	x 1.609	= Kilometres per hour (km/hr; kph)	x 0.621	=	Miles per hour (miles/hr; mph)

Fuel consumption*
Miles per gallon (mpg)	x 0.354	= Kilometres per litre (km/l)	x 2.825	=	Miles per gallon (mpg)

Temperature
Degrees Fahrenheit = (°C x 1.8) + 32   Degrees Celsius (Degrees Centigrade; °C) = (°F - 32) x 0.56

*It is common practice to convert from miles per gallon (mpg) to litres/100 kilometres (l/100km), where mpg x l/100 km = 282

MOT Test Checks REF•27

About the MOT Test

In the UK, all vehicles more than three years old are subject to an annual test to ensure that they meet minimum safety requirements. A current test certificate must be issued before a machine can be used on public roads, and is required before a road fund licence can be issued. Riding without a current test certificate will also invalidate your insurance.

For most owners, the MOT test is an annual cause for anxiety, and this is largely due to owners not being sure what needs to be checked prior to submitting the motorcycle for testing. The simple answer is that a fully roadworthy motorcycle will have no difficulty in passing the test.

This is a guide to getting your motorcycle through the MOT test. Obviously it will not be possible to examine the motorcycle to the same standard as the professional MOT tester, particularly in view of the equipment required for some of the checks. However, working through the following procedures will enable you to identify any problem areas before submitting the motorcycle for the test.

It has only been possible to summarise the test requirements here, based on the regulations in force at the time of printing. Test standards are becoming increasingly stringent, although there are some exemptions for older vehicles. More information about the MOT test can be obtained from the TSO publications, *How Safe is your Motorcycle* and *The MOT Inspection Manual for Motorcycle Testing*.

Many of the checks require that one of the wheels is raised off the ground. If the motorcycle doesn't have a centre stand, note that an auxiliary stand will be required. Additionally, the help of an assistant may prove useful.

Certain exceptions apply to machines under 50 cc, machines without a lighting system, and Classic bikes - if in doubt about any of the requirements listed below seek confirmation from an MOT tester prior to submitting the motorcycle for the test.

Check that the frame number is clearly visible.

> **HAYNES HiNT** *If a component is in borderline condition, the tester has discretion in deciding whether to pass or fail it. If the motorcycle presented is clean and evidently well cared for, the tester may be more inclined to pass a borderline component than if the motorcycle is scruffy and apparently neglected.*

Electrical System

Lights, turn signals, horn and reflector

✔ With the ignition on, check the operation of the following electrical components. **Note:** *The electrical components on certain small-capacity machines are powered by the generator, requiring that the engine is run for this check.*

a) Headlight and tail light. Check that both illuminate in the low and high beam switch positions.
b) Position lights. Check that the front position (or sidelight) and tail light illuminate in this switch position.
c) Turn signals. Check that all flash at the correct rate, and that the warning light(s) function correctly. Check that the turn signal switch works correctly.
d) Hazard warning system (where fitted). Check that all four turn signals flash in this switch position.
e) Brake stop light. Check that the light comes on when the front and rear brakes are independently applied. Models first used on or after 1st April 1986 must have a brake light switch on each brake.
f) Horn. Check that the sound is continuous and of reasonable volume.

✔ Check that there is a red reflector on the rear of the machine, either mounted separately or as part of the tail light lens.
✔ Check the condition of the headlight, tail light and turn signal lenses.

Headlight beam height

✔ The MOT tester will perform a headlight beam height check using specialised beam setting equipment **(see illustration 1)**. This equipment will not be available to the home mechanic, but if you suspect that the headlight is incorrectly set or may have been maladjusted in the past, you can perform a rough test as follows.
✔ Position the bike in a straight line facing a brick wall. The bike must be off its stand, upright and with a rider seated. Measure the height from the ground to the centre of the headlight and mark a horizontal line on the wall at this height. Position the motorcycle 3.8 metres from the wall and draw a vertical line up the wall central to the centreline of the motorcycle. Switch to dipped beam and check that the beam pattern falls slightly lower than the horizontal line and to the left of the vertical line **(see illustration 2)**.

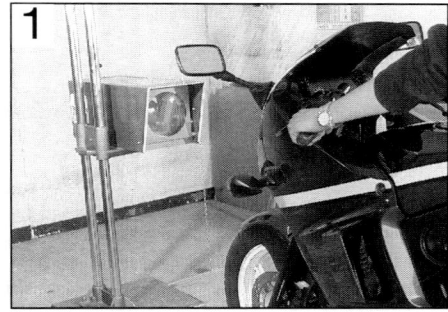

Headlight beam height checking equipment

Home workshop beam alignment check

REF•28 MOT Test Checks

Exhaust System and Final Drive

Exhaust

✔ Check that the exhaust mountings are secure and that the system does not foul any of the rear suspension components.
✔ Start the motorcycle. When the revs are increased, check that the exhaust is neither holed nor leaking from any of its joints. On a linked system, check that the collector box is not leaking due to corrosion.
✔ Note that the exhaust decibel level ("loudness" of the exhaust) is assessed at the discretion of the tester. If the motorcycle was first used on or after 1st January 1985 the silencer must carry the BSAU 193 stamp, or a marking relating to its make and model, or be of OE (original equipment) manufacture. If the silencer is marked NOT FOR ROAD USE, RACING USE ONLY or similar, it will fail the MOT.

Final drive

✔ On chain or belt drive machines, check that the chain/belt is in good condition and does not have excessive slack. Also check that the sprocket is securely mounted on the rear wheel hub. Check that the chain/belt guard is in place.
✔ On shaft drive bikes, check for oil leaking from the drive unit and fouling the rear tyre.

Steering and Suspension

Steering

✔ With the front wheel raised off the ground, rotate the steering from lock to lock. The handlebar or switches must not contact the fuel tank or be close enough to trap the rider's hand. Problems can be caused by damaged lock stops on the lower yoke and frame, or by the fitting of non-standard handlebars.
✔ When performing the lock to lock check, also ensure that the steering moves freely without drag or notchiness. Steering movement can be impaired by poorly routed cables, or by overtight head bearings or worn bearings. The tester will perform a check of the steering head bearing lower race by mounting the front wheel on a surface plate, then performing a lock to lock check with the weight of the machine on the lower bearing (see illustration 3).
✔ Grasp the fork sliders (lower legs) and attempt to push and pull on the forks (see illustration 4). Any play in the steering head bearings will be felt. Note that in extreme cases, wear of the front fork bushes can be misinterpreted for head bearing play.
✔ Check that the handlebars are securely mounted.
✔ Check that the handlebar grip rubbers are secure. They should by bonded to the bar left end and to the throttle cable pulley on the right end.

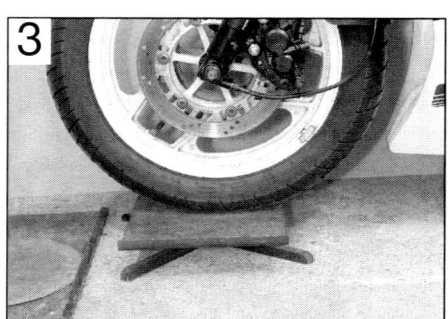

Front wheel mounted on a surface plate for steering head bearing lower race check

Front suspension

✔ With the motorcycle off the stand, hold the front brake on and pump the front forks up and down (see illustration 5). Check that they are adequately damped.

Checking the steering head bearings for freeplay

Hold the front brake on and pump the front forks up and down to check operation

MOT Test Checks REF•29

Inspect the area around the fork dust seal for oil leakage (arrow)

Bounce the rear of the motorcycle to check rear suspension operation

Checking for rear suspension linkage play

✔ Inspect the area above and around the front fork oil seals **(see illustration 6)**. There should be no sign of oil on the fork tube (stanchion) nor leaking down the slider (lower leg). On models so equipped, check that there is no oil leaking from the anti-dive units.

✔ On models with swingarm front suspension, check that there is no freeplay in the linkage when moved from side to side.

Rear suspension

✔ With the motorcycle off the stand and an assistant supporting the motorcycle by its handlebars, bounce the rear suspension **(see illustration 7)**. Check that the suspension components do not foul on any of the cycle parts and check that the shock absorber(s) provide adequate damping.

✔ Visually inspect the shock absorber(s) and check that there is no sign of oil leakage from its damper. This is somewhat restricted on certain single shock models due to the location of the shock absorber.

✔ With the rear wheel raised off the ground, grasp the wheel at the highest point and attempt to pull it up **(see illustration 8)**. Any play in the swingarm pivot or suspension linkage bearings will be felt as movement.

Note: *Do not confuse play with actual suspension movement.* Failure to lubricate suspension linkage bearings can lead to bearing failure **(see illustration 9)**.

✔ With the rear wheel raised off the ground, grasp the swingarm ends and attempt to move the swingarm from side to side and forwards and backwards - any play indicates wear of the swingarm pivot bearings **(see illustration 10)**.

Worn suspension linkage pivots (arrows) are usually the cause of play in the rear suspension

Grasp the swingarm at the ends to check for play in its pivot bearings

REF•30 MOT Test Checks

Brake pad wear can usually be viewed without removing the caliper. Most pads have wear indicator grooves (1) and some also have indicator tangs (2)

On drum brakes, check the angle of the operating lever with the brake fully applied. Most drum brakes have a wear indicator pointer and scale.

Brakes, Wheels and Tyres

Brakes

✔ With the wheel raised off the ground, apply the brake then free it off, and check that the wheel is about to revolve freely without brake drag.
✔ On disc brakes, examine the disc itself. Check that it is securely mounted and not cracked.
✔ On disc brakes, view the pad material through the caliper mouth and check that the pads are not worn down beyond the limit **(see illustration 11)**.
✔ On drum brakes, check that when the brake is applied the angle between the operating lever and cable or rod is not too great **(see illustration 12)**. Check also that the operating lever doesn't foul any other components.
✔ On disc brakes, examine the flexible hoses from top to bottom. Have an assistant hold the brake on so that the fluid in the hose is under pressure, and check that there is no sign of fluid leakage, bulges or cracking. If there are any metal brake pipes or unions, check that these are free from corrosion and damage. Where a brake-linked anti-dive system is fitted, check the hoses to the anti-dive in a similar manner.
✔ Check that the rear brake torque arm is secure and that its fasteners are secured by self-locking nuts or castellated nuts with split-pins or R-pins **(see illustration 13)**.
✔ On models with ABS, check that the self-check warning light in the instrument panel works.
✔ The MOT tester will perform a test of the motorcycle's braking efficiency based on a calculation of rider and motorcycle weight. Although this cannot be carried out at home, you can at least ensure that the braking systems are properly maintained. For hydraulic disc brakes, check the fluid level, lever/pedal feel (bleed of air if its spongy) and pad material. For drum brakes, check adjustment, cable or rod operation and shoe lining thickness.

Wheels and tyres

✔ Check the wheel condition. Cast wheels should be free from cracks and if of the built-up design, all fasteners should be secure. Spoked wheels should be checked for broken, corroded, loose or bent spokes.
✔ With the wheel raised off the ground, spin the wheel and visually check that the tyre and wheel run true. Check that the tyre does not foul the suspension or mudguards.
✔ With the wheel raised off the ground, grasp the wheel and attempt to move it about the axle (spindle) **(see illustration 14)**. Any play felt here indicates wheel bearing failure.

Brake torque arm must be properly secured at both ends

Check for wheel bearing play by trying to move the wheel about the axle (spindle)

MOT Test Checks REF•31

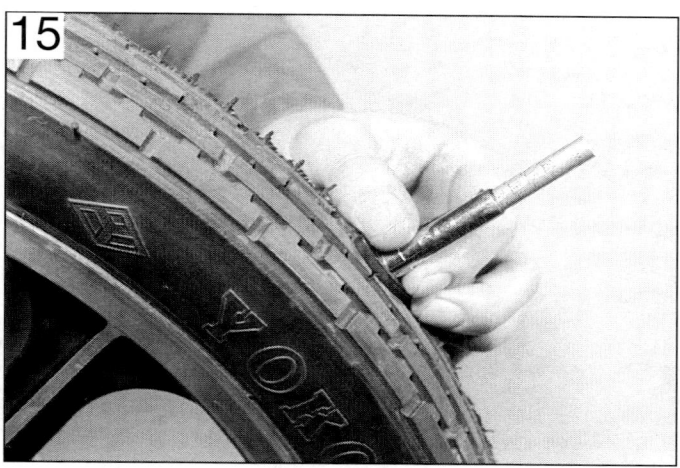
Checking the tyre tread depth

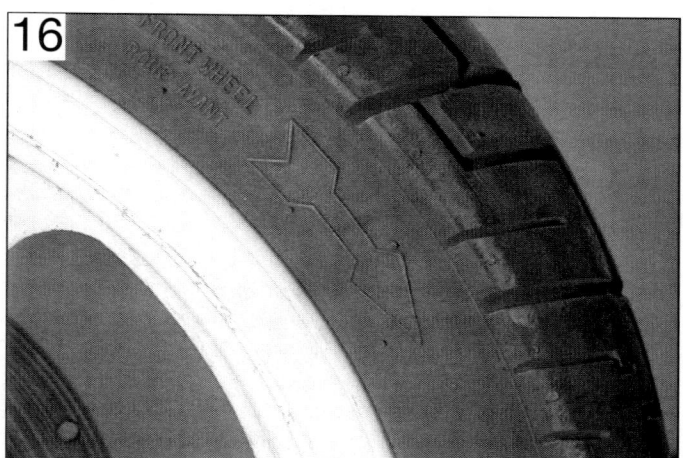
Tyre direction of rotation arrow can be found on tyre sidewall

Castellated type wheel axle (spindle) nut must be secured by a split pin or R-pin

Two straightedges are used to check wheel alignment

✔ Check the tyre tread depth, tread condition and sidewall condition **(see illustration 15)**.
✔ Check the tyre type. Front and rear tyre types must be compatible and be suitable for road use. Tyres marked NOT FOR ROAD USE, COMPETITION USE ONLY or similar, will fail the MOT.
✔ If the tyre sidewall carries a direction of rotation arrow, this must be pointing in the direction of normal wheel rotation **(see illustration 16)**.
✔ Check that the wheel axle (spindle) nuts (where applicable) are properly secured. A self-locking nut or castellated nut with a split-pin or R-pin can be used **(see illustration 17)**.
✔ Wheel alignment is checked with the motorcycle off the stand and a rider seated. With the front wheel pointing straight ahead, two perfectly straight lengths of metal or wood and placed against the sidewalls of both tyres **(see illustration 18)**. The gap each side of the front tyre must be equidistant on both sides. Incorrect wheel alignment may be due to a cocked rear wheel (often as the result of poor chain adjustment) or in extreme cases, a bent frame.

General checks and condition

✔ Check the security of all major fasteners, bodypanels, seat, fairings (where fitted) and mudguards.
✔ Check that the rider and pillion footrests, handlebar levers and brake pedal are securely mounted.
✔ Check for corrosion on the frame or any load-bearing components. If severe, this may affect the structure, particularly under stress.

Sidecars

A motorcycle fitted with a sidecar requires additional checks relating to the stability of the machine and security of attachment and swivel joints, plus specific wheel alignment (toe-in) requirements. Additionally, tyre and lighting requirements differ from conventional motorcycle use. Owners are advised to check MOT test requirements with an official test centre.

Storage

Preparing for storage

Before you start

If repairs or an overhaul is needed, see that this is carried out now rather than left until you want to ride the bike again.

Give the bike a good wash and scrub all dirt from its underside. Make sure the bike dries completely before preparing for storage.

Engine

● Remove the spark plug(s) and lubricate the cylinder bores with approximately a teaspoon of motor oil using a spout-type oil can **(see illustration 1)**. Reinstall the spark plug(s). Crank the engine over a couple of times to coat the piston rings and bores with oil. If the bike has a kickstart, use this to turn the engine over. If not, flick the kill switch to the OFF position and crank the engine over on the starter **(see illustration 2)**. If the nature on the ignition system prevents the starter operating with the kill switch in the OFF position, remove the spark plugs and fit them back in their caps; ensure that the plugs are earthed (grounded) against the cylinder head when the starter is operated **(see illustration 3)**.

 Warning: It is important that the plugs are earthed (grounded) away from the spark plug holes otherwise there is a risk of atomised fuel from the cylinders igniting.

 On a single cylinder four-stroke engine, you can seal the combustion chamber completely by positioning the piston at TDC on the compression stroke.

● Drain the carburettor(s) otherwise there is a risk of jets becoming blocked by gum deposits from the fuel **(see illustration 4)**.

● If the bike is going into long-term storage, consider adding a fuel stabiliser to the fuel in the tank. If the tank is drained completely, corrosion of its internal surfaces may occur if left unprotected for a long period. The tank can be treated with a rust preventative especially for this purpose. Alternatively, remove the tank and pour half a litre of motor oil into it, install the filler cap and shake the tank to coat its internals with oil before draining off the excess. The same effect can also be achieved by spraying WD40 or a similar water-dispersant around the inside of the tank via its flexible nozzle.

● Make sure the cooling system contains the correct mix of antifreeze. Antifreeze also contains important corrosion inhibitors.

● The air intakes and exhaust can be sealed off by covering or plugging the openings. Ensure that you do not seal in any condensation; run the engine until it is hot,

Squirt a drop of motor oil into each cylinder

Flick the kill switch to OFF . . .

. . . and ensure that the metal bodies of the plugs (arrows) are earthed against the cylinder head

Connect a hose to the carburettor float chamber drain stub (arrow) and unscrew the drain screw

Storage

Exhausts can be sealed off with a plastic bag

Disconnect the negative lead (A) first, followed by the positive lead (B)

Use a suitable battery charger - this kit also assess battery condition

then switch off and allow to cool. Tape a piece of thick plastic over the silencer end(s) **(see illustration 5)**. Note that some advocate pouring a tablespoon of motor oil into the silencer(s) before sealing them off.

Battery

● Remove it from the bike - in extreme cases of cold the battery may freeze and crack its case **(see illustration 6)**.

● Check the electrolyte level and top up if necessary (conventional refillable batteries). Clean the terminals.
● Store the battery off the motorcycle and away from any sources of fire. Position a wooden block under the battery if it is to sit on the ground.
● Give the battery a trickle charge for a few hours every month **(see illustration 7)**.

Tyres

● Place the bike on its centrestand or an auxiliary stand which will support the motorcycle in an upright position. Position wood blocks under the tyres to keep them off the ground and to provide insulation from damp. If the bike is being put into long-term storage, ideally both tyres should be off the ground; not only will this protect the tyres, but will also ensure that no load is placed on the steering head or wheel bearings.
● Deflate each tyre by 5 to 10 psi, no more or the beads may unseat from the rim, making subsequent inflation difficult on tubeless tyres.

Pivots and controls

● Lubricate all lever, pedal, stand and footrest pivot points. If grease nipples are fitted to the rear suspension components, apply lubricant to the pivots.
● Lubricate all control cables.

Cycle components

● Apply a wax protectant to all painted and plastic components. Wipe off any excess, but don't polish to a shine. Where fitted, clean the screen with soap and water.
● Coat metal parts with Vaseline (petroleum jelly). When applying this to the fork tubes, do not compress the forks otherwise the seals will rot from contact with the Vaseline.
● Apply a vinyl cleaner to the seat.

Storage conditions

● Aim to store the bike in a shed or garage which does not leak and is free from damp.
● Drape an old blanket or bedspread over the bike to protect it from dust and direct contact with sunlight (which will fade paint). This also hides the bike from prying eyes. Beware of tight-fitting plastic covers which may allow condensation to form and settle on the bike.

Getting back on the road

Engine and transmission

● Change the oil and replace the oil filter. If this was done prior to storage, check that the oil hasn't emulsified - a thick whitish substance which occurs through condensation.
● Remove the spark plugs. Using a spout-type oil can, squirt a few drops of oil into the cylinder(s). This will provide initial lubrication as the piston rings and bores comes back into contact. Service the spark plugs, or fit new ones, and install them in the engine.

● Check that the clutch isn't stuck on. The plates can stick together if left standing for some time, preventing clutch operation. Engage a gear and try rocking the bike back and forth with the clutch lever held against the handlebar. If this doesn't work on cable-operated clutches, hold the clutch lever back against the handlebar with a strong elastic band or cable tie for a couple of hours **(see illustration 8)**.
● If the air intakes or silencer end(s) were blocked off, remove the bung or cover used.
● If the fuel tank was coated with a rust

Hold clutch lever back against the handlebar with elastic bands or a cable tie

Storage

preventative, oil or a stabiliser added to the fuel, drain and flush the tank and dispose of the fuel sensibly. If no action was taken with the fuel tank prior to storage, it is advised that the old fuel is disposed of since it will go off over a period of time. Refill the fuel tank with fresh fuel.

Frame and running gear

● Oil all pivot points and cables.
● Check the tyre pressures. They will definitely need inflating if pressures were reduced for storage.
● Lubricate the final drive chain (where applicable).
● Remove any protective coating applied to the fork tubes (stanchions) since this may well destroy the fork seals. If the fork tubes weren't protected and have picked up rust spots, remove them with very fine abrasive paper and refinish with metal polish.
● Check that both brakes operate correctly. Apply each brake hard and check that it's not possible to move the motorcycle forwards, then check that the brake frees off again once released. Brake caliper pistons can stick due to corrosion around the piston head, or on the sliding caliper types, due to corrosion of the slider pins. If the brake doesn't free after repeated operation, take the caliper off for examination. Similarly drum brakes can stick due to a seized operating cam, cable or rod linkage.
● If the motorcycle has been in long-term storage, renew the brake fluid and clutch fluid (where applicable).
● Depending on where the bike has been stored, the wiring, cables and hoses may have been nibbled by rodents. Make a visual check and investigate disturbed wiring loom tape.

Battery

● If the battery has been previously removal and given top up charges it can simply be reconnected. Remember to connect the positive cable first and the negative cable last.
● On conventional refillable batteries, if the battery has not received any attention, remove it from the motorcycle and check its electrolyte level. Top up if necessary then charge the battery. If the battery fails to hold a charge and a visual checks show heavy white sulphation of the plates, the battery is probably defective and must be renewed. This is particularly likely if the battery is old. Confirm battery condition with a specific gravity check.
● On sealed (MF) batteries, if the battery has not received any attention, remove it from the motorcycle and charge it according to the information on the battery case - if the battery fails to hold a charge it must be renewed.

Starting procedure

● If a kickstart is fitted, turn the engine over a couple of times with the ignition OFF to distribute oil around the engine. If no kickstart is fitted, flick the engine kill switch OFF and the ignition ON and crank the engine over a couple of times to work oil around the upper cylinder components. If the nature of the ignition system is such that the starter won't work with the kill switch OFF, remove the spark plugs, fit them back into their caps and earth (ground) their bodies on the cylinder head. Reinstall the spark plugs afterwards.
● Switch the kill switch to RUN, operate the choke and start the engine. If the engine won't start don't continue cranking the engine - not only will this flatten the battery, but the starter motor will overheat. Switch the ignition off and try again later. If the engine refuses to start, go through the fault finding procedures in this manual. **Note:** *If the bike has been in storage for a long time, old fuel or a carburettor blockage may be the problem. Gum deposits in carburettors can block jets - if a carburettor cleaner doesn't prove successful the carburettors must be dismantled for cleaning.*
● Once the engine has started, check that the lights, turn signals and horn work properly.
● Treat the bike gently for the first ride and check all fluid levels on completion. Settle the bike back into the maintenance schedule.

Fault Finding

This Section provides an easy reference-guide to the more common faults that are likely to afflict your machine. Obviously, the opportunities are almost limitless for faults to occur as a result of obscure failures, and to try and cover all eventualities would require a book. Indeed, a number have been written on the subject.

Successful troubleshooting is not a mysterious 'black art' but the application of a bit of knowledge combined with a systematic and logical approach to the problem. Approach any troubleshooting by first accurately identifying the symptom and then checking through the list of possible causes, starting with the simplest or most obvious and progressing in stages to the most complex.

Take nothing for granted, but above all apply liberal quantities of common sense.

The main symptom of a fault is given in the text as a major heading below which are listed the various systems or areas which may contain the fault. Details of each possible cause for a fault and the remedial action to be taken are given, in brief, in the paragraphs below each heading. Further information should be sought in the relevant Chapter.

1 Engine doesn't start or is difficult to start
- [ ] Starter motor doesn't rotate
- [ ] Starter motor rotates but engine does not turn over
- [ ] Starter works but engine won't turn over (seized)
- [ ] No fuel flow
- [ ] Engine flooded
- [ ] No spark or weak spark
- [ ] Compression low
- [ ] Stalls after starting
- [ ] Rough idle

2 Poor running at low speed
- [ ] Spark weak
- [ ] Fuel/air mixture incorrect
- [ ] Compression low
- [ ] Poor acceleration

3 Poor running or no power at high speed
- [ ] Firing incorrect
- [ ] Fuel/air mixture incorrect
- [ ] Compression low
- [ ] Knocking or pinging
- [ ] Miscellaneous causes

4 Overheating
- [ ] Engine overheats
- [ ] Firing incorrect
- [ ] Fuel/air mixture incorrect
- [ ] Compression too high
- [ ] Engine load excessive
- [ ] Lubrication inadequate
- [ ] Miscellaneous causes

5 Clutch problems
- [ ] Clutch slipping
- [ ] Clutch not disengaging completely

6 Gearchanging problems
- [ ] Doesn't go into gear, or lever doesn't return
- [ ] Jumps out of gear
- [ ] Overselects

7 Abnormal engine noise
- [ ] Knocking or pinking
- [ ] Piston slap or rattling
- [ ] Valve noise
- [ ] Other noise

8 Abnormal driveline noise
- [ ] Clutch noise
- [ ] Transmission noise
- [ ] Final drive noise

9 Abnormal frame and suspension noise
- [ ] Front end noise
- [ ] Shock absorber noise
- [ ] Brake noise

10 Excessive exhaust smoke
- [ ] White smoke
- [ ] Black smoke
- [ ] Brown smoke

11 Poor handling or stability
- [ ] Handlebar hard to turn
- [ ] Handlebar shakes or vibrates excessively
- [ ] Handlebar pulls to one side
- [ ] Poor shock absorbing qualities

12 Braking problems
- [ ] Brakes are spongy, don't hold
- [ ] Brake lever or pedal pulsates
- [ ] Brakes drag

13 Electrical problems
- [ ] Battery dead or weak
- [ ] Battery overcharged

1 Engine doesn't start or is difficult to start

Starter motor doesn't rotate
- [ ] Engine kill switch OFF.
- [ ] Fuse blown. Check main fuse and ignition circuit fuse (Chapter 9).
- [ ] Battery voltage low. Check and recharge battery (Chapter 9).
- [ ] Starter motor defective. Make sure the wiring to the starter is secure. Make sure the starter relay clicks when the start button is pushed. If the relay clicks, then the fault is in the wiring or motor.
- [ ] Starter relay faulty. Check it according to the procedure in Chapter 9.
- [ ] Starter switch not contacting. The contacts could be wet, corroded or dirty. Disassemble and clean the switch (Chapter 9).
- [ ] Wiring open or shorted. Check all wiring connections and harnesses to make sure that they are dry, tight and not corroded. Also check for broken or frayed wires that can cause a short to ground (earth) (see wiring diagram, Chapter 9).
- [ ] Ignition (main) switch defective. Check the switch according to the procedure in Chapter 9. Replace the switch with a new one if it is defective.
- [ ] Engine kill switch defective. Check for wet, dirty or corroded contacts. Clean or replace the switch as necessary (Chapter 9).
- [ ] Faulty neutral, sidestand or clutch switch, or starter circuit cut-off relay. Check the wiring to each switch and the switch itself according to the procedures in Chapter 9.

Starter motor rotates but engine does not turn over
- [ ] Starter clutch defective. Inspect and repair or replace (Chapter 2).
- [ ] Damaged idler or starter gears. Inspect and replace the damaged parts (Chapter 2).

Starter works but engine won't turn over (seized)
- [ ] Seized engine caused by one or more internally damaged components. Failure due to wear, abuse or lack of lubrication. Damage can include seized valves, followers, camshafts, pistons, crankshaft, connecting rod bearings, or transmission gears or bearings. Refer to Chapter 2 for engine disassembly.

No fuel flow
- [ ] No fuel in tank.
- [ ] Fuel tank breather hose obstructed.
- [ ] Fuel tap strainer or in-line filter clogged. Remove the tap and clean it and check the filter (Chapters 1 and 4).
- [ ] Fuel line clogged. Pull the fuel line loose and carefully blow through it.
- [ ] Float needle valve clogged. For all of the valves to be clogged, either a very bad batch of fuel with an unusual additive has been used, or some other foreign material has entered the tank. Many times after a machine has been stored for many months without running, the fuel turns to a varnish-like liquid and forms deposits on the inlet needle valves and jets. The carburettors should be removed and overhauled if draining the float chambers doesn't solve the problem.
- [ ] Fuel pump faulty. Check the fuel pump flow and renew the pump if necessary (Chapter 4).

Engine flooded
- [ ] Fuel level (float height) too high. Check as described in Chapter 4.
- [ ] Float needle valve worn or stuck open. A piece of dirt, rust or other debris can cause the valve to seat improperly, causing excess fuel to be admitted to the float chamber. In this case, the float chamber should be cleaned and the needle valve and seat inspected. If the needle and seat are worn, then the leaking will persist and the parts should be replaced with new ones (Chapter 4).
- [ ] Starting technique incorrect. Under normal circumstances (i.e., if all the carburettor functions are sound) the machine should start with little or no throttle. When the engine is cold, the choke should be operated and the engine started without opening the throttle. When the engine is at operating temperature, only a very slight amount of throttle should be necessary. If the engine is flooded, turn the fuel tap OFF or disconnect the vacuum hose (according to model - see Chapter 4) and hold the throttle open while cranking the engine. This will allow additional air to reach the cylinders. Remember to turn the fuel tap back ON or attach the vacuum hose.

No spark or weak spark
- [ ] Ignition switch OFF.
- [ ] Engine kill switch turned to the OFF position.
- [ ] Battery voltage low. Check and recharge the battery as necessary (Chapter 9).
- [ ] Spark plugs dirty, defective or worn out. Locate reason for fouled plugs using spark plug condition chart and follow the plug maintenance procedures (Chapter 1).
- [ ] Spark plug caps or secondary (HT) wiring faulty. Check condition. Renew either or both components if cracks or deterioration are evident (Chapter 5).
- [ ] Spark plug caps not making good contact. Make sure that the plug caps fit snugly over the plug ends.
- [ ] Ignition control unit defective. Check the unit (Chapter 5).
- [ ] Pick-up coil defective. Check the coil (Chapter 5).
- [ ] Ignition HT coils defective. Check the coils (Chapter 5).
- [ ] Ignition or kill switch shorted. This is usually caused by water, corrosion, damage or excessive wear. The switches can be disassembled and cleaned with electrical contact cleaner. If cleaning does not help, renew the switches (Chapter 9).
- [ ] Wiring shorted or broken between:
    - a) Ignition (main) switch and engine kill switch (or blown fuse)
    - b) Ignition control unit and engine kill switch
    - c) Ignition control unit and ignition HT coils
    - d) Ignition HT coils and spark plugs
    - e) Ignition control unit and pick-up coil
- [ ] Make sure that all wiring connections are clean, dry and tight. Look for chafed and broken wires (Chapters 5 and 9).

Compression low
- [ ] Spark plugs loose. Remove the plugs and inspect their threads. Reinstall and tighten to the specified torque (Chapter 1).
- [ ] Cylinder head not sufficiently tightened down. If the cylinder head is suspected of being loose, then there's a chance that the gasket or head is damaged if the problem has persisted for any length of time. The head nuts should be tightened to the proper torque in the correct sequence (Chapter 2).
- [ ] Improper valve clearance. This means that the valve is not closing completely and compression pressure is leaking past the valve. Check and adjust the valve clearances (Chapter 1).
- [ ] Cylinder and/or piston worn. Excessive wear will cause compression pressure to leak past the rings. This is usually accompanied by worn rings as well. A top-end overhaul is necessary (Chapter 2).
- [ ] Piston rings worn, weak, broken, or sticking. Broken or sticking piston rings usually indicate a lubrication or carburation problem that causes excess carbon deposits or seizures to form on the pistons and rings. Top-end overhaul is necessary (Chapter 2).
- [ ] Piston ring-to-groove clearance excessive. This is caused by excessive wear of the piston ring lands. Piston renewal is necessary (Chapter 2).
- [ ] Cylinder head gasket damaged. If the head is allowed to become loose, or if excessive carbon build-up on the piston crown and combustion chamber causes extremely high compression, the head gasket may leak. Retorquing the head is not always sufficient to restore the seal, so gasket renewal is necessary (Chapter 2).

Fault Finding REF•37

1 Engine doesn't start or is difficult to start (continued)

- ☐ Cylinder head warped. This is caused by overheating or improperly tightened head nuts. Machine shop resurfacing or head renewal is necessary (Chapter 2).
- ☐ Valve spring broken or weak. Caused by component failure or wear; the springs must be renewed (Chapter 2).
- ☐ Valve not seating properly. This is caused by a bent valve (from over-revving or improper valve adjustment), burned valve or seat (improper carburation) or an accumulation of carbon deposits on the seat (from carburation or lubrication problems). The valves must be cleaned and/or replaced and the seats serviced if possible (Chapter 2).

Stalls after starting

- ☐ Improper choke action. Make sure the choke linkage shaft is getting a full stroke and staying in the out position (Chapter 4).
- ☐ Ignition malfunction (Chapter 5).
- ☐ Carburettor malfunction (Chapter 4).
- ☐ Fuel contaminated. The fuel can be contaminated with either dirt or water, or can change chemically if the machine is allowed to sit for several months or more. Drain the tank and float chambers (Chapter 4).
- ☐ Intake air leak. Check for loose carburettor-to-intake manifold connections, loose or missing vacuum gauge adapter screws or hoses, or loose carburettor tops (Chapter 4).
- ☐ Engine idle speed incorrect. Turn idle adjusting screw until the engine idles at the specified rpm (Chapter 1).

Rough idle

- ☐ Ignition malfunction (Chapter 5).
- ☐ Idle speed incorrect (Chapter 1).
- ☐ Carburettors not synchronised. Adjust carburettors with vacuum gauge or manometer set as described in Chapter 1.
- ☐ Carburettor malfunction (Chapter 4).
- ☐ Fuel contaminated. The fuel can be contaminated with either dirt or water, or can change chemically if the machine is allowed to sit for several months or more. Drain the tank and float chambers (Chapter 4).
- ☐ Intake air leak. Check for loose carburettor-to-intake manifold connections, loose or missing vacuum gauge adapter screws or hoses, or loose carburettor tops (Chapter 4).
- ☐ Air filter clogged. Renew the air filter element (Chapter 1).

2 Poor running at low speeds

Spark weak

- ☐ Battery voltage low. Check and recharge battery (Chapter 9).
- ☐ Spark plugs fouled, defective or worn out. Refer to Chapter 1 for spark plug maintenance.
- ☐ Spark plug cap or HT wiring defective. Refer to Chapters 1 and 5 for details on the ignition system.
- ☐ Spark plug caps not making contact. Make sure they are securely pushed on to the plugs.
- ☐ Incorrect spark plugs. Wrong type, heat range or cap configuration. Check and install correct plugs listed in Chapter 1.
- ☐ Ignition control unit defective (Chapter 5).
- ☐ Pick-up coil defective (Chapter 5).
- ☐ Ignition HT coils defective (Chapter 5).

Fuel/air mixture incorrect

- ☐ Pilot screws out of adjustment (Chapter 4).
- ☐ Pilot jet or air passage clogged. Remove and overhaul the carburettors (Chapter 4).
- ☐ Air bleed holes clogged. Remove carburettor and blow out all passages (Chapter 4).
- ☐ Air filter clogged, poorly sealed or missing (Chapter 1).
- ☐ Air filter housing poorly sealed. Look for cracks, holes or loose clamps and renew or repair defective parts.
- ☐ Fuel level too high or too low. Check the level (Chapter 4).
- ☐ Fuel tank breather hose obstructed.
- ☐ Carburettor intake manifolds loose. Check for cracks, breaks, tears or loose clamps. Renew the rubber intake manifold joints if split or perished.

Compression low

- ☐ Spark plugs loose. Remove the plugs and inspect their threads. Reinstall and tighten to the specified torque (Chapter 1).
- ☐ Cylinder head not sufficiently tightened down. If the cylinder head is suspected of being loose, then there's a chance that the gasket and head are damaged if the problem has persisted for any length of time. The head nuts should be tightened to the proper torque in the correct sequence (Chapter 2).
- ☐ Improper valve clearance. This means that the valve is not closing completely and compression pressure is leaking past the valve. Check and adjust the valve clearances (Chapter 1).
- ☐ Cylinder and/or piston worn. Excessive wear will cause compression pressure to leak past the rings. This is usually accompanied by worn rings as well. A top-end overhaul is necessary (Chapter 2).
- ☐ Piston rings worn, weak, broken, or sticking. Broken or sticking piston rings usually indicate a lubrication or carburation problem that causes excess carbon deposits or seizures to form on the pistons and rings. Top-end overhaul is necessary (Chapter 2).
- ☐ Piston ring-to-groove clearance excessive. This is caused by excessive wear of the piston ring lands. Piston renewal is necessary (Chapter 2).
- ☐ Cylinder head gasket damaged. If the head is allowed to become loose, or if excessive carbon build-up on the piston crown and combustion chamber causes extremely high compression, the head gasket may leak. Retorquing the head is not always sufficient to restore the seal, so gasket renewal is necessary (Chapter 2).
- ☐ Cylinder head warped. This is caused by overheating or improperly tightened head nuts. Machine shop resurfacing or head renewal is necessary (Chapter 2).
- ☐ Valve spring broken or weak. Caused by component failure or wear; the springs must be renewed (Chapter 2).
- ☐ Valve not seating properly. This is caused by a bent valve (from over-revving or improper valve adjustment), burned valve or seat (improper carburation) or an accumulation of carbon deposits on the seat (from carburation, lubrication problems). The valves must be cleaned and/or replaced and the seats serviced if possible (Chapter 2).

Poor acceleration

- ☐ Carburettors leaking or dirty. Overhaul the carburettors (Chapter 4).
- ☐ Timing not advancing. The pick-up coil or the ignition control unit may be defective. If so, they must be renewed, as they can't be repaired.
- ☐ Carburettors not synchronised. Adjust them with a vacuum gauge set or manometer (Chapter 1).
- ☐ Engine oil viscosity too high. Using a heavier oil than that recommended in Chapter 1 can damage the oil pump or lubrication system and cause drag on the engine.
- ☐ Brakes dragging. Usually caused by debris which has entered the brake piston seals, or from a warped disc or bent axle. Repair as necessary (Chapter 7).
- ☐ Fuel pump flow rate insufficient. Check the pump (Chapter 4).

3 Poor running or no power at high speed

Firing incorrect
- ☐ Air filter restricted. Clean or renew filter (Chapter 1).
- ☐ Spark plugs fouled, defective or worn out. See Chapter 1 for spark plug maintenance.
- ☐ Spark plug caps or HT wiring defective. See Chapters 1 and 5 for details of the ignition system.
- ☐ Spark plug caps not in good contact (Chapter 5).
- ☐ Incorrect spark plugs. Wrong type, heat range or cap configuration. Check and install correct plugs listed in Chapter 1.
- ☐ Ignition control unit defective (Chapter 5).
- ☐ Ignition HT coils defective (Chapter 5).

Fuel/air mixture incorrect
- ☐ Main jet clogged. Dirt, water or other contaminants can clog the main jets. Clean the fuel tap strainer, the float chamber area, and the jets and carburettor orifices (Chapter 4). Renew the in-line fuel filter (Chapter 1).
- ☐ Main jet wrong size. The standard jetting is for sea level atmospheric pressure and oxygen content.
- ☐ Air bleed holes clogged. Remove and overhaul carburettors (Chapter 4).
- ☐ Air filter clogged, poorly sealed, or missing (Chapter 1).
- ☐ Air filter housing poorly sealed. Look for cracks, holes or loose clamps, and renew or repair defective parts.
- ☐ Fuel level too high or too low. Check the level (Chapter 4).
- ☐ Fuel tank breather hose obstructed.
- ☐ Carburettor intake manifolds loose. Check for cracks, breaks, tears or loose clamps. Renew the rubber intake manifolds if they are split or perished (Chapter 4).

Compression low
- ☐ Spark plugs loose. Remove the plugs and inspect their threads. Reinstall and tighten to the specified torque (Chapter 1).
- ☐ Cylinder head not sufficiently tightened down. If the cylinder head is suspected of being loose, then there's a chance that the gasket and head are damaged if the problem has persisted for any length of time. The head nuts should be tightened to the proper torque in the correct sequence (Chapter 2).
- ☐ Improper valve clearance. This means that the valve is not closing completely and compression pressure is leaking past the valve. Check and adjust the valve clearances (Chapter 1).
- ☐ Cylinder and/or piston worn. Excessive wear will cause compression pressure to leak past the rings. This is usually accompanied by worn rings as well. A top-end overhaul is necessary (Chapter 2).
- ☐ Piston rings worn, weak, broken, or sticking. Broken or sticking piston rings usually indicate a lubrication or carburation problem that causes excess carbon deposits or seizures to form on the pistons and rings. Top-end overhaul is necessary (Chapter 2).
- ☐ Piston ring-to-groove clearance excessive. This is caused by excessive wear of the piston ring lands. Piston renewal is necessary (Chapter 2).
- ☐ Cylinder head gasket damaged. If the head is allowed to become loose, or if excessive carbon build-up on the piston crown and combustion chamber causes extremely high compression, the head gasket may leak. Retorquing the head is not always sufficient to restore the seal, so gasket renewal is necessary (Chapter 2).
- ☐ Cylinder head warped. This is caused by overheating or improperly tightened head nuts. Machine shop resurfacing or head renewal is necessary (Chapter 2).
- ☐ Valve spring broken or weak. Caused by component failure or wear; the springs must be renewed (Chapter 2).
- ☐ Valve not seating properly. This is caused by a bent valve (from over-revving or improper valve adjustment), burned valve or seat (improper carburation) or an accumulation of carbon deposits on the seat (from carburation or lubrication problems). The valves must be cleaned and/or renewed and the seats serviced if possible (Chapter 2).

Knocking or pinking
- ☐ Carbon build-up in combustion chamber. Use of a fuel additive that will dissolve the adhesive bonding the carbon particles to the crown and chamber is the easiest way to remove the build-up. Otherwise, the cylinder head will have to be removed and decarbonised (Chapter 2).
- ☐ Incorrect or poor quality fuel. Old or improper grades of fuel can cause detonation. This causes the piston to rattle, thus the knocking or pinking sound. Drain old fuel and always use the recommended fuel grade.
- ☐ Spark plug heat range incorrect. Uncontrolled detonation indicates the plug heat range is too hot. The plug in effect becomes a glow plug, raising cylinder temperatures. Install the proper heat range plug (Chapter 1).
- ☐ Improper air/fuel mixture. This will cause the cylinders to run hot, which leads to detonation. Clogged jets or an air leak can cause this imbalance. See Chapter 4.

Miscellaneous causes
- ☐ Throttle valve doesn't open fully. Adjust the throttle grip freeplay (Chapter 1).
- ☐ Clutch slipping. May be caused by loose or worn clutch components. Refer to Chapter 2 for clutch overhaul procedures.
- ☐ Engine oil viscosity too high. Using a heavier oil than the one recommended in Chapter 1 can damage the oil pump or lubrication system and cause drag on the engine.
- ☐ Brakes dragging. Usually caused by debris which has entered the brake piston seals, or from a warped disc or bent axle. Repair as necessary.
- ☐ Fuel pump flow rate insufficient. Check the pump (Chapter 4).

Fault Finding REF•39

4 Overheating

Engine overheats
- ☐ Coolant level low. Check and add coolant (Chapter 1).
- ☐ Leak in cooling system. Check cooling system hoses and radiator for leaks and other damage. Repair or renew parts as necessary (Chapter 3).
- ☐ Thermostat sticking open or closed. Check and renew as described in Chapter 3.
- ☐ Faulty radiator cap. Remove the cap and have it pressure tested.
- ☐ Coolant passages clogged. Have the entire system drained and flushed, then refill with fresh coolant.
- ☐ Water pump defective. Remove the pump and check the components (Chapter 3).
- ☐ Clogged radiator fins. Clean them by blowing compressed air through the fins from the backside.
- ☐ Cooling fan or fan switch fault (Chapter 3).

Firing incorrect
- ☐ Spark plugs fouled, defective or worn out. See Chapter 1 for spark plug maintenance.
- ☐ Incorrect spark plugs.
- ☐ Ignition control unit defective (Chapter 5).
- ☐ Faulty ignition HT coils (Chapter 5).

Fuel/air mixture incorrect
- ☐ Main jet clogged. Dirt, water and other contaminants can clog the main jets. Clean the fuel tap strainer, the float chamber area and the jets and carburettor orifices (Chapter 4). Renew the in-line fuel filter (Chapter 1).
- ☐ Main jet wrong size. The standard jetting is for sea level atmospheric pressure and oxygen content.
- ☐ Air filter clogged, poorly sealed or missing (Chapter 1).
- ☐ Air filter housing poorly sealed. Look for cracks, holes or loose clamps and renew or repair.
- ☐ Fuel level too low. Check the level (Chapter 4).
- ☐ Fuel tank breather hose obstructed.
- ☐ Carburettor intake manifolds loose. Check for cracks, breaks, tears or loose clamps. Renew the rubber intake manifold joints if split or perished.

Compression too high
- ☐ Carbon build-up in combustion chamber. Use of a fuel additive that will dissolve the adhesive bonding the carbon particles to the piston crown and chamber is the easiest way to remove the build-up. Otherwise, the cylinder head will have to be removed and decarbonised (Chapter 2).
- ☐ Improperly machined head surface or installation of incorrect gasket during engine assembly.

Engine load excessive
- ☐ Clutch slipping. Can be caused by damaged, loose or worn clutch components. Refer to Chapter 2 for overhaul procedures.
- ☐ Engine oil level too high. The addition of too much oil will cause pressurisation of the crankcase and inefficient engine operation. Check Specifications and drain to proper level (Chapter 1).
- ☐ Engine oil viscosity too high. Using a heavier oil than the one recommended in Chapter 1 can damage the oil pump or lubrication system as well as cause drag on the engine.
- ☐ Brakes dragging. Usually caused by debris which has entered the brake piston seals, or from a warped disc or bent axle. Repair as necessary.

Lubrication inadequate
- ☐ Engine oil level too low. Friction caused by intermittent lack of lubrication or from oil that is overworked can cause overheating. The oil provides a definite cooling function in the engine. Check the oil level (Chapter 1).
- ☐ Poor quality engine oil or incorrect viscosity or type. Oil is rated not only according to viscosity but also according to type. Some oils are not rated high enough for use in this engine. Check the Specifications section and change to the correct oil (Chapter 1).

Miscellaneous causes
- ☐ Modification to exhaust system. Most aftermarket exhaust systems cause the engine to run leaner, which make them run hotter. When installing an accessory exhaust system, always rejet the carburettors.

5 Clutch problems

Clutch slipping
- ☐ Incorrectly adjusted cable (see Chapter 1).
- ☐ Friction plates worn or warped. Overhaul the clutch assembly (Chapter 2).
- ☐ Plain plates warped (Chapter 2).
- ☐ Clutch release mechanism defective. Renew any defective parts (Chapter 2).
- ☐ Clutch centre or housing unevenly worn. This causes improper engagement of the plates. Renew the damaged or worn parts (Chapter 2).

Clutch not disengaging completely
- ☐ Incorrectly adjusted cable (see Chapter 1).
- ☐ Clutch plates warped or damaged. This will cause clutch drag, which in turn will cause the machine to creep. Overhaul the clutch assembly (Chapter 2).
- ☐ Clutch spring(s) broken or weak (Chapter 2).
- ☐ Engine oil deteriorated. Old, thin, worn out oil will not provide proper lubrication for the plates, causing the clutch to drag. Change the oil and filter (Chapter 1).
- ☐ Engine oil viscosity too high. Using a heavier oil than recommended in Chapter 1 can cause the plates to stick together, putting a drag on the engine. Change to the correct weight oil (Chapter 1).
- ☐ Clutch needle bearing seized on input shaft. Lack of lubrication, severe wear or damage can cause the guide to seize on the shaft. Overhaul of the clutch, and perhaps transmission, may be necessary to repair the damage (Chapter 2).
- ☐ Clutch release mechanism defective. Overhaul it (Chapter 2).
- ☐ Loose clutch centre nut. Causes housing and centre misalignment putting a drag on the engine. Engagement adjustment continually varies. Overhaul the clutch assembly (Chapter 2).

6 Gearchanging problems

Doesn't go into gear or lever doesn't return
- [ ] Clutch not disengaging. See above.
- [ ] Selector fork(s) bent or seized. Often caused by dropping the machine or from lack of lubrication. Overhaul the transmission (Chapter 2).
- [ ] Gear(s) stuck on shaft. Most often caused by a lack of lubrication or excessive wear in transmission gears and bushes. Overhaul the transmission (Chapter 2).
- [ ] Selector drum binding. Caused by lubrication failure or excessive wear. Renew the drum and bearing (Chapter 2).
- [ ] Gearchange lever return spring weak or broken (Chapter 2).
- [ ] Gearchange lever broken. Splines stripped out of lever or shaft, caused by allowing the lever to get loose or from dropping the machine. Renew necessary parts (Chapter 2).
- [ ] Gearchange mechanism stopper arm broken or worn. Full engagement and rotary movement of selector drum results. Renew the arm (Chapter 2).
- [ ] Stopper arm spring broken. Allows arm to float, causing sporadic gearchange operation. Renew spring (Chapter 2).

Jumps out of gear
- [ ] Selector fork(s) worn. Overhaul the transmission (Chapter 2).
- [ ] Gear groove(s) worn. Overhaul the transmission (Chapter 2).
- [ ] Gear dogs or dog slots worn or damaged. The gears should be inspected and renewed. No attempt should be made to service the worn parts.

Overselects
- [ ] Stopper arm spring weak or broken (Chapter 2).
- [ ] Gearchange shaft return spring post broken or distorted (Chapter 2).

7 Abnormal engine noise

Knocking or pinking
- [ ] Carbon build-up in combustion chamber. Use of a fuel additive that will dissolve the adhesive bonding the carbon particles to the piston crown and chamber is the easiest way to remove the build-up. Otherwise, the cylinder head will have to be removed and decarbonised (Chapter 2).
- [ ] Incorrect or poor quality fuel. Old or improper fuel can cause detonation. This causes the pistons to rattle, thus the knocking or pinking sound. Drain the old fuel and always use the recommended grade fuel (Chapter 4).
- [ ] Spark plug heat range incorrect. Uncontrolled detonation indicates that the plug heat range is too hot. The plug in effect becomes a glow plug, raising cylinder temperatures. Install the proper heat range plug (Chapter 1).
- [ ] Improper air/fuel mixture. This will cause the cylinders to run hot and lead to detonation. Clogged jets or an air leak can cause this imbalance. See Chapter 4.

Piston slap or rattling
- [ ] Cylinder-to-piston clearance excessive. Caused by improper assembly. Inspect and overhaul top-end parts (Chapter 2).
- [ ] Connecting rod bent. Caused by over-revving, trying to start a badly flooded engine or from ingesting a foreign object into the combustion chamber. Renew the damaged parts (Chapter 2).
- [ ] Piston pin or piston pin bore worn or seized from wear or lack of lubrication. Renew damaged parts (Chapter 2).
- [ ] Piston ring(s) worn, broken or sticking. Overhaul the top-end (Chapter 2).
- [ ] Piston seizure damage. Usually from lack of lubrication or overheating. Renew the pistons and crankcases, as necessary (Chapter 2).
- [ ] Connecting rod upper or lower end clearance excessive. Caused by excessive wear or lack of lubrication. Renew worn parts.

Valve noise
- [ ] Incorrect valve clearances. Adjust the clearances by referring to Chapter 1.
- [ ] Valve spring broken or weak. Check and renew weak valve springs (Chapter 2).
- [ ] Camshaft or cylinder head worn or damaged. Lack of lubrication at high rpm is usually the cause of damage. Insufficient oil or failure to change the oil at the recommended intervals are the chief causes. Since there are no replaceable bearings in the head, the head itself will have to be renewed if there is excessive wear or damage (Chapter 2).

Other noise
- [ ] Cylinder head gasket leaking.
- [ ] Exhaust pipe leaking at cylinder head connection. Caused by improper fit of pipe(s) or loose exhaust flange. All exhaust fasteners should be tightened evenly and carefully. Failure to do this will lead to a leak.
- [ ] Crankshaft runout excessive. Caused by a bent crankshaft (from over-revving) or damage from an upper cylinder component failure. Can also be attributed to dropping the machine on either of the crankshaft ends.
- [ ] Engine mounting bolts loose. Tighten all engine mount bolts (Chapter 2).
- [ ] Crankshaft bearings worn (Chapter 2).
- [ ] Cam chain, tensioner or guide blades defective. Renew according to the procedure in Chapter 2.

Fault Finding

8 Abnormal driveline noise

Clutch noise
- [ ] Clutch housing/friction plate clearance excessive (Chapter 2).
- [ ] Loose or damaged clutch pressure plate and/or bolts (Chapter 2).

Transmission noise
- [ ] Bearings/bushes worn. Also includes the possibility that the shafts are worn. Overhaul the transmission (Chapter 2).
- [ ] Gears worn or chipped (Chapter 2).
- [ ] Metal chips jammed in gear teeth. Probably pieces from a broken clutch, gear or selector mechanism that were picked up by the gears. This will cause early bearing failure (Chapter 2).
- [ ] Engine oil level too low. Causes a howl from transmission. Also affects engine power and clutch operation (Chapter 1).

Final drive noise
- [ ] Chain not adjusted properly (Chapter 1).
- [ ] Front or rear sprocket loose. Tighten fasteners (Chapter 6).
- [ ] Sprockets worn. Renew sprockets (Chapter 6).
- [ ] Rear sprocket warped. Renew sprockets (Chapter 6).
- [ ] Loose or worn rear wheel or sprocket coupling bearings. Check and renew as needed (Chapter 7).

9 Abnormal frame and suspension noise

Front end noise
- [ ] Low fluid level or improper viscosity oil in forks. This can sound like spurting and is usually accompanied by irregular fork action (Chapter 6).
- [ ] Spring weak or broken. Makes a clicking or scraping sound. Fork oil, when drained, will have a lot of metal particles in it (Chapter 6).
- [ ] Steering head bearings loose or damaged. Clicks when braking. Check and adjust or renew as necessary (Chapters 1 and 6).
- [ ] Fork yokes loose. Make sure all clamp pinch bolts are tightened to the specified torque (Chapter 6).
- [ ] Fork tube bent. Good possibility if machine has been dropped. Replace tube with a new one (Chapter 6).
- [ ] Front axle bolt or axle clamp bolt loose. Tighten them to the specified torque (Chapter 7).
- [ ] Loose or worn wheel bearings. Check and renew as needed (Chapter 7).

Shock absorber noise
- [ ] Fluid level incorrect. Indicates a leak caused by defective seal. Shock will be covered with oil. Renew shock or seek advice on repair from a Yamaha dealer (Chapter 6).
- [ ] Defective shock absorber with internal damage. This is in the body of the shock and can't be remedied. The shock must be replaced with a new one (Chapter 6).
- [ ] Bent or damaged shock body. Replace the shock with a new one (Chapter 6).
- [ ] Loose or worn suspension linkage components. Check and renew as necessary (Chapter 6).

Brake noise
- [ ] Squeal caused by pad shim not installed or positioned correctly (where fitted) (Chapter 7).
- [ ] Squeal caused by dust on brake pads. Usually found in combination with glazed pads. Clean using brake cleaning solvent (Chapter 7).
- [ ] Contamination of brake pads. Oil, brake fluid or dirt causing brake to chatter or squeal. Clean or renew pads (Chapter 7).
- [ ] Pads glazed. Caused by excessive heat from prolonged use or from contamination. Do not use sandpaper, emery cloth, carborundum cloth or any other abrasive to roughen the pad surfaces as abrasives will stay in the pad material and damage the disc. A very fine flat file can be used, but pad renewal is suggested as a cure (Chapter 7).
- [ ] Disc warped. Can cause a chattering, clicking or intermittent squeal. Usually accompanied by a pulsating lever and uneven braking. Renew the disc (Chapter 7).
- [ ] Loose or worn wheel bearings. Check and renew as needed (Chapter 7).

10 Excessive exhaust smoke

White smoke
- [ ] Piston oil ring worn. The ring may be broken or damaged, causing oil from the crankcase to be pulled past the piston into the combustion chamber. Replace the rings with new ones (Chapter 2).
- [ ] Cylinders worn, cracked, or scored. Caused by overheating or oil starvation. Check the cylinder bores, lubrication system and cooling system (see Chapters 2 and 3).
- [ ] Valve oil seal damaged or worn. Replace oil seals with new ones (Chapter 2).
- [ ] Valve guide worn. Perform a complete valve job (Chapter 2).
- [ ] Engine oil level too high, which causes the oil to be forced past the rings. Drain oil to the proper level (Daily checks).
- [ ] Head gasket broken between oil return and cylinder. Causes oil to be pulled into the combustion chamber. Replace the head gasket and check the head for warpage (Chapter 2).
- [ ] Abnormal crankcase pressurisation, which forces oil past the rings. Clogged breather is usually the cause.

Black smoke
- [ ] Air filter clogged. Clean or replace the element (Chapter 1).
- [ ] Main jet too large or loose. Compare the jet size to the Specifications (Chapter 4).
- [ ] Choke cable or linkage shaft stuck, causing fuel to be pulled through choke circuit (Chapter 4).
- [ ] Fuel level too high. Check and adjust the float height(s) as necessary (Chapter 4).
- [ ] Float needle valve held off needle seat. Clean the float chambers and fuel line and replace the needles and seats if necessary (Chapter 4).

Brown smoke
- [ ] Main jet too small or clogged. Lean condition caused by wrong size main jet or by a restricted orifice. Clean float chambers and jets and compare jet size to Specifications (Chapter 4).
- [ ] Fuel flow insufficient - float needle valve stuck closed due to chemical reaction with old fuel; fuel level incorrect; restricted fuel line; faulty fuel pump (Chapter 4).
- [ ] Carburettor intake manifold clamps loose (Chapter 4).
- [ ] Air filter poorly sealed or not installed (Chapter 1).

11 Poor handling or stability

Handlebar hard to turn
- [ ] Steering head bearing adjuster nut too tight. Check adjustment as described in Chapter 1.
- [ ] Bearings damaged. Roughness can be felt as the bars are turned from side-to-side. Renew bearings and races (Chapter 6).
- [ ] Races dented or worn. Denting results from wear in only one position (e.g., straight ahead), from a collision or hitting a pothole or from dropping the machine. Renew races and bearings (Chapter 6).
- [ ] Steering stem lubrication inadequate. Causes are grease getting hard from age or being washed out by high pressure car washes. Disassemble steering head and repack bearings (Chapter 6).
- [ ] Steering stem bent. Caused by a collision, hitting a pothole or by dropping the machine. Renew damaged part. Don't try to straighten the steering stem (Chapter 6).
- [ ] Front tyre air pressure too low (Chapter 1).

Handlebar shakes or vibrates excessively
- [ ] Tyres worn or out of balance (Chapter 7).
- [ ] Swingarm bearings worn. Renew worn bearings (Chapter 6).
- [ ] Wheel rim(s) warped or damaged. Inspect wheels for runout (Chapter 7).
- [ ] Wheel bearings worn. Worn front or rear wheel bearings can cause poor tracking. Worn front bearings will cause wobble (Chapter 7).
- [ ] Handlebar clamp bolts loose (Chapter 6).
- [ ] Fork yoke bolts loose. Tighten them to the specified torque (Chapter 6).
- [ ] Engine mounting bolts loose. Will cause excessive vibration with increased engine rpm (Chapter 2).

Handlebar pulls to one side
- [ ] Frame bent. Definitely suspect this if the machine has been dropped. May or may not be accompanied by cracking near the bend. Renew the frame (Chapter 6).
- [ ] Wheels out of alignment. Caused by improper location of axle spacers or from bent steering stem or frame (Chapter 6).
- [ ] Swingarm bent or twisted. Caused by age (metal fatigue) or impact damage. Renew the arm (Chapter 6).
- [ ] Steering stem bent. Caused by impact damage or by dropping the motorcycle. Renew the steering stem (Chapter 6).
- [ ] Fork tube bent. Disassemble the forks and renew the damaged parts (Chapter 6).
- [ ] Fork oil level uneven. Check and add or drain as necessary (Chapter 6).

Poor shock absorbing qualities
- [ ] Too hard:
    a) Fork oil level excessive (Chapter 6).
    b) Fork oil viscosity too high. Use a lighter oil (see the Specifications in Chapter 6).
    c) Fork tube bent. Causes a harsh, sticking feeling (Chapter 6).
    d) Fork internal damage (Chapter 6).
    e) Shock shaft or body bent or damaged (Chapter 6).
    f) Shock internal damage.
    g) Tyre pressure too high (Daily checks).
- [ ] Too soft:
    a) Fork or shock oil insufficient and/or leaking (Chapter 6).
    b) Fork oil level too low (Chapter 6).
    c) Fork oil viscosity too light (Chapter 6).
    d) Fork springs weak or broken (Chapter 6).
    e) Shock internal damage or leakage (Chapter 6).

12 Braking problems

Brakes are spongy, don't hold
- [ ] Air in brake line. Caused by inattention to master cylinder fluid level or by leakage. Locate problem and bleed brakes (Chapter 7).
- [ ] Pad or disc worn (Chapters 1 and 7).
- [ ] Brake fluid leak. See paragraph 1.
- [ ] Contaminated pads. Caused by contamination with oil, grease, brake fluid, etc. Renew pads. Clean disc thoroughly with brake cleaner (Chapter 7).
- [ ] Brake fluid deteriorated. Fluid is old or contaminated. Drain system, replenish with new fluid and bleed the system (Chapter 7).
- [ ] Master cylinder internal parts worn or damaged causing fluid to bypass (Chapter 7).
- [ ] Master cylinder bore scratched by foreign material or broken spring. Repair or renew master cylinder (Chapter 7).
- [ ] Disc warped. Renew disc (Chapter 7).

Brake lever or pedal pulsates
- [ ] Disc warped. Renew disc (Chapter 7).
- [ ] Axle bent. Renew axle (Chapter 7).
- [ ] Brake caliper bolts loose (Chapter 7).
- [ ] Wheel warped or otherwise damaged (Chapter 7).
- [ ] Wheel bearings damaged or worn (Chapter 7).

Brakes drag
- [ ] Master cylinder piston seized. Caused by wear or damage to piston or cylinder bore (Chapter 7).
- [ ] Lever balky or stuck. Check pivot and lubricate (Chapter 7).
- [ ] Brake caliper piston seized in bore. Caused by wear or ingestion of dirt past deteriorated seal (Chapter 7).
- [ ] Brake pad damaged. Pad material separated from backing plate. Usually caused by faulty manufacturing process or from contact with chemicals. Renew pads (Chapter 7).
- [ ] Pads improperly installed (Chapter 7).

Fault Finding

13 Electrical problems

Battery dead or weak
- [ ] Battery faulty. Caused by sulphated plates which are shorted through sedimentation. Also, broken battery terminal making only occasional contact (Chapter 9).
- [ ] Battery cables making poor contact (Chapter 9).
- [ ] Load excessive. Caused by addition of high wattage lights or other electrical accessories.
- [ ] Ignition (main) switch defective. Switch either grounds (earths) internally or fails to shut off system. Renew the switch (Chapter 9).
- [ ] Regulator/rectifier defective (Chapter 9).
- [ ] Alternator stator coil open or shorted (Chapter 9).
- [ ] Wiring faulty. Wiring grounded (earthed) or connections loose in ignition, charging or lighting circuits (Chapter 9).

Battery overcharged
- [ ] Regulator/rectifier defective. Overcharging is noticed when battery gets excessively warm (Chapter 9).
- [ ] Battery defective. Renew battery (Chapter 9).
- [ ] Battery amperage too low, wrong type or size. Install manufacturer's specified amp-hour battery to handle charging load (Chapter 9).

REF•44 Fault Finding Equipment

Checking engine compression

● Low compression will result in exhaust smoke, heavy oil consumption, poor starting and poor performance. A compression test will provide useful information about an engine's condition and if performed regularly, can give warning of trouble before any other symptoms become apparent.
● A compression gauge will be required, along with an adapter to suit the spark plug hole thread size. Note that the screw-in type gauge/adapter set up is preferable to the rubber cone type.
● Before carrying out the test, first check the valve clearances as described in Chapter 1.

1 Run the engine until it reaches normal operating temperature, then stop it and remove the spark plug(s), taking care not to scald your hands on the hot components.
2 Install the gauge adapter and compression gauge in No. 1 cylinder spark plug hole (see illustration 1).

Screw the compression gauge adapter into the spark plug hole, then screw the gauge into the adapter

3 On kickstart-equipped motorcycles, make sure the ignition switch is OFF, then open the throttle fully and kick the engine over a couple of times until the gauge reading stabilises.
4 On motorcycles with electric start only, the procedure will differ depending on the nature of the ignition system. Flick the engine kill switch (engine stop switch) to OFF and turn the ignition switch ON; open the throttle fully and crank the engine over on the starter motor for a couple of revolutions until the gauge reading stabilises. If the starter will not operate with the kill switch OFF, turn the ignition switch OFF and refer to the next paragraph.
5 Install the plugs back in their caps and arrange the plug electrodes so that their metal bodies are earthed (grounded) against the cylinder head; this is essential to prevent damage to the ignition system (see illustration 2). Position the plugs well away from the plug holes otherwise there is a risk of

All spark plugs must be earthed (grounded) against the cylinder head

atomised fuel escaping from the plug holes and igniting. As a safety precaution, cover the cylinder head cover with rag and disconnect the fuel pump wiring connector (see Chapter 4). Turn the ignition switch and kill switch ON, open the throttle fully and crank the engine over on the starter motor for a couple of revolutions until the gauge reading stabilises.
6 After one or two revolutions the pressure should build up to a maximum figure and then stabilise. Take a note of this reading and on multi-cylinder engines repeat the test on the remaining cylinders.
7 The correct pressures are given in Chapter 1 Specifications. If the results fall within the specified range and on multi-cylinder engines all are relatively equal, the engine is in good condition. If there is a marked difference between the readings, or if the readings are lower than specified, inspection of the top-end components will be required.
8 Low compression pressure may be due to worn cylinder bores, pistons or rings, failure of the cylinder head gasket, worn valve seals, or poor valve seating.
9 To distinguish between cylinder/piston wear and valve leakage, pour a small quantity of oil into the bore to temporarily seal the piston rings, then repeat the compression

Bores can be temporarily sealed with a squirt of motor oil

tests (see illustration 3). If the readings show a noticeable increase in pressure this confirms that the cylinder bore, piston, or rings are worn. If, however, no change is indicated, the cylinder head gasket or valves should be examined.
10 High compression pressure indicates excessive carbon build-up in the combustion chamber and on the piston crown. If this is the case the cylinder head should be removed and the deposits removed. Note that excessive carbon build-up is less likely with the used on modern fuels.

Checking battery open-circuit voltage

⚠ *Warning: The gases produced by the battery are explosive - never smoke or create any sparks in the vicinity of the battery. Never allow the electrolyte to contact your skin or clothing - if it does, wash it off and seek immediate*

Fault Finding Equipment REF•45

Measuring open-circuit battery voltage

Float-type hydrometer for measuring battery specific gravity

- Before any electrical fault is investigated the battery should be checked.
- You'll need a dc voltmeter or multimeter to check battery voltage. Check that the leads are inserted in the correct terminals on the meter, red lead to positive (+ve), black lead to negative (-ve). Incorrect connections can damage the meter.
- A sound fully-charged 12 volt battery should produce between 12.3 and 12.6 volts across its terminals (12.8 volts for a maintenance-free battery). On machines with a 6 volt battery, voltage should be between 6.1 and 6.3 volts.

1 Set a multimeter to the 0 to 20 volts dc range and connect its probes across the battery terminals. Connect the meter's positive (+ve) probe, usually red, to the battery positive (+ve) terminal, followed by the meter's negative (-ve) probe, usually black, to the battery negative terminal (-ve) **(see illustration 4)**.

2 If battery voltage is low (below 10 volts on a 12 volt battery or below 4 volts on a six volt battery), charge the battery and test the voltage again. If the battery repeatedly goes flat, investigate the motorcycle's charging system.

Checking battery specific gravity (SG)

> ⚠️ **Warning: The gases produced by the battery are explosive - never smoke or create any sparks in the vicinity of the battery. Never allow the electrolyte to contact your skin or clothing - if it does, wash it off and seek immediate medical attention.**

- The specific gravity check gives an indication of a battery's state of charge.
- A hydrometer is used for measuring specific gravity. Make sure you purchase one which has a small enough hose to insert in the aperture of a motorcycle battery.
- Specific gravity is simply a measure of the electrolyte's density compared with that of water. Water has an SG of 1.000 and fully-charged battery electrolyte is about 26% heavier, at 1.260.
- Specific gravity checks are not possible on maintenance-free batteries. Testing the open-circuit voltage is the only means of determining their state of charge.

1 To measure SG, remove the battery from the motorcycle and remove the first cell cap. Draw

Digital multimeter can be used for all electrical tests

Battery-powered continuity tester

some electrolyte into the hydrometer and note the reading **(see illustration 5)**. Return the electrolyte to the cell and install the cap.

2 The reading should be in the region of 1.260 to 1.280. If SG is below 1.200 the battery needs charging. Note that SG will vary with temperature; it should be measured at 20°C (68°F). Add 0.007 to the reading for every 10°C above 20°C, and subtract 0.007 from the reading for every 10°C below 20°C. Add 0.004 to the reading for every 10°F above 68°F, and subtract 0.004 from the reading for every 10°F below 68°F.

3 When the check is complete, rinse the hydrometer thoroughly with clean water.

Checking for continuity

- The term continuity describes the uninterrupted flow of electricity through an electrical circuit. A continuity check will determine whether an **open-circuit** situation exists.
- Continuity can be checked with an ohmmeter, multimeter, continuity tester or battery and bulb test circuit **(see illustrations 6, 7 and 8)**.

Battery and bulb test circuit

REF•46 Fault Finding Equipment

Continuity check of front brake light switch using a meter - note split pins used to access connector terminals

Continuity check of rear brake light switch using a continuity tester

- All of these instruments are self-powered by a battery, therefore the checks are made with the ignition OFF.
- As a safety precaution, always disconnect the battery negative (-ve) lead before making checks, particularly if ignition switch checks are being made.
- If using a meter, select the appropriate ohms scale and check that the meter reads infinity (∞). Touch the meter probes together and check that meter reads zero; where necessary adjust the meter so that it reads zero.
- After using a meter, always switch it OFF to conserve its battery.

Switch checks

1 If a switch is at fault, trace its wiring up to the wiring connectors. Separate the wire connectors and inspect them for security and condition. A build-up of dirt or corrosion here will most likely be the cause of the problem - clean up and apply a water dispersant such as WD40.

2 If using a test meter, set the meter to the ohms x 10 scale and connect its probes across the wires from the switch (see illustration 9). Simple ON/OFF type switches, such as brake light switches, only have two wires whereas combination switches, like the ignition switch, have many internal links. Study the wiring diagram to ensure that you are connecting across the correct pair of wires. Continuity (low or no measurable resistance - 0 ohms) should be indicated with the switch ON and no continuity (high resistance) with it OFF.

3 Note that the polarity of the test probes doesn't matter for continuity checks, although care should be taken to follow specific test procedures if a diode or solid-state component is being checked.

4 A continuity tester or battery and bulb circuit can be used in the same way. Connect its probes as described above (see illustration 10). The light should come on to indicate continuity in the ON switch position, but should extinguish in the OFF position.

Wiring checks

- Many electrical faults are caused by damaged wiring, often due to incorrect routing or chaffing on frame components.
- Loose, wet or corroded wire connectors can also be the cause of electrical problems, especially in exposed locations.

1 A continuity check can be made on a single length of wire by disconnecting it at each end and connecting a meter or continuity tester across both ends of the wire (see illustration 11).

2 Continuity (low or no resistance - 0 ohms) should be indicated if the wire is good. If no continuity (high resistance) is shown, suspect a broken wire.

Checking for voltage

- A voltage check can determine whether current is reaching a component.
- Voltage can be checked with a dc voltmeter, multimeter set on the dc volts scale, test light or buzzer (see illustrations 12 and 13). A meter has the advantage of being able to measure actual voltage.
- When using a meter, check that its leads are inserted in the correct terminals on the meter, red to positive (+ve), black to negative (-ve). Incorrect connections can damage the meter.
- A voltmeter (or multimeter set to the dc volts scale) should always be connected in parallel (across the load). Connecting it in series will not harm the meter, but the reading will not be meaningful.
- Voltage checks are made with the ignition ON.

Continuity check of front brake light switch sub-harness

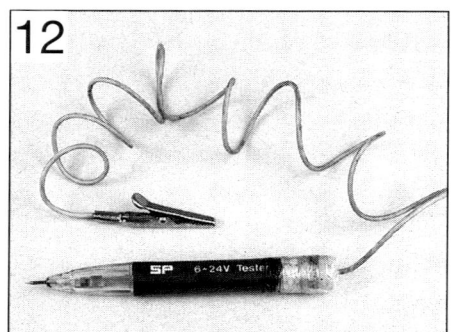

A simple test light can be used for voltage checks

A buzzer is useful for voltage checks

Fault Finding Equipment   REF•47

Checking for voltage at the rear brake light power supply wire using a meter . . .

1 First identify the relevant wiring circuit by referring to the wiring diagram at the end of this manual. If other electrical components share the same power supply (ie are fed from the same fuse), take note whether they are working correctly - this is useful information in deciding where to start checking the circuit.

2 If using a meter, check first that the meter leads are plugged into the correct terminals on the meter (see above). Set the meter to the dc volts function, at a range suitable for the battery voltage. Connect the meter red probe (+ve) to the power supply wire and the black probe to a good metal earth (ground) on the motorcycle's frame or directly to the battery negative (-ve) terminal **(see illustration 14)**. Battery voltage should be shown on the meter

A selection of jumper wires for making earth (ground) checks

. . . or a test light - note the earth connection to the frame (arrow)

with the ignition switched ON.

3 If using a test light or buzzer, connect its positive (+ve) probe to the power supply terminal and its negative (-ve) probe to a good earth (ground) on the motorcycle's frame or directly to the battery negative (-ve) terminal **(see illustration 15)**. With the ignition ON, the test light should illuminate or the buzzer sound.

4 If no voltage is indicated, work back towards the fuse continuing to check for voltage. When you reach a point where there is voltage, you know the problem lies between that point and your last check point.

Checking the earth (ground)

● Earth connections are made either directly to the engine or frame (such as sensors, neutral switch etc. which only have a positive feed) or by a separate wire into the earth circuit of the wiring harness. Alternatively a short earth wire is sometimes run directly from the component to the motorcycle's frame.
● Corrosion is often the cause of a poor earth connection.
● If total failure is experienced, check the security of the main earth lead from the negative (-ve) terminal of the battery and also the main earth (ground) point on the wiring harness. If corroded, dismantle the connection and clean all surfaces back to bare metal.

1 To check the earth on a component, use an insulated jumper wire to temporarily bypass its earth connection **(see illustration 16)**. Connect one end of the jumper wire between the earth terminal or metal body of the component and the other end to the motorcycle's frame.

2 If the circuit works with the jumper wire installed, the original earth circuit is faulty. Check the wiring for open-circuits or poor connections. Clean up direct earth connections, removing all traces of corrosion and remake the joint. Apply petroleum jelly to the joint to prevent future corrosion.

Tracing a short-circuit

● A short-circuit occurs where current shorts to earth (ground) bypassing the circuit components. This usually results in a blown fuse.

● A short-circuit is most likely to occur where the insulation has worn through due to wiring chafing on a component, allowing a direct path to earth (ground) on the frame.

1 Remove any bodypanels necessary to access the circuit wiring.
2 Check that all electrical switches in the circuit are OFF, then remove the circuit fuse and connect a test light, buzzer or voltmeter (set to the dc scale) across the fuse terminals. No voltage should be shown.
3 Move the wiring from side to side whilst observing the test light or meter. When the test light comes on, buzzer sounds or meter shows voltage, you have found the cause of the short. It will usually shown up as damaged or burned insulation.
4 Note that the same test can be performed on each component in the circuit, even the switch.

Technical Terms Explained

A

ABS (Anti-lock braking system) A system, usually electronically controlled, that senses incipient wheel lockup during braking and relieves hydraulic pressure at wheel which is about to skid.
Aftermarket Components suitable for the motorcycle, but not produced by the motorcycle manufacturer.
Allen key A hexagonal wrench which fits into a recessed hexagonal hole.
Alternating current (ac) Current produced by an alternator. Requires converting to direct current by a rectifier for charging purposes.
Alternator Converts mechanical energy from the engine into electrical energy to charge the battery and power the electrical system.
Ampere (amp) A unit of measurement for the flow of electrical current. Current = Volts ÷ Ohms.
Ampere-hour (Ah) Measure of battery capacity.
Angle-tightening A torque expressed in degrees. Often follows a conventional tightening torque for cylinder head or main bearing fasteners **(see illustration)**.

Angle-tightening cylinder head bolts

Antifreeze A substance (usually ethylene glycol) mixed with water, and added to the cooling system, to prevent freezing of the coolant in winter. Antifreeze also contains chemicals to inhibit corrosion and the formation of rust and other deposits that would tend to clog the radiator and coolant passages and reduce cooling efficiency.
Anti-dive System attached to the fork lower leg (slider) to prevent fork dive when braking hard.
Anti-seize compound A coating that reduces the risk of seizing on fasteners that are subjected to high temperatures, such as exhaust clamp bolts and nuts.
API American Petroleum Institute. A quality standard for 4-stroke motor oils.
Asbestos A natural fibrous mineral with great heat resistance, commonly used in the composition of brake friction materials. Asbestos is a health hazard and the dust created by brake systems should never be inhaled or ingested.
ATF Automatic Transmission Fluid. Often used in front forks.
ATU Automatic Timing Unit. Mechanical device for advancing the ignition timing on early engines.
ATV All Terrain Vehicle. Often called a Quad.
Axial play Side-to-side movement.
Axle A shaft on which a wheel revolves. Also known as a spindle.

B

Backlash The amount of movement between meshed components when one component is held still. Usually applies to gear teeth.
Ball bearing A bearing consisting of a hardened inner and outer race with hardened steel balls between the two races.
Bearings Used between two working surfaces to prevent wear of the components and a build-up of heat. Four types of bearing are commonly used on motorcycles: plain shell bearings, ball bearings, tapered roller bearings and needle roller bearings.
Bevel gears Used to turn the drive through 90°. Typical applications are shaft final drive and camshaft drive **(see illustration)**.

Bevel gears are used to turn the drive through 90°

BHP Brake Horsepower. The British measurement for engine power output. Power output is now usually expressed in kilowatts (kW).
Bias-belted tyre Similar construction to radial tyre, but with outer belt running at an angle to the wheel rim.
Big-end bearing The bearing in the end of the connecting rod that's attached to the crankshaft.
Bleeding The process of removing air from an hydraulic system via a bleed nipple or bleed screw.
Bottom-end A description of an engine's crankcase components and all components contained there-in.
BTDC Before Top Dead Centre in terms of piston position. Ignition timing is often expressed in terms of degrees or millimetres BTDC.
Bush A cylindrical metal or rubber component used between two moving parts.
Burr Rough edge left on a component after machining or as a result of excessive wear.

C

Cam chain The chain which takes drive from the crankshaft to the camshaft(s).
Canister The main component in an evaporative emission control system (California market only); contains activated charcoal granules to trap vapours from the fuel system rather than allowing them to vent to the atmosphere.
Castellated Resembling the parapets along the top of a castle wall. For example, a castellated wheel axle or spindle nut.
Catalytic converter A device in the exhaust system of some machines which converts certain pollutants in the exhaust gases into less harmful substances.
Charging system Description of the components which charge the battery, ie the alternator, rectifer and regulator.
Circlip A ring-shaped clip used to prevent endwise movement of cylindrical parts and shafts. An internal circlip is installed in a groove in a housing; an external circlip fits into a groove on the outside of a cylindrical piece such as a shaft. Also known as a snap-ring.
Clearance The amount of space between two parts. For example, between a piston and a cylinder, between a bearing and a journal, etc.
Coil spring A spiral of elastic steel found in various sizes throughout a vehicle, for example as a springing medium in the suspension and in the valve train.
Compression Reduction in volume, and increase in pressure and temperature, of a gas, caused by squeezing it into a smaller space.
Compression damping Controls the speed the suspension compresses when hitting a bump.
Compression ratio The relationship between cylinder volume when the piston is at top dead centre and cylinder volume when the piston is at bottom dead centre.
Continuity The uninterrupted path in the flow of electricity. Little or no measurable resistance.
Continuity tester Self-powered bleeper or test light which indicates continuity.
Cp Candlepower. Bulb rating commonly found on US motorcycles.
Crossply tyre Tyre plies arranged in a criss-cross pattern. Usually four or six plies used, hence 4PR or 6PR in tyre size codes.
Cush drive Rubber damper segments fitted between the rear wheel and final drive sprocket to absorb transmission shocks **(see illustration)**.

Cush drive rubbers dampen out transmission shocks

D

Degree disc Calibrated disc for measuring piston position. Expressed in degrees.
Dial gauge Clock-type gauge with adapters for measuring runout and piston position. Expressed in mm or inches.
Diaphragm The rubber membrane in a master cylinder or carburettor which seals the upper chamber.
Diaphragm spring A single sprung plate often used in clutches.
Direct current (dc) Current produced by a dc generator.

Technical Terms Explained REF•49

Decarbonisation The process of removing carbon deposits - typically from the combustion chamber, valves and exhaust port/system.

Detonation Destructive and damaging explosion of fuel/air mixture in combustion chamber instead of controlled burning.

Diode An electrical valve which only allows current to flow in one direction. Commonly used in rectifiers and starter interlock systems.

Disc valve (or rotary valve) A induction system used on some two-stroke engines.

Double-overhead camshaft (DOHC) An engine that uses two overhead camshafts, one for the intake valves and one for the exhaust valves.

Drivebelt A toothed belt used to transmit drive to the rear wheel on some motorcycles. A drivebelt has also been used to drive the camshafts. Drivebelts are usually made of Kevlar.

Driveshaft Any shaft used to transmit motion. Commonly used when referring to the final driveshaft on shaft drive motorcycles.

E

Earth return The return path of an electrical circuit, utilising the motorcycle's frame.

ECU (Electronic Control Unit) A computer which controls (for instance) an ignition system, or an anti-lock braking system.

EGO Exhaust Gas Oxygen sensor. Sometimes called a Lambda sensor.

Electrolyte The fluid in a lead-acid battery.

EMS (Engine Management System) A computer controlled system which manages the fuel injection and the ignition systems in an integrated fashion.

Endfloat The amount of lengthways movement between two parts. As applied to a crankshaft, the distance that the crankshaft can move side-to-side in the crankcase.

Endless chain A chain having no joining link. Common use for cam chains and final drive chains.

EP (Extreme Pressure) Oil type used in locations where high loads are applied, such as between gear teeth.

Evaporative emission control system Describes a charcoal filled canister which stores fuel vapours from the tank rather than allowing them to vent to the atmosphere. Usually only fitted to California models and referred to as an EVAP system.

Expansion chamber Section of two-stroke engine exhaust system so designed to improve engine efficiency and boost power.

F

Feeler blade or gauge A thin strip or blade of hardened steel, ground to an exact thickness, used to check or measure clearances between parts.

Final drive Description of the drive from the transmission to the rear wheel. Usually by chain or shaft, but sometimes by belt.

Firing order The order in which the engine cylinders fire, or deliver their power strokes, beginning with the number one cylinder.

Flooding Term used to describe a high fuel level in the carburettor float chambers, leading to fuel overflow. Also refers to excess fuel in the combustion chamber due to incorrect starting technique.

Free length The no-load state of a component when measured. Clutch, valve and fork spring lengths are measured at rest, without any preload.

Freeplay The amount of travel before any action takes place. The looseness in a linkage, or an assembly of parts, between the initial application of force and actual movement. For example, the distance the rear brake pedal moves before the rear brake is actuated.

Fuel injection The fuel/air mixture is metered electronically and directed into the engine intake ports (indirect injection) or into the cylinders (direct injection). Sensors supply information on engine speed and conditions.

Fuel/air mixture The charge of fuel and air going into the engine. See **Stoichiometric ratio**.

Fuse An electrical device which protects a circuit against accidental overload. The typical fuse contains a soft piece of metal which is calibrated to melt at a predetermined current flow (expressed as amps) and break the circuit.

G

Gap The distance the spark must travel in jumping from the centre electrode to the side electrode in a spark plug. Also refers to the distance between the ignition rotor and the pickup coil in an electronic ignition system.

Gasket Any thin, soft material - usually cork, cardboard, asbestos or soft metal - installed between two metal surfaces to ensure a good seal. For instance, the cylinder head gasket seals the joint between the block and the cylinder head.

Gauge An instrument panel display used to monitor engine conditions. A gauge with a movable pointer on a dial or a fixed scale is an analogue gauge. A gauge with a numerical readout is called a digital gauge.

Gear ratios The drive ratio of a pair of gears in a gearbox, calculated on their number of teeth.

Glaze-busting see **Honing**

Grinding Process for renovating the valve face and valve seat contact area in the cylinder head.

Gudgeon pin The shaft which connects the connecting rod small-end with the piston. Often called a piston pin or wrist pin.

H

Helical gears Gear teeth are slightly curved and produce less gear noise that straight-cut gears. Often used for primary drives.

Installing a Helicoil thread insert in a cylinder head

Helicoil A thread insert repair system. Commonly used as a repair for stripped spark plug threads **(see illustration)**.

Honing A process used to break down the glaze on a cylinder bore (also called glaze-busting). Can also be carried out to roughen a rebored cylinder to aid ring bedding-in.

HT (High Tension) Description of the electrical circuit from the secondary winding of the ignition coil to the spark plug.

Hydraulic A liquid filled system used to transmit pressure from one component to another. Common uses on motorcycles are brakes and clutches.

Hydrometer An instrument for measuring the specific gravity of a lead-acid battery.

Hygroscopic Water absorbing. In motorcycle applications, braking efficiency will be reduced if DOT 3 or 4 hydraulic fluid absorbs water from the air - care must be taken to keep new brake fluid in tightly sealed containers.

I

lbf ft Pounds-force feet. An imperial unit of torque. Sometimes written as ft-lbs.

lbf in Pound-force inch. An imperial unit of torque, applied to components where a very low torque is required. Sometimes written as in-lbs.

IC Abbreviation for Integrated Circuit.

Ignition advance Means of increasing the timing of the spark at higher engine speeds. Done by mechanical means (ATU) on early engines or electronically by the ignition control unit on later engines.

Ignition timing The moment at which the spark plug fires, expressed in the number of crankshaft degrees before the piston reaches the top of its stroke, or in the number of millimetres before the piston reaches the top of its stroke.

Infinity (∞) Description of an open-circuit electrical state, where no continuity exists.

Inverted forks (upside down forks) The sliders or lower legs are held in the yokes and the fork tubes or stanchions are connected to the wheel axle (spindle). Less unsprung weight and stiffer construction than conventional forks.

J

JASO Quality standard for 2-stroke oils.

Joule The unit of electrical energy.

Journal The bearing surface of a shaft.

K

Kickstart Mechanical means of turning the engine over for starting purposes. Only usually fitted to mopeds, small capacity motorcycles and off-road motorcycles.

Kill switch Handebar-mounted switch for emergency ignition cut-out. Cuts the ignition circuit on all models, and additionally prevent starter motor operation on others.

km Symbol for kilometre.

kmh Abbreviation for kilometres per hour.

L

Lambda (λ) sensor A sensor fitted in the exhaust system to measure the exhaust gas oxygen content (excess air factor).

Technical Terms Explained

Lapping see **Grinding**.
LCD Abbreviation for Liquid Crystal Display.
LED Abbreviation for Light Emitting Diode.
Liner A steel cylinder liner inserted in a aluminium alloy cylinder block.
Locknut A nut used to lock an adjustment nut, or other threaded component, in place.
Lockstops The lugs on the lower triple clamp (yoke) which abut those on the frame, preventing handlebar-to-fuel tank contact.
Lockwasher A form of washer designed to prevent an attaching nut from working loose.
LT Low Tension Description of the electrical circuit from the power supply to the primary winding of the ignition coil.

M

Main bearings The bearings between the crankshaft and crankcase.
Maintenance-free (MF) battery A sealed battery which cannot be topped up.
Manometer Mercury-filled calibrated tubes used to measure intake tract vacuum. Used to synchronise carburettors on multi-cylinder engines.
Micrometer A precision measuring instrument that measures component outside diameters **(see illustration)**.

Tappet shims are measured with a micrometer

MON (Motor Octane Number) A measure of a fuel's resistance to knock.
Monograde oil An oil with a single viscosity, eg SAE80W.
Monoshock A single suspension unit linking the swingarm or suspension linkage to the frame.
mph Abbreviation for miles per hour.
Multigrade oil Having a wide viscosity range (eg 10W40). The W stands for Winter, thus the viscosity ranges from SAE10 when cold to SAE40 when hot.
Multimeter An electrical test instrument with the capability to measure voltage, current and resistance. Some meters also incorporate a continuity tester and buzzer.

N

Needle roller bearing Inner race of caged needle rollers and hardened outer race. Examples of uncaged needle rollers can be found on some engines. Commonly used in rear suspension applications and in two-stroke engines.
Nm Newton metres.
NOx Oxides of Nitrogen. A common toxic pollutant emitted by petrol engines at higher temperatures.

O

Octane The measure of a fuel's resistance to knock.
OE (Original Equipment) Relates to components fitted to a motorcycle as standard or replacement parts supplied by the motorcycle manufacturer.
Ohm The unit of electrical resistance. Ohms = Volts ÷ Current.
Ohmmeter An instrument for measuring electrical resistance.
Oil cooler System for diverting engine oil outside of the engine to a radiator for cooling purposes.
Oil injection A system of two-stroke engine lubrication where oil is pump-fed to the engine in accordance with throttle position.
Open-circuit An electrical condition where there is a break in the flow of electricity - no continuity (high resistance).
O-ring A type of sealing ring made of a special rubber-like material; in use, the O-ring is compressed into a groove to provide the sealing action.
Oversize (OS) Term used for piston and ring size options fitted to a rebored cylinder.
Overhead cam (sohc) engine An engine with single camshaft located on top of the cylinder head.
Overhead valve (ohv) engine An engine with the valves located in the cylinder head, but with the camshaft located in the engine block or crankcase.
Oxygen sensor A device installed in the exhaust system which senses the oxygen content in the exhaust and converts this information into an electric current. Also called a Lambda sensor.

P

Plastigauge A thin strip of plastic thread, available in different sizes, used for measuring clearances. For example, a strip of Plastigauge is laid across a bearing journal. The parts are assembled and dismantled; the width of the crushed strip indicates the clearance between journal and bearing.
Polarity Either negative or positive earth (ground), determined by which battery lead is connected to the frame (earth return). Modern motorcycles are usually negative earth.
Pre-ignition A situation where the fuel/air mixture ignites before the spark plug fires. Often due to a hot spot in the combustion chamber caused by carbon build-up. Engine has a tendency to 'run-on'.
Pre-load (suspension) The amount a spring is compressed when in the unloaded state. Preload can be applied by gas, spacer or mechanical adjuster.
Premix The method of engine lubrication on older two-stroke engines. Engine oil is mixed with the petrol in the fuel tank in a specific ratio. The fuel/oil mix is sometimes referred to as "petroil".
Primary drive Description of the drive from the crankshaft to the clutch. Usually by gear or chain.
PS Pfedestärke - a German interpretation of BHP.
PSI Pounds-force per square inch. Imperial measurement of tyre pressure and cylinder pressure measurement.
PTFE Polytetrafluoroethylene. A low friction substance.
Pulse secondary air injection system A process of promoting the burning of excess fuel present in the exhaust gases by routing fresh air into the exhaust ports.

Q

Quartz halogen bulb Tungsten filament surrounded by a halogen gas. Typically used for the headlight **(see illustration)**.

Quartz halogen headlight bulb construction

R

Rack-and-pinion A pinion gear on the end of a shaft that mates with a rack (think of a geared wheel opened up and laid flat). Sometimes used in clutch operating systems.
Radial play Up and down movement about a shaft.
Radial ply tyres Tyre plies run across the tyre (from bead to bead) and around the circumference of the tyre. Less resistant to tread distortion than other tyre types.
Radiator A liquid-to-air heat transfer device designed to reduce the temperature of the coolant in a liquid cooled engine.
Rake A feature of steering geometry - the angle of the steering head in relation to the vertical **(see illustration)**.

Steering geometry

Technical Terms Explained

Rebore Providing a new working surface to the cylinder bore by boring out the old surface. Necessitates the use of oversize piston and rings.

Rebound damping A means of controlling the oscillation of a suspension unit spring after it has been compressed. Resists the spring's natural tendency to bounce back after being compressed.

Rectifier Device for converting the ac output of an alternator into dc for battery charging.

Reed valve An induction system commonly used on two-stroke engines.

Regulator Device for maintaining the charging voltage from the generator or alternator within a specified range.

Relay A electrical device used to switch heavy current on and off by using a low current auxiliary circuit.

Resistance Measured in ohms. An electrical component's ability to pass electrical current.

RON (Research Octane Number) A measure of a fuel's resistance to knock.

rpm revolutions per minute.

Runout The amount of wobble (in-and-out movement) of a wheel or shaft as it's rotated. The amount a shaft rotates 'out-of-true'. The out-of-round condition of a rotating part.

S

SAE (Society of Automotive Engineers) A standard for the viscosity of a fluid.

Sealant A liquid or paste used to prevent leakage at a joint. Sometimes used in conjunction with a gasket.

Service limit Term for the point where a component is no longer useable and must be renewed.

Shaft drive A method of transmitting drive from the transmission to the rear wheel.

Shell bearings Plain bearings consisting of two shell halves. Most often used as big-end and main bearings in a four-stroke engine. Often called bearing inserts.

Shim Thin spacer, commonly used to adjust the clearance or relative positions between two parts. For example, shims inserted into or under tappets or followers to control valve clearances. Clearance is adjusted by changing the thickness of the shim.

Short-circuit An electrical condition where current shorts to earth (ground) bypassing the circuit components.

Skimming Process to correct warpage or repair a damaged surface, eg on brake discs or drums.

Slide-hammer A special puller that screws into or hooks onto a component such as a shaft or bearing; a heavy sliding handle on the shaft bottoms against the end of the shaft to knock the component free.

Small-end bearing The bearing in the upper end of the connecting rod at its joint with the gudgeon pin.

Spalling Damage to camshaft lobes or bearing journals shown as pitting of the working surface.

Specific gravity (SG) The state of charge of the electrolyte in a lead-acid battery. A measure of the electrolyte's density compared with water.

Straight-cut gears Common type gear used on gearbox shafts and for oil pump and water pump drives.

Stanchion The inner sliding part of the front forks, held by the yokes. Often called a fork tube.

Stoichiometric ratio The optimum chemical air/fuel ratio for a petrol engine, said to be 14.7 parts of air to 1 part of fuel.

Sulphuric acid The liquid (electrolyte) used in a lead-acid battery. Poisonous and extremely corrosive.

Surface grinding (lapping) Process to correct a warped gasket face, commonly used on cylinder heads.

T

Tapered-roller bearing Tapered inner race of caged needle rollers and separate tapered outer race. Examples of taper roller bearings can be found on steering heads.

Tappet A cylindrical component which transmits motion from the cam to the valve stem, either directly or via a pushrod and rocker arm. Also called a cam follower.

TCS Traction Control System. An electronically-controlled system which senses wheel spin and reduces engine speed accordingly.

TDC Top Dead Centre denotes that the piston is at its highest point in the cylinder.

Thread-locking compound Solution applied to fastener threads to prevent slackening. Select type to suit application.

Thrust washer A washer positioned between two moving components on a shaft. For example, between gear pinions on gearshaft.

Timing chain See **Cam Chain**.

Timing light Stroboscopic lamp for carrying out ignition timing checks with the engine running.

Top-end A description of an engine's cylinder block, head and valve gear components.

Torque Turning or twisting force about a shaft.

Torque setting A prescribed tightness specified by the motorcycle manufacturer to ensure that the bolt or nut is secured correctly. Undertightening can result in the bolt or nut coming loose or a surface not being sealed. Overtightening can result in stripped threads, distortion or damage to the component being retained.

Torx key A six-point wrench.

Tracer A stripe of a second colour applied to a wire insulator to distinguish that wire from another one with the same colour insulator. For example, Br/W is often used to denote a brown insulator with a white tracer.

Trail A feature of steering geometry. Distance from the steering head axis to the tyre's central contact point.

Triple clamps The cast components which extend from the steering head and support the fork stanchions or tubes. Often called fork yokes.

Turbocharger A centrifugal device, driven by exhaust gases, that pressurises the intake air. Normally used to increase the power output from a given engine displacement.

TWI Abbreviation for Tyre Wear Indicator. Indicates the location of the tread depth indicator bars on tyres.

U

Universal joint or U-joint (UJ) A double-pivoted connection for transmitting power from a driving to a driven shaft through an angle. Typically found in shaft drive assemblies.

Unsprung weight Anything not supported by the bike's suspension (ie the wheel, tyres, brakes, final drive and bottom (moving) part of the suspension).

V

Vacuum gauges Clock-type gauges for measuring intake tract vacuum. Used for carburettor synchronisation on multi-cylinder engines.

Valve A device through which the flow of liquid, gas or vacuum may be stopped, started or regulated by a moveable part that opens, shuts or partially obstructs one or more ports or passageways. The intake and exhaust valves in the cylinder head are of the poppet type.

Valve clearance The clearance between the valve tip (the end of the valve stem) and the rocker arm or tappet/follower. The valve clearance is measured when the valve is closed. The correct clearance is important - if too small the valve won't close fully and will burn out, whereas if too large noisy operation will result.

Valve lift The amount a valve is lifted off its seat by the camshaft lobe.

Valve timing The exact setting for the opening and closing of the valves in relation to piston position.

Vernier caliper A precision measuring instrument that measures inside and outside dimensions. Not quite as accurate as a micrometer, but more convenient.

VIN Vehicle Identification Number. Term for the bike's engine and frame numbers.

Viscosity The thickness of a liquid or its resistance to flow.

Volt A unit for expressing electrical "pressure" in a circuit. Volts = current x ohms.

W

Water pump A mechanically-driven device for moving coolant around the engine.

Watt A unit for expressing electrical power. Watts = volts x current.

Wear limit see **Service limit**

Wet liner A liquid-cooled engine design where the pistons run in liners which are directly surrounded by coolant **(see illustration)**.

Wet liner arrangement

Wheelbase Distance from the centre of the front wheel to the centre of the rear wheel.

Wiring harness or loom Describes the electrical wires running the length of the motorcycle and enclosed in tape or plastic sheathing. Wiring coming off the main harness is usually referred to as a sub harness.

Woodruff key A key of semi-circular or square section used to locate a gear to a shaft. Often used to locate the alternator rotor on the crankshaft.

Wrist pin Another name for gudgeon or piston pin.

Index

Note: *References throughout this index are in the form - "Chapter number" • "Page number"*

A

Air filter
　cleaning and renewal – 1•10
　housing – 4•4
Air/fuel mixture adjustment – 4•4
Air induction system (AIS) – 1•12, 4•20
Alternator – 9•20

B

Battery
　charging – 9•3
　check – 1•15
　removal and installation – 9•3
Brake
　calipers – 7•4, 7•10
　discs – 7•5, 7•12
　general information – 7•2
　fault finding – REF•42
　fluid level check – 0•14
　hoses and unions – 1•24, 7•15
　lever – 6•2
　light bulbs – 9•7
　light switches – 9•8
　master cylinder – 7•6, 7•12
　pads – 1•13, 7•2, 7•9
　pedal – 6•2
　seal renewal – 1•24
　specifications – 7•1
　system bleeding – 7•15
　system check – 1•13
Bulbs
　headlight and sidelight – 9•6
　instrument and warning light bulbs – 9•11
　tail light – 9•7
　turn signal – 9•8
　wattage – 9•2

C

Cables
　choke – 1•17, 4•15
　clutch – 1•14, 2•27
　throttle – 1•17, 4•13
Calipers
　front brake – 7•4
　rear brake – 7•12
Cam chain and blades – 2•10
Camshaft and followers – 2•12 to 2•16
Carburettor
　disassembly and inspection – 4•6
　overhaul – 4•4
　reassembly, float height and fuel level check – 4•11
　removal and installation – 4•5
　separation and joining – 4•9
　synchronisation – 1•9
　throttle position sensor – 5•5
Chain (cam) – 2•10
Chain (final drive) – 1•6, 6•17
Charging system
　alternator – 9•20
　battery – 9•3
　charging system – 9•19
　regulator/rectifier – 9•22
　testing – 9•19

Choke cable – 1•17, 4•15
Clutch
　cable – 2•27
　check and adjustment – 1•14
　fault finding – REF•39
　removal, inspection and installation – 2•21
　switch – 9•13
Connecting rods – 2•42
Conversion factors – REF•26
Coolant
　change – 1•23
　general information – 3•2
　hoses, pipes and unions – 3•7
　level check – 0•15
　reservoir – 3•2
　temperature warning LED and thermo unit – 3•3
Cooling fan and relay – 3•2
Cooling system check – 1•16
Crankcase and cylinder bore inspection and servicing – 2•39
Crankcase separation and reassembly – 2•36
Crankshaft and main bearings – 2•40
Cylinder head and valve overhaul – 2•17
Cylinder head removal and installation – 2•16

D

Disc (brake) – 7•5, 7•12
Drive chain and sprocket check, adjustment and lubrication – 1•6
Drive chain removal and installation – 6•17

E

Electrical system – 9•1 *et seq*
　alternator – 9•20
　battery charging – 9•3
　battery removal and installation – 9•3
　brake light switches – 9•8
　brake/tail light bulbs – 9•7
　charging system – 9•19
　clutch switch – 9•13
　fault finding – 9•2, REF•43
　fuel pump and relay – 4•18
　fuses – 9•4
　general information – 9•2
　handlebar switch check – 9•12
　handlebar switch housing removal and installation – 9•12
　headlight aim check and adjustment – 1•25
　headlight assembly – 9•6
　headlight and sidelight bulbs – 9•6
　horn – 9•14
　ignition (main) switch – 9•11
　instrument and warning light bulbs – 9•11
　instrument cluster removal and installation – 9•9
　instrument check and disassembly – 9•10
　lighting system check – 9•5
　neutral switch – 9•12
　oil level switch – 9•14
　regulator/rectifier – 9•22
　relay assembly – 9•14
　sidestand switch – 9•13
　specifications – 9•1
　starter motor overhaul – 9•16
　starter motor removal and installation – 9•15
　starter relay – 9•15

Index REF•53

tail light assembly – 9•7
turn signals – 9•8
turn signal bulbs – 9•8
turn signal circuit check – 9•7
wiring diagrams – 9•24
Engine – 2•1 *et seq*
  bearings – 2•40
  cam chain, tensioner and blades – 2•10
  camshaft and followers – 2•12
  connecting rods – 2•42
  crankcases – 2•36
  crankshaft and main bearings – 2•40
  cylinder bores – 2•39
  cylinder compression check – 1•25, REF•44
  cylinder head removal and installation – 2•16
  disassembly and reassembly general information – 2•8
  fault finding – REF•37, REF•39
  general information – 2•4
  oil cooler – 2•9
  oil and filter change – 1•12, 1•20
  oil level check – 0•13
  oil pressure check – 1•25
  oil pump – 2•33
  piston rings – 2•46
  pistons – 2•44
  removal and installation – 2•5
  running-in – 2•54
  specifications – 2•1
  starter clutch and idle/reduction – 2•27
  valve clearances – 1•21
  valve covers – 2•10
Engine number – 0•9
Exhaust system – 4•15
EXUP system – 1•11, 4•16

F

Fairing and body panels – 8•2
Fault finding – 9•2, REF•35
Front forks
  adjustment – 6•14
  overhaul – 6•7
  oil change – 1•25, 6•6
  removal and installation – 6•5
Footrests – 6•2
Frame – 6•2
Frame number – 0•9
Front fork oil change – 1•25, 6•6
Front mudguard – 8•4
Fuel filter – 1•11, 1•21
Fuel gauge and level sensor – 4•19
Fuel hose renewal – 1•25
Fuel level sensor check – 4•13
Fuel pump and relay – 4•18
Fuel tank and fuel tap – 4•2
Fuses – 9•2, 9•4

G

Gearbox shafts – 2•29
Gearchange lever – 6•2
Gearchange mechanism – 2•29

H

Headlight
  assembly – 9•6
  beam adjustment – 1•25
  bulbs – 9•2, 9•6

Handlebars and levers – 6•4
Handlebar switch check – 9•12
HT coils – 5•2
Horn – 9•14
Hoses and unions (brake) – 7•15

I

Idle speed check and adjustment – 1•8
Ignition
  control unit – 5•4
  HT coils – 5•2
  (main) switch – 9•11
  spark plugs – 1•7
  system check – 5•2
  throttle position sensor – 5•5
  timing – 5•4
Input shaft (gearbox) – 2•49
Instrument
  check and disassembly – 9•10
  cluster removal and installation – 9•9
  warning light bulbs – 9•11

L

Lights
  brake – 9•7
  bulbs – 9•2
  tail light assembly – 9•7
Lighting system check – 9•5
Lubrication (cable and pivots) – 1•6
Lubricants and fluids – REF•23

M

Main and connecting rod bearings information – 2•39
Maintenance schedule – 1•4
Master cylinder
  front – 7•6
  rear – 7•12
Mirrors – 8•4
MOT test checks – REF•27
Mudguard (front) – 8•4

N

Neutral switch – 9•12
Nut and bolt tightness check – 1•16

O

Oil and filter change – 1•12, 1•20,
Oil cooler – 2•9
Oil level check – 0•13
Oil level switch – 9•14
Oil pressure check – 1•25
Oil pump – 2•33
Oil sump, oil strainer and relief valve – 2•31
Output shaft (gearbox) – 2•50

P

Pads – 1•13, 7•2, 7•9
Pick-up coil – 5•3
Pistons – 2•44
Piston rings – 2•46
Pump
  fuel – 4•18
  oil – 2•33
  water – 3•6

Index

R

Radiator – 3•5
Radiator pressure cap – 3•2
Rear sprocket coupling/rubber dampers – 6•19
Rear shock absorber – 6•12
Rear suspension linkage – 6•13
Rear view mirrors – 8•4
Regulator/rectifier – 9•22
Relay
　fuel pump – 4•18
　starter cut-off – 9•14
　turn signal – 9•7
　starter – 9•15
Running-in procedure – 2•54

S

Seat – 8•2
Security – REF•20
Selector drum and forks – 2•53
Sensors
　fuel level – 4•13
　oil level – 9•14
　throttle position – 5•5
　tip-over – 5•6
Shock absorber (rear) – 6•12
Sidestand and centrestand removal and installation – 6•3
Sidestand switch – 9•13
Spark plugs – 1•7
Specifications – 0•10, 1•2, 2•1, 3•1, 4•1, 5•1, 6•1, 7•1, 9•1
Sprockets – 1•6, 6•18
Sprocket coupling bearing – 7•21
Starter clutch and idle/reduction gear – 2•27
Stand, lever pivot and cable lubrication – 1•17
Starter cut-off relay – 9•14
Starter motor
　overhaul – 9•16
　removal and installation – 9•15
Starter relay – 9•15
Steering head bearing
　check and adjustment – 1•18
　inspection – 6•11
　lubrication – 1•21
Steering stem and head bearings – 6•10
Storage – REF•32
Suspension
　adjustments – 6•14
　checks – 0•16, 1•18
Swingarm and suspension linkage bearing lubrication – 1•20
Swingarm and bearing inspection – 6•17
Swingarm removal and installation – 6•15
Switches
　brake light – 9•9
　clutch – 9•13
　handlebar – 9•12
　ignition (main) – 9•11
　neutral – 9•12
　oil level – 9•14
　sidestand – 9•13

T

Tail light assembly – 9•7
Technical terms explained – REF•48
Thermostat and housing – 3•3, 3•4
Throttle cables – 1•17, 4•13
Throttle position sensor – 5•5
Tip-over sensor – 5•6
Tools and workshop tips – REF•2
Torque settings – 1•2, 2•4, 3•1, 4•2, 5•1, 6•2, 7•2, 9•2
Transmission shafts
　disassembly, inspection and reassembly – 2•48
　removal and installation – 2•47
　specifications – 2•3
Tyres
　checks and pressures – 0•16
　fitting – 7•22
　sizes – 0•11, 7•1
Turn signal
　bulbs – 9•8
　circuit check – 9•7
　relay – 9•7

V

Valve clearance check and adjustment – 1•21
Valve cover – 2•10
Valve (engine) – 2•21
Valve (EXUP) – 4•16

W

Water pump – 3•6
Weights – 0•10
Wheel
　alignment check – 7•16
　bearing check – 1•15
　bearing replacement – 7•19
　checks – 1•15
　inspection and repair – 7•16
　removal and installation – 7•17 to 7•19
Wiring diagrams – 9•24 to 9•29

Reference

Left blank for Motorcycle Manual listing

Preserving Our Motoring Heritage

< The Model J Duesenberg Derham Tourster. Only eight of these magnificent cars were ever built – this is the only example to be found outside the United States of America

Almost every car you've ever loved, loathed or desired is gathered under one roof at the Haynes Motor Museum. Over 300 immaculately presented cars and motorbikes represent every aspect of our motoring heritage, from elegant reminders of bygone days, such as the superb Model J Duesenberg to curiosities like the bug-eyed BMW Isetta. There are also many old friends and flames. Perhaps you remember the 1959 Ford Popular that you did your courting in? The magnificent 'Red Collection' is a spectacle of classic sports cars including AC, Alfa Romeo, Austin Healey, Ferrari, Lamborghini, Maserati, MG, Riley, Porsche and Triumph.

A Perfect Day Out

Each and every vehicle at the Haynes Motor Museum has played its part in the history and culture of Motoring. Today, they make a wonderful spectacle and a great day out for all the family. Bring the kids, bring Mum and Dad, but above all bring your camera to capture those golden memories for ever. You will also find an impressive array of motoring memorabilia, a comfortable 70 seat video cinema and one of the most extensive transport book shops in Britain. The Pit Stop Cafe serves everything from a cup of tea to wholesome, home-made meals or, if you prefer, you can enjoy the large picnic area nestled in the beautiful rural surroundings of Somerset.

> John Haynes O.B.E., Founder and Chairman of the museum at the wheel of a Haynes Light 12.

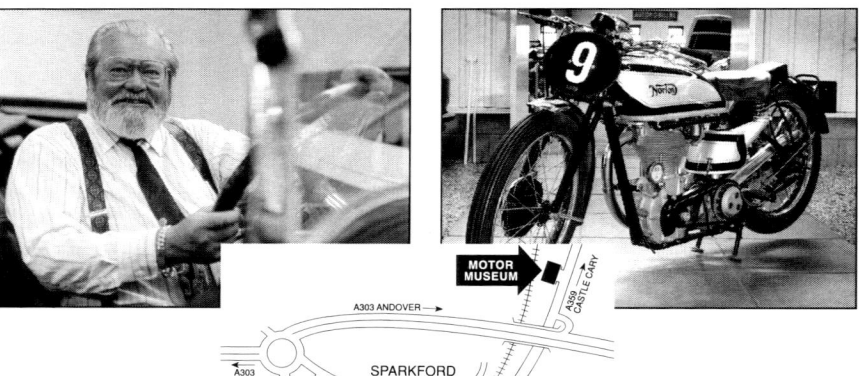

< The 1936 490cc sohc-engined International Norton – well known for its racing success

The Museum is situated on the A359 Yeovil to Frome road at Sparkford, just off the A303 in Somerset. It is about 40 miles south of Bristol, and 25 minutes drive from the M5 intersection at Taunton.
Open 9.30am - 5.30pm (10.00am - 4.00pm Winter) 7 days a week, *except Christmas Day, Boxing Day and New Years Day*
Special rates available for schools, coach parties and outings Charitable Trust No. 292048